The Politics of State Intervention

The Politics of State Intervention

Gender Politics in Pakistan, Afghanistan, and Iran

Shireen K. Burki

LEXINGTON BOOKS
Lanham • Boulder • New York • Toronto • Plymouth, UK

Published by Lexington Books
A wholly owned subsidiary of Rowman & Littlefield
4501 Forbes Boulevard, Suite 200, Lanham, Maryland 20706
www.rowman.com

10 Thornbury Road, Plymouth PL6 7PP, United Kingdom

Copyright © 2013 by Lexington Books

All rights reserved. No part of this book may be reproduced in any form or by any electronic or mechanical means, including information storage and retrieval systems, without written permission from the publisher, except by a reviewer who may quote passages in a review.

British Library Cataloguing in Publication Information Available

Library of Congress Cataloging-in-Publication Data

Burki, Shireen, 1964–
 The politics of state intervention : gender politics in Pakistan, Afghanistan, and Iran / Shireen K. Burki.
   pages cm.
 Includes bibliographical references and index.
 ISBN 978-0-7391-8432-5 (cloth : alk. paper) — ISBN 978-0-7391-8433-2 (electronic)
 1. Women's rights—South Asia. 2. Women's rights—Islamic countries. 3. Feminism—South Asia. 4. Feminism—Islamic countries. 5. Women—Government policy—South Asia. 6. Women—Government policy—Islamic countries. I. Title.
 HQ1236.5.S66B87 2013
 305.420954—dc23
                                                                                                    2013019742

∞™ The paper used in this publication meets the minimum requirements of American National Standard for Information Sciences Permanence of Paper for Printed Library Materials, ANSI/NISO Z39.48-1992.

Printed in the United States of America

Contents

Acknowledgments vii

Introduction 1

I: Pakistan 9

1   The Politics of Gender in Pakistan, 1947–1977: A Historical Overview   11

2   Islamization and Female Status: Life under General Zia-ul-Haq, 1977–1988   41

3   State Policies and Female Status in the Post-Zia State   67

II: Afghanistan 99

4   The Politics of Gender in Afghanistan (1919–1994): A Historical Overview   101

5   Rise of the Taliban and Female Practice: The Politics of Repression, 1996–2001   127

6   Gender Politics in the Post–Taliban Afghan State: The Politics of Accommodation?   147

III: Iran 175

7   The Politics of Gender in Iran, 1906–1941: From Constitutional Revolution to Monarchical "Modernization"   177

8   Modernization and Female Status: Life under the Second Pahlavi Shah, 1941–1979   201

9   Trials and Tribulations in Iran: Gender Politics in a Theocracy   227

Conclusion: Prospects for Pakistani, Afghan, and Iranian Women in
    the Twenty-first Century   263

Bibliography   283

Index   299

About the Author   307

Acknowledgments

This work is dedicated to all past and present female activists/warriors who have worked tirelessly to protect and defend female rights and/or willingly laid their lives on the line for individual freedom and justice. A few honorable mentions: Malala Yousafzai, Mukhtar Mai, Ghazala Javed (1988–2012), Begum Liaquat Ali Khan (1905–1990), and Bilquis Edhi (Pakistan); Bobo Jan (d:1912), Mina (1956–1987), Malalai Joya, Fawzia Koofi, and Sima Samar (Afghanistan); Neda Agha Soltan (1983–2009), Farrokhroo Parsa (1922–1980), Shirin Ebadi, Farah Pahlavi, and Zahra Rahnavard (Iran).

Many thanks, and deepest gratitude, to so many along the way whose personal stories, research, and/or teachings have inspired me to write this book. The superb professors at the State University of New York at Plattsburgh left an early imprint. Professor Patricia Higgins, a cultural anthropologist, was my first mentor. Her love for all things Persian (and Middle Eastern) was contagious. She's been an inspiration and a role model. So were Professors Martin Lubin and Professor Jon Gottschall at the Political Science Department. During my M.A. studies at the University of Virginia, Professor R. K. Ramazani's prescient insights on unfolding events in the Middle East were invaluable and fondly remembered. Professor Ramazani pushed us to "think outside the box" in his kindly professorial style: A humble, great man. Ambassador (ret) David Newsom (Virginia), an expert on Pakistan and the Middle East, was generous with sharing his knowledge and vast experience. Professor Susan Olson at the University of Utah's Political Science Department stood out for her high academic and ethical standards. She mentored me during some of the hardest times. Professor Howard Lehman (Utah), unbeknownst to him, provided me with invaluable insight for which I'm very grateful; while Professor Lee L. Bean (Utah) shared his vast expertise on Pakistan in memorable seminars.

On a more personal note, my late father (Hamidullah Khan Burki) encouraged critical thinking; to critique ideas and concepts from various prisms rather than taking things at face value; while my mother (Catherine Leech Burki) encouraged my love of reading by bringing loads of books for me to read. And last, but never least, my husband Vern's support and encouragement has never wavered.

Introduction

> And revere the womb that bore you, for God is ever watchful over you.
> —Qur'an Sura An Nisa (4:1)

The decision to focus on female status in Muslim majority states is a personal one. As a female of Pushtun and Irish heritage who grew up in Pakistan, I attended an all girls' school where independent thinking was discouraged and rote learning was the norm. In 1976, as part of the Prime Minister Zulfiqar Ali Bhutto's Islamization efforts as he sought generous financial support from the Saudi government and other Persian Gulf states, our school curriculum was revised to make it more Islamic compliant with an "Islamic" narrative. The curriculum changes were not limited to our history books, as mandatory Arabic language instruction was introduced for all Muslim (overwhelming majority) students. *Islamiat* (Islamic studies) was already a compulsory core of our daily curriculum since first grade, from which only a sprinkling of Christian girls were exempt.

Besides the "Islamization" of our school curriculum, we were now required to cover our heads when we left the school premises with our *dupattas* (scarfs) or *chadors* (full body length covering). By the late seventies, Islamization was in full swing as General Zia ul Haq tried to justify his military coup by leveraging Islam. Beer and alcohol were banned, dance halls closed, thieves' hands were chopped off, violent female harassment in public for not dressing "modestly" increased, and public whippings were introduced. In hindsight, these incremental state-led measures were the beginning of a process that has been detrimental to Pakistani society as a whole. Although one can argue that such measures are not illegitimate in an "Islamic republic," the fact remains that many of these changes were merely the tip of the iceberg: they were the first steps by the state to determine social norms and mores rather than leave such matters to the individual and civil society. *Shariah* inspired Hudood Ordinances of 1979 turned out to be a harbinger of the road ahead. Females and the religious minorities have borne the brunt of these laws over the course of time.

My father, who paid a heavy price for his criticism of the military autocracy, was prescient enough to encourage me to strike out on my own. Privileged to have been born in the United States, I left home for America. Looking back I acknowledge with much gratitude being born to an unusually enlightened father who inculcated in his children his firm belief in the equality of all human beings and every individual's right to freedom and justice. There are other men like him in Pakistan, Afghanistan, and Iran, but due to state or societal pressures are forced to comply with a herd mentality that increasingly restricts individual choice and freedom through often draconian measures. It is this personal "escape"—albeit with much sadness and nostalgia for one of my ancestral homelands—that has inspired, or perhaps compelled, me to undertake such a study to delve into "what went wrong?" which has led to the current predicament of females. A precarious existence across state lines where, in the name of religion (Islam), girls are being forced to avoid going to school for fear of an acid attack (Pakistan and Afghanistan), child marriage received state sanction (Iran's current theocracy and Afghanistan's Taliban), domestic violence is widespread and stoning women to death for adultery has been carried out with state or societal support (Iran, Afghanistan, and Pakistan). But this disturbing trend isn't limited to these three countries.

The entire Middle East and Southwest Asia is in turmoil. The self immolation of a Tunisian fruit vendor was the spark that lit the "Jasmine Revolution" in December 2010. What followed caught many by surprise as civil society throughout the Arab world took to the streets to demand the removal of autocratic regimes. Like dominoes, governments in Tunisia, Egypt, Libya, and Yemen were ousted; while Syria's Alawite-dominated Assad regime resorted to brute force in order to retain control over the reins of power despite international condemnation. The traditionally uneasy relationship between state institutions and civil society in the Muslim world has now entered a new phase where the talk of "democracy" permeates but without any clear idea of what "real democracy" would look like: Secular or *Shariah* (Islamic Law) based state institutions in an electoral system? This state of flux is understandably disconcerting to many within and without the region. But it is especially worrisome to the female populace in the Muslim world as their status has more often than not been a kind of litmus test of what form state institutions would assume.

One could, however, argue that it was Iran's "Green Movement" of June 2009 which provided the original impetus for this public discontent: millions of frustrated Iranian citizens, many women from all socioeconomic backgrounds, poured into the streets to protest what they perceived were rigged elections by a theocratic state which favored the incumbent, President Ahmadinejad, over the other challengers like Mir Hossein Mousavi and Mehdi Karroubi. The protestors were from all walks of life and chanted "*raye-man kojast*" (Persian: Where is my vote?). The videotaped death of Neda Agha-Soltan at the hands of a government militiaman came to symbolize the brutal misogyny of a theocracy notwithstanding the gains Iranian women had made in civil society. The Iranian regime struggled to quell the widespread public demonstrations through brute force by its militia and police, leaving many dead and wounded; but the discontent of the Iranian populace toward the autocratic rule of Grand Ayatollah Ali Khomenei continues to simmer just beneath the surface.

Unlike Iran, the Afghan state under NATO oversight has not experienced similar grumblings in the form of large public protests. Despite his growing unpopularity, President Karzai—who like his Iranian counterpart was re-elected in late 2009 in an election tainted by allegations of fraud at the ballot box—can rely on the presence of well-equipped foreign forces for the absence of any version of the "Arab Spring." But this could well be the calm before the storm given the populace's displeasure with the brazen corruption which permeates the Karzai government at all levels, and is viewed as obscene even by the traditionally lax standards of Afghan society. As Afghans warily watch the ongoing turmoil in the Middle East to their west, and the increasing instability in Pakistan to their east; urban women and the non-Pushtun women in Afghanistan remain especially anxious over their future. Many are worried over NATO's planned withdrawal from Afghanistan as the clout of the Taliban grows and is evident in their increasingly aggressive tactics at the grassroots level. These terror measures have included poisoning drinking wells in girls' schools; throwing acid in school girls' faces and/or executing teachers; in addition to public executions for violations of "Shariah" as defined by the Taliban's draconian worldview. Worse, the Karzai government has begun to accommodate the Taliban and has backed the Ulema Council's restrictive "code of conduct" for women in order to placate the conservative social elements such as the mullahs, warlords, and Taliban militias.[1]

In Pakistan's turbulent provinces of Baluchistan and Khyber Pukhtunkhwa, women are worried about pressure being brought to bear upon their families by the Islamist social elements: girls are being forced to abandon going to school due to kidnappings, acid attacks, and other physical hazards (such as the assassination attempt on fourteen-year-old Malala Yousefzai in October 2012) or because of verbal threats made to their male family members. The Pakistani state is unable or unwilling to protect them. While in the cities and the other two provinces of Sind and Punjab, the chasm between the "modernists" and the "traditionalists" grows exacerbated by a deteriorating economic situation and uncontrolled population growth.

Given the precariousness of the current situation in the region characterized by increasing intolerance and violence toward females, this book is a timely comparative work which aims to shed light on how females have fared in three neighboring states—Pakistan, Afghanistan, and Iran. Utilizing a historical context, it examines the gender specific policies of these states to assess whether or not shared cultural, religious, and social characteristics translate into similar gender policies and social outcomes, and if not, why not; to identify possible reasons or explanations for divergent outcomes when there have been similar independent variables/factors involved in order to better understand structurally or socially derivative impediments to improvements in women's status in these countries. Lastly, it seeks to address the question: Is the state indeed sufficiently autonomous from social elements to enact and implement controversial gender policies?

Excellent scholarly publications which have examined women's status in these countries include Mumtaz and Shaheed's *Women of Pakistan* (1984), Emadi's *Repression, Resistance, and Women in Afghanistan* (2002), Afary's *Sexual Politics in Modern Iran* (2009), and Heath and Zahedi's *Land of the Unconquerable: The Lives of Contemporary Afghan Women* (2011). These insightful studies, however, have comprised of individual country case studies. Surprisingly, there are few comparative scholarly works on gender politics in the Muslim world or the Middle East. The first is the edited volume by Lois Beck and Nikki Keddie titled *Women in the Muslim World* (1978). This book came to my attention in a Middle Eastern culture undergraduate seminar. It is still considered a classic notwithstanding being a bit outdated in light of all that has transpired in the region since 1979. A few others include Valentine Moghadam's *Globalization and Social Movements: Islamism, Feminism, and the Global Justice Movement* (2008) and *Modernizing Women: Gender and Social Change in the Middle East* (2003), Deniz Kandiyoti's edited volume, *Women, Islam and the State* (1991), and Mahnaz Afkhami's *Faith and Freedom: Women's Human Rights in the Muslim World* (1995). These books on gender politics in the Muslim world are some of the few examples of comparative scholarly studies which incorporate two or more gender country case studies, notwithstanding the level of interest in recent years. This is puzzling in light of the numerous linkages—ethnic, linguistic, religious and cultural—which exist between them. This book aims to address this scholarly gap to illuminate on how women have fared in these countries under progressive or regressive policies of certain state entities. Through such an examination of three "Islamic Republics" it seeks to glean prospects not only for women in these three countries but also to postulate on future trends vis-à-vis women as citizens in a region plagued by violence and instability.

The remainder of this book is divided into three parts. Part 1 covers Pakistan's gender policies since independence; part 2 examines Afghanistan's gender related policy since its independence; the third focuses on how Persia/Iran's females have fared since the early twentieth century; and the final chapter comparatively illuminates on the findings of this study in the conclusion chapter. The following is a synopsis of what each chapter will examine:

Chapter 1, The Politics of Gender in Pakistan, 1947–1977: A Historical Overview, examines the evolution of women's rights in Pakistan from the pre-partition days of colonial rule until the introduction of Shariah (Islamic) law in 1979 which began the process of reversing the gradual legal and social gains Pakistani women had made. It investigates the Pakistani state's actions to identify what successes and failures the state encountered during the implementation of specific ordinances and laws. It explores if, when, and what, specific social elements were involved in hampering or assisting this process as determined by the state's direction.

Chapter 2, Islamization and Female Status: Life under General Zia-ul-Haq (1977–1988), analyzes a critical time in identity and gender politics in Pakistan. During this period the state under military rule moved to introduce "Islamization" through the enactment of Shariah compliant ordinances and laws. The first section of this chapter examines specific legislative and structural measures taken by the state under military rule to implement its version of an Islamic agenda. The second half of the chapter explores the gender policies of this state under General Zia. It examines how urban women, over time, became adept at mobilizing both nationally and internationally to become a real threat to the state's gender agenda. Did the state's metamorphosis succeed? What does this attempt to redefine national identity, and more specifically, gender identity, suggest about state resiliency or lack thereof? And what does the evidence suggest in terms of social resistance when faced with unpalatable state measures?

Chapter 3, State Policies and Female Status in the Post-Zia State, examines the Pakistani state's gender policy following the death of General Zia-ul-Haq. Questions addressed here include: Did the removal of the architect of "Islamization" lead to any changes in the state's agenda on women's status (including the reversal of the unpopular Hudood ordinances) as demanded by women's organizations? Or did the state's perceived mission to clarify what the state of Pakistan represents (Islamic versus secular interests) continue unabated and what impact has its ongoing identity dilemma had on women's status in Pakistan? How does the politics of the post–Zia era inform us on the subject of gender politics in Pakistan? What are the impediments to reversal of draconian laws enacted under Zia? Did the state appear to be following a specific agenda vis-à-vis women and state identity? Has it been willing to bear the costs/risks associated with the liberalization of laws that grant women more public space and opportunities than conservative elements would like?

Chapter 4 on Afghanistan, The Politics of Gender in Afghanistan (1919–1994): A Historical Overview, examines state policy as it pertains to women's status since the establishment of the Afghan state to its disintegration into a violent civil war from which emerged the Taliban's draconian rule in 1994. It seeks to answer the following questions: Did the state seek to improve women's status for reasons independent of social demands or were these efforts meant to legitimize the leader's rule? In its attempts to improve women's status was the state autonomous enough from social forces to implement controversial policies in a very traditional milieu? What sort of opposition did the state encounter on the subject of women's rights and what was the state's reaction? Did it capitulate to social pressures or did it continue to work toward progress in women's status? Does this historical record suggest a pattern on the politics of gender relations that explains—or does not—the rise of the Taliban and their zest to "control" Afghan women?

Chapter 5, Rise of the Taliban and Female Practice: The Politics of Repression, 1996–2001, examines whether or not the Taliban's gender policy was really based on their ideology and religious (Deobandi influenced) beliefs, or did legitimacy concerns also play a part? What success or failure did the Taliban have in implementing their gender policies in the context of a failed state? What was the level of resistance from certain segments of the female populace and how successful were women in trying to reverse draconian policies? Given the brutal treatment of women at the hands of the Taliban, especially toward non-Pushtun, urban and educated women, was the social response nonexistent, faint, or did various social elements mobilize to influence state policy and action?

Chapter 6, Gender Politics in the Post–Taliban Afghan State: The Politics of Accommodation?, explores state-society relations in the context of external influences on state policies with regards to Afghan women. The key question is this: Does the evolving state of Afghanistan under foreign tutelage offer women sustainable opportunities necessary to improve their status in Afghan society regardless of ethnicity or socioeconomic position? Do recent events at the local and provincial levels encourage women to be involved in the process of reconstructing this shattered state? Or does the state, pressured by powerful social elements, appear to be involved in the politics of accommodating specific interests (the warlords, mullahs, and the former Taliban) at the expense of Afghan women?

Chapter 7, The Politics of Gender in Iran, 1906–1941: From Constitutional Revolutioin to Monarchical "Modernization," briefly explores state-society relations in Persia (which was renamed "Iran" in 1935) since the early twentieth century to place events that followed during Reza Shah reign within their proper context. It examines how, and why, the state under Reza Shah moved to rapidly implement alien, and controversial, gender policies in order to "modernize" Persian/Iranian society; what sort of resistance did the state encounter from specific social elements and how these issues were resolved?

Chapter 8, Modernization and Female Status: Life Under the Second Pahlavi Shah, 1941–1979, examines the continuation and expansion of Reza Shah's "modernization" program of Iranian society under his son's tutelage in order to determine what impact this state led process had on the lives of Iranian women; what, if any, social resistance—particularly from the ulema—threatened this process and if the state was able and willing to continue rapid implementation of gender policies that aimed to bring Iran into the modern (read: Western) age? The degree of support for the Shah's emancipation efforts from various socioeconomic, ethnic and regional social groups and how this was, or was not, leveraged to sustain implementation of controversial gender policies despite growing opposition.

Chapter 9, Trials and Tribulations in Iran: Gender Politics in a Theocracy, unveils the equally aggressive and rapid reversal/rejection of the Shah's White Revolution (with its emphasis on "modernization" and "progress" as determined through the lens of the ruler) by the clerics in charge. What impact has the establishment of a Shia theocracy had on women's status in Iran? Is this impact (of the state) on gender relations less clear cut than readily understood in the West? Does this theocratic state continue to enact, and implement, gender policies independent of popular opinion based solely on ideological considerations? Or has its actions on gender matters evolved based on pragmatic considerations?

The final, conclusive chapter, Prospects for Iranian, Afghan, and Pakistani Women in the Twenty-first Century, synthesizes the findings of the three country case studies. Today, all three are "Islamic republics" struggling with how best to mollify warring social factions on sensitive gender-related matters (marital and divorce laws, dress codes, female participation in the workforce, etc.). Comparatively, what does the historical record reveal in terms of outcomes: Did these states experience comparable outcomes from the enactment of similar, and controversial, gender policies by the state apparatus? If not, what differentiated social response in one state from another? Given the findings from this comparative study on gender relations and policies in three Muslim majority states, what are the future prospects for females in the region given the current trend?

This book hopes to encourage additional comparative research on gender politics in Muslim majority countries at a time when there seems to be increasing intolerance, cruelty, and violence toward females from all socioeconomic backgrounds and religions in the region. With the vocalized desire emanating out of a segment of the populace in Egypt, Tunisia, Turkey, and elsewhere for the enactment and implementation of Shariah derivative laws, it will be interesting to see if this enthusiastic endorsement (of Islamic law) continues if Shariah becomes the only law of the land a la Saudi Arabia. In contrast to the ongoing turmoil in Egypt and elsewhere, with much of the populace clamoring for "Shariah" as the proper antidote to secular autocrats, citizens in Pakistan, Afghanistan, and Iran with duel legal systems have now lived under various degrees of "Shariah" in action for almost three decades. In these states enthusiasm has somewhat waned, especially among females and the well educated. Perhaps the same will be the case in other states in the region if their people personally experience the effects of living under the strict stipulations of Shariah. Time will tell.

NOTE

1. Emily Dyer, "The War on Women Being Waged in Afghanistan," *Telegraph,* June 26, 2012. Accessed at: http://www.telegraph.co.uk/news/worldnews/asia/afghanistan/9356291/The-war-on-women-being-waged-in-Afghanistan.html

I

Pakistan

Chapter One

The Politics of Gender in Pakistan, 1947–1977

A Historical Overview

> You may belong to any religion, caste, color or creed—that has nothing to do with the business of the State. . . . We are starting with this fundamental system that we are all citizens and equal citizens of one State.
> —Muhammad Ali Jinnah, Quaid-i-Azam, 1st Governor General, Pakistan

Pakistan as a state is a fairly recent construct established in 1947 after the British decided to withdraw from India. Before departing, the British carved up their Indian Empire into two states using a single demographic criterion: religious affiliation. Thus the Indian sub-continent was divided into India and Pakistan on the basis of Hindu and Muslim religious majorities. Although theoretically Pakistan was created as a homeland for Muslims, some Muslim leaders who sought such a state (Muhammad Ali Jinnah, Liaquat Ali Khan, etc.) were not motivated by religion. They did not advocate the establishment of an *Islamic* state where *Shariah* (Islamic) law would prevail over secular legal institutions. Rather, they were *secular pragmatists* who sought the creation of a separate Muslim state from mother India in order to both safeguard, and further, their community's interests. They were quite clear on what would constitute state identity of this new Muslim state: one in which the rights of *all citizens regardless of religious affiliation* would be guaranteed under a written constitution. Furthermore, they envisioned a state where women would have the same rights and protections as men under the law.

Many scholars have emphasized the progressive nature of this movement for a separate state for Muslims by extensively quoting from Jinnah's speeches. Jinnah envisioned a modern Western-oriented country where religious minorities would enjoy the same rights and privileges as Muslims. Jinnah never imagined the Muslim polity as a theocracy. For Jinnah, "*Islam*" and "*Muslim*" (emphasis added) were two different constructs, the former more particularistic; while the latter involved an ethnocultural identity. Many Pakistanis argue that Jinnah, ever the pragmatist, recognized the conceptual utility of "Muslim nationalism" as a means to overcome conflicting identities of different ethnic groups within Pakistan's borders.[1]

Some scholars have even argued that initially the leaders of the Pakistan movement had *not* sought a separate Muslim state.[2] Rather their political demands evolved from seeking greater autonomy and political rights for Indian Muslims to a Muslim homeland within an Indian federation to the outright partition of the Indian subcontinent into separate states. Furthermore, until the passage of the Pakistan Resolution in 1940, these secular Muslim leaders—led by Muhammad Ali Jinnah—leveraged the concept of an independent Muslim state as part of a negotiating strategy in order to extract the best possible political concessions for the Muslim community from the British, whose departure from the subcontinent seemed imminent. These leaders represented the fears of the Muslim community, which were based on a demographic reality: the perception that their Muslim interests would be threatened by the sheer numbers of non-Muslims (i.e., Hindus) in a postcolonial Indian state. Muslim politicians sought what they believed were vital concessions from the British by upping the ante vis-à-vis their demand for the creation of a separate state (or states) in order to protect Muslim interests. And, in the end, they got what they had demanded—a separate Muslim state—and, quite conceivably, not what they had wanted, given the challenges the new Muslim state would face from its very inception.

Other scholars support the thesis that the "*Pakistan movement was not a movement of Islam but of Muslims.*"[3] This endeavor did not seek a divinely ordained political and social system (i.e., imposition of *Shariah*). Rather, it was a movement in which diverse Muslim ethnic groups of India sought material objectives through the establishment of a separate homeland for themselves. Leaders like Muhammad Ali Jinnah and Liaquat Ali Khan never considered that if such a state was indeed established it would be a theocracy. Although their struggle sought secular objectives, it did not acknowledge the irony of leveraging its primary conceptual card "Muslim identity" as the raison d'etre of this movement. This discrepancy was justified by explanations that their "Muslim" identity was more cultural than religious.

This distinction, which seemed self-serving and "un-Islamic" to devout Muslims, inevitably pitted these politicians against certain Muslim religious figures like Abul Ala Maududi[4] who never sought a separate Muslim state. Maududi, the founder of the religious party, the Jamaat-i-Islami[5] (the Islamic Party), despised Jinnah and his cohorts as being "*mushrik*" (deviants) because they were willing to settle for only a small portion of the subcontinent and were not devout Muslims who sought to regain lost ground for Dar al Islam (Abode of Islam). Maududi stressed that an Islamic revival would in fact lead to a dissipation of hostility between Hindus and Muslims; therefore there was no need for Muslims to seek a separate homeland. In stark contrast to Jinnah, the Islamists envisioned a return to the past: rule of the Indian subcontinent by the Muslim minority as had been the case during Mughal rule prior to the arrival of the British. The chasm between the Islamists led by Maududi and the secularists (led first by Jinnah) would become self-evident and widen after Pakistan's creation. While Jinnah, Liaquat Ali Khan and others visualized a secular Muslim state that was tolerant of its minorities and provided women with equal status and opportunities; Maududi and his ideological comrades entertained a completely different vision: subjugation/ conversion of minorities and seclusion/segregation of its women.[6]

Muhammad Ali Jinnah, as the founding father of the Pakistani state, was a firm believer in women's right to participate in the social and political affairs of the state. According to him, no nation could progress if half of its population were to remain passive and uninvolved from national affairs.[7] Jinnah, in his famous speech at Aligarh in 1944, said:

> It is a crime against humanity that our women are shut up within the four walls of the houses as prisoners. There is no sanction anywhere for the deplorable conditions in which our women have to live. You should take your women along as your comrades in every sphere of life.[8]

MUSLIM WOMEN'S STATUS: THE PRE-PARTITION PERIOD, 1885–1940

Although women played a prominent role in the Pakistan movement (1940–1947), their demands for equal status, the right to vote, et cetera, were not new. Their activism began in the late nineteenth century with the encouragement of prominent Muslim male leaders who were inspired by ideas of Sir Syed Ahmed Khan.[9] When the Indian legal system was Anglicized in 1790, local laws based on religious and customary traditions were replaced by British law in all legal fields with one notable exception: family law. In deference to the locals, the British allowed Muslim and Hindu laws to continue to determine interpersonal relations and the status in the family, marriage, divorce, maintenance, guardianship of minors, succession and inheritance, religious usages and the disposition of property by *hiba* (gift), will and *waqf* (trust). In essence, laws involving social interaction between the sexes were unchanged.

In the late nineteenth century, female activists in India organized the Women's Reform Movement, which advocated the right to an education for Indian women. In order to legitimize their demands for access to educational opportunities, Muslim women specifically sought acceptance for this effort by utilizing the framework of Islam in their quest to legitimize this concept; and, secondly, to silence the naysayers most notably the maulvis or mullahs.

The *Anjuman-e-Himayat-e-Islam* (Society for the Promotion of Islam), which played an important role in promoting women's education in Lahore, opened five elementary schools in 1885 with the aim of preserving Islamic values. The Mohammedan Educational Congress in Bombay in 1903 for the first time included women. The 1903 MEC conference passed a resolution calling for the establishment of a Normal School for female teachers, which was opened in 1913. From 1904 onward, the Women's Reform Movement grew as the need for educating Muslim women gained traction among prominent Muslim men. It had the support of a couple, Maulvi Sayyid Mumtaz Ali and Muhammadi Begum who started a newspaper called *Tahzib-i-Niswan* (Women's Rights) in which they encouraged the establishment of societies dedicated to the promotion of women's education in order to unite women.[10]

Between 1904 and 1911, many Muslim girls' schools were established in Bombay, Calcutta, Aligarh, Lahore, and Karachi. At the same time, women's newspapers and journals were created that contributed to the recognition of Muslim women in India as an independent entity able and willing to speak for themselves. In Lahore alone at least three newspapers emerged: *Akhbar-i-Niswan, Sharif Bibi,* and *Tahzib-i-Niswan*. These papers aimed at a female audience were established by men, but women helped run them and also contributed articles to them.[11] While education of women progressed at a slow pace, it was a significant departure from centuries old tradition which discounted or discouraged female education. By 1924, there were approximately 137,800 literate Indian Muslim women of whom only 3,940, or fewer than 3 percent, had received a secular education. Two prominent families—who actively worked to promote Muslim women's education- were the Faizi family of Bombay and the Suhrawardy family of Bengal. In 1922, the first Indian Muslim woman to receive a master of arts degree was Sultan Begum of Bengal. Around this time the Faizi sisters (Attiya, Zuhra, and Nazli)—who came to play an active role in promoting women's rights—were the first Indian Muslim women to go abroad for higher education.[12]

Despite cultural obstacles, the concept of women's education gained popularity particularly within the Muslim elite during the years 1886 to 1917. Sir Mohammad Shafi of Lahore argued for more radical steps to improve women's status and position in society. He worked to improve the status of Indian Muslim women upon his return from Great Britain in 1892. His female relatives abandoned the veil, while he argued for the end to the dowry system, and demanded that all girls be given their share of inheritance as outlined in the Quran. Many of his landowning friends in the Muslim community were not pleased with these recommendations which made him rather unpopular with them.[13]

In 1908, Sir Shafi founded the *Anjuman-e-Khawateen-e-Islam* (Muslim Women's Organization) which began social work in rural communities in its efforts to better the lives of Muslim women.[14] In 1915, the first All-India Muslim Ladies' Conference took place which was attended by relatives of the leading Muslim educators and professionals. The main focus of this conference was on education.[15] In 1917, a delegation of various women's organizations from all over India, including a Muslim woman, Begum Hasrat Mohani, met Secretary of State E. S. Montagu, to demand increased educational facilities for women, improved health and maternity services, and equal franchise in the forthcoming reforms. The Montagu-Chelmsford proposals, however, did not mention women's franchise. It stated that at this stage it was inadvisable to widen the electorate.[16] In 1918, both the All India Muslim League and the Indian National Congress announced their support of the women's franchise. Notwithstanding various efforts to obtain the franchise for women in India, the British government refused to accommodate these demands on the grounds that the current circumstances in India did not lend themselves to such a move. Due to continued pressure from women, the British decided to allow the provinces to deal with the issue of female franchise in India. Madras took the lead in granting women the right to vote in 1921. By 1925, all the provinces, except Orissa and Bihar, had followed Madras in granting the franchise to Indian women. In 1935, due to the results of social activism at the provincial level, the Government of India Act enfranchised six million women and for the first time seats were reserved for women in both the Council of State and in the February Assembly (6/150 and 9/250 seats, respectively). It is significant that India, a country steeped in traditions of female subservience, followed the example of European countries in granting women the right to vote early on. In fact, Indian women enjoyed this right seventeen years before French women, who were not granted the right to vote until 1945.[17]

FEMALE ACTIVISM AND THE PAKISTAN MOVEMENT, 1940–1947

Muslim women played an active role in demanding a separate homeland for Muslims. This was a time of mass mobilization of women which led the Muslim League to form a women's wing. In 1940, a large number of women attended the Muslim League's annual public gathering in Lahore where the Pakistan Resolution was unanimously passed advocating a separate Muslim homeland.[18] For the first time in 1940, Muslim women participated in a demonstration in Lahore to protest the arrest of Muslim leaders and the banning of the *Khaksars* (a Muslim religious group which was hostile toward maulvis like Maududi).[19]

In 1941, a Muslim Girls' Student Federation was formed to promote the concept of a separate homeland. The members went to various college campuses seeking support for the idea of an independent Muslim state of Pakistan. It was the vanguard of the Women's Sub-Committee which was formed in the Muslim League.[20] Muhammad Ali Jinnah took a personal interest in the women's committees and in his tours addressed these women at large public gatherings. A subcommittee was formed with members selected from the Muslim League's Central Committee for the purpose of drafting a program aimed at improving the social, economic, and cultural status of Muslim women.

In 1943, thousands of women participated in the All India Muslim League annual session held in Karachi. The newly created Women's National Guard was present as well. In the 1946 elections, two Muslim women stood as candidates, Begum Salma Tassadduque Hussain and Begum Shah Nawaz. These national elections were important as they were a test for the Muslim League's claim of being the sole representative of the Muslims of British India. When the party was not allowed to form a ministry based on its emergence as the party representing the majority of Muslim Indians, women came out to demonstrate in protest and were arrested. This launched the civil disobedience movement in January 1947, which successfully rallied women's support even in some of the most conservative areas of the subcontinent like the North West Frontier Province.[21]

What is remarkable about this period is how Indian Muslim women quickly emerged from confinement in their homes to becoming political activists through participation in the nationalist movement which would morph into a struggle for a separate homeland for Muslims of India. What is particularly noteworthy here is the *rapidity* with which this role transformation in women's status in political matters occurred. This is especially remarkable when compared to the timeline of the political struggle for suffrage by European women who strove under less restrictive conditions. The nationalist struggle gave Indian Muslim women an opportunity to challenge traditional mores all in the name of "Islamic nationalism." It also provided them with an umbrella of legitimacy as they worked to improve their status through participation in the larger struggle. These women sought implementation of specific laws which legalized their new rights, such as the right to vote, seek office, demonstrate, and be members of a political party.

It is important to mention that the Muslim women's movement in India during this period was not opposed by Muslim men probably *because such female activism did not directly challenge their authority*. Instead, both groups sought the same objective: an independent Muslim state carved out of British India. Which raises the question: Was the public support by Muslim men for the promotion of women's interests (the right to vote; the right to an education and to employment outside the home) due to the necessity of galvanizing their women to further *their* (men's) larger cause of promoting Muslim political interests?[22] Thus the question arises: had conditions been different—which mitigated the need for women's public support—would these Muslim (male) leaders have pursued women's concerns vis-à-vis the British to the same degree, if at all? The evidence does seem to suggest that Jinnah, and those immediately around him, were sincerely concerned about female inclusion as productive citizens and supported a more public role for women. The same, however, cannot be said for the majority of the male Muslim League members who regarded this effort (to encourage female activism) as one based on necessity rather than on any strongly held convictions.

THE STATUS OF PAKISTANI WOMEN: THE EARLY YEARS, 1948–1958

Following the establishment of the Pakistani state, many women—specifically in urban centers—expected to play a more active role in this state's affairs. Such women believed that the newly created state would provide them with *additional opportunities* to further their status in society.[23] It was Begum Ra'ana Liaquat Ali Khan,[24] the wife of the first prime minister of Pakistan, who was instrumental in working to further the gains women had made during the latter stages of colonial rule. Toward this end, with a few other women, she created the Women's Voluntary Service in 1948. The purpose of the organization was to encourage women to volunteer to assist the seven plus million refugees who fled across the border into West Pakistan during an unprecedented forced cross migration of populations. Muslims, threatened due to their minority status in certain Hindu dominant areas, struggled to get across the border to Pakistan; while the reverse was the case in Pakistan, with Hindus similarly threatened, trying to flee to India.

Pakistani women who joined the Voluntary Service performed a variety of services including food distribution, administering first aid, provision of clothing and tents, and dealing with a myriad of problems associated with refugees with no resources. These women were socially popular in the new state and received the support of the newly formed Pakistani government, private organizations and grateful citizens. Given its agenda of social work and refugee assistance, the Women's Voluntary Service was not seen as a threat by the state as it did not challenge the status quo.

Begum Liaquat Ali Khan's efforts to establish a women's defense force, however, were considered controversial. The Begum justified her support for the establishment of the Pakistan's Women's National Guard (PWNG) and the Pakistan's Women's Naval Reserve (PWNR) as being necessary for the defense of the new state during the 1948 war with India over Kashmir. She believed that women would be useful in the military once they had been appropriately trained. The PWNG was administered by the Army; while the PWNR was controlled by the Navy. The Begum was made the Chief Controller of both with the rank of Brigadier General. The response of Pakistani women was phenomenal which quickly led to the establishment of a trained National Guard Corps of three battalions with 2,400 women who were scattered across the country.[25]

This unprecedented move of organizing, training, and equipping women to be part of the military system was revolutionary for the times. But the Begum believed that given all the sacrifices Muslim women had made in the establishment of an independent Muslim homeland, it was

> our duty to work toward the defense, development and betterment of the country and this was not the time for the 40 million women of Pakistan to sit quietly in their homes. They have to come out of their homes to learn to work and then teach others to do so.[26]

Begum Liaquat Ali Khan's vision for the activist role for women in the newly established state of Pakistan was not popular, and the creation of the Women's National Guard and Naval Reserve units was widely denounced. Women who wanted to serve in these two military organizations faced intense family pressure to remain at home. A primary concern of these families in a traditional milieu was what the neighbors, extended family, and friends would think, and the concomitant loss of face that would ensue if one of their females embarked on such an unorthodox undertaking among unrelated men. To appease and assuage religious and social elements, both of these services adopted the *dupatta* (a head covering) as part of their uniform. Far from appeasing religious elements like the maulvis; this only served to further incense them and their supporters as a mere ploy that sought to leverage Islamic traditions of female modesty in order to justify an un-Islamic act of having "their women" serve in the military.[27]

The PWNG and the PWNR ceased to exist soon after Begum Ra'ana Liaquat Ali was sent abroad as Pakistan's ambassador to the Netherlands in 1954. That these controversial military organizations managed to survive for six years, and were disbanded only after their powerful mentor and advocate had left the country, was a testimony to the Begum's sheer force of personality.[28]

While the PWNG and the PWNR did not survive because women were seen to be challenging men's traditional "warrior" role, the Women's Voluntary Service (WVS) gained in popularity as it provided useful social services and was viewed as an extension of women's domestic role of nurturer. Men viewed women's role in WVS favorably because it was voluntary unpaid work that did not threaten the domestic status quo. The PWNG and PWNR on the other hand involved paid positions which were perceived by some to have emboldened women and, worse, involved provision of martial training to women, which most Pakistani men felt threatened existing gender roles.

During these early years, women in less controversial venues were successful in organizing themselves: in 1949, the All Pakistan Women's Association (APWA) was formed; in 1956, the Federation of University Women (FUW) was created which provided membership to women with bachelor's and advanced degrees.[29] It was affiliated with APWA and one of its first tasks was the establishment of a college for women in Karachi. This college was created for girls who wanted to continue their higher education but could not do so in the government-sponsored colleges because of lower grades in the college entrance exams. The Federation spread to the major cities of Pakistan and also became associated with the International Federation of University Women.[30]

Other organizations were created that involved women or women's concerns. These included Business and Professional Women's Clubs (BPW),[31] Family Planning Association of Pakistan, the Pakistan Child Welfare Council, the Pakistan Red Cross, the Pakistan Nurses' Federation, the Housewives' Association, Girls Guides' Association, Democratic Women's Association (DWA), and the International Women's Club. The establishment of these women's organizations in the years right after independence suggested a fledgling women's movement whose objective was a more active and visible role of women in the new state much to the displeasure of the very vocal and active religious elements led by Maulana Maududi and his Jamaat-i-Islami.

The United Front for Women's Rights was established in 1955 to improve women's rights and status in Pakistani society. Its sole mission was to push for reforms in the legislative arena that would improve the status of Pakistani women and provide them with greater social and economic opportunities. Due to the promulgation of the Muslim Family Laws Ordinance in 1961 and restrictions imposed upon political parties by the Ayub regime, the United Front became inactive and eventually ceased to exist.[32]

It is important to note two points here: first, the efforts of Pakistani women to seek an improvement of their status both socially, and politically, was a very limited one pursued by influential educated women with a secular outlook in a conservative, primarily Muslim, society; second, at every step of the way, they encountered strong resistance from other social groups—primarily from the *maulvis* both in the mosques and in the two Islamist parties, Jamaat-e-Islami and the Jamaat-e-Ulema-e-Islam. Thus this struggle to improve women's status was bound to face challenges on multiple fronts given that it was (a) limited in size; and (b) being pursued solely in the urban areas in a country where most people lived in rural communities. Nonetheless, these comparatively affluent women sought an improvement in the status of *all* Pakistani women regardless of their socioeconomic background and geographic location, and at great social and economic cost to themselves.

THE ESTABLISHMENT OF THE ALL PAKISTAN WOMEN'S ASSOCIATION (1949)[33]

Begum Ra'ana Liaquat Ali Khan convened a women's conference in Karachi on February 22, 1949, attended by over a hundred female activists. She feared that Pakistani women, who had been involved in the WVS and had provided invaluable services in helping with the refugee assistance program, would now be pressured to return to the confines of their homes. She envisioned the establishment of a permanent women's organization where their acquired skills and energy could be applied to activities that would continue to help Pakistani women in some way.

The Karachi convention ended with the formation of the All Pakistan Women's Association (APWA) with Begum Ra'ana Liaquat Ali as its first president. She was later elected its president for life, an honor that highlighted her vital role in APWA's formation. APWA was created as a voluntary nonpolitical organization in which membership was open to all Pakistani women who were over sixteen years of age, regardless of class, caste, color, or religious affiliation. Its stated objective was the welfare of Pakistan's women, creating educational, social, and cultural consciousness among them and improving opportunities for participation in economic development.[34]

Although membership in APWA was open to all women, its members were overwhelmingly from the urban middle and upper classes. APWA membership was quite popular because it provided the only acceptable venue for women to participate in activities outside their homes. APWA set about the task of opening girls' schools, health centers, and industrial homes which trained women in income-generating opportunities. APWA programs focused exclusively on the needs of impoverished women and their children. The problem with these programs was that most of APWA's activities were concentrated in the urban areas; though the greatest need for social services was in the countryside where most of Pakistan's impoverished women lived. Thus APWA came to be an *urban phenomenon* primarily benefiting low-income women in urban centers. A plausible explanation for this urban focus had to do with the fact that almost all of APWA's members were from more affluent *urban* backgrounds which confined their social activism to projects closer to home.

Since APWA was the brainchild of the Prime Minister's wife, Begum Ra'ana Liaquat Ali, and generally regarded as a harmless entity that could play a useful role helping low-income women and children, the government did not object to its mission. During the Pakistani state's early years, while the government supported APWA's mission, it expected APWA to generate funding for its own programs. This was because the state itself had few resources available to provide the kind of services that APWA was willing to as an organization. In fact, APWA was seen as a godsend by both the state and society. State approval of APWA was evident in that in every province the local governor was the patron of the provincial branch of APWA. Furthermore, the wife of the civil administrator in each district was almost always an honorary chief of the local wing of the organization which resulted in the rapid expansion of APWA. It was the wife of the chief administrator who often determined the level of success of the local APWA chapter by facilitating bureaucratic processes in the pursuit of APWA's objectives. For example, in getting land allocated for schools and raising funds, the wives of senior administration officials as members of APWA were very successful in obtaining these resources on behalf of APWA projects.[35]

APWA also worked hard as an advocate for Pakistani women in demanding an improvement in women's status and rights in Pakistani society. Toward this end, APWA created a women's rights and legal section, which not only provides free legal advice to women who seek its services, but also carries out research on legal issues that affect women and children and makes recommendations to the government of Pakistan.

APWA lobbied for the Family Laws Commission which finally came up with the draft of the Muslim Family Laws Ordinance of 1961. This ordinance was viewed as the first step in protecting women's rights in marriage. APWA got directly involved in the political process in 1953 when it recommended that the government reserve ten women's seats in the National and Provincial Assemblies for at least ten years.[36]

APWA faced stiff resistance from the *maulvis* (the mullahs) who did not approve of its actions which encouraged the empowerment of women in Pakistan. The religious parties such as the Jamaat-e-Islami led by Maulana Maududi, criticized APWA's founder, Begum Ra'ana Liaquat Ali and other women members for encouraging "un-Islamic" behavior in Pakistani women. Although APWA enjoyed the support and cooperation of the government due to its primary concentration on social welfare work, its members were chastised for not wearing the veil and they were referred to as "prostitutes" by the Majlis-e-Ahrar, an extreme right-wing orthodox party, which had opposed the creation of Pakistan and the Muslim League.[37] The two other Islamist parties, the Jamaat-e-Islami and Jamiat-e-Ulema-e-Islam, also disapproved of APWA which was seen as promoting women's *azadi* (Urdu for "freedom/independence"). It was a concept that the Islamists viewed as being un-Islamic since according to Islamic precepts women belonged within the confines of the home.[38]

PAKISTANI WOMEN IN THE POLITICAL AND LEGISLATIVE PROCESSES

Pakistani women sought a very active role in the legislative and political processes after independence.[39] During this early period of the Pakistani state, an important piece of legislation concerning women was the Muslim Personal Law of Shariat which went into effect in 1951 after the first legislative struggle between women activists and their opponents. In 1948, in one of the very first legislative attempts to secure economic rights for women during the Budget Session debate, a bill that advocated for improved economic opportunities for women was to be presented to the House by a select committee in this session was removed from the agenda. Women were furious and the female members of the Punjabi Provincial Assembly brought this matter before the Muslim League Women's Committee. Thousands of women marched in the streets of Lahore in protest led by Begum Jahanara Shah Nawaz as they arrived at the Assembly Chambers.[40] After the first prime minister of Pakistan, Liaquat Ali Khan, personally intervened, the Muslim Personal Law of Shariat of 1948 was passed by the legislature. The passage of this law was significant in that it legally recognized a woman's right to inherit property, including agricultural land, a right that had been denied to them during British rule.[41] It was a remarkable feat that in a parliament dominated by the landed aristocracy (of men), the two female representatives were successful in getting this law passed. Begum Jahanara Shah Nawaz, a member of the Muslim League,[42] and Begum Shaista Ikramullah, were the two female representatives in the first Pakistani legislature and they worked hard on behalf of women. For example, while the laws on the books reflected a women's right to inherit property, the reality was that the implementation of this bill would be difficult and sporadic given the prevalent custom of denying Muslim women their rights under Islam to inherit a specific amount of property as inheritance. The Muslim Personal Law of Shariat's failure to bring about tangible changes in inheritance matters as outlined in this bill led to the government intervening once again in 1961 to pass additional legislation on the matter that tried to address these failures at the implementation stage.

The first Constituent Assembly of Pakistan had several special committees—the Fundamental Rights Committee, the Basic Principles Committee, the Franchise Committee, and the Nationality Committee. Begum Jahanara Shah Nawaz and Shaista Ikramullah both faced heavy opposition in these committees from the religious ulema and from some of their male colleagues. For example, in the Zakat Committee set up by the finance minister, Mr. Ghulam Mohammad, the elected ulema refused to sit with their female colleagues arguing that only *burqa*-clad (i.e., veiled) women above the age of fifty should be allowed to sit in the Assembly.[43] The acrimony between the religious elements and women parliamentarians would continue to characterize relations between the two in their dealings with each other on legislative matters involving women's rights.

In 1954, when the draft bill for the Charter of Women's Rights prepared by Begum Shah Nawaz was discussed in the Constituent Assembly, the two women members (Nawaz and Ikramullah) demanded a very reasonable 3 percent quota of reserved seats for women in both the Central and Provincial Assemblies. The charter demanded that, under the Islamic Personal Law of Shariat, Muslim women were granted equality of status, equal opportunity, equal pay for equal work. This provision had widespread support in the Assembly and passed unanimously. This was a remarkable achievement for Pakistani women in the new state, especially since the bill was initially opposed by Sir Zafarullah who chaired the committee, on the grounds that even in Britain, Churchill had refused to accept a bill that sought equal pay for equal work in England.[44]

Pakistan's first Constitution—the 1956 Constitution—would accept the principle of female suffrage for women's reserved seats on the basis of special women's territorial constituencies, thus giving dual voting rights to women for general seats and reserved women's seats.[45]

THE RASHID COMMISSION, AUGUST 1955–JUNE 1956

By the mid-1950s there was an ongoing campaign by a small, but vocal, group of women in the urban centers, especially Karachi, who demanded that polygamy be banned. The incident which, however, added fuel to this fire, occurred on April 2, 1955, when Prime Minister Muhammad Ali Bogra married his secretary and thus took a second wife. His action enraged female activists, especially those affiliated with the influential APWA. Fifty women in Karachi led a protest march to the prime minister's home chanting slogans against polygamy.[46] This was followed by "social boycotts" of second wives by society's elite who emphasized that Islam's ultimate aim had been the prohibition of this social behavior that hurt women's status in a Muslim society. The activism of these women and their supporters was so effective that Prime Minister Bogra—one can only surmise that his second wife might have begged him to do something to end her social isolation—personally intervened in the matter and demanded the establishment of a special commission to look into the matter and to recommend social reforms.[47]

The Rashid Commission was established to examine the existing laws of marriage, divorce, maintenance, and custody of children, and to determine if any of the laws on these matters needed to be amended to make the laws more equitable to women as outlined in Islam. It consisted of seven members headed by the chief justice of the Supreme Court, Justice Rashid. The composition of this seven member committee—in addition to Justice Rashid—included three women and three men. Only one of these members was an Islamic scholar, Maulana Ehtishamul Haq, who apparently incensed that the other members of the commission also considered themselves to be "experts" on Islamic law. Nonetheless, he felt it essential to sit on this committee as so much was at stake for "true Muslims" and for Islam.[48] It submitted its majority report on June 20, 1956. The sole dissenter of the Rashid Commission, Maulana Ehtishamul Haq, submitted a lengthy "Note of Dissent" on August 30, 1956. By this time, however, the majority report had been widely disseminated and read much to the chagrin of the religious elements who opposed any kind of state intervention into affairs that concerned the Ulema (learned Muslim scholars). There was, however, limited interest in the dissent report as public interest on the subject had waned.[49]

The Majority Report of the Rashid Commission called for the registration of all marriages and divorces with specific governmental entities and not by the mullah in their mosques. This was in order to prevent false accusations of adultery and/or property disputes. The argument used to justify such action by the government was as follows: "The Quran urges that important transactions should be in writing."[50] This interpretation of the Quran by the secular component of the Rashid Commission infuriated the Islamists and their allies among the citizenry, especially men. It challenged the status quo control over interpreting religious doctrine normally considered the exclusive purview of Muslim scholars and religious figures. The other recommendation of the majority was that the three successive pronouncements of the required term *talaq* (Urdu for "divorce") should only count for one. Thus for a divorce to be effective this process must be repeated two additional times at later dates over a period of three months. They defended this process as being necessary to reduce the number of hasty divorces made in a fit of rage or emotion.[51] Notwithstanding the reasonableness of these recommendations, the religious establishment took umbrage that phony experts on Islam were trying to muscle in on their traditional sphere of influence on social and marital issues. They exerted intense pressure on the government through their support base, which was not insignificant; this pressure ultimately led the government to set aside the Rashid Commission's report.[52] This success by the more conservative—and well entrenched at the lower social echelons—elements was a harbinger of things to come. It also was indicative that, in the face of strong social opposition, a relatively weak state will consider backing down.

WOMEN'S LEGAL STRUGGLE DURING GENERAL AYUB KHAN'S RULE, 1958–1969

The military junta takeover in 1958 ironically inaugurated a period of greater opportunities for women in Pakistan. It was led by Sandhurst-trained General Ayub Khan[53]—a Muslim secularist in an army whose senior officers had served under the British before and during World War II. They absorbed— and were greatly influenced by—British military and political traditions. Women—specifically those who lived in the urban areas and were educated—had greater choices than ever before in the fields of science and civil service. Furthermore, the Pakistani civil service, which continued to perform under military rule, comprised of "Westernized" Muslims with more favorable attitudes toward women in the workplace than the "traditionalists" (the Islamists and their supporters). Ayub Khan himself was strongly opposed to the religious parties and the more orthodox elements in society because he regarded them as impediments to progress.[54] Female activists felt that this was the perfect time to try to seek the enactment of the Rashid Commission's recommendations, which had been shelved soon after its completion due to successful pressure applied by the Ulema and the religious parties.

THE MUSLIM FAMILY LAW ORDINANCE OF 1961[55]

The Muslim Family Law Ordinance (MFLO) of 1961 was based on the findings of the Rashid Commission and represented a major legal victory for Pakistani women. At the time, however, female activists had actually voiced their disappointment with the stipulations of the MFLO in that this ordinance did not go far enough in addressing women's (i.e., urban and educated) concerns. While it did not incorporate all the Rashid Commission recommendations, it was indeed a step forward for women in general without being precipitous. The MFLO was the first statutory reform measure carried out by the state on the subject of marital relations since the Dissolution of Muslim Marriages Act of 1939 (effective in both India and Pakistan) that allowed a Muslim (Sunni Hanafi Fiqh) wife to seek a judicial divorce on such grounds as desertion, cruelty, failure to maintain, leprosy and venereal disease, if she could provide satisfactory evidence in court.[56] The main aim of the MFLO was to discourage polygamy and to regulate divorce by prescribing procedures for both. The ordinance stipulated that a man who wants to have more than one wife had to first obtain the written consent of his first wife. Then he was required to present his request—along with reasons for the second marriage to an "arbitration council" consisting of a representative from each party and the chairman of the local council. The final decision on whether or not he could take a second wife would then rest with the arbitration council.[57]

An important clause of the MFLO required mandatory registration of all marriages and a standard marriage contract, the *nikah nama,* thus making it possible for the wife to seek enforcement through the courts. The *nikah nama* contains clauses which, if agreed upon at the time of the marriage, protect the position of the wife. For example, the *nikah nama* included the provision of *talaq-e-tafwid* (delegated right of divorce) to the wife. This provision permits the wife to end the marriage without having to go to a court, but she is required to send a notice of the dissolution to the chairman of the Local Council. The MFLO also provided for *mubara'at* (divorce by mutual consent). This ordinance—by mandating that marriages and divorces had to be registered to be legal—imposed certain conditions and restrictions upon the institution which favored or protected women who had traditionally been victimized due to the arbitrariness of the process under the complete control of the mullahs.

The MFLO also raised the minimum marriageable age of girls from fourteen to sixteen (and of boys from eighteen to twenty-one years) and it tried to protect a woman's right to *haq mehr* (dower) by specifying the entire amount of dower should be payable upon demand unless otherwise specified in the *nikah nama.* It provided that maintenance disputes to be settled by arbitration council, giving the council jurisdiction to grant maintenance retrospectively. Prior to the MFLO, maintenance could only be claimed through the courts under criminal procedure (Section 144 of the Criminal Procedure Code).[58]

In the matter of divorce, this ordinance eliminated the customary practice of declaring-by-repudiation divorce (pronouncing the word *talaq* thrice). In order to obtain a divorce, a husband was now required to send a written notice to the chairman of the Local Council, along with a copy to his wife (in Ayub's time the notice was sent to the chairman of the Basic Democracy). Once notified, there was a ninety-day wait period in the hopes of a possible reconciliation between the parties with the help of an arbitration council. Only if this reconciliation process failed, did the divorce become effective at the end of the ninety-day period, and if the wife was pregnant, after delivery. If reconciliation was achieved, the husband revoked the notice.[59]

The MFLO was, not surprisingly, rejected by the *ulema* and the religious parties as being "un-Islamic." Religious leaders throughout the country opposed it and strongly condemned the law as yet another attempt to distort the Quran. Pakistani women in an effort to challenge the allegations of the religious elements of society launched a movement in support of the MFLO, and in Lahore, Begum Nasim Jehan led a procession which ended in the burning of the effigy of Maulana Abbas Ali Khan who was one of the most vocal opponents of the MFLO (from East Pakistan) in front of the Punjab Assembly.

The specific clauses of the MFLO that the religious and conservative elements chose to attack included: Section 4 (grandchildren's right of inheritance of a living grandfather's property in the case of a deceased father); Section 5 (registration of nikah nama with local council); Section 6 (restrictions on polygamy); Section 7 (procedures for divorce) and Section 12 (ban on child marriage and raising minimum age for marriage).

The maulvis were concerned that this legislation posed a threat to their influence over people's lives by virtue of their former monopoly over family matters. Both historically and traditionally, the maulvi/mullah had exerted influence over society by regulating social contracts such as marriage and divorce. With the introduction of this ordinance, the legal and political structures were now granted by the state the role of being the primary interpreters and executors of social issues. Therefore, at least on paper, these secular entities had replaced the maulvis, whose social importance was thereby reduced to sermons and classes in the local mosque on the teachings of the Quran and the Hadith. The maulvis, who had historically considered "family matters" to be under their exclusive oversight and regulation, believed this legislation would permanently undermine their social position. This concern propelled them to exert enormous pressure on both social and governmental forces to get this ordinance repealed.

Although the concerted effort by the religious parties on behalf of the maulvis failed, since the military government under General Ayub Khan supported the enactment of the MFLO, the actual implementation of this law was limited due to the influence of the religious elements on society as a whole.[60] Instead of implementation of the measures specified in the MFLO, deeply entrenched traditions and customs prevailed. While it appeared that the procedures outlined in the MFLO legislation were being adhered to, such as use of specific documents like the nikah nama, the reality was that loopholes enabled the pre–MFLO status quo to prevail. For example, the required *nikah nama* (marriage certificate) was completed as stipulated but with the sections that involved the woman's rights in the marriage being intentionally left blank by the maulvi. Since the matrimonial process was unchanged what with the maulvi presiding over the traditional Muslim wedding service, the opportunities to circumvent the *spirit* of the MFLO were exploited always at the expense of the woman. Even in the urban areas, many educated women did not read the marriage certificate and just compliantly signed the document where required as they felt intimidated, shy, or secure that their interests were being protected. It was only those women with fathers and/or brothers who wished to legally protect them who made sure that specific, and favorable, language was included in the nikah nama in the advent of a talaq (divorce). The explanation for women's lack of assertiveness in this process involving a marriage contract has a cultural basis. During marriage proceedings women were supposed to act sad, shy, and compliant, while in reality such an event required a more active role in ensuring that their rights under the law were safeguarded. Thus, while the laws pertaining to marriage, inheritance, and divorce had been either enacted or amended to protect women, the reality was that the religious establishment through coercion, tradition or bribery managed to, by and large, maintain the pre–MFLO marital status quo.

The MFLO of 1961 was quickly judged as inadequate by many female activists. They thought its mere enactment failed to provide women in marital positions with adequate rights as implementation measures remained circumscribed due to embedded cultural and social mores and strong public opposition from the maulvis and other conservative elements. It was, nonetheless, a success from an enactment standpoint since it clearly outlined what was legally acceptable in marital relations in the future. Thus, as a legal blueprint on marital and inheritance matters it could be consulted and applied to specific cases. In the decades that followed its enactment, the MFLO would remain a lightening rod for Pakistani women as they fought to improve their status, and also for their equally vocal opponents, namely the religious/conservative elements in society who would continue to seek its abolishment.

THE POLITICS OF JUSTIFICATION: FATIMA JINNAH'S CANDIDACY FOR PRESIDENT

During the Ayub period, the other significant event involving women was the presidential candidacy of Fatima Jinnah (the sister of the Quaid-e-Azam, Muhammad Ali Jinnah) in the 1965 presidential elections. Fatima Jinnah was selected by the Combined Opposition Parties (COP) when their original candidate, Khawaja Nazimuddin, died in October 1964, during the election campaign. Fatima Jinnah's nomination was probably due to her status as the beloved younger sister of the Father of the Nation, Muhammad Ali Jinnah, and Pakistanis high regard for her services to the country as a prominent social worker. Her political experience, however, was limited to shadowing her famous brother as Jinnah campaigned on behalf of Muslim interests, and later for a Muslim homeland in India.

Interestingly enough, as a party in the COP coalition, the conservative Jamaat-e-Islami (JI) party found itself supporting Jinnah's candidacy in contradiction to its stated position that, under Islam, a woman could not be Head of State.[61] JI justified its support for Fatima Jinnah by releasing a statement that in "extraordinary circumstances" women could hold this office. While President Ayub Khan's—who was regarded as being sympathetic to women's demands for more rights—military government tried to make the candidacy of Ms. Jinnah controversial by questioning its legitimacy under

Islamic law.[62] Ayub's government had several *ulema* (Muslim scholars) issue *fatwas* (religious edicts) against a woman seeking to be the head of state in an Islamic country, which only served to encourage the controversy surrounding her candidacy. Fatima Jinnah's candidacy not only demonstrated the limits of Ayub's "feminism," but it also revealed the primacy of the political process over ideological rigidities.[63] Although the government tried to paint a picture of an unstable woman, the public came out in large numbers to show their support for her candidacy. She drew enormous crowds from Peshawar to Chittagong. In the election, Fatima Jinnah carried the urban centers of Karachi, Dacca, and Chittagong, and it has been speculated that absent a strictly-controlled indirect elections process by an electoral college of approximately 100,000 Basic Democrats, she would have been the country's first female head of state.[64]

Fatima Jinnah's nomination illustrates an important finding: in their quest for political power even the most dogmatic and rigid political groups are often willing to compromise on their stated core principles in the name of political expediency. In this particular case, not only did Maulana Maududi's ultraconservative religious party, the Jamaat-e-Islami, support a woman running for head of state of an "Islamic" country; but its opponent—Ayub's increasingly autocratic regime—which was regarded as being progressive on matters involving gender relations, chose to take a step back from its traditional position and seek the support of certain *ulema* to issue *fatwas* which challenged the right of a Muslim woman to become the head of a Muslim state. Ayub Khan, who was well known for his strong dislike of the religious elements in society, had done a complete about-face that challenged his longstanding views on women's right to equal treatment. This demonstrates the lengths that political groups or entities will go to in their quest for political power.

WOMEN'S STATUS IN THE BHUTTO ERA, 1970–1977

The establishment of the Pakistan People's Party (PPP) in the late 1960s in West Pakistan led to an effective mobilization campaign of people belonging to all socioeconomic groups. It was led by Zulfikar Ali Bhutto—a former member of Ayub Khan's cabinet—whose oratory skills and charismatic personality mesmerized the crowds he addressed in West Pakistan. Wherever Bhutto went, huge crowds gathered to hear him speak. Always dressed in *Shalwar Kameez* (traditional Pakistani attire), often with a Mao cap on his head, Bhutto successfully portrayed himself as one of *them*: the peasants and the workers. His speeches inspired these attendees (almost always men) to encourage their womenfolk to become political activists on behalf of the PPP and the country. Bhutto's popularity soared when he invoked the slogan of "roti, kapra aur makan."[65] Since its inception in 1967, the PPP strongly encouraged its female activists to go out into neighborhoods, towns, and even villages, in order to mobilize women from all walks of life to come out and cast their votes and to man polling booths in Pakistan's first general election held in December 1970.

The PPP's party manifesto promised women equal rights.[66] Following the election, many women who had participated in the electoral process joined the PPP drive to form *mohalla* (neighborhood) committees. These women, who were from middle to upper income backgrounds, visited poverty stricken areas for the first time to mobilize the women who lived there. Following the upheaval and the civil war which led to the break up of the state into two states (Pakistan and Bangladesh), the National Assembly (the Legislature) finally convened in 1972. One of its first tasks was the formation of a Constitution Committee, which included two women—Begum Nasim Jehan and Ashraf Abbasi—to draft the new Constitution.[67]

WOMEN'S STATUS UNDER THE 1973 CONSTITUTION

Although specific articles of the 1973 Constitution have been criticized by various segments of Pakistani society, it was adopted with the consensus of all of Pakistan's political parties who were represented in the National Assembly at the time. Thus, the document represented inevitable compromises and concessions to specific interests. What was significant about the 1973 Constitution as enacted, however, was the provision of specific rights and protections to the women of Pakistan *as equal citizens under the law*.[68] Article 25 of the Fundamental Rights stipulated equal status before the law for all citizens of Pakistan, as well as equal protection provides an additional safeguard for women by stipulating that there would be no discrimination on the basis of sex.[69] Article 27 of the Fundamental Rights clause prohibits discrimination on the basis of race, religion, caste, or sex for appointment in the service of Pakistan. Article 32 of the Basic Principles of state policy guarantees reservation of seats for women in the Local Bodies. Article 34 of the same Principles lays down that steps shall be taken to ensure the participation of women in all spheres of national life, and Article 35 stipulates that the state shall protect marriage, the family, the mother, and the child. Significantly, once the Constitution was ratified by the National Assembly, the Assembly amended Article 228 of the Constitution to accept the principle of at least one female member on the proposed Council of Islamic Ideology.[70] Women, however, consistently failed to achieve women's suffrage for a specified number of reserved seats for women in the National and Provincial Assemblies. Under the 1973 Constitution, women continued to be indirectly elected by the members of the Assemblies which placed women at a permanent disadvantage vis-à-vis their male colleagues.[71] Although the Bhutto government would amend this constitution eight times, women's rights were not affected since the primary aim was to limit judicial powers and, with the Second Amendment, to declare a Muslim minority, the Qadianis, "non-Muslims."[72]

WOMEN'S ACTIVISM DURING THE BHUTTO PERIOD

The 1970s were a period of increased mobilization of Pakistani women in universities, *mohallas* (neighborhoods), and factories resulting in a greater demand for more legislation that both protected and expanded gains made by women since independence.[73] Under the Bhutto government, changes were implemented to raise the status of women. For the first time a woman, Begum Ra'ana Liaquat Ali, was appointed as the governor of Sind; another woman, Kaniz Fatima, was appointed the vice-chancellor of a university; and Ashraf Abbasi, was elected deputy speaker of the National Assembly. All Government departments were now required to hire women thanks to the administrative reforms of 1972. For the first time in Pakistan's turbulent history, women could seek any governmental position which were previously not open to them, such as in the Foreign Service and district management groups of the Civil Service. Based on the stipulations of the 1973 Constitution, the government recognized that women were capable of holding any senior government position to include that of prime minister, governor, or a cabinet minister. Discrimination toward women in senior governmental positions was now limited to those who were non-Muslim (to include the Qadianis/Ahmedis).[74] One important specification of this Constitution under Article 227, that both the head of state (the president) and the prime minister had to be "Muslim," conflicted with the letter, if not the spirit, of Article 25 (Fundamental Rights). Since Article 25 stressed the equality of *all* citizens before the law; the barring of non-Muslims from holding one or both of these leadership positions could be interpreted as contradicting Article 25. Furthermore, this religious requirement of Article 227 implicitly divided Pakistani women into two categories: those who could run for the highest offices in the land (Muslim) and those who could not under the law (Christian, Hindu, Sikh, Ahmedi, etc.). Thus, under Article 227, not *all* women were equal, nor were men for that matter.

As a consequence of these legislatively enacted reforms, a large number of women entered the Foreign Service. In 1975, the International Women's Year was launched with much publicity and the prime minister's wife, Begum Nusrat Bhutto, represented Pakistan at the Mexico Conference on Women that year. Pakistan was a signatory to the Mexico Declaration and a semi-autonomous Pakistan Women's Institute was set up in Lahore that year in honor of the first International Women's Year.[75]

In January 1976, a thirteen-member Women's Rights Committee was formed under the chairmanship of Yahya Bakhtiar, attorney general of Pakistan, which included nine women, some of whom were pressing for a commission to determine the status of women in Pakistan and to make recommendations on how to improve their situation. The women activists included Nasim Jehan, Miriam Habib, Rashida Patel, and Zari Sarfraz. They managed to persuade the commission to examine legislative reforms that would improve the status of women and ensure better enforcement mechanisms to protect and provide women with appropriate relief in matters involving child custody and spousal support in the advent of a divorce.[76] In July 1976, the Women's Rights Commission presented its report on the Law Reforms. Interestingly enough, the commission's report was neither ratified nor implemented by the National Assembly, nor was it ever made public.[77]

It was during the Bhutto period that a variety of women's organizations flourished. While APWA's emphasis changed, new women's organizations emerged. The early seventies witnessed a shift in objectives vis-à-vis women's groups. Women were no longer satisfied in just undertaking social work–related projects but wanted an equal voice in more substantial developmental issues that concerned the country as a whole.

The United Front for Women's Rights was reinstated when the Constitution Committee was formed to draft the new constitution. Its primary objective was to get a number of reserved women's seats to be elected directly through female suffrage, embedded in the new Constitution. While it lobbied hard and tried various pressure tactics to achieve this objective, it failed to get this included in the Constitution and dispersed once the 1973 Constitution was finalized.[78]

Some of the more militant feminist groups that emerged during this period included *Shirkat Gah* (Women's Resource Center), the Women's Front, and *Aurat*. Shirkat Gah was established by a number of Western-educated women who perceived existing women's organizations to not be structurally up to the task of effectively promoting women's interests. Given their frame of reference (the women's movement in the West in the 1960s and early 1970s), these women believed that *desi*[79] groups like APWA and Behbud had too narrow a focus (improving women's existing status). Infused with Western notions of women's liberation and/or feminism, they confidently believed that such concepts (which were completely alien to existing cultural strictures) could, and should, be quickly introduced. In their minds, "liberation" and "feminism" needed to constitute the foundation upon which Pakistani women's "status" and well-being would be built. In November 1975, the group was informally established and called *Shirkat Gah* (Women's Resource Center). It was formally registered as an organization in August 1976.

Its seven founding members were professional women who belonged to the middle and upper-middle class. According to its Memorandum of Association the key goal was:

> to encourage a woman to play a full and equal role in her society by promoting and protecting the social and economic development of women already participating in or wanting to participate in the national development.[80]

Shirkat Gah goals included: to raise awareness among Pakistani women and to undertake research on women's issues in Pakistani society; to provide legal and medical assistance; to advocate in order to safeguard the rights of working women; and to publish on such matters. It also acted as a reference agency and kept directories of women who needed accommodation, day care centers, or jobs, and of working women who could work as "consultants" to the center and to future working women.

The organization of Shirkat Gah/Women's Resource Center was established on the principle that all members were equal. The center's first project was to set up a hostel for single working women in Islamabad. This hostel was opened in August 1976 and in addition to providing housing for single working women, it also was the Shirkat Gah's office. This hostel provided much needed accommodations for working women and it was transferred to the Pakistan government's Social Welfare Department in 1978, which continued to run it.[81]

Although Shirkah Gah's members had dispersed by 1977, it was later reestablished in 1979 by two of the original members in Karachi. Given its emphasis on concepts of "liberation" and "feminism" over the more pragmatic concerns of the overwhelming majority of Pakistani women, Shirkat Gah found itself isolated as existing women's organizations and the government distanced themselves from it. APWA, for example, did not see the utility of yet another women's organization and encouraged Shirkat Gah's members to join APWA instead. It was snubbed by other women's organizations possibly because its members were feminists and were politically "nonaligned." In comparison to other women's organizations, Shirkat Gah chose to work outside the political realm and sought change through "enlightenment" of Pakistani women. This was its undoing because it promoted itself as an *indigenous* movement when, in actuality, its ideology and goals were really a reflection of the ideological influences of the Western feminist movement on Shirkat Gah's leaders. It prided itself on being "nonpolitical" in comparison to the predominant women's organizations; when, in reality, by focusing on ideological "victories," instead of provision of tangible benefits, it understandably came to be viewed with suspicion by other women's organizations like Behbud who were trying to expand social services to lower-income women and their families. Shirkat Gah would evolve and come into its own during the more oppressive Zia-ul-Haq period when it would morph into the Women's Action Forum (WAF) and lead a popular and effective struggle against state-led oppression of women. It was quite visible on college campuses until it disappeared in 1977.[82]

CONCLUSION

The activism of urban Muslim women of the Indian subcontinent prior to the establishment of Pakistan was impressive in its scope and degree of success. It highlighted their ability to challenge traditional mores all in the name of Islamic nationalism which ultimately led to the—albeit reluctant—granting of the franchise to all Indian women by the British. This successful process of activism is indicative of a vibrant society willing to challenge the state apparatus in order to attain specific goals. Furthermore, these women continued their activism under the auspices of the new state of Pakistan and expected progression in their social, political, and economic position within this new state.

On the subject of gender policies during Pakistan's first three decades, the historical record suggests that these policies were not autonomous constructs of the state but were a consequence of social influences as exemplified by the ongoing power struggle between the religious elements on the one hand and the elite (including influential women's groups) on the other. The gradual legal progression in women's status, as specified in the MFLO of 1961, reflected the enormous influence of the urban elite on the policy processes of the state. Furthermore, how one woman, Begum Ra'ana Liaquat Ali Khan, could single-handedly influence the government to enact, and implement, a widely unpopular public policy (the establishment of two female military units) suggests that even in a conservative Muslim majority state a determined—albeit from a wealthy and influential family—woman can influence governmental decisions on matters pertaining to social issues. Her example suggests that the policy-making process even in a quasi-democracy is influenced by vying social actors and responds to various social pressures.

Notwithstanding the state's actions in consideration of these social pressures, implementation of state measures (state capacity) was problematic due to social resistance from opponents of these policies. An example of this "limited state capacity" was the enactment of the MFLO of 1961 wherein women's marital rights were to be protected through specific measures. Although, on paper, the MFLO did indeed bolster women's marital position in general and was widely unpopular with the religious establishment whose exclusive turf this had been prior to the passage of the MFLO; the reality was that, in practice, many of the stipulations of this law were deliberately ignored. Conservative social forces opposed what was regarded as state meddling at the behest of the elite, and found ways around it. For example, due to deeply entrenched customs, the marital document (the *nikah nama*) which was required now to legitimate a union had sections left blank that involved women's rights in the marriage. Second, the role of the maulvi in the conduct of marital ceremonies informally remained unchanged and he continued to influence the official documentation process to the detriment of the female.

Another important point that needs further exploration is that Pakistani state actors—although cognizant of social pressure brought to bear upon its apparatus on policy matters—are first, and foremost, concerned about their survival at the helm and are willing to conduct state business in a politically expedient manner if political survival is at stake. Thus, General Ayub sought the support of the ulema—a group he despised in general—by asking them to issue specific *fatwas* (religious decrees) against his female opponent (Fatima Jinnah) during the 1965 presidential election campaign. This was in contradiction to his longstanding, publicly enunciated, views on both the ulema and on women's status.

NOTES

1. Iftikhar H. Malik, "The State and Civil Society in Pakistan: From Crisis to Crisis," *Asian Survey* 36, no. 7 (1996): 673–690.
2. For more on the criticism of the thesis that Jinnah was a communalist from the very beginning of his political career see Ayesha Jalal, *The Sole Spokesman* (Cambridge: Cambridge University Press, 1985); Ian Bryant Wells, *Jinnah: Ambassador of Hindu-Muslim Unity* (London: Seagull Books, 2005); Akbar S. Ahmed, *Jinnah, Pakistan and Islamic Identity: The Search for Saladin* (London: Routledge, 1997).
3. Hamza Alavi, "Ethnicity, Society, and Ideology," in *Islamic Reassertion in Pakistan: The Application of Modern Laws in an Islamic State*, ed. Anita Weiss (Syracuse, NY: Syracuse University Press, 1986), 22.
4. Maulana Abul A'la Maududi (1903–1979) is widely considered within Pakistan's elite circles and by female activists to have been the most detrimental figure (after General Zia-ul-Haq) to the promotion/protection of women's interests and to the improvement of women's status in civil society. Under his tutelage, the Jamaat-e-Islami party waged an unrelenting political and social campaign to relegate women to second class status within the confines of their homes all in the name of Islam. Maududi's writing which justified the need to keep women in *purdah* (seclusion) was his book titled: *Purdah and the Status of Women in Islam* (New Dehli: Markizi Maktaba Islami Publisher, 1998). This book was originally published in 1939. For more on Maududi's views on how Shariah and its role in an Islamic State see Abul A'la Maududi, *The Islamic Law and Constitution* (Lahore, Pakistan: Islamic Publications Ltd., 1980). See also C. J. Adams, "The Ideology of Maulana Maududi" in *South Asia Politics and Religion*, ed. E. D. Smith (Princeton, NJ: Princeton University Press, 1966).
5. Jamaat-e-Islami was founded by Abul A'la Maududi around 1939–1940. The party was established in what was then British India in order to pursue Muslim interests and to seek greater concessions for Muslims. JI objected to the founding of a separate Muslim state because it saw such an event as destroying any chances of returning the Indian subcontinent as a whole to Muslim rule/subjugation. The JI's position was redefined in 1947 to support an Islamic State in Pakistan. Their goal was to realize this by purging society of "deviant behavior," which would lead to the establishment of Islamic (Shariah) law in the region. Once Maududi and the JI's cadre moved to Pakistan, they quickly became active in the political system, and especially

sought to disrupt the secular tendencies of the state. After General Zia-ul-Haq's coup d'etat, Zia became a staunch ally of JI's ideology/cause much to the chagrin of most Pakistanis.

6. See Stephen P. Cohen, *The Pakistan Army* (University of California Press, 1984), 87–88.

7. Zulfikar Khalid Maluka, "Islamic Theory and Practice," in *The Myth of Constitutionalism in Pakistan*, ed. Zulfikar Khalid Maluka (Oxford: Oxford University Press, 1995), 74.

8. Muhammad Ali Jinnah's famous speech delivered at Aligarh in 1944 that is widely quoted today as proof of Jinnah's enlightened approach toward the role of Muslim women in society.

9. Khawar Mumtaz and Farida Shaheed, *Women of Pakistan: Two Steps Forward, One Step Back?* (London: Zed; Karachi: Vanguard, 1987), 7. In this gem of a book, the authors provide a succinct and valuable historical framework on the condition and activism of Muslim women in pre-partition India. See also Siobhan Lambert-Hurley, *Muslim Women, Reform and Princely Patronage: Nawab Sultan Jahan Begum of Bhopal* (London: Routledge, 2007). Although Lambert-Hurley's primary focus is on the efforts of the Begum of Bhopal who—by gingerly navigating social and religious obstacles to reform efforts—helped Indian women secure better access to education. This fascinating account highlights the Begum's modus operandi: endorsing incremental change within the traditional context by employing Islamic precepts to legitimate the objective. Another book which examines social reform efforts in nineteenth-century India challenges the conventional wisdom of the day (of scholars)—that the lives of Muslim women were characterized by a monolithic identity (of passivity and submission)—given evidence to the contrary is Gail Minault's *Secluded Scholars: Women's Education and Muslim Social Reform in Colonial India* (Oxford: Oxford University Press, 1999). For more on the Sir Syed Ahmed Khan and his Aligarh Movement see Anita Weiss "The Slow Yet Steady Path to Women's Empowerment in Pakistan," in *Islam, Gender and Sociopolitical Change: Case Studies*, ed. Anita Weiss (New York: Oxford University Press, 1998), 124–126, 131–132.

10. Amar Nath Prasad and S. John Peter Joseph, *Indian Writing in English* (New Dehli: Sarup and Sons, 2006), 255.

11. Mumtaz and Shaheed, 40.

12. Mumtaz and Shaheed, 40.

13. Mumtaz and Shaheed, 41; see also Iftikhar H. Malik, *State and Civil Society in Pakistan: Politics of Authority, Ideology and Ethnicity* (New York: Palgrave Macmillan, 1997), 142.

14. Malik, 142; see also Mumtaz and Shaheed, 41.

15. For more on this historic conference see Siobhan Lambert-Hurley, "Fostering Sisterhood: Muslim Women and the All India Ladies' Association," *Journal of Women's History* 16, no. 2 (Summer 2004): 40–65.

16. Laura Dudley Jenkins, *Identity and Identification in India: Defining the Disadvantaged* (London: Routledge, 2003), 160.

17. Mumtaz and Shaheed, 42.

18. For a detailed examination of the events leading up to the Pakistan Resolution, see Muhammad Aslam Malik, *The Making of the Pakistan Resolution* (Oxford: Oxford University Press, 2001); Stanley Wolpert, *Jinnah of Pakistan* (New York: Oxford University Press, 1984), 184–187. Hamid Khan, *Constitutional and Political History of Pakistan* (Oxford: Oxford University Press, 2001), 34–36.

19. Farhat Haq, "Women, Islam, and the State in Pakistan," *The Muslim World* (April 1996): 160–161.

20. Malik (1997), 144.

21. Mumtaz and Shaheed, 47.

22. Mumtaz and Shaheed, 47. Mumtaz and Shaheed on page 48 make a strong case, based on the historical record, that women's issues or concerns were often only addressed during times of political crisis or war when their support was vital. They argue that once the conflict or issue was resolved or disappeared, women would often find their concerns ignored or were sidelined.

23. Sarah Ansari, "Polygamy, Purdah and Political Representation: Engendering Citizenship in 1950s Pakistan," *Modern Asian Studies*, December 5, 2008. See also Haq (1996): 158–175;

Ayesha Jalal, "The Convenience of Subservience: Women and the State of Pakistan," in *Women, Islam and the State*, ed. Deniz Kandiyoti (Philadelphia: Temple University Press, 1991), 77–114.

24. Begum Ra'ana Liaquat Ali Khan has been often regarded as the female equivalent of the Quaid-e-Azam, Muhammad Ali Jinnah. An energetic and passionate advocate on behalf of all women she inspired many young girls to follow their dreams/ambitions. For more on her, see Kay Miles, *The Dynamo in Silk: A Brief Biographical Sketch of Begum Ra'ana Liaquat Ali Khan* (Karachi: All Pakistan Women's Association, 1974); Mihr Nigar Masrur, *Ra'ana Liaquat Ali Khan: A Biography* (Karachi: All Pakistan Women's Association, 1980).

25. Mumtaz and Shaheed, 51.

26. Begum H. I. Ahmed, *Begum Ra'ana Liaquat Ali Khan* (Karachi: Kifayat Academy, 1975), 35.

27. "Maulvis" in Urdu is the equivalent to a Catholic father or priest. Such a person, however, generally does not have any religious training but came into this "profession" via contacts.

28. For more on this fascinating woman during this period, see "The Glory of Moguls," *Time*, May 8, 1950. Accessed at: http://www.time.com/time/magazine/article/0,9171,812405,00.html.

29. Mumtaz and Shaheed, 55.

30. Mumtaz and Shaheed, 55.

31. Ahmed (1975), 78.

32. Mumtaz and Shaheed, 55.

33. The "Sophia Smith Collection Series-National Organizations" at Smith College (Northampton, MA) contains the All Pakistan Women's Association (APWA) annual reports, pamphlets, newsletters, clippings and program papers from 1957–1964. See also Sylvia Chipp, "Tradition and Change: The All Pakistan Women's Association," *Islam and the Modern Age*. 1(1970): 69–90; Sylvia Chipp-Kraushaar, "The All Pakistan Women's Association and the 1961 Muslim Family Laws Ordinance," in *The Extended Family: Women and political participation in India and Pakistan*, ed. Gail Manault (Delhi: South Asia Books, 1989), 265–273.

34. Mumtaz and Shaheed, 52; see Haq (1996):164.

35. Mumtaz and Shaheed, 53.

36. Mumtaz and Shaheed, 53.

37. Anwar Syed, *Pakistan: Islam, Politics and National Solidarity* (Lahore: Vanguard Books Ltd, 1984).

38. Mumtaz and Shaheed, 54.

39. Nabeela Afzal, *Women and Parliament in Pakistan, 1947–1977* (Lahore: Pakistan Study Centre, University of Punjab, 1999); H. Alavi, "Pakistani Women in a Changing Society," in *Economy and Culture in Pakistan: Migrants and Cities in a Muslim Society*, eds. Hastings Donnan and P. Werbner (New York: St. Martin's Press, 1991).

40. Anis Mirza, "Women's Role in the Pakistan Movement and the Formative Years," *Women in Public Life* (October 1972), 4.

41. Mumtaz and Shaheed, 56.

42. Begum Jahanara Shah Nawaz had been elected to the All India Muslim League Council in 1937.

43. Mumtaz and Shaheed, 56.

44. Mumtaz and Shaheed, 56.

45. For more details see "The Constitution of 1956" in Hamid Khan, *Constitutional and Political History of Pakistan* (Oxford University Press, 2005), 102–120; Mumtaz and Shaheed, 56.

46. As reported in *The Pakistan Times*, Lahore, April 16, 1955.

47. In light of the timeline—the activism to abolish polygamy of the mid-1950s; the prime minister's decision to take a second wife served to infuriate those who sought the end to polygamy; the social activism of influential women which followed included social ostracism of second wives of wealthy men. A second "weapon" leveraged was APWA and the United Front for Women's Rights (UNFR) bringing public pressure to bear on the government on the subject and the need to abolish/ban it. These actions appeared to have lead to the prime

minister's decision to respond by establishing a commission to look into the matter and to recommend social reform.

48. Freeland Abbott, "Pakistan's New Marriage Law: A Reflection of Qur'anic Interpretation." *Asian Survey* 1, no. 11 (January 1962): 28–29.

49. Abbott, "Pakistan's New Marriage Law," 29.

50. "Report of the Commission on Marriage and Family Laws," *Gazette Extraordinary*, June 20, 1956, 1229.

51. "Report of the Commission on Marriage and Family Laws," 1212.

52. Mumtaz and Shaheed, 56.

53. For more on Ayub Khan, see Mohammad Ayub Khan, *Friends Not Masters: A Political Autobiography* (Oxford: Oxford University Press, 1967).

54. Khan, 106–107.

55. For more on the MFLO see Shaheen Sardar Ali, "Limits of Family Law Reforms in Pakistan: A Critical Analysis of the Muslim Family Law Ordinance of 1961," *International Survey of Family Law* (2002): 317–335; Javaid Rehman, "The Sharia, Islamic Family Laws and International Human Right Law: Examining the Theory and Practice of Polygamy and Talaq," *International Journal of Law Policy and the Family* 21 (2007), 108–127; Farida Shaheed, "Controlled or Autonomous: Identity and the Experience of the Network, Women Living Under Muslim Laws," *SIGNS: Journal of Women in Culture and Sociology* 19, no. 4 (1994): 997–1019; David Pearl, "Three Decades of Executive, Legislative and Judicial Amendments to Islamic Family Law in Pakistan," in *Islamic Family Law (Arab and Islamic Laws)*, eds. Chibli Mallet and Jane Connors (London: Graham and Trotman, 1990), 322–328; Riazul Hasan Gilani, "A Note on Islamic Family Law and Islamisation in Pakistan" in *Islamic Family Law(Arab and Islamic Laws)*, 342–347; Lucy Carroll, "The Muslim Family Laws Ordinance, 1961: Provisions and Procedures," *Contributions to Indian Sociology* 13, no. 1 (1979).

56. For an excellent scholarly study on *talaq* (Muslim divorce) in South Asia, see Lucy Carroll, "Talaq-i-Tafwid and Stipulations in a Muslim Marriage Contract: Important Means of Protecting the Position of the South Asian Muslim Wife," *Modern Asian Studies* 16, no. 2 (1982): 277–309.

57. Malik (1997), 145; Mumtaz and Shaheed, 58; Haq, 165.

58. Malik (1997), 145; Mumtaz and Shaheed, 58; Haq, 165.

59. Ian Talbot. *Pakistan: A Modern History* (New York: Palgrave Macmillan, 2005), 167–168.

60. Seyyed Vali Reza Nasr, *Islamic Leviathan: Islam and the Making of State Power* (Oxford: Oxford University Press, 2001), 63.

61. See Haq, 165.

62. For more on Ayub's strategy and use of Islamic symbols for legitimacy purposes, especially during the 1965 election, see S. V. R. Nasr, "Islamic Opposition in the Political Process: Lessons from Pakistan," in *Political Islam: Revolution, Radicalism or Reform?* ed. John Esposito (Boulder: Lynne Rienner, 1997), 142–144; see also Mumtaz Ahmed, "Islam and the State: The Case of Pakistan," in *The Religious Challenge to the State*, eds. Mathew Moen and Lowell Gustafson (Philadelphia: Temple University Press, 1992), 239–267; and Lawrence Ziring, *The Ayub Khan Era: Politics of Pakistan, 1958–69* (Syracuse, NY: Syracuse University Press, 1971).

63. Haq (1996), 165.

64. Malik (1997), 145–146; Khan (2005), 169–177; Hasan-Askari Rizvi, *Military, State and Society in Pakistan* (Lahore: Sang-e-Meel Publications, 2003), 114.

65. "Roti, Kapra aur Makan, (Urdu: food, clothes and house in Urdu) was a key slogan at PPP rallies to convince the audience that the PPP government intended to alter the status quo by leveraging the powers of the State to implement social change (i.e., socialism) that would benefit the masses. It resonated with PPP audiences and especially when Bhutto himself spoke of this promise at public venues.

66. For more on Bhutto refer to Ashok Kapur's *Pakistan in Crisis* (New York: Routledge, 1991), 155–158.

67. Mumtaz and Shaheed, 63.

68. For a detailed examination of the Pakistan Constitution of 1973 see Paula R. Newberg, *Judging the State: Courts and constitutional politics in Pakistan* (Cambridge: Cambridge University Press, 1995), 138–140; Khan (2005), 274–290;

69. Haq, 166.

70. The Council of Islamic Ideology was created to provide recommendations to Parliament and the Provincial Assemblies for bringing the existing laws into conformity with the injunctions of Islam and as to the procedures required to enable this process per Articles 228 and 230.

71. Mumtaz and Shaheed, 63.

72. K. M. Arif, "The Role of the Judiciary," *Khaki Shadows: Pakistan 1947–1997* (Oxford University Press, 2001), 281. See also Swarna Rajagopalan, *State and Nation in South Asia* (Boulder, CO: Lynne Rienner Publishers, 2001), 45–46.

73. Malik, 146; Samina Yasmeen, "Islamisation and Democratisation in Pakistan: Implications for Women and Religious Minorities," in *South Asia: Journal of South Asian Studies* 22, no. 1 (1987): 183–198.

74. Mumtaz and Shaheed, 63.

75. Mumtaz and Shaheed, 63.

76. Mumtaz and Shaheed, 64.

77. Mumtaz and Shaheed, 64.

78. Mumtaz and Shaheed, 65; see also Malik (1997), 146.

79. "Desi" is an Urdu term that means "native" or home grown. It can have both derogatory or positive connotations depending on the context within which it is used.

80. Mumtaz and Shaheed, 67.

81. Mumtaz and Shaheed, 68.

82. Mumtaz and Shaheed, 68.

Chapter Two

Islamization and Female Status

Life under General Zia-ul-Haq, 1977–1988

> My only ambition in life is to complete the process of Islamization so that there will be no turning back.
> —General Zia ul-Haq, President of Pakistan, August 14, 1983

General Zia-ul-Haq's determined efforts to "Islamize" Pakistani society during his dictatorial rule particularly impacted women and minorities. New laws—such as the *Hudood* Ordinances[1]—were the primary means to implement *Shariah* (Islamic) law. These laws placed the lives of some women in grave danger and ensured the reversal of the slow but significant gains Pakistani women had legally made since Pakistan's creation in 1947.[2] As Haq writes, "The 1977 military coup was a turning point for the women's movement in Pakistan."[3] General Zia-ul-Haq, in March 1978, announced he intended to Islamize the penal code of Pakistan thus succeeding to persuade certain religious elements in two political parties, the Pakistan Muslim League (Pagara group) and the Jamaat-e-Islami to join his cabinet.[4]

There has been much speculation on General Zia-ul-Haq's motives and timing in his efforts to bring Pakistani society into conformance with "Islamic" values as defined by his orthodox Sunni worldview, which mirrored the view of Maududi's Jamaat-i-Islami, an Islamist political party.[5] Some have argued that Zia's efforts to launch an "Islamization" campaign had more to do with seeking political and social legitimacy for his regime by appealing to specific social elements.[6] The only real constituency General Zia and his cohorts could seek support from was the religious elements that historically were on the sidelines in the Pakistani political process.[7] Jinnah, the Father of the Nation, was reinvented as being an Islamist and not a secular politician, and an effort was made to depict Jinnah as one who had favored the establishment of an *Islamic* state with rigorous Islamic codes and laws.[8]

Once the Zia regime successfully managed to get the Jamaat-e-Islami and the Pakistan Muslim League (Pagara group) to join the government, it launched a general campaign in the media that urged people to be more "Islamic" in their behavior and to make sure that their neighbors were too. The social climate began to change: first subtly, and then in more overt ways, which would have an adverse impact on the lives of urban women. General Zia's embarked on his "identity politics" crusade by launching a campaign for "Islamic morality." Overnight, women became the target of the religious clerics that began a campaign to keep women out of the public sphere in the name of Islam. Notwithstanding the gains women had made—both in the political and social arenas—they were the weakest political group, while the more moderate factions were inclined to support the ousted Prime Minister Bhutto's party, the PPP.

Pakistan's identity politics were, however, already well underway when General Zia assumed power. While it was Bhutto's government that set this reinterpretation process in motion by invoking a more "Islamic" theme for consolidation and legitimation purposes, it was careful not to dismantle or challenge the slow but steady gains Pakistani women had made both legally and socially to date. It did this by means of interpretation: Pakistan would be an "Islamic Socialist" state, where women would have equal opportunities as guaranteed by the 1973 Constitution. For Bhutto, his government's emphasis on making Pakistan an "Islamic" state was more a rhetorical exercise than a sincere effort to transform the secular core of the state itself. Cosmetic changes, such as declaring Friday the official day off, and banning the use of alcohol, were considered adequate measures in enforcing the "Islamic" character of the state.

From the very beginning, General Zia justified his takeover of the reins of power in 1977 with the following reasons: the political instability that characterized the country and threatened the nation's survival; and the need to bring the state into conformity with Pakistan's raison d'être through an "Islamization process."[9] In sharp contrast to former rulers of Pakistan, Zia became the first leader to argue for the introduction of an Islamic system as being a prerequisite for the "Islamic" state. He considered himself a "guardian" whose temporary role was to correct the political system.[10]

The "Islamization" process, as Zia interpreted it, would involve far more consequential measures on the part of the State: implementation of the Shariah (Islamic) laws that would take precedence over secular legal procedures and laws. In his bid for legitimacy, and to consolidate power, Bhutto however never conceived such an actual legal transformation from secular to theocratic as being a necessary basis for making Pakistan a more "Islamic" state. It can be surmised that perhaps Bhutto was never a proponent of a genuine

"Islamization" program, and merely leveraged this concept for purposes of legitimacy and/or consolidation after the loss of East Pakistan in 1971. Why? Because Bhutto was a Shia, and the actual enactment and implementation of Shariah would undoubtedly have to be based on Sunni (Hanafi Fiqh) jurisprudence in a country where over 85 percent of the Muslim majority were Sunni adherents to the Hanafi school of jurisprudence (fiqh). Furthermore, for Bhutto to advocate on behalf of a controversial program, would have led to criticism (even cries of heresy and betrayal from the Shia) being levied on him by both the Sunni and Shia factions. However, the first, and most significant, casualty of Zia's Islamization project was women's rights in society.

THE STATE'S ISLAMIZATION PROCESS AND ITS IMPACT ON WOMEN'S LIVES, 1977–1988

Under General Zia's tutelage, "Islamization" acquired legitimacy and the backing of the State.[11] After declaring Martial Law, and initial consolidation efforts, the Zia regime set about implementing its stated agenda of "Islamizing" of Pakistani society via its judicial system. In 1978, Zia announced that Pakistan's legal system would be based on *Nizam-i-Mustafa* (the law of the Prophet).[12] *The regime announced that the Shariah would be the basis of all law in Pakistan.* This would mean that any law passed by Parliament or the provincial assemblies had to be in conformance with Shariah.[13] Any laws found to be in violation of the criteria outlined in Shariah laws would be null and void and would be discarded or revised.[14]

On February 7, 1979, through a Presidential Order (Provisional Constitution Order 3 of 1979), special Shariat benches were established in all four provincial High Courts with the authority to strike down any law found to be in violation of Islamic law (i.e., Shariah) by invalidating it by a specific date. Every High Court was required to constitute a bench of three Muslim judges, called the Shariat Bench for exercise of jurisdiction being conferred based on this Order. Appeal of a High Court's decision lay in the Supreme Court, which was to constitute a bench which three Muslim judges (*qadis*) and was to be called the Shariat Appellate Bench.[15]

By early 1980, the Zia regime decided that these Shariat Benches—which were meant to supplement, not replace, the conventional court system—were not performing adequately. Thus, the President's Order No. 1 of 1980, as incorporated in the 1973 Constitution of Pakistan, under Chapter 3A, established the Federal Shariat Court (FSC) in order to review cases to ensure legal compliance with Islam. This move also reflected the state's mistrust of the Superior Courts. This Presidential Order disbanded the system of Shariat benches on High Courts and replaced it with the FSC in 1980 which originally consisted of five justices, including the chairman. The court appoints its own staff and frames its own rules of procedure. The FSC judges are appointed by the president of Pakistan who selects them from serving or retired members of the Supreme Court or a High Court, or from among persons with the appropriate qualifications for a High Court position. The judges hold office for a period of three years, which can be extended by the president.[16] The FSC is headquartered in Islamabad, the country's capital but also has provincial branches or offices.

When the FSC's ruled that the sentence of *rajm* (stoning to death) for *zina* (fornication) was repugnant to the injunctions of Islam (*Hazoor Bakhsh v. Federation of Pakistan*, PLD 1981 F.S.C. 145.), it infuriated the ulema. The FSC's "interpretation" was condemned as being contrary to Shariah and the judges were accused of being ignorant of both Islamic scripture and law; as well as being too "Westernized." The furious ulema demanded the Zia regime revamp the FSC by replacing its incompetent, "Western oriented," judges with trained qadis/ulemas (Muslim judges/scholars). This led to another constitutional amendment (President's Order 5 of 1981) which added three judges who were ulema and well versed in Shariah law, raising the number of judges who sat on the FSC bench to eight. These ulema were selected by a panel of ulema and then approved by the president in consultation with the chairman of the court. The reason for the addition of three ulema on the FSC bench was a direct consequence of the cacophony of complaints by the religious/conservative supporters of Zia and the concern Zia had that the five judges were too "liberal and secular" in their decisions and needed to be reined in by expanding the size of the FSC bench. Cognizant of other powerful social groups, Zia stopped short of making the FSC an exclusive venue for the ulema by retaining judges with actual legal credentials.

Jurisdiction to hear appeals to FSC decisions now resides in the Shariat Appellate Bench of the Supreme Court consisting of three (Muslim) judges of the Supreme Court and two ulema, appointed by the president. If any part of a law is declared to be in violation of Shariah, the government is required to take necessary steps to amend such law appropriately. Zia's Islamization agenda, as well as his consolidation (of power) concerns, led him in March 1981, to promulgate a Provisional Constitutional Order (PCO) which would serve as Pakistan's "constitution" while most of the 1973 Constitution was held in abeyance with the exception of Articles related to the daily workings of both the Federal and Provincial governments. The PCO, in the words of Mortimer "must be an almost unequalled document in world history in the frankness with which it institutionalizes the unfettered arbitrary power of a single man."[17]

Under the powers granted by the PCO, Zia established a *Majlis-i-Shura* or Muslim Consultative Assembly. It consisted of almost three hundred members, and this was the President's answer to his political critics and their demand for representative government. The *Majlis-i-Shura* was an appointed, not an elected body, and its powers were defined in the presidential order that created it. It had the power to recommend laws and was meant to satisfy certain Islamic traditions. It was seen as another legitimacy tool of the regime in its quest for Islamic credentials.[18]

The immediate, and most visible, impact of this so-called Islamization policy was to limit women's role in the public sphere. The state-controlled media implemented censorship measures. Women were required to wear headdress and "decent" clothes before they appeared on state-controlled television. The Federal government issued "chador" directives to all women employees.[19] Television programs depicted women as the root cause of corruption, as those who forced poor men into accepting bribes, smuggling, or pilfering funds, all in order to satisfy the insatiable female desire for clothes and jewelry. Similarly, working women were the cause of lax morality and the disintegration of the family and social values.[20]

The Zia's regime's overnight embrace of a conservative perspective vis-à-vis women created an unfriendly, almost threatening, atmosphere for urban women. At this juncture it is important to point out that although these measures would eventually impact the lives of all women in Pakistan in that a culture of intimidation and threat toward women's safety and well-being would emerge; initially those specifically affected were the urban, middle-class women who were a small minority. The lives of most Pakistani women at the outset were not adversely impacted by the Zia regime's efforts as they went about their daily lives. Rural women, as they had done for centuries, continued to work alongside their menfolk in the fields unveiled and outside their homes.[21] In the urban areas, however, it was a different story: numerous incidents of harassment of women by strangers in the streets of Lahore and other major cities; restrictions placed on women's participation in "spectator sports"; pressure to wear the chador (large sheet covering the body) in public areas to name a few.

Between 1978 and 1988, when the Zia government set in motion a series of measures that had an adverse impact upon the lives of females,[22] the only political party that the regime was able to garner support from was the Jamaat-i-Islami whose head, Maulana Mawdudi, enthusiastically endorsed Zia's initiatives in implementing the Nizam-i-Mustafa movement. Maududi praised Zia's efforts as the "renewal of the covenant" between government and Islam.[23] Zia managed to convince the Jamaat-i-Islami members to join his government and agreed to that party's longstanding demand that a separate women's university be established vice coeducational arrangements. It also began implementing the Jamaat's position on female attire in public by issuing various directives in 1979 that specified what type of appropriate attire women could wear to government offices. And, in 1980, the government decided to ban women from spectator sports.

THE HUDOOD ORDINANCES AND THEIR IMPACT ON WOMEN'S LIVES, 1979–1988

Zia-ul-Haq amended the Pakistan Penal Code through Presidential Decree to introduce the Hudood Ordinances in 1979.[24] These were a collection of five criminal laws: (1) The *Offenses Against Property Ordinance* pertains to cases of theft and armed robbery; (2) The *Offense of Zina Ordinance* relates to crimes of rape, abduction, adultery, and fornication; (3) The *Offense of Qazf Ordinance* deals with false testimony in *zina* cases (i.e., false accusations); (4) The *Prohibition Order* prohibits the use of alcohol and narcotics; and (5) The *Execution of Punishment of Whipping Ordinance* which prescribes the type of whipping to be implemented for those convicted under the *Hudood* ordinances. Zia justified his decision to promulgate these ordinances as being based on the recommendations of the *Majlis-i-Shura* (Council of Islamic Ideology), whose members were appointed by him.[25]

Zia's stated objective was to bring the criminal legal system of the country into conformity with the injunctions of Islam as specified in the Quran and the *Sunnah*. Thus the Hudood Ordinances of 1979 required the application of Shariah in cases involving murder, adultery, fornication (*zinâ bil raza*), rape and prostitution, perjury (*qazf*), theft and intoxication. One section of this ordinance details the types of punishment to be prescribed for a particular crime, including stoning by death (*rajm*) for adultery and amputation of a hand for theft.[26] These laws are considered to be the most controversial, and detrimental, legacy of the Zia period. Enactment of these ordinances was seen as the first step in Zia's process of "Islamization." Pakistani women, however, have borne the disproportional brunt of the enactment of these ordinances. These Shariah compliant laws reversed most of the gains women had slowly made since the establishment of the Pakistani state.[27] Worse, as Izzud-Din Pal writes, the dire effect or impact of the Hudood Ordinances was a *psychological* one. Furthermore, it was a political victory for the normally marginalized religious establishment, at least in the short run.[28]

One of the most controversial sections of the Hudood Ordinances involved Ordinance VII of 1979. In this section, this ordinance provides two contradictory markers of adulthood. The first criteria of adulthood is "one who has attained, being a male, the age of eighteen years or, being a female, the age of sixteen years. The second, alternate and contradictory, criterion for adulthood is "*or has attained puberty.*" Provision of these two competing criteria gave the enforcement elements wide latitude in terms of determining the applicability of Section VII of this ordinance by adding the "puberty" test in its prosecution criteria. Prior to these identifying criteria under the Pakistan Penal Code which this ordinance replaced, girls below the age of fourteen were not considered competent to give legal consent. Under the *Zina Ordinance*, however, children of both sexes could be prosecuted under these

Shariah compliant laws and face imprisonment, lashes or, worst of all, stoning. The fact that their youth may preclude them from understanding the seriousness of the charges under the new laws was considered irrelevant.

Significantly, the Quran or Hadith do not mention the use of puberty as a criterion for imposing *hadd* punishments probably because puberty is a biological process that spans an age range starting as early as nine or ten for girls, and is not specifically identifiable in boys. The use of such a varied biological marker (of puberty) that does not necessarily suggest actual mental and emotional maturity would be challenged in specific cases especially in light of the severity of the charges and punishments involved if convicted.

Furthermore, Ordinance VII, in accordance with the teachings of the Quran and the Sunna, requires four male witnesses as proof for adultery and fornication (*zina*). Where this legislation departs from the Quran and Sunna is in its requirement that there be four male witnesses for proving rape (*zina bil jabr*). Rape or *zina bil jabr* is defined as "the forced sexual intercourse by a man or woman with someone to whom the accused is not married." Punishment for *zina bil jabr* is the same as that prescribed for *zina*: one hundred lashes for the unmarried and stoning for the married. The ordinance states that if the convict is not an adult, punishment for *zina* and *zina bil jabr* will include imprisonment which may extend to five years, and/or a fine, as well as whipping "not exceeding thirty stripes." By requiring that rape take place in a place that is open or where there is the potential of having male witnesses present, this law in essence makes it unlikely that any rape cases would ever be brought up for prosecution. The mere fact that if four Muslim men did indeed witness the sexual assault of a woman, they might be disqualified from testifying on the grounds that they do not meet the high moral standards required of witnesses in an Islamic court. No prosecutorial rape case would be possible under the Hudood ordinances due to the unlikelihood of obtaining testimony from four *honorable* Muslim men who would certainly have intervened to stop the assault rather than stand idly by as witnesses. Under this ordinance, the only way a *zina bil jabr* case could be successfully prosecuted is if the rapist himself confessed to the charges.

The law proved to be a catch-22 for females in that if a female filed a criminal case charging rape but could not provide the required four male witnesses to the assault, she then faced the real possibility of being charged for the crime of fornication and/or adultery (*zina*) as she has confessed to a sexual act outside the bounds of matrimony. As ludicrous as this logic appears, the reality is that under the Hudood Ordinances there are a number of cases on record where a rape victim has been charged as co-accused for the crime of *zina* (fornication) while the rapist has gone free.[29] For example, in 1982, fifteen-year-old Jehan Mina became pregnant as a result of a reported rape. Lacking the testimony of four eyewitnesses that the intercourse was in fact rape, Jehan was convicted of zina on the evidence of her illegitimate pregnancy (*Mina v. State*, 1983 P.L.D. Fed. Shariat Ct 183) and her child was born in prison.[30]

Rape committed by police officers is a well-established fact in Pakistan and widely reported on by the Pakistani media, Amnesty International, and Human Rights Watch. One victim of police brutality, Shajida Parveen, was confronted with being charged with zina when she tried to file a complaint against two police officers who broke into her house on July 1994 and raped her after they locked her children in another room. Her medical examination stated that she was raped by more than one person, but the police refused to register her complaint. She had to go to the High Court to have the First Information Report registered, but even then no action was apparently taken against the police officers alleged to have raped her. While in other cases, media exposure has forced police to register a complaint brought by a woman. On January 3, 1995 Kaki, a fifteen-year-old Hindu girl, was abducted by two armed soldiers. She had gone to pray at a Hindu temple in Giddu, Hyderabad district. The soldiers took her to a nearby field and raped her, leaving her unconscious and injured. One of the soldiers absconded, while the other was turned over to the police by local people. Police initially refused to file a complaint. However, local newspapers reported the incident and the army ordered an inquiry. Only then did the police file a complaint and a senior police officer told journalists that a preliminary medical report had confirmed that Kaki had been raped. According to reports, Kaki's parents were threatened by police to make them drop the charges. To Amnesty International's knowledge, the findings of the army inquiry have not been published and no action appears to have been taken against the alleged rapists.[31]

Worse, for many women/girls reporting their rape to the authorities (read: police) sometimes results in further victimization. One poor family in Lahore sent their daughter, Shahnaz, to work as a housemaid for a restaurant owner whose son allegedly raped her and then threatened to kill her if she told anyone. Shahnaz's parents approached the employer, who reportedly filed a false case of theft against Shahnaz. She was arrested in October 1994 but was not brought before a magistrate as required under the law. Her family did not know where she was. After Shahnaz's brother filed a *habeas corpus* petition in the Lahore High Court, she was found in the living quarters of a subinspector of police in Model Town. There was no record of her arrest. Upon her release, Shahnaz reportedly stated that she had been repeatedly raped in custody. It is not known if any action has been taken against the police officer. In another case, Shameem, a twenty-one-year-old mother of three, went to the police to file a rape complaint. She was raped again—*this time by the police*. Shameem, from North Nazimabad in Karachi, was kidnapped with two of her children and raped by a cleric in July 1991. Shameem's mother filed a complaint with the police. Several months later, the accused cleric was detained in police custody for questioning but he was released in June 1992, reportedly for lack of evidence. Shameem escaped from the cleric's house after almost thirteen months of captivity. She and her mother went to Peerabad police station to file a complaint about the abduction and rape. The police officers refused to register Shameem's complaint, stating that she must have acquiesced in the act, and charged her with zina. The police then detained Shameem and demanded a bribe of Rs. 15,000 (US$500) for her release. Shameem said the police officers beat her regularly and insulted her. She reported that at night:

> two of them beat me and held me down while the third one raped me. Then the other ones raped me, one after another. They took turns holding me down and raping me, every night. They threatened to kill me and my children if I told anyone about it.[32]

Another problem with the Hudood ordinances and zina bil jabr cases had to do with their insistence that the four eyewitnesses be *honorable males*. By disallowing the testimony of other women who were more likely to witness such an assault of their sister, mother, aunt, friend, etc., it further eliminated the possibility of prosecution of a male aggressor. The women most vulnerable to sexual assault tend to reside outside of their family homes and villages, often in major urban centers. For these women—who might be pursuing a higher education or employment away from home in metropolitan areas and have to reside in a women's hotel or hostel—the failure to consider testimony of women was a major hurdle for female rape victims. Such laws, it can be argued, discouraged women from pursuing higher education or employment opportunities that involved a move to another area and living with other women or on their own since predators were protected by the discriminatory prosecutorial requirements of zina bil jabr cases.[33]

Although the Quran does not specifically mention zina bil jabar (rape), the Hadith briefly do. In the *Al-Muwatta* collection of Hadith, in a section titled "Judgment about Raped Women, Virgin and Non-Virgin," it is recommended that hadd punishment be applied to the rapist only, and no punishment for the raped woman. Importantly, it does not suggest the need for witnesses to the crime, nor does it specify what punishment should be awarded to the rapist.[34] One of two historical examples provided in the Hadith is an incident involving a woman in the desert who was forced to consent to intercourse with a man in order to receive water to drink. Ali (Muhammad's cousin and son-in-law) exonerated her when he discovered that she had been compelled by circumstances beyond her control.[35] The other recorded incident, also traced to Ali, involved a man and a woman accused of adultery and ordered to be stoned to death. When Ali was told by the woman that she had actually been raped by the man, he did not allow the punishment to be carried out.[36]

Another important area of discrepancy between the Hudood Ordinance and Sunnah (the Quran and the Hadith) is the criteria used for proof for adultery and fornication cases. Given the severity of the punishment—flogging or stoning to death—the Quran specifies stringent criteria for prosecution, namely provision of four male adult witnesses of good character. If four witnesses to *zina* (adultery) cannot be produced, the Quran is unambiguous: the accusers are to be flogged as they are "wicked transgressors."[37]

While the Hudood Ordinances also require four eyewitnesses to the event, they caveat this requirement by allowing the judge to use his judgment based on "the evidence of record," in deciding the punishment if one of the four witnesses retracts his testimony. This is an important deviation in that it does not prosecute—as is prescribed in the Sunna—cases involving slander for which the Quran prescribes hadd punishments.[38] Instead, the Hudood Ordinances cases involving slander were placed in the *ta'azir*[39] category in which judicial discretion is allowed. The record suggests that Pakistani courts have, on the basis of ta'azir, handed down fines and imprisonment for frivolous accusations according to the Hudood Ordinances. Muslim scholars believe the stringent requirements for establishing guilt are due to the severity of the hadd punishments (the worst being stoning to death) if convicted. In fact, in the Hadiths the only convictions cited which involved sexual misconduct were obtained through confessions not witnesses.[40]

While the Hudood Ordinances required the courts to be diligent in ensuring that the witnesses to zina be men of good moral character, they did not provide any criteria or guidelines as to how this is to be evaluated and decided. Furthermore, the record suggests that Pakistani judges have tended to use ad hoc measures for determining the credibility of the witnesses, which have ranged from cross examination, to eliciting public opinions, or to none at all. The absence of specific criteria, and the failure of the ordinances to follow the guidelines of the Quran in their treatment of slander charges in zina cases, removed an essential safeguard against the real possibility of false accusations. This safeguard would be especially pertinent in light of the fact that the punishments for zina cases are so severe.[41]

Ordinance VIII specifically deals with the punishment for false accusations. It defines *qazf* as "whoever by words either spoken or intended to be heard, or by signs or by visible representations, publishes an imputation of zina concerning any person intending to harm, or knowing or having reason to believe that such imputation will harm the reputation or hurt the feelings of such person is said, *except in cases hereinafter excepted* (emphasis added), to commit qazf. The "excepted" cases when hadd punishment for slander would not be awarded include instances in which "the imputation is being made or published for public good." The other instance or exception is if an accusation of zina has been made in "good faith" against an individual "to any of those who have lawful authority over that person with respect to the subject matter of accusation."[42] These broad exceptions are problematic in that they open up the process to subjective interpretation "that clearly dilute the punishment for qazf as a deterrent against false accusations of zina." Furthermore, they have no precedent in the Quran, nor the Hadith, as neither make any such allowances for recanting of eyewitness testimony, and they are unambiguous in meting out harsh hadd punishment to those who recant or withdraw their testimony.

Under these ordinances, Pakistani courts allowed the accusation of qazf to be made formally in court. The Pakistani courts have only allowed consideration of hadd for slander punishment once they decided that the individual made a false accusation of zina or if four witnesses had not been produced. These courts have not convicted those accused of slander in zina cases if it is "proved" that the accusation was made "in good faith." Furthermore, the onus of proving that the allegation was mala fide is on the complainant. This whole process clearly provides little protection to women against false accusations and from social humiliation contrary to the spirit of what was intended in both the Quran and the Hadith traditions.[43]

The impact of Ordinance VII on women's lives was swift, as it was severe, as evident in the numbers: In 1980 and 1981, there were a total of seventy female prisoners in all of Pakistan and twenty had been convicted of a number of sex related crimes.[44] By 1984, four years after the passage of Ordinance VII, 1,843 cases of zina had been registered according to police records. By 1987, in the province of Punjab alone, 125 women were in jail, almost half imprisoned for committing or abetting zina. There is little doubt that the number of convictions and cases registered for zina against both sexes, but especially against women, increased due to the institution of the Hudood ordinances.[45]

The Federal Shariat Court, although part of the state apparatus created to implement its policies, such as the Hudood Ordinances, quickly became a moderating influence on the ongoing Islamization process through its interpretation of these ordinances during appeal hearings. To its credit, it examined individual Hudood cases using the more stringent evidentiary requirements as outlined in the Hadith thus signifying a departure from the criteria established during the state's enactment phase. Nonetheless, the adverse psychological, and physical, impact of the enactment of the Hudood Ordinances on Pakistani women's lives cannot be overstated.

One of the first cases that helped to catapult some urban women to become activists was the 1982 case of Safia Bibi (*Bibi v. State*, 1985 P.L.D. Fed. Shariat Ct. 120); a blind unmarried eighteen-year-old woman raped by her landlord and his son.[46] When she became pregnant, her father lodged a complaint of rape against the two men. Since Safia unsurprisingly could not provide four witnesses, her pregnancy was taken as circumstantial evidence of zina. In a stunning verdict, the court acquitted the men, giving them the benefit of the doubt, but sentenced the young woman to three years' imprisonment and fifteen lashes for having sex outside marriage. This judgment set off a wave of protests and appeals on her behalf. The *Khwateen Mahaz-e-Amal* or Women's Action Forum (WAF), founded in 1981, investigated the details of the case and publicized their findings. WAF, along with other women's groups, filed a writ in the Federal Shariat Court challenging the Zina Ordinance.[47]

Due to WAF's efforts, the Federal Shariat Court agreed to take up the case for review. It rescinded the lower court's judgment and severely criticized the methodology used by the Session Judge to arrive at the decision.[48] In its hearing on the case, the Federal Shariat Court did differentiate between adultery and rape. Safia's sentence was dismissed and she was finally released after having served six months in jail.[49] Thus the pressure exerted within the country, and also due to the international outrage at her conviction, the case was dismissed.[50] Less known was what Mumtaz and Shaheed in their seminal book called "the enlightening outlook" of the FSC's presiding judge, Justice Aftab Hussein, who opined that if a man was acquitted due to lack of evidence (four witnesses or a confession), and thus given the benefit of the doubt, the female must also be given the benefit of the doubt as the mere fact of her pregnancy did not in of itself prove guilt.[51]

The successful reversal of Safia Bibi's conviction for rape by the Federal Shariat Court was widely celebrated by various women organizations. They had come onboard with WAF to litigate on behalf of specific cases, as well as to promote and to protect women's rights under the 1973 Constitution and the MFLO of 1961. This victory was a watershed moment for female activists in that it highlighted how, through effective mobilization by various women's groups in different parts of the country, they were able to get this new Shariah Court to review and reverse a ruling that had been made on the basis of the new Hudood ordinances.

While the significance of the activism of women's groups and their supporters within the country cannot be overstated, external influences also played a determining role in this outcome. When Representative Clarence D. Long, chairman of the powerful House Appropriations Committee read an article that recounted the details of this case, he furiously threatened to cut off all funding to Pakistan for the Afghan war effort if General Zia did not ensure that the girl was immediately pardoned, put in a home, and cared for. The very next day, Pakistan's ambassador, General Ajaz Azim, appeared in the chairman's office and announced that President Zia had told him to personally convey that the matter had been resolved exactly as the chairman requested. Because of this assurance, Representative Long agreed to cooperate in ensuring that Pakistan got the allocated funds.[52]

In recognition of a disturbing new trend of the Pakistani state which sought reversal of gains women had made since Independence, the Karachi based women's organization, Shirkah Gah, decided to take action. It moved toward the establishment of a platform which would represent as many women's organizations as possible. Toward this end, it called for a meeting of all women's organization, including APWA (the All Pakistan Women's Association) which had historically been an informal social arm of the State and enjoyed extensive support of the state in its actions/efforts.[53]

The first public flogging of a woman for having sex outside marriage took place in 1983. The judge was particularly infuriated that the thirty-five-year-old mother of five, Lal Mai, refused to divulge the name of the man who fathered her youngest child. Dressed in white, in a tent-like Islamic veil, she was tied to a pole, her hands and feet outstretched, and given fifteen lashes with a heavy strip of leather. The flogging of Lal Mai led to protests by women's organizations all over the country. As a result, women were no longer flogged in public. Instead the floggings were held in prisons in front of other female inmates. After martial law was lifted in 1985, no court has since sentenced a woman to flogging.[54]

In early 1988, the conviction of Shahida Parveen and Mohammad Sarwar sparked public criticism. Both were to be stoned to death but because of public outcry and the actions of various groups on their behalf, they were retried and later acquitted by the Federal Shariat Court. In this case, the FSC took the view that the notice of divorce by Shahida's former husband, Khusi Mohammad, should have been given to the chairman of the Local Council, as stipulated under Section 7(3) of the MFLO, 1961. This section states that any man who divorces his wife must register it with the Union Council. Otherwise, the court concluded that the divorce stood invalidated and the couple became liable to conviction under the Zina Ordinance.

ENACTMENT OF THE *QANOON-E-SHAHADAT* (LAW OF EVIDENCE)

Unfazed by the challenges posed by WAF and others, the various government entities established to promote Zia's Islamization agenda, continued to work toward the implementation of Islamic laws. In 1982, the Council of Islamic Ideology recommended the promulgation of the Law of Evidence stipulating that in Hudood cases two male or four female witnesses would be needed to prove a crime.[55] In 1984, Zia ordered that the Evidence Act of 1872 be replaced by the Law of Evidence (*Qanoon-e-Shahadat*) which initially stated that in all cases other than those covered by the Hudood Ordinances and by other "special laws," two male witnesses, and in the absence of two male witnesses, one male and two female witnesses, would be required for proving a crime.[56] As Shahnaz Khan explains:

> The onus of providing proof of rape rests with the victim under the Hudood Ordinances and there are severe ramifications if she does not provide that proof. If she is unable to convince the court, her allegation of rape is in itself considered as confession of Zina and the victim effectively implicates herself and is liable to Tazir punishment. Furthermore, the woman can be categorized as the rapist herself since it is often assumed that she seduced the man.[57]

During the two years between October 1982 and October 1984, when the Law of Evidence was finally enacted, it was the focal point of women activists. The WAF and other women's organizations launched a major campaign against what was perceived to be a discriminatory law which equated the evidence of two women to one man in all matters. WAF spent most of 1983 and 1984 protesting against the proposed Law of Evidence. WAF highlighted what it considered were the unfair, and un-Islamic, aspects of the proposed ordinance for women. It consulted lawyers and Islamic scholars to indicate that the ordinance was not within the framework of the Quran and the Hadith.

The most dramatic moment of WAF's campaign against General Zia's Islamization program occurred in February 1983 while protesting the Law of Evidence. WAF organized a public protest against this proposed ordinance, which led to a clash with the police and the arrest of female activists.[58] This incident involved women's groups who had responded to a call from the Punjab Women Lawyers' Association to join a march down the Mall road of Lahore (the main artery of the city) to the Punjab High Court to present a memorandum against the proposed law to the Chief Justice, on behalf of women's organizations. About three hundred women from different walks of life gathered to march down the Mall and were greeted by a large police force who tear gassed them. Some of the women were seriously injured and fifty women were arrested.[59]

The Pakistan Women's Lawyers Association brought suit against the government on Islamic legal grounds that the police, as unrelated men, had no right to touch the demonstrating women. Although this public protest received considerable media coverage, it was not the first time women had publicly demonstrated: In 1982 women had demonstrated against the discriminatory Hudood ordinances and were assaulted by *lathis* (sticks) by the police to disperse the demonstrators. This was the first large street protest against martial law in Pakistan and it had been carried out by women. Due to the press coverage of the incident, the Zia government was forced to recognize the fact that they had a formidable opponent (female activists) on their hands.

This incident convinced the regime that women's groups had to be taken more seriously as a possible threat to their social agenda. The significance of the actions by these women during a period of martial law was not lost on politicians either who had been sidelined by the regime: women, to date, had been the only social entity that was willing to engage the regime through protest in the streets. The same could not be said for the political parties who had been reticent to challenge the Zia regime on the streets. In fact, this incident led some of the political parties to seek an alliance with women's groups like WAF, but they were quickly rebuffed. As a result of the large-scale public protest against the Qanoon-e-Shahadat, the interpretation finally decreed into law included the caveat that this evidentiary requirement would be the case in matters involving financial cases only and would not pertain to other matters. This was seen by female activists as a needed validation that their efforts to reverse the discriminatory legal trend against women was working, but they recognized that it was going to be a long struggle.

The Proposed Law of Qisas and Diyat

While the stipulations of the Law of Evidence were revised before passage of this law, women experienced another setback in 1983 when the nominated *Majlis-e-Shura* (Consultative Assembly) passed a law drafted in 1980 by the Council of Islamic Ideology regarding *Qisas* (retribution) and *Diyat* (blood money). The proposed law stipulated that the blood money for a female victim would be half that of a man. Another section of the proposed law declared abortion illegal under any circumstances. Punishment for abortion would carry a penalty of seven years of imprisonment. The word *qisas* literally means retribution, and according to its guidelines, punishment is based on "an eye for an eye," while *diyat* is "blood money" for murder, or financial compensation for physical injury in lieu of retribution.[60]

The original draft proposal of the law stated in Section 25(b), that the *diyat* for a female victim of an offense of *qatl-e-khata* (unintentional murder) would be half of that of a male. The law proposed that in a case of death, the blood money for a man should be fixed at 30.63 kg of silver (or its equivalent), and only half of this amount for a woman. Similarly, in all instances of compensation for bodily injury, an injured or maimed woman would receive only half the compensation due to a man for the same injury. On the other hand, women guilty of murder, or causing bodily injury, would be liable to the same punishment as men.

Women organizations rejected this proposed law for two reasons. First, they opposed the legal practice of placing a price on human life. Second, they argued that the Quran does not specify any amount of *diyat*, nor does it mention the question of gender in this regard. In Sura *An-Nisa* (4:92), the Quran on *diyat* says:

> It never is it for a believer to kill a believer except by mistake; and he who kills a believer by mistake should free a believing slave and pay blood money to the victim's family unless they forgo it as an act of charity.[61]

WAF and other women's organizations challenged this proposed compensation under the *diyat* on the basis that the above verse from the Quran on *diyat does not make any reference to gender of any of those involved* (emphasis added), nor does it mention greater or lesser amounts of compensation among the believers. The justification for this discretion, the supporters of the *diyat* argued had to do with the fact that a man was the breadwinner of the family and support of the family depended on him. With his death, the proponents of this Law argued, the family lost its sole provider; whereas in the case of a woman, this was not the case, hence the difference in compensation.

Women activists saw this proposed law as yet another attempt to delegate women to the status of second class citizens under the law. They argued that proponents of this law overlooked the daily contribution women made within the confines of their homes, and failed to include the contribution that women in the rural areas made in agricultural production as they worked in the fields doing back breaking agricultural work without the benefit of technology. WAF and other women activists also objected to the provisions of *Qisas*. The clause that they objected to was Section 10(b) in the proposed draft Ordinance. According to this section, proof of murder liable to qisas required the testimony of two Muslim male witnesses (fulfilling the requirement of *tazkia-e-shahood*). Women as witnesses would be admissible for awarding *ta'azir* (lesser punishment). Thus a woman's eyewitness evidence would be reduced to the status of circumstantial evidence in all instances of murder or bodily injury. Women were concerned that under this law, if a murder was committed in the presence of women, the murderers could go unpunished. Furthermore, the law would not accept the testimony of women or non-Muslims in cases involving maximum punishment.[62] The Law of Qisas and Diyat were not enacted until 1997 when Nawaz Sharif's Pakistan Muslim League (PML) and his supporters in the National Assembly enacted the Qisas and Diyat Ordinance.

The Proposed Shariat Bill and Amendments to the Constitution

The passage of the Eighth Amendment to the Constitution was a huge blow to the women's movement that sought to legislatively remove the *Hudood* Ordinances and the 1984 *Qanoon-e-Shahadat*. This amendment stated that any ordinance, laws and acts made during Zia-ul-Haq's rule stand validated and cannot be questioned in any court of law on any ground whatsoever. It effectively ensured that the "Islamic" laws enacted to date would not be able to be repealed.[63] The Eighth Amendment to the 1973 Constitution successfully embedded Zia's Islamization program into the state's blueprint. Ever since, opponents of this amendment have faced an uphill battle to reverse this process with limited success.

The Shariat Bill of 1985 was introduced in Parliament by two members of the Jamaat-i-Islami. The bill stipulated that the legislature will have no powers to make any laws in conflict with Shariah. The definition of Shariah was that it included not only the Quran and Sunnah, but also *ijma* (consensus), *ijtihad* (independent reasoning), and *qiyas* (ascertaining) evolved over the centuries. The problem with this broad definition of Shariah, as provided in this bill, was that since some of these concepts involved consensus, no laws would be passed, as differing opinions would prevent any changes, making the passage of laws static.[64]

The Shariat bill sought to establish an Islamic state based on the Hanafi fiqh. It also recommended that only "recognized ulema" be appointed to the courts. There would be no court of appeal against a judgment of the Shariat courts which would retain jurisdiction over all matters, thus undermining the power of the legislative body; while the Ninth Amendment sought that all laws in Pakistan should be in conformance with Shariah laws.

Opposition to the Shariat bill, and the Ninth Amendment, did not only come from women this time, but also from the sizeable Shia minority (around 20 percent of the population), the Ahmedis, the Ismailis, and all the major political parties which had been allowed to resume functioning once martial law was lifted in December 1985. The first objection involved the selection of a particular school of Muslim jurisprudence (*Hanafi fiqh*) would encourage sectarian violence and lead to deep schisms within society where one group, namely Muslims belonging to the *Hanafi* school, would be seen as being accorded privileged status by the state. The second concern was that by imposing Islamic laws based on the tenets of one Muslim school of jurisprudence, the principles of justice and the fundamental rights of citizens as being equal under the law would be negated. General Zia believed that between the two Muslim sects, Sunni and Shia, there were little differences in their belief in one God, the Quran, the Prophet, and the Hadith. Zia's logic was small consolation for the Shias who began to voice their own objections to these proposed bills.

When the Shariat bill was introduced in the NA it was not approved in spite of Zia's efforts. He did manage to get it approved by the Senate which was dominated by Zia loyalists, but the bill was kept pending by the NA through various stalling methods. This move by members of the National Assembly enjoyed the tacit support of the appointed Prime Minister Junejo and served to infuriate Zia and would lead Zia to unceremoniously dismiss Junejo and dissolve the National Assembly on May 29, 1988. The Senate was not, however, dissolved given its carte blanche support for Zia's efforts to introduce Shariah laws.[65]

The Ninth Constitution Amendment Bill was introduced in the Senate on July 7, 1986 by the ruling Pakistan Muslim League (PML) to counter the proposed Shariat bill. The Ninth Amendment varied from the Shariat bill in that it reduced the power of the ulema, and it also proposed that financial and economic matters be kept separate and out of the jurisdiction of the Shariat courts. It was passed the next day by a two-thirds majority. Out of eighty-seven members, sixty-seven voted in favor of the bill.[66]

The Shariat Bill of 1988 and Its Impact on Women's Status

On June 15, 1988, two weeks after dissolving the national and provincial assemblies (elected on non-party basis), and disbanding ministries (formed on party basis), General Zia enacted "The Enforcement of Shariah Ordinance of 1988," which declared Shariah as the supreme law of the land. [67] Article 3 of the Shariah Act stated that "the Shariah that is to say, the injunction of Islam as laid down in the Holy Quran and Sunnah, shall be the supreme law of Pakistan."[68]

Upon promulgating the Shariah Ordinance, Zia stressed: "Nifaz-i-Shariah is not only the basis of our existence but also is a guarantee for our survival."[69] To some supporters of this legislation, Zia's ordinance had fallen short in that it did not specify that the Shariah was supra-constitutional. Clause 4 enabled the Constitution to remain exempt from the scrutiny of the courts. Zia's ordinance gave the High Courts jurisdiction to interpret matters that were outside the purview of the Federal Shariat Court as per Article 203-B. Interestingly, the judges of Pakistan's four High Courts were not known to be "Islamic judicial activists," nor were they known to be informed on Islamic law.[70] Thus supporters of these ordinances were concerned that due to Clause 4, the Islamization program would not be appropriately implemented.

Opposition in the parliament was voiced by the Opposition Parliamentary Group (OPG) and the extra-parliamentary Movement for the Restoration of Democracy (MRD) who agreed that the passage of any Shariah legislation was neither necessary nor desirable. They argued that this legislation was merely an attempt on part of an unpopular regime in its efforts to gain legitimacy. The MRD leader, Benazir Bhutto continued to argue that, "Zia's Islamization policy was reactionary, barbaric, and discriminatory to the rights of women."[71]

MOBILIZATION OF WOMEN: FROM SOCIAL WELFARE TO POLITICAL ACTIVISM, 1981–1988

After General Zia's military takeover in 1977, the reaction of Pakistani urban women was one of private indignation at the subtle, and not so subtle, attempts of the new regime's to "Islamize" them.[72] The challenges posed by the State to their various freedoms were greeted with indignation, such as the social debate on whether or not a woman had the right to dress as she wanted; her right to drive a car (which was brought up in the Sind Assembly); her right to participate in spectator sports; even her right to leave the house alone was questioned. But when speculation began that there was a state sponsored plan to repeal the Muslim Family Laws Ordinance of 1961, urban women grew alarmed and many realized they would have to take a more proactive approach.

Although the Hudood Ordinances were promulgated in 1979, the implications of these ordinances were initially underestimated by urban women until the fall of 1981 when the specific court case of Fehmida and Allah Bux versus the State was tried under these ordinances. This case propelled Pakistani women in the urban areas to become activists rather than remain passive observers.[73] With the successful activist past of their mothers and grandmothers dating back to the colonial times in mind, these women shifted gears by getting involved in the political process during a period of martial law. It was the punishment prescribed for Fehmida and Allah Bux's *zina* case (the man to be stoned to death and the woman to receive a hundred lashes) that galvanized educated women in the urban areas to mobilize.

FORMATION OF THE WOMEN'S ACTION FORUM

The formation of the *Khawateen Mahaz-e-Amal* (Women's Action Forum) can be viewed as a critical event as, through its activist agenda, it would become a formidable opponent of the state. The Women's Action Forum (WAF) wanted to provide both a platform, as well as a forum, for women and women's organizations. The key word that defined this group was "action": it saw a state moving toward reducing women status through draconian laws and sought to counteract this trend. In its very first meeting, WAF members discussed how to best mobilize to intervene in the Fehmida-Allah Bux case. This required the procurement of the case proceedings, as well as an investigation into the Hudood Ordinance itself. It was decided that WAF would appeal on behalf of the defendants but this proved to be unnecessary as one of the prominent attorneys in matters of Islamic jurisprudence, Khalid Ishaq, offered to represent the defendants in the proceedings. While WAF established and maintained contact with Mr. Ishaq, it focused on other matters that concerned women at that time.

WAF was concerned about two things: first, the ongoing implications of the Hudood Ordinances; second, the possibility that the government would repeal the MFLO of 1961 in order to strengthen its position vis-à-vis certain social elements. The first action WAF took was a signature campaign which emphasized five basic points:

> that the Family Laws Ordinance be strengthened to protect women, and not be repealed; that women be given protection in police custody; that the ban on women participating in spectator sports be lifted; that scarce financial resources be put into basic literacy for women and not into the luxury of a separate women's university; and that the ban on cultural activities in educational institutions be lifted.[74]

As a platform, WAF was quickly endorsed by five different organizations in Karachi where it originated. This was soon followed by the opening of a WAF chapter in Lahore, to be followed by WAF chapters in Islamabad and Peshawar. Within six months of its formation, WAF had chapters in four major cities in three of the four provinces of Pakistan. By 1983, WAF had the support of more than a dozen organizations. Significantly, as a platform, WAF was endorsed by the oldest and most established women's organization, APWA. APWA had always enjoyed tremendous respect and had been viewed favorably by the state as a legitimate organization dedicated to helping women and children. The fact that this organization—historically part of the status quo—had endorsed WAF's platform was not lost on the regime and its allies, namely the Jamaat-i-Islami.

When WAF started its signature campaign in September 1981, Begum Ra'ana Liaquat Ali Khan, the founding member and life president of APWA was the first woman to sign this document. It was her name that headed the 10,000 signatures collected from all over the country. Her endorsement gave WAF the legitimacy it needed to get started with challenging the state's new approach to women's issues and rights.[75] The Fehmida-Allah Bux case not only was a wakeup call but, more importantly, it mobilized educated urban women who were the first to realize that, unlike previous governments, both civilian and military, who had continued to introduce policies that improved the status of Pakistani women, Zia's regime was a misogynistic one which sought through regressive policies to reduce women's status in society. Women groups and other civic organizations campaigned against the ordinances for being anti-women laws and urged the government to be a signatory of the United Nations CEDAW.[76]

While WAF was successful in mobilizing a coordinated effort by various organizations and individuals to challenge implementation of the Hudood Ordinances in certain cases, it was not able to exert sufficient influence to get these ordinances repealed; a goal which had been, and remains, one of its key objectives. Its actions did, however, compel a public debate and helped to raise awareness on the inequities inherent in these ordinances. WAF's successful legal actions in challenging specific rulings by lower courts in the Federal Shariat Court, helped female activists leverage the very legal mechanism of the Zia regime, the FSC, in acting as a sort of checks and balances to the whole process. Since almost all the cases tried under the Hudood Ordinances involved women from lower income groups who did not have the means to challenge a ruling by a lower court in the FSC, the significance of this activism on part of WAF, other women's organizations and certain individual lawyers cannot be overstated.

It is important to note that not all urban women rejected Zia's "Islamization" program. Zia's support in urban areas came from the lower middle classes and included women. According to General Arif, a protégé of Zia: "Barring the English-speaking intelligentsia and the elite, a great majority of the middle and the lower classes in the country support the process of Islamization of society."[77]

The Majlis-e-Khawateen-i-Pakistan (a women's organization) rejected the CEDAW by arguing that it was antithetical to Islam. The Jamaat-i-Tulaba, a student group affiliated with the Jamaat-i-Islami which had a women's wing, also opposed the actions of female activists like WAF. It is noteworthy that women's groups affiliated with Islamic fundamentalist movements have posed the strongest challenge to the secularly oriented mainstream women's groups like WAF.

CONCLUSION

General Zia's sudden, and violent, demise in August of 1988 ended a period in the Pakistani state's short history that can best be characterized as being regressive on matters involving women's rights and status in society. Critics of the state's legal maneuvers—including women activists opposed to the imposition of *shariah* over secular law—thought that Zia's policies had a detrimental impact not only on women's lives but also on society as a whole.

The problem with Zia's "Islamization" program was that it quickly became a legitimate, State supported, mechanism, through the institution of Shariah compliant laws such as the draconian Hudood Ordinances of 1979. Perhaps for many Pakistanis, such laws which "empowered" males in a Muslim majority country would not have been of much concern if it did not involve draconian punishments as "justice" that overwhelmingly placed women in danger of being lashed or, worse, being stoned to death for adultery. Nasir Aslam Zahid, a former Supreme Court Judge and Chair of the National Commission on the Status of Women (NCSW), which advised the

Zia regime in 1997 to repeal the Hudood ordinances, argued that prior to the passage of these ordinances, adultery was not a criminal offense, but was considered a personal matter: "only directly affected persons, a wife or husband, could register cases, but only against men as a protection for women in a male dominated feudal society where women are rarely in control of their lives."[78]

Under Zia's rule, women and the press emerged as the major challengers to his autocratic regime. It was a period that witnessed a major shift in female activism: From an emphasis on social work and family issues to challenging the policies of the junta led government. Asma Jahangir, a prominent woman activist and a Lahore-based attorney, observed: "The woman's movement put Pakistan on the map of the world as a country where women were aware and struggling for rights."[79]

The legacy of the Zia period, as viewed from the perspective of women activists, was summed up by Nighat Said Khan who wrote:

> the process (of Islamization) has been very detrimental to the nation. It has given legitimacy to fundamentalism and has put the nation, especially the middle class on the defensive, by constantly having to prove its identity.[80]

The reality of the Zia years was that, although by all appearances the state had moved toward Islamization, the process of enactment (of state policy) was far more successful than that of implementation (state capacity) which was half hearted at best. The Zia state's metamorphosis into an "Islamic" country through the state's attempts at reconfiguration of national and gender identities was seen by many Pakistanis as a legitimacy tool that fooled no one. Instead what emerged was a widespread cynicism toward the whole exercise.[81] The process of Islamization once begun, however, proved hard to reverse. This had a lot to do with the fact that the process was embedded in the 1973 Constitution through the Eighth Amendment, which upheld all laws made during Zia's rule as being valid and could not be challenged in a Court of Law. Only another constitutional amendment could invalidate the stipulations of the Eighth Amendment, and this would require a two thirds majority support in parliament. The religious conservatives, however, had gained sufficient clout in parliament during General Zia's rule to make this difficult but not impossible.

In order to garner wider support from all segments of Pakistani society, groups like WAF would need to seriously engage with women affiliated with organizations like Jamaat-i-Islami.[82] Contemplation, let alone action, meant to reach out to their sisters at the opposite end of the ideological spectrum has been anathema to groups like WAF to their own detriment. Given their limited resources and pool of activists, WAF and other similar secular groups experienced limited success in challenging detrimental gender policies of the Zia regime.

NOTES

1. In Arabic *hudood* is plural for limits and fixed punishments as defined in the *Quran* and the traditions of the Muslim prophet Muhammad (the hadiths).
2. Prior to the enactment of the *Hudood* Ordinances in 1979, most laws since Pakistan's establishment were a continuation of British colonial laws. The Pakistan Penal Code didn't include specific punishments for women involved in fornication or adultery. Furthermore, adultery was a matter for private complaint and the police could not exercise jurisdiction. It was a bailable offence for men and the complainant could withdraw the allegations.
3. Farhat Haq, "Women, Islam, and the State in Pakistan," *The Muslim World* (April 1996): 166.
4. Iftikhar H. Malik, *State and Civil Society in Pakistan: Politics of Authority, Ideology and Ethnicity* (New York: Palgrave Macmillan, 1997), 146.
5. For more on the Jamaat-i-Islami see Syed Vali Reza Nasr, *The Vanguard of the Islamic Revolution: The Jamaat-i-Islami of Pakistan* (Berkeley: University of California Press, 1994).
6. See Richard Reeves. *Passage to Peshawar: Pakistan Between the Hindu Kush and the Arabian Sea* (New York: Simon and Schuster, 1984), 99–101; Hussain Haqqani, *Pakistan: Between Mosque and Military* (Washington, DC: Carnegie Endowment for International Peace, 2005), 131–136; Mary Anne Weaver, *Pakistan: In the Shadow of Jihad and Afghanistan* (New York: Farrar, Straus and Giroux, 2002), 43; Charles H. Kennedy. "Islamization and Legal Reform in Pakistan, 1979–1989," *Pacific Affairs* 63, no. 1 (Spring 1990), 62.
7. For more on the influence of social and political forces on Zia's process of "Islamization" see Riaz Hassan, "Islamization: An Analysis of Religious, Political and Social Change in Pakistan," *Middle Eastern Studies* 21, no. 3 (July 1985): 263–284.
8. Ian Bryant Wells, *Jinnah: Ambassador of Hindu-Muslim Unity* (Oxford: Seagull Books, 2005), 2; Sharif Al Mujahid, *Quaid-i-Azam Jinnah* (South Asia Books, 1982), 228–277.
9. Anwar Hussain Syed, *Islam, Politics, and National Solidarity* (Lahore: Vanguard Books 1984), 136–152. For more on the Zia-ul Haq period, see Lawrence Ziring, *Pakistan in the 20th Century: A Political History* (Oxford: Oxford University Press, 1997), 423–502.
10. See Eric Nordlinger's *Soldiers in Politics: Military Coups and Governments* (Englewood Cliffs, NJ: Prentice Hall 1977), 138–147 for a more detailed look at military regimes.
11. Stephen Cohen, *The Idea of Pakistan* (Washington, DC: Brookings Institution Press, 2004), 170. On the issue of "legitimacy" see Craig Baxter's chapter "Conclusion: Legitimacy for Zia and His Regime?" in *Zia's Pakistan: Politics and Stability in a Frontline State,* ed. Craig Baxter (Boulder, CO: Westview Press, 1985), 111–117; Tariq Ali, *Can Pakistan Survive?* (London: Penguin Books, 1983), 133–163.
12. For Zia's efforts to bring the judiciary under his control see Haqqani (2005), 142–146.
13. *Shariah* (Islamic) laws are based on interpretation of the *Quran* and the *Sunnah* (stories of the life of the Prophet Muhammad by the Sunni *ulema* (religious scholars) on a specific subject involving human behavior within society. There are no specific, established, guidelines which allow the *ulema* to base their interpretations on how they *perceive* the intent of Allah. The conservative traditionalists, however, argue that only a literalist reading of the Quran and *Hadith* will suffice. While, other *ulema* (the rationalists) stress the importance of flexibility in application of *Shariah* in order to incorporate current social and political mores.
14. Shahid Javed Burki, *Zia's Eleven Years* (Boulder, CO: Westview Press), 36.
15. Hamid Khan. *Constitutional and Political History of Pakistan* (Oxford: Oxford University Press, 2005), 353–354.
16. For more details on the FSC please refer to http://www.ljcp.gov.pk .
17. Edward Mortimer, "Pakistan-Islam as Nationality," *Faith and Power: The Politics of Islam* (London: Faber and Faber Limited, 1982), 222.
18. Ziring (2003), 183. See also *Constitutional and Political History of Pakistan,* 370.

19. Haq, 166.
20. Khawar Mumtaz and Farida Shaheed, *Women of Pakistan: Two Steps Forward, One Step Back?* (London: Zed Books, 1987), 82.
21. See Richard Kurin, "Islamisation in Pakistan: A View from the Countryside," *Asian Survey* 25 (August 1985), 115–128.
22. Hasan Askari Rizvi, "Return of the Military," *The Military and Politics in Pakistan, 1947–1986* (Lahore: Sang-e-Meel Publications, 2000), 233–234; for a detailed account of Zia's early drive for Islamization see S. S. Bindra, *The Politics of Islamisation: With Special Reference to Pakistan* (New Delhi: South Asian Books, 1990), 197–279; Anita Weiss, ed., *Islamic Reassertion in Pakistan: The Application of Islamic Laws in a Modern State.* Syracuse, NY: Syracuse University Press, 1986.
23. Nasr (1994), 189. For more on Maududi's conception of an "Islamic State," see Zafaryab Ahmed, "Maudoodi's Islamic State," in *Islam, Politics, and the State: The Pakistan Experience,* ed. Asghar Khan (Lahore: Zed Books, 1985), 95–113.
24. Bindra (1990), 241–242; Asma Jahangir and Hina Jilani, *A Divine Sanction? The Hudood Ordinances* (Lahore: Rhotas Books, 1990), 23–33.
25. For more on these ordinances see Asma Jahangir and Hina Jilani, *The Hudood Ordinances: A Divine Sanction?* Lahore, Pakistan: Sang-e-Meel Publications, 2003.
26. Farhat Moazam, "The Hudood Ordinances of Pakistan," *Journal of South Asian and Middle Eastern Studies* (Fall 2004), 36.
27. For a detailed examination of the Hudood Ordinances see Rashida Patel, *Islamisation of Laws in Pakistan?* (Karachi: Saad Publishers, 1986), 36–61.
28. Izzud-Din Pal, "Women and Islam in Pakistan," *Middle Eastern Studies* 26 (October 1990), 460.
29. Sana Bucha, "When Rapists Go Free," *pkarticleshub.com*, April 24, 2011, Accessed at: http://www.pkarticleshub.com/2011/04/24/when-rapists-go-free/ .
30. Rubya Mehdi, "The Offence of Rape in the Islamic Law of Pakistan." *International Journal of Society and Law* 18 (1990), 19–29.
31. "Women in Pakistan: Disadvantaged and Denied Their Rights," *Amnesty International*, December 1995, 14. Accessed at: http://www.amnesty.org/en/library/info/ASA33/023/1995 .
32. "Women in Pakistan" 14.
33. Rahat Imran, "Legal Injustices: The Zina Ordinance of Pakistan and Its Implications," *Journal of International Women's Studies* 7, no. 2 (November 2005), 89.
34. Moazam, 46. As quoted from Imam Malik ibn Anas, *al-Muwatta*, section 36.16. Accessed at: http://www.sunnipath.com/library/Hadith/H0001P0036.aspx .
35. Moazam, 47. As quoted from *Manaqib*, vol.II, 190; Ibne Qaiyum Zakheeratul Uqba, Turuqui Hikmia 81. Accessed at: http://www.duas.org/selectedjudgements.htm .
36. *Selected Judgments of Hazrat Ali,* Wafi, Vol. 9 (Light, Knowledge, Truth), as cited in Moazam, 46.
37. Sura Nur (24): 4.
38. Sura Nur (24): 7, 11, 13 and 15.
39. Ta'azir in Shariah are discretionary and corrective punishments for *minor* crimes.
40. For a detailed case study on the "moral regulation" of Pakistani women by both their families and the state, to include interviews with women incarcerated under the *zina* ordinance, see Shahnaz Khan, "Zina and the Moral Regulation of Pakistani Women," *Feminist Review* 75 (2003), 75–100.
41. Moazam, 51.
42. Moazam, 52.
43. Moazam, 52.
44. Asma Jahangir, "Women's Commission and Hudood Ordinances," *Daily Times,* September 12, 2003, http://www.hrsolidarity.net/mainfile.php/2003vol13no04-05/2292/ .
45. Jahangir and Jilani, 132–133.
46. *Safia Bibi v. The State* PLD 1985 FSC 120; Safia Bibi v The State PLD 1986 SC 132.
47. For more on WAF see Amina Jamal, "Feminist Selves and Feminism's Others: Feminist Representation of Jamaat-i-Islami Women in Pakistan," *Feminist Review* 81 (2005), 58–60.
48. Haq, 169–170.

49. Malik (1997), 148.
50. Shahid Rehman Khan, "Under Pakistan's Form of Islamic Law, Rape is a Crime for the Victims," *Los Angeles Times,* May 25, 1986. Accessed at: http://articles.latimes.com/1986-05-25/news/mn-7291_1_islamic-law .
51. Mumtaz and Shaheed, 103–104.
52. George Crile, *Charlie Wilson's War* (Boulder, CO: Grove Press 2003), 206–207.
53. Mumtaz and Shaheed, 74.
54. Moazam, 27.
55. For a detailed examination of the Laws of Evidence refer to Patel (1986), 78–86.
56. Rahat Imran, "Legal Injustices: The Zina Ordinance of Pakistan and Its Implications," *Journal of International Women's Studies* 7, no.2 (November 2005), 87–93.
57. Shahnaz Khan, "Gender, Religion, Sexuality and the State: Mediating the Hudood Laws in Pakistan," *Center for Research on Violence against Women and Children* (Ontario, Canada, 2001). Accessed at: www.uwo.ca/violence.
58. Haq, 170.
59. Mumtaz and Shaheed, 107.
60. For more on Quranic ayats on qisas see Al-Qisas (Sura 28).
61. As quoted in the Quran in Sura An-Nisa (4:92).
62. Mumtaz and Shaheed,112.
63. Shehla Zia, "The Legal Status of Women in Pakistan," in *Finding Our Way: Readings on Women in Pakistan,* ed. Fareeha Zafar (Lahore: ASR Publications, 1991), 34.
64. For more details on this bill and previous legal measures, refer to Rashida Patel's *Islamisation of Laws in Pakistan? 1986.*
65. Surendra Nath Kaushik, *Politics of Islamization in Pakistan: A Study of the Zia Regime* (New Delhi: South Asian Publishers, 1993), 107.
66. Kaushik, 120.
67. Golam Wahed Choudhury, *Pakistan: Transition from Military to Civilian Rule* (Essex: Scorpion Publishing Co., 1988), 151–152.
68. "Enforcement of Shariah Ordinance, 1988 (Ordinance I of 1988), June 15, 1988." PLD 1988 Central Statutes 29 as cited in Charles Kennedy's *Pakistan: 1982* (Boulder, CO: Westview Press, 1993), 62.
69. Choudhury, 129.
70. Kennedy, 1993, 62.
71. Kennedy, 1993, 61.
72. Imran, 93–96.
73. Khawar Mumtaz and Yameena Mitha, *Pakistan: Tradition and Change* (Oxford: Oxfam, 1996), 46.
74. Mumtaz and Shaheed, 74.
75. Mumtaz and Shaheed, 75.
76. Malik (1997), 148.
77. General Khalid Mahmud Arif, *Working with Zia: Pakistan's Power Politics, 1977–1988* (Oxford and Karachi: Oxford University Press, 1995), 413; Khawar Mumtaz's Identity Politics and Women: "Fundamentalism and Women in Pakistan," in *Identity Politics and Women: Cultural Reassertions and Feminism in International Perspectives,* ed. Valentine Moghadem (Boulder, CO: Westview Press, 1993), 228–242.
78. As quoted in Imran, 89–90.
79. As quoted in Malik, 1997, 161.
80. Nighat Said Khan, "The New Global Order: Politics and the Women's Movement," in *Pakistan: The Contours of State and Society,* eds. Mumtaz, Soofia, Racine, Jean Luc and Imran Anwar Ali (Oxford: Oxford University Press, 2002), 143.
81. Anwar Hussain Syed, "Pakistan: Ideology and Politics," in *Islam, Politics and National Solidarity* (Lahore: Vanguard Books, 1984), 151.
82. Jamal, 53.

Chapter Three

State Policies and Female Status in the Post-Zia State

> This is a second life. I want to serve the people. I want every girl, every child, to be educated.
> —Malala Yousafzai, Pakistani school girl and education activist [1]

General Zia ul-Haq's sudden demise in 1988 raised immediate, and unrealistic, expectations in certain social circles. With Benazir Bhutto at the helm as prime minister, urban female activists were especially confident that Bhutto would work hard to improve the lives of Pakistani women. For a myriad of reasons, Bhutto's efforts to counter and reverse the detrimental impact of the Hudood ordinances were slow and limited. This served to infuriate those segments of civil society bitterly opposed to Zia's tinkering with the 1973 Constitution and his establishment of a parallel, Shariah-based, judicial system.

WOMEN'S STATUS UNDER THE BHUTTO GOVERNMENT, 1988–1990

Benazir Bhutto's rapid ascension to power as the first female head of state in the Muslim world astonished Pakistanis. With Bhutto as chief executive, various women's organizations were optimistic. They wanted Bhutto to move quickly to reverse the process of Islamization begun by her predecessor, and nemesis, General Zia. Thus Bhutto's election was seen as a major boost to the women's movement opposed to Zia's "Islamization" process.

The October 1988 elections reflected a victory for the mainstream secular parties over the religious ones. Notwithstanding the state's emphasis during the previous eleven years on transforming political and social institutions to make them congruent with Islamic traditions and norms, the 1988 election did not indicate a central role for Islam in the elected government.[2] Events, however, would suggest that the art of politics is far more complex: like most politicians, Bhutto's primary concern became how to remain in office. In her defense, Bhutto inherited a difficult state of affairs and lacked full authority at the helm. Nonetheless, the fact that a woman held the country's highest office was not lost on anyone. It was a significant departure from the policies and inclinations of the state under Zia.

Bhutto could not live up to the high expectations placed on her by urban women's groups because her hands were tied by circumstances: her party, the PPP, did not have a significant majority in Parliament. Disillusionment replaced enthusiasm among women's groups who had supported Bhutto's candidacy as she was forced to adopt a more defensive, and conservative, approach in matters related to human rights and women's rights. This had to do with trying to deflate the nonstop criticism from those on her right, the Ulema and religious parties, who vociferously attacked her credentials and right to lead an Islamic state. Bhutto was forced to back-track from her campaign promises to women that she would repeal the unpopular Hudood Ordinances and the Qanoon-e-Shahadat.

Furthermore, Bhutto's government did not enjoy a clear majority in the legislature which inhibited it from attempting to reverse the state's conservative trend under Zia toward Islamization. Bhutto's PPP knew it would have to garner strong support to move away from the Seventh Five-Year Plan (1988–1993) drafted under Zia. Although this government plan acknowledged its own dismal record in matters involving women's status, it provided poorly thought-out solutions to problems associated with women in Pakistan. Bhutto did not have enough political capital to move away from this agenda and steer the state toward a policy of empowerment (of women) as she had promised on the campaign trail. In order to win the 1988 election, the PPP aligned itself with a variety of allies at the local level, many of whom were not enthusiastic about the idea of women's empowerment and did not favor the reversal of the Islamization process. Since the survival of her government depended on these alliances, she could not risk their defection over what was considered a controversial issue, namely, women's rights.

Female activists accused her of selling out to conservative elements, which was unfair especially since Bhutto herself was personally committed to improving human rights and women's rights. Some in the women's movement felt that Bhutto abandoned them when she adopted a more "Islamic" demeanor by covering her head with a *dupatta* (head scarf) and not shaking men's hands. They refused to make any allowances in light of Bhutto's position. As activists, they unrealistically expected overnight reversals of policies they opposed. The reality was that they faced formidable opponents within civil society to their goals: The religious and conservative elements of

Pakistani society were just as determined to continue the path of Islamization and to set up various roadblocks to any change in course by the state. The prime minister and her government did not have a wide enough mandate to aggressively pursue gender-related policies as it tried to consolidate its support base.

During her eighteen month tenure, Bhutto also faced continuous criticism from conservative elements for being—as a female—the head of state of a Muslim country. The reality was that most Pakistanis did not care about the gender of their leader. Rather, their concerns involved what reforms would be undertaken to improve their lives of basic subsistence. They wanted Bhutto to deliver on the promises her father had made to the Pakistani people of *roti, kapra aur makan* (Urdu: food, clothes, and shelter).

Bhutto's government did take certain actions to improve women's situation. First, many female prisoners were released. Second, in July 1989, the government took an important symbolic step when it elevated the Women's Division to become the Ministry for Women's Development and sought the establishment of a women's bank. Critics, however, felt that the Bhutto government could have taken more measures that would not have been considered controversial by the conservatives. These included releasing the Report of the Pakistan Commission on the Status of Women (whose members had been appointed by Zia); signing the United Nations Convention on the Elimination of All Forms of Discrimination against Women (CEDAW); and allowing the continuation of reserved seats for women in Parliament, which expired in 1988.

At the outset, the government did ensure that the "revised" Shariah ordinance that had been promulgated by the interim government of Ghulam Ishaq Khan on October 15, 1988, was allowed to expire without legislative action. Bhutto's government also attempted to bury the issue of the Shariat bill by not making any attempts to reintroduce a similar bill once it expired. In fact, Bhutto took the position that Zia's Islamization plan should be dismantled ideally through the repeal of the Eighth Amendment and restoration of the 1973 Constitution.[3] Bhutto faced continued political resistance to her efforts to steer the state on to a secular track that recognized women and minorities as equal citizens under the law. The Senate, controlled by the conservative Islami Jamhoori Ittehad (IJI-Islamic Democratic Alliance), wanted to restore Zia's Islamization program. As Bhutto's popularity dwindled, proponents of Zia's plan moved to reintroduce his Shariat bill in the legislature.

In a climate of growing unpopularity due to its failure to deliver on campaign promises, the Bhutto government faced emboldened proponents for a modified version of Zia's program. Any bill they believed was better than no bill whose passage would force the National Assembly to consider its version of a Shariah bill, a move the conservatives believed would embarrass Bhutto's vulnerable coalition government.

In May 1990, the Senate passed a less controversial version of Zia's ordinance: "Shariat Bill (Senate version), 1990," which tightened the wording of Article 3 of Zia's 1988 act to read: "Shariah shall be the supreme law of Pakistan . . . and shall have effect notwithstanding anything contained in any other law, custom or usage." Like Zia's ordinance, it adopted the process of assigning jurisdiction to the High Courts in matters that were not under the Federal Shariat Court's jurisdiction.[4]

Bhutto's government was dismissed by President Ghulam Ishaq Khan on August 6, 1990, on charges of corruption and incompetence and the president installed an interim coalition government under Prime Minister Ghulam Mustapha Jatoi. At the end of Bhutto's short-lived government, none of the discriminatory laws that targeted women had been repealed or amended much to the disappointment of women's organizations which had become critical of Bhutto's government.

THE STATE UNDER NAWAZ SHARIF AND WOMEN'S STATUS, 1990–1993

The October 1990 general election victory of Nawaz Sharif's Pakistan Muslim League (PML) was viewed as a "back to the future" event by female activists since he was a protégé of Zia. Once in office, Sharif did not waste time making Zia's program of "Islamization" his number one priority. During the electoral process, he received the support of the Islamist parties such as the Jamaat-i-Islami and the Jamaat-Ulema-Pakistan who were strongly opposed to Bhutto and the PPP. Cognizant of the support his party had received from the religious elements in the election, and to appease some PML party members, Nawaz Sharif lent his support to the Shariat Bill which *stipulated that all laws must be in agreement with Shariah.*

The first indication of state regression during Sharif's tenure on women's status occurred when, on March 6, 1991, the Senate passed the Qisas and Diyat laws that categorized women as less than equal in value for compensation purposes. The introduction of the Islamic concepts of Qisas, roughly "an eye for an eye," and Diyat, "blood money," into the penal code was a setback for women. The Qisas and Diyat ordinances allowed compensation to be paid to a victim's family in lieu of the accused receiving punishment. As a result, wealthy or influential people were provided with a loop hole to avoid punishment for such crimes as murder and injury. The right to seek pardon or commutation was not available to defendants under this ordinance. Like the Hudood ordinances, the Qisas and Diyat ordinances applied to ordinary criminal courts and Shariah courts.

In late March 1991, Sharif established a committee of senators, judges, members of the national assembly (MNAs), lawyers and ulema to draft another version of the Shariah legislation. This was soon followed in May of 1991 with the introduction of the Sami-Latif Bill in the Senate which was dominated by Zia's ideological successors. The Sami-Latif Bill, introduced by two Senators, Maulana Sami-ul-Haq and Qazi Abdul Latif, dealt with the overall Islamization of society and the imposition of Shariah.[5]

SOCIAL MOBILIZATION AGAINST THE SHARIAH BILL

The Women's Action Forum (WAF), and other women organizations, launched a concerted effort against the enactment of the Sami-Latif bill.[6] WAF called a meeting attended by intellectuals, minority leaders, women's organizations, and lawyers to form a unified front to oppose the passage of this bill in the National Assembly. As a result, the Joint Action Committees for People's Rights, which included forty organizations, was formed. Representing not only women and minorities, it was meant to represent all who were opposed to Islamization through legislative means. This organization held seminars and protest meetings, published pamphlets and articles, and sent letters to members of the National Assembly to convince them of the long terms effects of this bill.[7]

The "Enforcement of Shariah Act, 1991" was passed in the National Assembly on April 11, 1991.[8] Sharif managed to ensure the passage of a less controversial version of Zia's Shariat bill by removing the gender discriminatory clause that was met by a strong opposition during Zia's rule. In addition, this bill did not amend the constitutional provisions that limited the scope of the Superior Courts' jurisdiction. It also addressed the huge controversy that surrounded Zia's earlier version of the bill, which stipulated that the interpretation of the Hanifi School of Islamic jurisprudence (*fiqh*) would prevail over other schools or sects. This had infuriated the Shias, around a quarter of the population. In the 1991 version of the Shariat bill, "Shariah" was narrowly defined as the "Quran and Sunnah," and "with respect to the personal law of any Muslim sect, the expression Quran and Sunnah shall mean *the Quran and Sunnah as interpreted by that sect.*"[9]

Although some Pakistani scholars such as Iftikhar H. Malik[10] have questioned whether Nawaz Sharif's government was really inclined to implement Zia's policies of Islamization, others believe Nawaz Sharif was set on carrying out Zia's agenda. Toward this end, under Nawaz's government, the State's ideological stance once again took a conservative turn vis-à-vis women's issues.

The passage of "Enforcement of Shariah Act" was seen as a huge blow to the women's efforts to force the state to reverse the direction it was taking and to ensure that the provisions of the 1973 Constitution be upheld which guaranteed women equal opportunities. In 1992, in a significant blow to the marital safeguards of Pakistani women, the Supreme Court invalidated the requirement, as stipulated under the MFLO of 1961, that a husband must give written notice of a divorce to a local union council. The husband's statement, with or without witnesses, was the defining legal step. Without written proof of divorce, the woman would become legally and socially vulnerable. Women activists expressed concern that removal of this protective mechanism of validating a divorce through registration would place women in the precarious position of possibly being charged for *zina* (adultery) if she remarried and her former husband denied that he'd divorced her. They feared this Supreme Court decision was the beginning of an assault by the conservative elements in society to repeal the minimum protections afforded women with the passage of the MFLO in 1961.

The PML government did try to appease women's groups by incorporating "women's issues" into its Eight Five-Year Plan (1993-1998). It enlisted the help of representatives from certain women's groups to provide feedback on a number of important issues that concerned women. It commissioned the well-known female activist Khawar Mumtaz to write a prescriptive paper on women in development for its "National Conservation Strategy Report."

When elections were scheduled for October 6, 1993, both the major parties—Bhutto's PPP and Nawaz's PML—campaigned on platforms that included women's rights. This was a significant testament to the fact that since 1981, through an activist stance toward the enactment of regressive gender policies by the state, the women's movement had managed to build up significant capital to compel the political parties to acknowledge their concerns in their parties' platforms.

BHUTTO'S RETURN AND STATE POLICIES TOWARD WOMEN, 1993–1997

The reactions of women activists to Bhutto's reelection in October 1993 ran the gamut from cautious optimism to complete skepticism. Events would prove the skeptics right due to a myriad of factors which prevented Bhutto from taking a more proactive approach to addressing the concerns of women regarding their status in society and their rights. Due to the close election results, Bhutto was forced to cater to certain religious elements in order to obtain their support in the legislature. The Bhutto government moved away from its secular stance on the Islamization issue by appointing the secretary general of the Jamiat Ulema-e-Islam - Fazal-ur-Rehman Group (JUI-F), closely linked to the Anjuman Sipah-e-Sahaba Pakistan, as the head of the Parliamentary Committee for Foreign Affairs. Under Bhutto's government, women continued to experience growing violence toward them both on the domestic front and in society in general. In spite of political restrictions, Bhutto vowed to introduce a new social contract.

THE COMMISSION OF INQUIRY FOR WOMEN

One of the first measures undertaken by the Bhutto government was to establish a Commission of Inquiry for Women in 1994 mandated to "review all the existing laws which are discriminatory to women or affect their right of being equal citizens of Pakistan," and to recommend amendments to bring laws and rules "in accordance with the injunctions of Islam as enshrined in the Quran and Sunnah," as well as other remedial measures.[11]

This commission consisted of human rights lawyers, Islamic scholars, and legislators and was headed by a Supreme Court judge. It examined family laws, labor and service laws, criminal laws, various social practices which involve violence against women, developmental rights which women have been deprived of and the lack of suitable institutions to promote women's rights. The commission sent a questionnaire to women's organizations and published it in newspapers. It visited relevant institutions, including women's prisons, women's police stations, and women's shelters. The commission's report detailed the deprivation of rights suffered by women through discriminatory legislation and the effects of various policies on women at all social levels and in all parts of the country. It recommended inter alia:

- removal of discriminatory clauses in the Constitution of Pakistan;
- legislative measures to increase political participation of women;
- changes in family laws, relating to marriage, divorce, maintenance, inheritance, guardianship, and child marriage which currently disadvantaged women;
- changes in labor laws relating to conditions of employment, pay, and child care;
- amendment of criminal laws, including identifying honor killings as a criminal offense;
- the repeal of the Hudood laws as they contravene the injunctions of Islam, constitutional provisions of equality before the law;
- repeal of the Qanoon-e-Shahadat (Evidence Act) as it discriminates against women;
- strengthen legislation on domestic violence and to monitor its implementation.[12]

The commission's report concluded: "The Commission urges decision makers, including political party leadership, the legislators and the judiciary, to give the issue of women's rights the critical priority it deserves, not as a favor or protective gesture, but as their fundamental inalienable right."[13] Although the commission's report was praised by women's organizations, and by Amnesty International, as being a positive step forward in addressing women's concerns, there was never an official acknowledgment of the importance of this report: the Parliament never brought up the issues enunciated in it in order to take steps to implement its recommendations. Women's and human rights groups in Pakistan repeatedly called on the government to urgently consider and adopt its recommendations, namely to repeal discriminatory laws, adopt and implement provisions protecting women against custodial, domestic, and societal violence.[14]

The Bhutto government brought up the issue of reinstatement of women's reserved seats in the National Assembly through the use of a constitutional amendment. Legislative disputes with the PML, however, prevented its passage. While both the PPP and the PML had expressed support for this amendment, the religious parties such as the Jamaat-i-Islami had opposed this move. A Jamaat member reportedly said that women should have their own assembly, and if they are allotted special seats in the National Assembly, they should not be allowed to contest general elections.

The Bhutto government opened women's police stations staffed only by women in an attempt to protect women from what was perceived was rampant and violent abuse by male officers toward women in their custody. This was a significant step in safeguarding women's safety while in police custody where, according to a Human Rights Watch study conducted in 1991, more than 70 percent of women in police custody were subjected to physical and sexual abuse by law enforcement agents.[15]

Soon after Bhutto's reelection, the Ministry for Women's Development and Youth Affairs outlined four areas of concentration with regards to women's issues:

- human resource development on public-private partnership basis
- improvement in women's educational status
- expansion of health care facilities
- provision of free legal aid and protection to women.

Toward this end, the Bhutto government pledged 64 percent more to these areas in the 1994–1995 budget (to a total of Rs. 141 million, US $3.5 million) than it had allocated in the preceding year. By June of 1994, the Ministry had also funded a total of 339 NGO projects involved in education, health, skill training, income generation and other similar projects.[16] Notwithstanding Bhutto's efforts to address some of the problems facing women as enunciated by women activist groups like WAF and Shirkat Gah, Bhutto realized that the Islamists had gained political ground over the years and she had to tread carefully.

One significant development for the women's movement occurred when Pakistan became a signateur to the *Convention on the Elimination of All Forms of Discrimination against Women (CEDAW)* in 1996.[17] By adopting this convention, Pakistan agreed to incorporate the provisions set forth in order to eliminate discrimination against women. This was a big step forward on part of a state that wavered, depending on who was in charge of the government, on matters involving women and their rights and status in society. The problem would be one of implementation of the provisions of CEDAW.

An important issue identified in CEDAW was the necessity of eliminating cultural practices and customs which discriminate against women. Both Articles 2(f) and 5(a) specifically state that state parties agree to modify customs and practices that discriminate against women. Pakistan, like many other states, believed that cultural practices are not a violation of human rights since they are customary.[18] Pakistan failed to submit its initial report that was due in 1997 to the CEDAW as provided for under Article 18 of this convention. This was a harbinger of Pakistan's approach to the CEDAW as it failed to implement and enforce many of CEDAW's provisions in both its legislative and judicial actions.

STATE APPROACHES TO WOMEN DURING NAWAZ SHARIF'S RULE, 1997–1999

With the return of Nawaz Sharif's PML government, the Pakistani state once again shifted gears on gender policies. The PML government began a slow reversal in its approach toward women's issues as it moved to reenergize Zia's "Islamization" plan. There has been much speculation as to the motives behind Nawaz's continued commitment to pursue Zia's Islamization program. Some have argued that ongoing legitimacy and consolidation concerns influenced the Nawaz government's policies. On a more personal note, others have suggested that this had more to do with implementing a program that was important to his conservative father. Or perhaps, as a protégé of Zia, Nawaz felt it was incumbent that he implement Zia's program.

PASSAGE OF THE QISAS AND DIYAT ORDINANCE

In 1997, Nawaz Sharif and his supporters in the National Assembly enacted the Qisas and Diyat Ordinance which had been first proposed during Zia's rule. Enactment of this ordinance instituted Shariah-based changes in Pakistan's criminal law thus making it a part of the Pakistan Penal Code rather than an ordinance subject to periodic renewal.[19] The Qisas and Diyat law posed a serious obstacle to justice in domestic violence cases.

Although the law gave women and their guardians or heirs the opportunity to pardon perpetrators, it was inadequate in cases involving domestic violence where the onus for making a decision regarding punishment, or pardoning, was placed on the victim. This requirement failed to recognize the power and control exercised over females that typifies abusive relationships. Pressure to pardon does not only come from the perpetrators themselves; the victim is also aware that she might face further violence as a result of her decision, as well as from her own family and the family of her abuser(s). Where perpetrators are the female's own relatives (she may be married to her cousin, for example), the pressure to pardon the perpetrator is often intense.[20]

In such an environment, under the Qisas and Diyat law, women were either discouraged or coerced into pardoning the perpetrators. The Qisas and Diyat law, by "privatizing" crimes created a threatening environment for females, and also provided a means for influential people who may have committed a serious crime-like murder, to be able to buy their way out of a prison sentence. The ability to make a financial settlement with the heirs and guardians of a victim of violence ensured the further reduction of status of women in society.

MFLO OF 1961 UNDER SIEGE

The MFLO of 1961, which was initially regarded by women's groups as inadequate family legislation, in due course came to be seen as an essential legislative step forward that had to be safeguarded against the growing movement led by the maulvis to get it repealed. Thirty-eight years after it was enacted, the MFLO was legally challenged in 1999 when the Federal Shariat Court (FSC) agreed to hear petitions against it.[21] A bench consisting of Chief Justice Mian Mehboob Ahmed, Justice Dr. Fida Muhammad Khan and Justice Ejaz Yousaf heard arguments that challenged and supported provisions of Section 4 (inheritance of orphan grandchildren), 5 (registration of marriage), 6 (polygamy), and 7 (divorce) of the MFLO.

The FSC decided to conduct proceedings in all the major metropolitan centers starting in February 25, 1999, in Lahore. During the Lahore proceedings prominent religious scholars, lawyers, and members of civil society made presentations before the court. Opponents of MFLO called it "un-Islamic"; while advocates such as Asma Jahangir and Syed Afzal Haider made presentations which bolstered the clauses of the MFLO. These hearings, which in Lahore lasted till March 4, 1999, were attended by women from diverse backgrounds.

Prominent human rights lawyer, Asma Jahangir, argued that MFLO was protected against scrutiny by the 1973 Constitution. She argued that after the introduction of the FSC Chapter to the Constitution in 1979, the protection granted to the MFLO and some other laws remained intact; therefore jurisdiction of the FSC and the Shariat Appellate Bench of the Supreme Court did not extend to the Constitution and the MFLO. Ms. Jahangir acknowledged that while the FSC could examine laws for repugnance to Islamic injunctions, it could not hold an open-ended inquiry. Unless something had been expressly prohibited or provided, its presence or absence could not be termed "un-Islamic." Opponents of the MFLO argued that the FSC was mandated to examine all laws to verify their legality under Islamic laws.

The judges on the FSC bench noted that while the FSC had unrestricted power to examine laws to ensure that they were in accordance with "Islamic laws," the FSC's jurisdiction was subject to a final order only of the Shariat Appellate Bench of the Supreme Court. On the subject of marriage under the MFLO, the religious scholars argued that it was not un-Islamic to register *nikahs* (marriage contracts) but it was un-Islamic to impose a punishment for nonregistration. They argued that just because a nikah was not registered did not make it (i.e., the marriage) invalid. Therefore, any imposition of punishment for nonregistration was not justified as the performer of the nikah (a mullah or religious figure) was not a criminal and had not committed an offense.

Supporters of the stipulations of MFLO on the issue of registration of marriages argued that nonregistration of nikahs (marriage) created numerous problems for women and generated chaos in society. Under the clear cut requirements of MFLO, these women had a paper trail that proved their marital status. Failure to enforce the registration requirement, they argued, would place a lot of women at the mercy of their husbands should they choose to divorce and eventually remarry. They cited cases in which women were unable to get justice because they could not provide proof of their marital status due to nonregistration of their nikahs and this had also embroiled some women in zina cases. Without enforcement of MFLO provisions of mandatory registration of marriages and divorces and punishment for failure to register this information, women would be vulnerable to prosecution and abuse. The FSC agreed with advocates of MFLO when it opined that the mechanism provided under MFLO protected the institution of marriage from a state of chaos. They also stated that punishment in cases of noncompliance with established procedures was only logical.

On the issue of polygamy, the religious camp argued that the MFLO requirement of asking permission of an existing wife prior to the contracting of another marriage was against the injunctions of Islam, which allowed a man to have four wives at a time provided he could treat them all equally. Advocates of the MFLO requirement challenged this argument by invoking the stringent requirements laid down in Islam which discouraged the practice; they also pointed out that in most Islamic countries a man could only have a second wife if the first gave her permission. It was therefore not un-Islamic that the provisions of Section 6 required this permission for such an act to be legal. The FSC court stated that there were very strict requirements for a man to fulfill before he was eligible to remarry.

On the matter of divorce, the religious scholars argued that sending the divorce notice to the chairman of the Union Council was un-Islamic. In Islam, they argued, divorce became effective as soon as the third *talaq* (the husband says: "I divorce you" three times) was pronounced. They argued that the three-month *iddat* period (waiting time) was also against the injunctions of Islam. The lawyers who supported the provisions of MFLO on divorce argued that sending notice to the Union Council safeguarded the rights of women and upheld the sanctity of marriage. The court was informed that several women who thought themselves divorced after the pronouncement of the third *talaq* were successfully charged with adultery when they remarried simply because their ex-husbands did not notify the authorities about the pronouncement of *talaq*. Consequently, a divorced woman's second marriage was challenged as being illegal and a vindictive ex-husband was thus able to have his former spouse charged with adultery when she sought a new life after her divorce. Repealing the present procedure they argued would make it much harder for a woman to seek a new life with another spouse. They argued that the ambiguity created by repealing this ordinance would damage the social fabric, as well as the sanctity of marriage and the institution of family.

In response the FSC bench stated that it might order replacement of notice of divorce under Section 7 of the MFLO with a notice of intention to divorce and allow a two-month reconciliation period between estranged spouses. The chief justice further observed that all matters pertaining to matrimonial disputes, such as restitution of conjugal rights or dissolution of marriage by divorce or otherwise, dowry or any other claim, custody of children and maintenance, should preferably be decided by one consolidated judgment and by the same court. While the FSC recognized the importance of reconciliation efforts under Islam, it dismissed the idea of transferring reconciliation proceedings from Union Councils (as set up by MFLO) to Family Courts since it saw such efforts as being of a nonjudicial nature.

The necessity of elaborating on these proceedings here is that it highlights the ongoing struggle between certain societal groups—the Islamists and the moderates—as they strive to influence state policies. Given the importance of the MFLO as a major battleground for these groups, the significance of these proceedings and the interpretation by the FSC should not be underestimated. The rulings of the FSC (a state apparatus) on each of the issues concerning marital relations as defined under MFLO essentially upheld the stipulations of the MFLO, which was viewed unfavorably by the prime minister and his conservative cabinet (another state entity). The only area in which the FSC recommended any change involved divorce initiatives, where it recommended that instead of a "notice of divorce" being issued as prescribed under Section 7 of MFLO, a "notice of intention" should be issued, and efforts at reconciliation be allowed.

The proceedings of the FSC in all the metropolitan areas to hear petitions against the MFLO of 1961, as requested by opponents of this Ordinance, resulted in an outcome that had not been foreseen, nor favored, by those religious scholars opposed to the MFLO. It was, however, viewed as a huge victory by supporters of the MFLO, including female activists. Also, the FSC by hearing the arguments against MFLO, and by upholding this ordinance, had in effect nullified the 1992 Supreme Court decision that had invalidated one of the requirements of the MFLO (that a husband no longer had to give written notice of divorce to a local union council).[22]

The significance of the Federal Shariat Court decision on the MFLO was that *a state entity established to uphold and legitimize the Islamization process had taken an independent, and unexpected, stance from the rest of the state apparatus* that was driven to pursue General Zia's Islamization agenda under the tutelage of his protégé, Nawaz Sharif.

In 1999, Nawaz Sharif then went one step further and tried to make Shariah laws part of Pakistan's Constitution through the enactment of the Fifteenth Amendment Bill.[23] The bill passed the lower house, the National Assembly, where the PML had a commanding majority, and Nawaz expected the process to be completed when the PML gained control of the Senate in 2000.[24]

During this period not all initiatives undertaken in the name of the State were detrimental to women. In fact several positive initiatives were implemented to improve women's situation in society. First, a crisis center for women in distress was opened in 1997 in Islamabad. The Crisis Center, the first of its kind in the country, was an initiative of the Ministry of Women's Development with the assistance of local NGOs. The Center offered legal and medical referrals from volunteer doctors and lawyers, counseling from trained psychologists and a hotline for women in distress. Later similar crisis centers would be opened in other parts of the country. Second, in 1998, Amnesty International reported that several court judgments over the previous few years had stated that adult Muslim women have the right to marry men of their own choice, irrespective of their father's consent.[25]

Third, on April 1, 1998, the Federal Cabinet announced its decision to increase women's representation in local councils by 100 percent. However, the Federal Cabinet's decision—to double women's seats in local councils, was not forwarded to the election authorities, nor was any concrete legislative steps taken to implement this cabinet announcement.[26]

Notwithstanding these state-led initiatives to improve women's status, women organizations and their supporters found themselves under attack from provincial and national entities. For example, in a press statement on Friday May 14, 1999, Punjab Social Welfare Minister, Pir Bin Yamin attacked by name the Human Rights Commission of Pakistan (HRCP), Shirkat Gah and Ajoka (a theater group), and charged them with "spreading vulgarity and obscenity in the name of human rights."[27] Later, this minister would order a "scrutiny" of all NGOs. All 1,941 organizations operating under the Voluntary Social Welfare Agencies (Registration and Control) Ordinance, 1961 were "deregistered" on May 10, 1999. Reasons given for being "deregistered" included the failure to inform the directorate of a change of address. This minister, Mr. Yamin, also stated that "all human rights and women's rights organizations in urban areas were fraudulent."[28]

In a significant departure from the usual cast of women activists (urban and affluent), forty rural women in the Kaghan Valley signed a resolution on August 5, 1999, accusing certain religious leaders and vested interests of stirring up trouble when they launched a "malicious campaign against *Sungi* (a prominent NGO) in June 1999.[29] Similar resolutions appeared in other rural areas of Hunza from both men and women. By working collectively with Sungi, many local problems had been collectively solved. The significance of this rural rebellion regarding the status quo was not lost on female activists who predominantly (and historically) were urban residents. It suggested that rural women—notwithstanding the limitations imposed due to a lack of education—while living a subsistence existence were indeed capable of getting on the activist bandwagon.

THE STATUS OF WOMEN UNDER MILITARY (1999–2008) AND CIVILIAN RULE (2008–2013)

Upon assumption of power in August 1999 via a military takeover,[30] General Pervez Musharraf, a self-declared moderate unlike his military predecessor, General Zia-ul-Haq, launched a Human Rights campaign that addressed some of women's concerns. But Musharaff's regime was initially reluctant to move quickly on the subject of women's status. In July 2000, it issued a new decree reviving Islamic provisions in the country's suspended constitution. The decree said all provisions in the Constitution embodying Islamic injunctions remained in force. The provisions included a ban on any law which conflicts with Islamic principles thus strengthening the Hudood ordinances. The government spokesman justified the enactment of the decree as a measure which underscored the government's commitment to the Islamic rules contained in the 1973 Constitution.[31] Critics have cited this reversal as the military junta's attempt to seek legitimacy and support from the conservative elements which have been critical of the state's ongoing efforts to appease Western powers.

To its credit, the regime moved to establish a National Commission on the Status of Women (NCSW) on September 1, 2000. Like previously established committees, the NCSW proceeded with examining the issues involving women's status and released its report in 2002. It resolved:

- The report that convicted women are being kept in death cells and not allowed to meet relatives is a matter of great concern.
- The Commission also expressed its serious concern over the reported incidents of abuse and misapplication of the Hudood Laws by the police.
- The Commission, therefore, called upon the authorities to take necessary measures to prevent the abuse of the process of law.[32]

In August of 2003, the NCSW called for the repeal of the Hudood Ordinances in order to raise the status of women in Pakistan. Retired Justice Majida Razvi, Chairwoman of the NCSW, told Inter Press Service that while she welcomed the announcement of the new Human Rights Commission, it needs to be "given independence to work with an independent secretariat and should not be linked to any ministry."[33]

As part of its efforts to improve women's status, the provision of reserving a small number of seats for women in the National Assembly was reintroduced. This was first introduced in 1956 as per the terms of Pakistan's first Constitution. The current Constitution, first adopted in 1973, contained a similar quota provision but also had expanded quotas to the provincial assemblies. Despite protests, lawsuits, and a prolonged campaign by women activists from 1988 (when the provision was allowed to expire) to the time of the military takeover by General Musharaff, this provision had not been reinstituted. In 2001, 33 percent of the seats in all elected local governmental bodies were reserved for women. In 2002, 20 percent of the seats in the provincial assemblies and the National Assembly were reserved for women.[34]

This move to ensure female representation in the legislative bodies was praised by the women's movement as a positive step toward including women in the political process although they questioned whether 20 percent was a sufficient quota to ensure adequate representation. They were concerned about political accountability in light of the fact that the elected female representatives would be completely dependent on the goodwill of their colleagues and parties in order to be elected. Without being directly elected they feared that these women would hesitate to take a stand on issues related to women's rights that were considered controversial. As a matter of fact, women from the upper classes tended to dominate the provincial and federal assemblies; while those from the lower-income groups tend to be represented at the lowest level of the local governing hierarchy—union and tehsil councils. They argued that the process created an inadequate dichotomy in female representation. This in turn would lead to a failure to address graver issues that concern the majority of Pakistani women but from which the privileged classes are generally exempt or protected. Women activists therefore launched a campaign to demand direct elections of women on reserved seats.[35]

In the National Assembly, 60 out of 342 seats were reserved for women; while in the Senate, a total of 17 out of a 100 seats were reserved for women. (In 2010, these percentages remained under the democratically elected government of the PPP.) In each of Pakistan's four provincial assemblies, about 20 percent of the total number of seats were now reserved for women. In the general election on October 10, 2002, twelve women were directly elected to general seats in the National Assembly; while sixty were selected by the party's leaders who nominated women and placed their name on the party's list of female candidates. For the 2002 election results, women representatives constituted 21 percent of those in the National Assembly (72 out of 342 seats). In the Senate, however, there is no distinction between general and women's seats in the election procedures. Both are elected by members of the provincial assemblies through a single transferable vote system. This process has enabled female senators to avoid the often discriminatory treatment that women elected on reserved seats can experience.[36]

This election witnessed social reaction to state interference in specific isolated regions of the country (tribal areas of the Khyber Pukhtunkhwa and Baluchistan provinces): women often were not allowed to vote by their male relatives due to a number of reasons, but especially because of social pressure by their respective communities. Coercive measures in certain tribal regions of NWFP (now Khyber Pukhtunkhwa), where tribal jirgas unanimously pledged to demolish the homes of any men who allowed their women to participate in the electoral or voting process, discouraged female participation. As a result of these pressure tactics, women in the tribal belt did not become candidates in the 2002 election.[37]

The significance of the election results was that the Muttahida Majlis-Amal (MMA), a collection of religious parties opposed to women's presence in the Parliament and seeking the complete imposition of shariah, were now forced to sit beside the elected women members. Consequently, the floor of the National Assembly became the scene of many a confrontation between members of MMA and female legislators over issues concerning women.[38]

IMPLEMENTATION OF THE HUDOOD ORDINANCES: TWO CASE STUDIES

Although the state under General Musharaff stressed the importance of restoring women's status and dignity in society, the trend toward moderation was slow as reflected in the continued implementation of the Hudood Ordinances. Critics, including the Alliance for the Repeal of Discriminatory Laws, argued that the military regime failed to follow through on its promises and that women were being prosecuted, abused, and discriminated against through the legal system which continued to enforce the Hudood Ordinances. Two well-publicized court cases, which prosecuted two women under the Hudood Ordinances, ignited a societal response which was both swift and effective in challenging these cases at the higher FSC level.

The first Hudood case illustrates the pitfalls of implementing the Hudood Ordinances when applied to specific cases involving pregnancy.[39] Zafran Bibi was convicted of adultery after she accused her brother-in-law of rape.[40] On April 17, 2002, Additional Sessions Judge Anwar Ali Khan pronounced Zafran Bibi guilty as charged, sentencing her to death by stoning at a public place "subject to confirmation of this judgment by Federal Shariat Court of Pakistan." In the nine-page judgment, he says that Zafran Bibi's two statements alleging zina "coupled with the presence of an illegitimate female child, amounts to confession of offence as envisaged by Section 8 of the offence of Zina (Enforcement of Hudood) Ordinance 1979."[41]

After spending eighteen months in solitary confinement in a death row cell in Kohat, Zafran Bibi was released after the Pakistan's Federal Shariat Court (FSC) took up her case and overturned the sentence.[42] The initial court's conviction was based on the criteria of the Zina Ordinance which required that Zafran Bibi produce four male witnesses of good character to support her allegations of rape by her brother-in-law while her husband, Naimat Khan, was incarcerated. Because Zafran Bibi could not produce the required witnesses, the court following the established criteria for zina offenses had concluded that since she was impregnated while her husband was in jail, she had engaged in an illicit relationship.[43] This sentence sparked an outcry from Pakistani human rights activists who launched a national protest campaign for the repeal of Hudood laws and release of Zafran Bibi.[44]

During the hearing by the Federal Shariat Court, Zafran Bibi and her husband, Naimat Khan testified that the baby girl in question was their daughter. Khan testified that Zafran Bibi actually became pregnant after a conjugal visit with him in jail. By making this assertion, Naimat Khan saved his wife's life and the daughter/family's "honor."[45] This paved the way for the FSC to rule: "Since Zafran Bibi and her husband have denied the commission of the offense, the question doesn't arise of their conviction." The court ordered her release.[46]

What was significant about the Zafran Bibi case in terms of state autonomy from social forces was that state actors themselves were not impartial, particularly at the higher federal echelons in the face of negative publicity. It can be argued that the FSC gave Ms. Bibi "a way out" of her predicament by accepting dubious testimony as to the father of her child given the fact that her husband had been in prison for a while. Following the FSC's acquittal of Zafran Bibi, the federal minister for Women's Development, Attiya Inayatullah expressed support for the FSC's verdict and disagreement with the Hudood Ordinances, which were state-enacted laws: "The judgment of the FSC is a source of relief for me and every Pakistani woman as it reflects the provision of justice for women who have fallen victim to misinterpretation of laws."[47]

Another case prosecuted under the Hudood Ordinance which attracted considerable international and domestic attention was the rape of Mukhtar Mai in June of 2002.[48] Mukhtar Mai was ordered raped as retribution by the village council after her brother was falsely accused of "associating" with a woman from a more prominent family. Within days of her public gang rape by four men, where she was raped, beaten, and thrown naked into the street to walk home, six men were behind bars, and a judge found them guilty and sentenced them to death in August 2002 while eight others were acquitted. Soon after this incident, Mukhtaran said she considered her options: "My choice was either to commit suicide or to fight back . . . I decided to fight back."[49]

According to rural Punjab's strict moral code, she had been forever "dishonored" despite the fact that her rape had been publicly carried out on the orders of the village council thereby sparing her the possible charge of zina (fornication) under the Hudood Ordinances. Even her clan, the Gujar, refused to support her. Mukhtaran took the unusual route of not killing herself as was expected and instead proposed the novel concept in rural Pakistan that *"real shame lay in the act of rape, rather than in the fact that she had been raped."* Just a week after her rape, a girl in the next village was gang-raped and took what was considered the traditional route of killing herself: she swallowed a bottle of pesticide and died.[50]

Mukhtaran chose the unprecedented path in rural Punjab to become a human rights and women rights advocate in spite of the obstacles she faced within her community. It was a significant event when, soon after her rape, the first "official" encouragement came from a local imam (an Islamic cleric) who called for her attackers to be brought before a civil court.[51] Soon, due to the efforts of the media and human rights organizations, this incident attracted the attention of the government and had led to an official investigation on the orders of Pakistan's Supreme Court.[52]

President Musharaff himself presented Mukhtaran with a check of about $8,300 (a large sum in Pakistan) in compensation and ordered the police to protect her. Instead of fleeing her village and the families of the rapists, Mukhtaran established schools for children in her village. Sarwar Bari of Pattan, an NGO, observed: "A lot people would have taken the money and run away, tried to forget. Mukhtaran had not only stayed but has launched a visible challenge to the feudal landlords to change the status quo."[53]

On March 3, 2005, in a huge setback for Ms. Mai's case, the Lahore High Court acquitted the five men, and reduced the death sentence on the March 6, 2005, to life in prison. The court justified its decision on the grounds that convictions could not be upheld for reasons of "insufficient evidence" and "faulty investigations." According to Khawaja Naveed Ahmed, a prominent lawyer in Karachi who deals mostly in criminal cases, what appears to be a miscarriage of justice is in fact a problem with Pakistan's criminal justice system: "In high profile cases such as that of Mukhtar Mai, the police find themselves under immense pressure—both from the government as well as influential people who may be supporting the accused."[54] Ahmed argues that differences between the trial and appellate court procedures also negatively impacted the case in that at the trial court level the judge is interacting with all parties on a one-on-one basis, while at the appellate level, only the recorded evidence is considered.[55]

When the Lahore High Court overturned the rape conviction in Mukhtar's case, the Pakistani prime minister, Shaukat Aziz, intervened by ordering the re-arrest of the accused who were acquitted. This move was also praised by other political parties, even the conservative PML whose vice president, Syed Kabir Ali Wasti, praised the PM's decision: "The LHC verdict has put Mukhtar Mai in grave peril. The Prime Minister has taken an appropriate step by ordering that the accused be put under custody . . . President Musharaff's concept of enlightened moderation is designed to rid the society of such medieval thinking and that the PM's orders reflected the government's determination to enforce the agenda of enlightened moderation."[56]

As soon as the LHC released its decision to acquit the accused rapists on the basis of insufficient evidence, the Federal Shariat Court stepped in suspending the judgment of the Lahore High Court. The FSC declared the LHC order to be *coram non judicie* or without jurisdiction.[57] The FSC judges said they were acting according to the Constitution which allows them to suspend judgment of any criminal court pending their own ruling. They ordered Mukhtar Mai, the six defendants, and the seven acquitted by the trial court to attend a new hearing. The FSC argued that this case should have been tried under the Hudood laws and not under the anti-terrorist legislation.[58] On the basis of the FSC's decision, the Punjab provincial government arrested all twelve men originally implicated in the case, including the five that had been acquitted by the trial court.[59]

Immediately after the FSC stepped in to hear the case, the Supreme Court Chief Justice, exercising *suo moto* powers, then stayed all proceedings in the case.[60] The Supreme Court decided to take over the case in order to prevent a turf war between the FSC and the Lahore High Court (LHC) in the full glare of the international media. This situation underscores the jurisdictional conflicts that have characterized Pakistan's higher judiciary since the establishment of the FSC in 1980.[61] Then, in June 2005, the LHC refused to extend a ninety-day detention order and said that the twelve men must be released on bail pending the Pakistan Supreme Court hearing on the case on June 27, 2005.[62] On June 28, 2005, the Supreme Court suspended the ruling of the LHC and ordered the arrest of all thirteen men accused of gang raping Mukhtar Mai.[63]

Mukhtar Mai's honeymoon period with the state, however, came to an abrupt end when she was perceived to represent a threat to the Pakistani state's attempts to improve its public image abroad in order to encourage foreign investment in Pakistan. State actors, who once lavished praise and assistance upon Mukhtar Mai, including President General Musharraf himself, eventually came to see her as a menace. First, her plans to travel to the United States (2005) to speak on the plight of Pakistani women were abruptly canceled when the government placed her name on the "Exit Control List" which prohibited her exit from the country. Then, Mukhtar was also placed under house arrest on the pretext of "protecting" her. At the same time, the LHC released her attackers who lived near her home.[64] The uproar over Mukhtar's inability to visit the United States led to the personal intervention of U.S. Secretary of State, Condoleeza Rice, who secured a pledge from Pakistan to allow Mukhtar Mai to visit the United States and address rights activists. In April 2011, the Supreme Court of Pakistan acquitted five of the six men in Mai's rape case. Despite this setback, Mai refused to give up and she tweeted: "No court can weaken my resolve to stand against injustice . . . the Supreme Court's verdict proves that police dictate system in Pakistan."[65]

Although Mukhtar Mai's life continues to be threatened, she refuses to end her legal battle and vows to keep fighting on behalf of women. Mukhtar views herself as a social activist and, in this capacity, established the Mukhtar Mai Women's Welfare Organization (MMWWO) to help support and educate Pakistani girls and women, and remains an outspoken advocate for women's rights.[66] The funds she accumulated through the international media attention have been used toward establishing two schools, setting up a shelter for abused women, and buying a van which is now used as an ambulance in the area—all making her something of a local heroine.

Both of these cases are illuminating on the internal conflict and tension within Pakistan's judicial system vis-à-vis implementation of "Shariah laws." Although the Musharaff-led state wasn't inclined to move toward repealing the Hudood (and especially the Zina) Ordinances, it was also not enthusiastic about implementing its stipulations. In fact, what is noteworthy is that the FSC (created by General Zia to ensure "Shariah" compliance) *acted as a moderating force, as well as a protector of the two women involved.* In the first case of Zafran Bibi, the FSC's acquittal of the defendant, based on dubious testimony, only infuriated the conservatives, while it pleased specific segments of the state apparatus and society. Furthermore, in the Mukhtar Mai case, the FSC was quick to jump into the legal fray as it took over the proceedings from the LHC in what appeared to become a turf war between the FSC and the Supreme Court on the question of jurisdiction.

The interesting question is why did the FSC, in its role as the premier enforcer of Shariah, consistently act to protect women from the damaging interpretations of Shariah? The answer to this question is multifaceted: international and domestic news coverage, coupled with pressure and appeals from various entities, as well as the makeup of the FSC, all contributed to varying degrees to the outcome in both cases. As to the makeup of the FSC itself: five of its eight judges are appointed from serving or retired judges of the Supreme Court or a High Court; while the remaining three are required to be ulema who are well versed in Islamic law. Thus the majority of judges on this—the highest Islamic Appeals Court of Pakistan—are from secular legal, not religious, backgrounds. This flavor of the FSC appears to have had a significant impact on how the FSC conducted itself in matters involving women's rights under the law.[67]

PASSAGE OF THE 2006 PROTECTION OF WOMEN (CRIMINAL LAWS AMENDMENT) BILL

Due to Musharaff's "liberalization" of the media, heated public debates on women's rights and status in Pakistani society were conducted by a dozen or so of the private television channels that were established ironically only after the reinstatement of military rule under Musharaff. The popular GEO TV's ("Geo" is Urdu for "live") chief executive, Mir Ibrahim Rahman, decided it was time for Pakistanis to debate the various clauses of the Hudood Ordinances. GEO produced and broadcast four groundbreaking episodes of a program called *"Zara Socieye"*—Urdu for "just think"—in June 2006. In this publicly aired program, twenty-seven prominent religious scholars debated various clauses of the Hudood Ordinances and agreed on a series of amendments. This public debate, and a general acknowledgment that changes were required in order to correct the misinterpretation of Islam on the subject of women, led Musharaff to personally ask the Council of Islamic Ideology—which advises the legislature on whether a certain law is repugnant to Islam or not—to draft an amendment to the Hudood Ordinances.[68] At the time, Jamaat-i-Islami's spokesman, Shahid Shamsi, said that his party was not opposed to changing the Hudood Ordinances, but would not support repealing them either.[69]

The bitter struggle within Pakistan's civil society over its identity and how this would determine women's role and status came to a head when the Women's Protection Bill of 2006 reached the National Assembly for a vote. On December 1, 2006, the Protection of Women (Criminal Laws Amendment) Bill, 2006 was granted assent by Musharaff. It passed in the National Assembly on November 15 and the Senate on November 23. Through this action, the Musharaff-led state took the first major step to reverse the precedents set under General Zia which denied women the ability to seek legal redress for crimes like rape and incest.[70]

The greatest impact of the Women's Protection Bill 2006 involved a change in the jurisdiction for prosecuting rape cases. In the future, victims of *zina bil jabr* (rape) now had the ability to legally pursue their rapists under the Pakistan Penal Code (PPC) procedures and not through the Shariah Courts, as had been the case since the enactment of the Hudood Ordinances. This amendment returned such cases to their original jurisdiction—the Criminal Courts—under PPC, thus eliminating the unattainable requirement of having to produce four honorable male witnesses to the act of *zina bil jabr* in order to obtain a verdict against the rapist.

Immediately after the passage of this bill, many Pakistani clerics began their efforts to undermine the law on the grounds that it was "un-Islamic." The Muttahida Majlis Amal (MMA) leader, Liaquat Baloch, stated that the United States and European countries continued to demand the repeal of the Hudood Ordinances because *it was an obstacle to changing the Islamic identity of Pakistan*.[71] Specifically, the clerics opposed four main clauses of this new bill as being repugnant to the Holy Quran and Sunnah and called for their repeal. These clauses included:

1. Exclusion of rape from *Hadd*.
2. Powers extended to the provincial governments to reduce punishment in adultery or consensual sex cases under Clause 5 of Section 20 of the bill.
3. Amendments to *Qazf* Ordinance regarding punishment for perjury.
4. Another amendment in which if a women voluntarily admits her offense she would remain exempted from *Hadd*.[72]

The Musharaff government, in meetings with members of the ulema, promised to take into consideration their concerns by referring them to the FSC for determination on whether this amendment violated Islamic injunctions. Interestingly, the ulema rejected this proposal—to seek the interpretation of the highest Islamic court (the FSC)—and demanded this bill be reviewed by the Parliament instead.[73] The ulema's reluctance to involve the highest Islamic Court in the land reflects the reality that the FSC has not been a reliable advocate of the ulema in enforcement, on appeal, of these "Shariah"-based ordinances. But the ulema needn't have worried as the FSC demanded that such a move was "unconstitutional" and, per its mandate, jurisdiction over such Shariah-related crimes had to remain with it.

Opponents of the clerics included an active, and relatively censor-free, media, various activist groups, and prominent members of the judiciary, including retired Supreme Court Justice, Javed Iqbal. Iqbal have argued that the Zina Ordinance, and the Hudood Ordinances in general, that were forcibly imposed were not laws passed by a parliament since at that time the parliament had been abolished by General Zia. Calling these ordinances "un-Islamic and unconstitutional" Iqbal stressed that the effects have been dire for women as the number of incarcerated women increased significantly while men went free. Iqbal argued that these "black laws" were also in contradiction to Quaid-i-Azam's views. Another former Lahore High Court chief justice, Allah Nawaz, proposed a joint seminar of the opponents and supporters of the Hudood Ordinance to resolve the dispute; while a Muslim scholar, Allama Ghulam Rasul Qasmi, proposed the establishment of a committee of religious scholars of all schools of thought to review it.

Notwithstanding criticism from various women groups and international organizations, the passage of this bill was a significant victory for Pakistani women in reversing the oppressive effects of the Hudood Ordinances. For the first time since the passage of these ordinances, a bill was passed to address the inequities inherent in them. Ironically none of the previous democratically elected governments (Bhutto and Sharif) had made any serious efforts to address the deficits of these ordinances as they pertained to the subject of rape and incest.[74]

As mentioned, the Protection of Women's Bill of 2006 amended only two of the five ordinances of the 1979 Hudood Ordinances, namely the Zina and Qazf Ordinances in order to restore jurisdiction for prosecution to the PPC as was the case prior to the enactment of the Hudood Ordinances. Procedural changes (Section 203(a), (b), and (c)) no longer allowed the police to issues arrest warrants; instead, summons was to be issued and, until and unless guilt was proven, no one was to be sent to prison. Any complaint regarding *zina* or *qazf* had to go through the district or session judge, along with the statement of four witnesses. If the judge decided the complaint is genuine, then only was the application accepted. This was due to a reinterpretation of what constituted a *hadd* case. *Zina* cases were now considered in the *ta'azir* category and thus jurisdiction would reside in the civil not the Shariah realm. This has been of an enormous relief to women since prior to the passage of this law, any woman could be accused of zina and thrown in prison until the matter came before the court. As a result, false accusations of zina appeared to have dropped dramatically.[75]

Notwithstanding these successes, however, women's activists in Pakistan accused the Musharraf government of promoting "an enlightened Islam" vision that excludes women. They also accused officials of trying to cover up the brutal justice of the tribal hinterlands as a matter of public relations. When *Time* magazine nominated Mukhtar Mai as one of Asia's heroes, it commented: "As long as the state refuses to fully challenge the brutality of tribal law, the plight of Pakistani women will continue. Mukhtar Mai is a symbol of their victimhood, but in her resilience she is also a symbol of their strength."

Those who had opposed the Women's Protection Law as being "un-Islamic" did not waste time setting in motion a variety of challenges to have this overturned. On November 23, 2010, the FSC reserved its verdict on petitions challenging the Women Protection Law. A three-member bench of FSC comprising Chief Justice Agha Rafiq Ahmed, Justice Afzal Haider, and Justice Shahzado Sheikh heard the petition[76] which challenged the Women Protection Law on the grounds that no law that was repugnant to both the Quran and Sunnah could be adopted.[77] On December 22, the FSC asserting jurisdiction declared Sections 11, 25, 28, and 29 of the Women's Protection Act 2006 "un-Islamic and unconstitutional" on the premise that the overriding effect of the Hudood Ordinances over other laws could not be stripped. It argued that it retained jurisdiction to hear appeals under any law relating to ten offences covered by the term "hudood" for the purpose of Article 203 DD of the constitution. The FSC decision to retain jurisdiction evoked strong criticism from women's groups who argued that the court sought to reverse the limited gains women had made over tyrannical and discriminatory laws.[78]

Prevention of Domestic Violence Bill of 2009

In Pakistan, honor killings and other forms of violence toward females is widespread. According to Ali Dayan Hasan, a senior South Asia researcher at Human Rights Watch, "victims of domestic violence have long faced a double injustice—abuse at home and then no protection from the government."[79] A female PPP member of the NA, Yasmeen Rahman introduced a "prevention of domestic violence" bill in the assembly. The passage of this twenty-eight clause bill was another, albeit short-lived, symbolic victory for women via the legislative process. The bill defined "domestic violence" as "*all intentional acts of gender-based or other physical or psychological abuse committed by an accused against women, children or other vulnerable persons, with whom the accused person is or has been in a domestic relationship.*"

In the "State of Human Rights in 2008" report, issued by the Human Rights Commission of Pakistan (HRCP), over 800 women were sexually harassed, 350 raped, 45 gang-raped, and 13 were stripped. It added that 185 women were killed due to domestic violence and 138 others injured. A total of 7,571 incidents of violence against women were reported in the country, according to the women's rights group Aurat Foundation's "Situation of Violence against Women in Pakistan, 2008."[80]

The bill stipulated that an aggrieved person had the right to approach a first class magistrate's court with an application, or through another authorized person, and the court must fix a hearing within three days and give a decision within thirty days. The Court Protection orders could prohibit the accused from committing or aiding or abetting domestic violence, dispossessing an aggrieved person of household, give monetary relief to meet expenses and losses as well as for maintenance. The first breach of a protection order would be punishable with imprisonment of up to one year, but not less than six months, and a minimum fine of 100,000 rupees which would be paid to the aggrieved person. But a violation for the second or third time, or more, will be punishable with up to two years' imprisonment and a fine of not less than 200,000 rupees payable to the aggrieved person. The offense of breach of a protection "shall be cognizable, non-bail able and compoundable," and convictions could be appealed in a session's court. However, filing a false complaint—which the complainant knows or has reason to believe to be false—in a court would be punishable with simple imprisonment of up to six months or with fine of up to 50,000 rupees or with both.

Termed a good piece of legislation, it was passed in the NA on August 4, 2009, in a rare show of unanimity by all parties.[81] According to Article 70 of the Constitution, the government had to get an affirmation to the bill from the Senate within ninety days of it being passed by the NA, but failed to achieve this due to objections raised by the Islamists and their supporters in the Senate. This meant that the process would have to start anew with the bill having to be passed again by both houses.[82] But before that could happen, the Bill had to be approved by a mediation committee comprising members of both houses.[83] Although supporters of the Bill in the NA were optimistic that it could be reintroduced with some slight changes and resubmitted, it remains in limbo.

Protection against Harassment of Women at Workplace Bill 2009

In another landmark move, under the tutelage of the democratically elected PPP government, on January 21, 2010, President Asif Zardari signed into law the "Protection against Harassment of Women at Workplace Bill 2009" following passage in the Parliament.[84] Human Rights Watch characterized this amendment to the PPC as a "step forward." The measure made sexual harassment or intimidation punishable by three years in prison, a 500,000 rupee fine (approximately US$6,000), or both. The bill included protection in public places such as markets, public transport, streets, or parks, and more private settings, such as workplaces, private gatherings, and homes. Human Rights Watch, however, observed that the new law provides legal protections without putting in place the mechanisms needed to give female workers access to the protections. It urged the Pakistani Parliament to also pass a companion bill to the sexual harassment measure which would provide the essential mechanisms for employers to abide by a code of conduct and to investigate complaints, offer victims counseling and medical treatment if necessary.[85] Although this recommendation has not been followed, the passage of the bill, which stipulates protecting women in the workplace, is another important legislative milestone for Pakistani women in ensuring them fundamental protections at the workplace.

In terms of enactment of legislation meant to restore women's rights to the pre-1979 era and/or to ameliorate conditions previously unaddressed legislatively, the PPP-led government's track record hasn't been a bad one. In February 2012, the Senate unanimously passed the National Commission on the Status of Women Bill 2012 to ensure women's rights against all forms of discrimination.[86] This legislative measure followed two earlier bills passed in December 2011. The Acid Control and Acid Crime Prevention Bill 2010 and the Prevention of Anti-Women Practices Act 2011, which was authored by the Pakistan Muslim League-Quaid Member National Assembly (PML-Q MNA), Dr. Donya Aziz. The bill on Acid Control and Acid Crime recommends fourteen-year to lifetime imprisonment sentences and levies fines up to Rs1 million for the perpetrators of the crime.[87] Although enactment of this favorable legislation was fairly uneventful, it remains to be seen how effective the actual implementation process will be in the long run.

The Elimination of the Custom of "Ghag" Law of 2013

The ratification of this bill enacted by the Khyber Pukhtunkhwa Provincial Assembly on January 8, 2013, was a huge victory for females in the province. This tribal custom (known as "ghag") compelled fathers to give their daughters in marriage to predatory males who had "cast their eyes upon their prey (their daughters)" in order to save the family's "honor." The passage of this bill was due to a father's personal mission to save his two daughters from this cruel tradition. Muhammad Nawaz refused to hand over his two daughters to his nephews in 2012 when they invoked "ghag." When the tribal jirga determined he was in violation of tribal custom and demanded he pay a hefty fine and comply, Nawaz refused. Instead, he appealed to the provincial government to help him save his daughters from ghag's tentacles. There were no laws on the books as no one had raised the issue before. But this new law, which punishes violators with long prison sentences and/or a fine, is a step forward for the province's females. Furthermore, it underscores the ongoing struggle within Pakistani society at all levels (local, provincial, and national) to determine female status (servitude or equal citizens) in the twenty-first century.[88]

CONCLUSION

During the eleven-year period of haphazard democracy (1988–1999) before the resumption of military rule (1999–2008), the Pakistani state addressed the gender issue with caution. The discourse on what constitutes women's identity in an Islamic state became a highly contentious one, pitting various social groups against each other. Furthermore, as the evidence suggests, the state was not immune from internal dissent on the subject of female rights in an "Islamic republic." One noteworthy source of dissent and unpredictability vis-à-vis female rights and status remains the state's judicial arm.

Female activist groups like WAF who envisioned a quick repeal of the "black laws," the Hudood Ordinances, once democracy was restored, have voiced their disappointment and vowed to continue to advocate and fight on to reverse this "Shariah" trend. Supporters of General Zia's Islamization efforts worry that these programs could be dismantled in the future thanks to this activism and media attention. Given deep social divisions, the controversial subject of female rights in an "Islamic republic" has become one of the most critical discourses in Pakistan today. One perception which gained some momentum over time is that the policies established under General Zia were not based on Islamic precepts but on misogynistic interpretations (of Islamic law) to the detriment of its female populace.

The politics of the Pakistani state since Zia's death to the return of the military in 1999 suggests that state policy on gender-related issues was determined by the narrow interests of those at the helm. State gender policy vacillated and was never consistent in following a specific trajectory. It was often impulsive and driven by the narrow agendas of those in charge (Bhutto or Sharif), since both of these leaders were beholden to specific social groups for their government's survival. Thus, the only constant was recognition by these politicians that their primary objective involved staying in office. It was this need that lent itself to concessions to the other side or to enact certain gender policies in order to appease social elements. Furthermore, within the state apparatus there was dissent and contradiction, especially when it came to implementation of controversial clauses within the Hudood Ordinances. The judiciary in particular has fought hard to retain some semblance of impartiality, which made it unpopular with those in charge.

The passage of the Protection of Women (Crimes Laws Amendment) Act of 2006 was due in no small part to the heated public discourse on various television shows which served to highlight the absurdity (and unfairness) of the existing stipulations of the Hudood Ordinances on zina and *zina bil jabr* cases. Public pressure and widespread awareness on the subject thanks to a free media led to passage of this important bill which represented the first major legislative effort to reverse Zia's gender policies. Emboldened, but not satisfied, female activists clamored for a complete repeal of the Hudood

Ordinances. Resumption of civilian rule in 2008 appears to have been a harbinger of additional legislation favorable to Pakistan's female populace. In the long run, however, enactment of legislative measures will not suffice unless there is broad public support, and entrenched social norms and mores are overcome despite the vanguard efforts of the conservative social and religious elements of society to treat females like possessions and chattel all in the name of Islam.

Although female activists and their supporters have witnessed hard-won successes in the legislative and judicial arenas; the social and security conditions for females in general continues to deteriorate. The near-fatal shooting by a Taliban assassin of fourteen-year-old Malala Yousefzai on October 9, 2012, in Mingora (Swat), was the shot heard around the world. The targeting of girls for simply attending school by Muslim terrorists is indicative of the degree of rot, and the pervasive (physical) insecurity, that now permeates the lives of all females irrespective of locale and socioeconomic background. The defiance of Malala Yousefzai in her first public appearance after being shot, however, is encouraging as it is necessary.[89] Her refusal to be cowed, and her determination to continue to advocate on behalf of females' right to an education, is a public relations nightmare for Islamists because such defiance emboldens others to challenge their brutal misogyny.

NOTES

1. Elise Garafolo, "Malala Devotes 'Second Life' to Girls' Rights," *PBS Newshour Extra*, February 14, 2013. Accessed at: http://www.pbs.org/newshour/extra/features/world/jan-june13/malala_02-14.html.
2. For more on this election and the religious parties refer to Syed Vali Reza Nasr, *The Vanguard of the Islamic Revolution* (Berkeley: University of California Press, 1994), 206–218.
3. Charles H. Kennedy, "Judicial Activism," in *Pakistan: 1992* (Boulder, CO: Westview Press, 1993), 63.
4. Kennedy, "Judicial Activism," on page 61 please refer to footnote 28.
5. Rubina Saigol, "The Shariat Bill and Its Impact on Education and Women," in *Against All Odds: Essays on Women, Religion and Development from India and Pakistan*, edited by Kamla Basin, Ritu Menon, and Nighat Said Khan (New Delhi: ISIS, 1998), 84.
6. Fauzia Gardezi, "Islam, Feminism, and the Women's Movement in Pakistan: 1981–91," in *Against All Odds*, 51–54.
7. Saigol, 85.
8. For text of the government sponsored official shariat bill see "*The News*," April 12, 1991.
9. Saigol, 64.
10. See Iftikhar H. Malik, *State and Civil Society in Pakistan: Politics of Authority, Ideology and Ethnicity* (New York: Palgrave Macmillan, 1997), 162–163.
11. Amnesty International Online Annual Human Rights Report on Pakistan, 1998: "*Pakistan: No Progress on Women's Rights*," 2. Accessed at: http://www.law.georgetown.edu/rossrights/docs/reports/packistan-amnestyhonour.html.
12. Amnesty International, "Pakistan," 2.
13. Amnesty International, "Pakistan," 3.
14. Amnesty International, "Pakistan," 3.

15. Dorothy Q. Thomas, "Double Jeopardy: Police Abuse of Women in Pakistan," *Human Rights Watch*, June 21, 1992. Accessed at: http://www.hrw.org/reports/1992/pakistan/.

16. Thomas, "Double Jeopardy."

17. For more background on CEDAW's history, see *The International Standards of Equality and Religious Freedom: Implications for the Status of Women*, eds. John Bale and David Drakaki-Smith (New York: UN, 1990), 425–435. Accessed at: http://untreaty.un.org/cod/avl/ha/cedaw/cedaw.html

18. Alice Bettencourt, "Violence Against Women in Pakistan," Human Rights Advocacy Clinic, Spring 2000, 15. Accessed at: http://8mars2009.files.wordpress.com/2009/03/violencepkstn.pdf.

19. "A Report by Refugee Women's Resource Project, Domestic Violence: Country Studies: Islamic Republic of Pakistan," *Asylum Aid*, September 2001/updated March 2002, 8. Accessed at: http://www.asylumaid.org.uk/data/files/publications/43/Refugee_Women_and_Domestic_Violence_Edition_2.pdf

20. "A Report by Refugee Women's Resource Project, Domestic Violence," 29.

21. For more on the FSC please access its website at: http://federalshariatcourt.gov.pk/.

22. For more on the Pakistan Judiciary and the various Constitutional Crises, refer to Javed Iqbal, "The Judiciary and Constitutional Crises in Pakistan," in *Pakistan: Founder's Aspirations and Today's Realities*, ed. Hafeez Malik (Oxford: Oxford University Press, 2001), 61–81.

23. For information on Sharif's other efforts to limit the judiciary's powers during this period see Hasan Abbas, *Pakistan's Drift into Extremism* (New York: M.E. Sharpe, 2005), 159–161, 164–165.

24. Stephen Cohen, *The Idea of Pakistan* (Washington, DC: Brookings Institution, 2004), 173.

25. Amnesty International Annual Country Report: Pakistan, 1998.

26. Amnesty International Annual Country Report: Pakistan, 1998, 3.

27. Sultan J. Quraishi, "NGOs under Attack in New Campaign," *The News*, May 25, 1999. Accessed at: http://www.sacw.net/aii/NGOsunderfire-News250599.html.

28. Tariq Butt, "Punjab Government Prepares to Regulate NGOs," *The Nation*, May 18, 1999. Accessed at: http://www.sacw.net/aii/regulNGOs18-5.html.

29. Omar Asghar Khan, "When Women Speak Out," *The News*, October 22, 1999. Accessed at: http://www.sacw.net/Wmov/WspeakOUT.html.

30. See Zulfikhar Khalid Maluka, "Reconstructing the Constitution for a COAS President: Pakistan, 1999 to 2002," in *Pakistan on the Brink: Politics, Economics, and Society*, ed. Craig Baxter (Lanham, MD: Lexington Books, 2004), 53–95.

31. "New Islamic Decree in Pakistan," *BBC News*, July 15, 2000. Accessed at: http://news.bbc.co.uk/2/hi/south_asia/835425.stm.

32. "Government of Pakistan: National Commission on the Status of Women," *Women's International Network News* (Lexington, MA, Autumn 2002), 76.

33. Zofeen Ebrahim, "Rights-Pakistan: Ancient Customs Trigger Debate on Women's Rights," *Global Information Network*, New York: June 9, 2004, 1.

34. Maluka, 92; Irene Graff, "Quota Systems in Pakistan under the Musharraf Regime," *Nordic Institute of Asian Studies, Asia Insights*, no. 1 (March 2004), 21.

35. Maluka, 22.

36. Maluka, 22, 92.

37. Maluka, 22, 92.

38. Maluka, 93.

39. Zafran Bibi's case illustrates the legal pitfalls that may befall a female impregnated by rape (Safia Bibi's case is another well-known case). Her case was one of many in which a court's conviction was set aside by the FSC upon appeal. For more on such cases see Moen H. Cheema, "Cases and Controversies: Pregnancy as Proof of Guilt under Pakistan's Hudood Laws," *Brooklyn Journal of International Law* 32, no. 1 (2007), 121–160). Cheema writes: "Repeated errors by the trial courts are due in part to the continuing inability of the Federal Shariat Court (FSC) to harmonise its jurisdiction, indicating that the relevant precedents have not been widely publicized, studied and brought to the court's attention by advocates."

40. Seth Mydans, "In Pakistan, Rape Victims Are the Criminals," *New York Times*, May 17, 2002. Accessed at: http://www.nytimes.com/2002/05/17/world/in-pakistan-rape-victims-are-the-criminals.html

41. Sanna Bucha, "Twice Damned," *Newsline*, May 7th, 2002. Accessed at: http://www.newslinemagazine.com/2002/05/twice-damned/

42. Nadeem Iqbal, "Rights-Pakistan: Death Sentence Lifted on Rape Victim," *Global Information Network*, June 11, 2002, 1; see also Mydans; Zofeen Ebrahim, "Rights-Pakistan: Despite Sound and Fury, "Hudood" Laws Still Stay," *Global Information Network*, New York: September 26, 2003, 1.

43. Hannah Bloch, "Blaming the Victim," *Time*, May 20, 2002. Accessed at: http://www.time.com/time/magazine/article/0,9171,238673,00.html.

44. Iqbal, 2.

45. Bloch. Accessed at: http://www.time.com/time/magazine/article/0,9171,238673,00.html#ixzz16RfEBZno.

46. Iqbal, 1.

47. Iqbal, 2.

48. Waseem Ahmed Shah, "Justice Under Fire: Should the Courts Make Legal Concessions in Cases Involving Marginalised Members of Society?" *The Herald*, April 2005, 29–33.

49. Ron Moreau and Zahid Hussain, "I Decided to Fight Back," *Newsweek*, March 28, 2005. Accessed at: http://www.thedailybeast.com/newsweek/2005/03/27/i-decided-to-fight-back.html.

50. Wendy McElroy, "Muslim Woman's Courage Sets Example," *Fox News*, March 16, 2005. Accessed at: http://www.foxnews.com/story/0,2933,150556,00.html.

51. McElroy.

52. Iqbal, 1.

53. Iqbal, 1.

54. Aamer Ahmed Khan, "Pakistan's Justice System in Spotlight," *BBC News*, March 12, 2005. Accessed at: http://news.bbc.co.uk/2/hi/south_asia/4315491.stm.

55. Khan.

56. "Re-arrest of Accused in Rape Case Lauded," *DAWN*, March 20, 2005. Accessed at: http://www.pakistanpressfoundation.org/news-archives/30465.

57. Waseem Ahmed Shah, "Counter Claims," *The Herald*, April 2005, 30.

58. "Rape Ruling in Pakistan Suspended," *BBC NEWS*, March 12, 2005. Accessed at: http://news.bbc.co.uk/2/hi/south_asia/4339927.stm.

59. "Passport Pledge to Rape Victim," *BBC News*, June 23, 2005. Accessed at: http://news.bbc.co.uk/2/hi/south_asia/4118624.stm.

60. Shah, 30.

61. Ali Dayan Hasan, "The Jurisdictional Dilemma," *DAWN News*, March 21, 2005. Accessed at: http://www.hrw.org/es/news/2005/03/20/jurisdiction-dilemma.

62. Jan McGirk, "Women's Rights in Pakistan: The Woman Who Dared to Cry Rape," *Independent News*, June 15, 2005. Accessed at: http://www.independent.co.uk/news/world/asia/womens-rights-in-pakistan-the-woman-who-dared-to-cry-rape-6144260.html.

63. Nadeem Saeed, "Swept under the Rug," *The Herald*, July 2005, 62-64. Accessed at: http://www.nadeemsaeed.com/mukhtarmai.html

64. Saeed 2005.

65. "Mukhtaran Mai Denied Justice in Pakistani Supreme Court Ruling," *Women's Revolution*, April 22, 2011. Accessed at: http://www.womensrevolution.com/2011/04/mukhtaran-mai-denied-justice-in.html

66. Chiade O'Shea, "The Rape Victim Who Fought Back," *BBC News*, March 12, 2005. Accessed at: http://news.bbc.co.uk/2/hi/south_asia/4330335.stm

67. Kennedy's (1988)—albeit somewhat dated—examination of 426 FSC cases (1980-1984) presented some interesting findings: (a)the FSC accepted most appeals from lower courts; (b)overwhelming majority of cases involved *zina*; (c) most convictions were overturned; and (d) overwhelmingly, those charged were not from middle class or affluent backgrounds. Charles Kennedy, "Islamization in Pakistan: Implementation of the Hudood Ordinances," *Asian Survey* 28, no. 3 (March 1988), 307–316.

68. "Pakistan Ponders Altering Islamic Rape Law," *New York Times*, July 9, 2006. Accessed at: http://www.sfgate.com/news/article/Pakistan-ponders-altering-Islamic-rape-law-2493175.php
69. "Pakistan ponders altering Islamic rape law," *New York Times*, July 9, 2006.
70. "Repeal of Hudood Ordinances Demanded," *DAWN*, July 31, 2006. Accessed at: http://archives.dawn.com/2006/07/31/nat13.htm.
71. "Amendments to Weaken Hudood Laws: Baloch," *DAWN*, August 4, 2006. Accessed at: http://archives.dawn.com/2006/08/04/nat24.htm
72. "Pakistani Clerics Continue Efforts to Undermine Women's Protection Bill," *Khaleej Times*, December 5, 2006.
73. "Pakistani Clerics Continue Efforts to Undermine Women's Protection Bill," *Khaleej Times*.
74. "Pakistan: Proposed Reforms to Hudood Laws Fall Short," *Human Rights Watch*, September 6, 2006. Accessed at: http://www.hrea.org/lists/women-rights/markup/msg00351.html
75. Rubya Mehdi, "The Protection of Women (Criminal Laws Amendment) Act, 2006 in Pakistan," *Droit Cultures* (2010), 191–206. Accessed at: http://droitcultures.revues.org/2016: Niaz. A.Shah, "The Women Protection Act 2006 of Pakistan: An Analysis," *Religion and Human Rights* 5 (2010), 1–10.
76. The petitioners were Muhammad Akhtar, Abdul Latif Sufi, and Mian Abdu Razzaq.
77. "FSC Reserves Verdict on Petitions Challenging Women Protection Law," *Business Recorder*, November 24, 2010. Accessed at: http://www.brecorder.com/news/general-news/pakistan/1127082:news.html
78. Iftikhar A. Khan, "Shariat Court Knocks Out 3 Sections of Women Protection's Act," *DAWN*, December 23, 2006. Accessed at: http://dawn.com/2010/12/23/shariat-court-knocks-out-3-sections-of-womens-protection-act/ ; "Do We Need a Moral Police?" *Daily Times*, December 24, 2010. Accessed at: http://www.dailytimes.com.pk/default.asp?page=2010\12\24\story_24-12-2010_pg3_1
79. "Pakistan: Expedite Domestic Violence Legislation," *Human Rights Watch*, January 11, 2010. Accessed at: http://www.hrw.org/en/news/2010/01/11/pakistan-expedite-domestic-violence-legislation
80. Zofeen T. Ebrahim, "Pakistan's Domestic Violence Survivors in a Blind Alley," *Women's Feature Service*, February 15, 2010. Accessed at: http://www.faqs.org/periodicals/201002/2041510071.html#ixzz16PtR8BSn
81. Raja Asghar, "NA Bill Outlaws Domestic Violence," *DAWN*, August 5, 2009. Accessed at: http://news.dawn.com/wps/wcm/connect/dawn-content-library/dawn/news/pakistan/11-pakistan-moves-to-outlaw-domestic-violence--il--04.
82. Pakistan has a bicameral federal legislature that consists of the Senate (upper house) and the National Assembly (lower house).
83. Ebrahim, Accessed at: http://www.faqs.org/periodicals/201002/2041510071.html#ixzz16PtR8BSn
84. Shamim ur-Rahman, "Women's Bill Sets Tough Penalties," *DAWN*, Jan 30, 2010. Accessed at: http://news.dawn.com/wps/wcm/connect/dawn-content-library/dawn/news/pakistan/04-zardari-signs-women-prot-bill-qs-08
85. Rebecca Buckwalter-Poza, "Troubled History of Domestic Violence Legislation," *Huffington Post*, October 7, 2010. Accessed at: http://www.huffingtonpost.com/rebecca-buckwalterpoza/troubled-history-of-omes_b_753400.html
86. "Senate Approves Women Protection Bill 2012," *Pak Tribune*. February 3, 2012. Accessed at: http://paktribune.com/news/Senate-approves-womens-protection-bill-2012-247235.html
87. Sumera Khan, "Women Specific Bill Passed: Fourteen Year Jail Term for Acid Throwers," *The Express Tribune*, December 12, 2011. Accessed at: http://tribune.com.pk/story/305482/unanimous-vote-senate-passes-women-protection-anti-acid-throwing-bills/
88. Umer Farooq, "A Story of Courage: Villager Rescues Women from Brutal Tribal Custom," *The Express Tribune*, January 14, 2013. Accessed at: http://tribune.com.pk/story/493706/a-story-of-courage-villager-rescues-women-from-brutal-tribal-custom/

89. See Robert Mackey, "Malala Yousafzai, Pakistani Girl Shot by Taliban Militants, Speaks in New Videos." *The New York Times,* February 4, 2013. Accessed at: http://thelede.blogs.nytimes.com/2013/02/04/a-video-statement-from-malala-yousafzai-the-pakistani-girl-shot-by-the-taliban/.

II

Afghanistan

Chapter Four

The Politics of Gender in Afghanistan (1919–1994)

A Historical Overview

> I'm the woman who has awoken, I've found my path and will never return.
> —Meena (1957–1987), founder RAWA

Since independence the Afghan state has embarked on various controversial programs that sought to directly influence the lives of its female populace with limited success. Prior to the establishment of what has been characterized as the "modern" Afghan state following the end of the Third Anglo-Afghan War (1919), social matters were local affairs with no outside interference. How women fared in terms of their daily lives and social position was contingent on a myriad of factors such as geographical location, ethnic affiliation, socioeconomic status, and educational background. This status quo came to an abrupt end when for the first time in its history, Afghanistan's Durrani ruler struggled to implement ambitious, even precipitous, social reforms.

STATE'S MODERNIZATION PROGRAM AND SOCIAL RESISTANCE (1919–1929)

Afghanistan comprised of a loose tribal confederation prior to 1919. There was no real middle class and the clerics to varying degrees dominated, and interpreted, social mores that included defining women's role in society. Soon after independence, King Amanullah formulated an ambitious plan to "modernize" a country that had changed little in centuries. His attempts were influenced by unfolding events in the region (Ataturk's Turkey and Persia under Reza Shah) and by his enunciated belief that Afghanistan's future interests were best served by such a transformation.

Under Amanullah, Afghanistan embarked on an ambitious project of overnight transformation of embedded social and cultural traditions in the name of modernization and progress. Due to certain state policies some Afghan females, particularly those in the urban areas, experienced certain changes which appeared to improve their social and physical condition but also left them bewildered as the state first moved sharply in one direction (as in implementing its modernization schemes) and then did an about-face (as it tried to appease, and co-opt, the outraged conservative elements). This ten-year period witnessed some sharp policy reversals in terms of the state's stipulations on women's rights and status.[1]

Upon assuming office, King Amanullah immediately pledged to not only modernize the country but also to free women from centuries' old traditions of social oppression. In a speech he declared:

> and by the grace of God our sublime government will employ such measures of reform as may prove suitable and useful to the country and nation so that the Government and nation of Afghanistan may make and gain great renown in the civilized world and take its proper place among the civilized powers of the world.[2]

In 1923, Amanullah established Afghanistan's first constitution, *Nizamnameh-ye-Asasi-e-Dawlat-e-Aliyah-e-Afghanistan* which comprised of seventy-three articles. This document was his roadmap on how to create a modern civil society: it outlined the responsibilities of the king and his government, as well as the rights of its citizens and it abolished slavery. The abolishment of slavery ended the common practice of slave ownership that existed even among state officials who often offered slaves as gifts to each other. This led to the freedom of seven hundred Hazara slaves in Kabul alone, which included young girls and boys.[3]

In the social arena, Amanullah's state sought to end illiteracy. Schools were established for boys and girls, but also adult classes were offered with Amanullah personally teaching some classes, and by recruiting itinerant teachers to serve nomadic citizens. He hoped modern education would complement religious education, not necessarily replace it. Elementary education was made compulsory and free of charge for both sexes, and the state provided some stipends and clothes to students beyond primary education to encourage poor and marginalized families to send their children to school. The state also established schools for girls. The first primary school for girls, Masturat School, was established in 1921 in Kabul, under the tutelage of Amanullah's wife, Soraya. Soraya's mother, Asma Rasmiyah, was the principal of the school, assisted by her two nieces, Belqis and Rohafza.[4] Civil service personnel were encouraged to send their daughters to school so that they could set an example for others to follow.

During 1920–1927, there were two primary schools and one middle school for girls, with an estimated seven hundred students. King Amanullah promoted a coeducational system and the Amaniya School, which was named after him, was coeducational. In 1928, the state sent fifteen female graduates of the Masturat middle school, who were daughters of prominent Kabulis, to Turkey for higher education.[5] In 1921, the state established a weekly paper called *Irshad-e-Niswan* (the Guide for Women) which was edited by Amanullah's mother-in-law, Asma Rasmiyah Tarzi.[6] The stated purpose of this paper for women was to increase women's awareness while also providing useful household tips like recipes.[7]

The first women's hospital, Masturat Hospital, in Kabul was established which was administered by Amanullah's sister, Bibi Gul, known as Seraj al-Banat. Al-Banat was also a social activist who participated in campaigns that aimed at raising social awareness among women. In 1923, she addressed a public gathering in Kabul in which she criticized the prevailing concept of women's inferiority:

> Some people are laughing at us, saying that women know only how to eat and drink. Old women discourage young women by saying their mothers never starved to death because they could not read and write. . . . But knowledge is not man's monopoly. Women also deserve to be knowledgeable.[8]

In August 1924, the *Nizamnamah-ye-Arusi* and the *Nikah wa Khatnasuri* laws were introduced which covered the subject of engagements and marriage. The *Nizamnamah* stressed gender equality and established minimum age for marriage. Girls were encouraged to choose their marriage partners without their parents' interference and women were urged to take legal action if their husbands did not treat them well. Such decrees were considered "un-Islamic" by most of the Afghan populace, who viewed them as a violation of their understanding of Shariah law. For many, such interference was also perceived as a attempt by the state to destroy their patriarchal, lineage based tribal society.

The *Nizamnameh* stated:

> If the wife of a polygamist man feels that her husband has failed to treat all of his wives fairly and equally, she can file a complaint against her husband in a court of Sharia, so that the unjust husbands should be punished accordingly. Moreover, punishment prescribed for husbands who would prevent their wives from petitioning against them. . . . Article 18 of this document prohibits a forced marriage between adults; it calls the arranger of such a forceful mar-

riage jabir, tyrant and states that the qazi (judge) who presides over this contract is to be reprimanded.[9]

Queen Soraya was also active in advocating on behalf of Afghan women. On the seventh anniversary of the country's independence, Soraya addressed a group of women:

> Do not think . . . that our nation needs only men to serve it. Women should also take part as women did in the early years of Islam. The valuable services rendered by women are recounted throughout history, from which we learn that women were not created solely for pleasure and comfort. From their examples we learn that we must all contribute toward the development of our nation and that this cannot be done without being equipped with knowledge.[10]

The State's social measures, under Amir Amanullah's influence and direction, faced stiff social resistance due to both their controversial nature and to the unprecedented meddling by the state on sensitive *zanana* (harem/household) issues. When a major rebellion broke out in Khost province in March 1924 (which was militarily suppressed), the threat posed by this rebellion convinced Amanullah of the need to temporarily halt some of his reforms and to modify others. For example, in a complete about-face, females were now directed to receive their education at home, religious studies were encouraged and men were once again allowed to have four wives.[11]

While the state's modernization program never resumed the same pace, some women did see improvements in their lives and status during this period. In 1928, Amanullah established *Anjuman-e-Niswan*, the Association for the Protection of Women. He appointed his sister, Kubra, to head the association and to work on matters involving women's liberation. The association had twelve active members who worked to promote women's issues.[12] When Amanullah held a Loya Jirga, a Grand Assembly of Tribal Elders in August 1928 to obtain their endorsement of the state's program, he brought along his wife, Queen Soraya. Oblivious to the shocking impact it would have, Amanullah on stage publicly asked the queen to remove her veil in front of the tribal elders who had been compelled to wear European clothes to the event provided to them by the state. Along with Queen Soraya, around a hundred other women, mostly wives of government employees who supported her, also removed their veils in front of these tribal elders. This symbolic move shocked the unprepared audience who hadn't imagined they would ever be privy to such a sight: seeing their Amir's wife tossing off her veil to expose herself to strange men; while some Kabuli applauded this act.[13] Furthermore, the theatrical acts of the queen were preceded by unpalatable economic demands placed on these tribal elders on behalf of the state.

Amanullah described his recent world tour to his uncomfortably dressed audience and stated his determination that Afghanistan should catch up with the more advanced nations he had visited. He announced that a new, more liberal constitution needed to be promulgated. These enunciated proposals on social matters aroused considerable discomfort among his captive audience of elders: monogamy for government employees, a minimum age limit for marriage, the further education for women, the end to *purdah* (veil) and the wearing of Western dress in public throughout Kabul.[14]

Although the tribal elders at the Jirga reluctantly pretended to endorse Amanullah's proposals, they did not waste time mobilizing public opinion against him as soon as they returned to their homes in the provinces on the grounds that these policies were un-Islamic.[15] The public display of obscene behavior by the queen was the final straw for these elders who thought the king had lost his mind. Prior to this forced, and awkward, gathering in Kabul, the state in Amanullah's name, had not only demanded additional taxes for the implementation of controversial political, social, and economic reforms as conceptualized by their modern king, but it had also declared that the traditional stipends and privileges of tribal chiefs and distant members of the Amir's family, as well as subsidies to the clergy, would eventually be abolished. It was this last stipulation of cutting subsidies that was the straw that broke the camel's back and led to open rebellion. As long as the state continued with sending its yearly stipends to the various power brokers in the provinces, the theatrics of the king and his entourage had been overlooked and were tolerated by the elders because implementation measures outside of the major cities of Kabul and Herat were nonexistent.

When the countryside began to take up arms against the state apparatus, and as elements within the state Bureaucracy began to turn against Amanullah, the king abruptly shelved his ambitious modernization program yet again in an effort toward stability and to cultivate state legitimacy. The first to feel the effects of this social whiplash were females in the urban areas. Girls that had been sent to Constantinople were recalled and schools for girls were closed. Women were again prohibited from appearing unveiled and cutting their hair. In essence, the Afghan state had reverted to its original state as a loose tribal confederation by the time King Amanullah was overthrown in March 1929.[16]

STATE REVERSALS ON GENDER POLICY UNDER BACHA-E-SAQAW'S RULE: 1929

Under Habibullah, the first Tajik ruler of Afghanistan, better known as Bacha-e-Saqaw (Dari: child of a water carrier), the state moved to introduce an "Islamic way of life" to consolidate the support from the religious leaders. Habibullah's move toward "Islamizing" society was a transparent attempt to seek legitimacy in light of the events of the previous decade which were characterized by unprecedented meddling by the state in sensitive matters involving the *zanana*. The first action of his rule was to close all the modern schools created during Amanullah's reign. During his short nine-month rule, Afghan women once again found themselves confined within four walls and without access to formal education.

Bacha's sharp reversal on matters related to women's status in Afghan society was a harbinger of the trend that would continue in Afghanistan: the state would enact measures under the rubric of "modernization" that would include women's social emancipation, this would be followed by reversals—once such a move was perceived as a "threat" to society as a whole—which would involve duplication of "rural" and traditional values in the urban setting only to be reversed again depending on the whims of those in power.

NADIR SHAH'S CAUTIOUS "MODERNIZATION": STATE POLICY AND WOMEN'S STATUS (1929–1933)

Unlike his royal predecessor, Zahir Shah, Nadir Shah was not interested in a program of rapid and erratic modernization. A conservative, he outlined a cautious process of state instituted change, within the context of a primarily conservative tribal social structure, as the correct template to address female status. Nadir Shah believed that Amanullah's radical attempts to implement change were not in line with the cultural and societal traditions of the Afghan people: "I am for a certain progress and for cultural reforms in the western sense, but I want such reforms to be introduced with a slower pace than those adopted by Amanullah."[17]

He stressed the importance of implementing social change that would incorporate *both* the religious strictures of Islam and customs across the country in order to make this process acceptable to all Afghans. Nadir stressed that religion and progress were not incompatible but could coexist. He quickly moved the state apparatus to abandon Amanullah's controversial reforms and to restore many preexisting social and cultural practices in order to consolidate his social base which included the conservative elements in the Pushtun belt.

After Nadir Shah consolidated his power and control over the state apparatus, he moved to convene a *Loya Jirga* to legitimize his rule. Members of this *Jirga*, or gathering, were assigned the task of drafting a new constitution. Enacted on October 31, 1931, this new constitution, *Usul-e-Asasi-ye-Dawlat-e-Aliyya-e-Afghanistan* (the Fundamental Principals of the Higher State of Afghanistan), placed restrictions on civic and political activities. Article 1 of the Constitution stipulated that the Hanafi School of Islam must be the official religion and that the king must be of Hanafi Sunni background. Article 5 confirmed Nadir as the king and the succession of leadership to his family, and Article 22 brought all educational institutions under state control.[18]

In 1932, Nadir Shah instituted additional statutes which involved women's status. These included prohibiting marriage between Muslim women and non-Muslim men. It also declared that foreign women who were married to Afghan men were Afghan citizens. If widowed, and they were Muslims, they were allowed to resume citizenship of their former country. But those women who had converted to Islam could only return to their birthplace if the government was satisfied that the widow would not abandon her adopted Muslim faith. Non-Muslim widows were not allowed to repudiate their Afghan citizenship. Article 100 ordered that women who possessed property in Afghanistan must sell their property and land if they married a foreigner.[19]

Nadir Shah reintroduced *purdah* (veil) and enforced the wearing of the *chadri* (long shawl). He moved to desecularize the educational system by delegating the supervision of educational materials to the clerics to ensure that the curriculum would be according to Islamic teachings. Nadir Shah and his family did not apply the same educational standards to their own children, who were sent to secular schools abroad. Nadir closed all girls' schools, recalled female students who were sent abroad during Amanullah's reign, and he reinstated the practice of polygamy. The Hanifi School of Jurisprudence was used as the basis for both criminal and civil law. Alcoholic consumption was banned and women were prohibited from wearing Western dress. Any symbols of progress associated with Amanullah were erased: the Amaniya School was renamed *Estiqlal* (Independence), and the Amani School was called *Nijat* (Salvation). In the final years of his rule, 1931–1933, girls were allowed to attend separate schools from men.[20] Nadir's regressive policies were widely unpopular with the progressive elements in Kabul (the elite), as well as with the pro-Abdullah intellectuals who sought the return of the ousted king. Nadir Shah was killed by a student at the Nijat School in Kabul during an award ceremony.[21] It has been speculated that Nadir Shah's conservative policies led to his assassination at the hands of a student from a middle-class background. Although widely regarded as regressive among the pro-Abdullah crowd, Nadir Shah's approach to women's issues has been regarded as one involving a policy of "gradualism": a process of reform that was deliberate and cautious and took into consideration potential social responses.[22]

ZAHIR SHAH'S APPROACH TO WOMEN RIGHTS: STEADY PROGRESS, 1933–1973

When Zahir Shah succeeded his father, Nadir Shah, on the throne following his assassination in 1933, he continued the cautious policies of his father vis-à-vis civil society. The state under Zahir Shah adopted a moderate approach which included gradual reversals of state-implemented policies under Bacha Khan and Nadir Shah that had reversed most of the rapid gains women had made in their status under state tutelage.[23]

During the early years of his reign, under the stewardship of his uncle Hashim Khan, who became prime minister, the state moved cautiously in introducing new schools for girls. The state did encourage employment of women in specific professions that were thought to be "appropriate" for them: teaching and healthcare. Toward this end, a few separate schools for girls were reopened and in 1950, the Women's College was established. While women continued to remain in seclusion in the urban areas in contrast to the Amanullah period, there was growing disgruntlement among the upper classes, including among men, that women were oppressed.[24]

With the consolidation of power, the ruling elite cautiously encouraged women to work in the public sectors. The first female announcer, Latifa Kabir Seraj, was employed at the Radio Station in 1947. The first female singer, Parwin was employed at the Radio Station in 1951. Habiba Askar became the first female actress in 1958. Before these changes, women entertainers performed in women only theaters.[25]

Women's Status and the Daoud Government, 1953–1963: An Era of Modernization

During Daoud's ten years as the prime minister of Afghanistan, Afghan society witnessed a period that was characterized as one of consistent development and modernization of the country. It was only in the early 1950s that certain educated urban women began to demand equality and more opportunities for women. While the state under Daoud's tutelage encouraged women's emancipation through greater participation of women in the public sphere, there were no significant overall changes in women's status in the provinces. The Daoud government, aware of the perils of Amanullah's rapid emancipation approach, moved to emancipate women in gradual steps: first, women were hired as receptionists and telephone operators in the Tele-Communications agency, and later a few women were hired to work as air hostesses for the national airline, Aryana.[26]

Emboldened by the absence of any large-scale protest to the state's new policies regarding women, Daoud's government began to accelerate the speed of "modernization" that mirrored to a certain extent Amanullah's programs. Events at a military parade on August 1959 were eerily reminiscent of Amanullah's disastrous public performance at the Loya Jirga meeting in 1928: the women of the royal family and wives of officials in attendance came unveiled, something that had not transpired since the times of Amanullah in the 1920s.[27]

Daoud's policies of accelerated emancipation of women were supported by a very small segment of the population: the upper and middle classes in the urban areas, primarily Kabul, and the intellectuals who supported the idea of unveiling as a necessary step toward female emancipation. In rural areas, however, just as during Amanullah's reign, Daoud's policies were met with opposition and rebellion by both the tribal chiefs and religious clerics in the southern and eastern provinces of Kandahar, Wardak, and Nangarhar. Clerics staged large demonstrations and attacked a number of state-owned institutions in these provinces with the objective of compelling the state to retract its gender policies. In some cities, the demonstrators beat to death women who removed their veils. In response Daoud moved to crush this growing opposition to his objective of "empowering women" through use of the military. Within two days, the government forces had put down the resistance, imprisoned around six hundred people, and executed some key organizers. After destroying the resistance, the state continued with its programs aimed at "emancipating women."[28]

In an effort to embarrass the clerics who were opposed to his "women's movement," Daoud set out to challenge them ideologically by ordering a debate between his aides and the clerics on the subject of women. Daoud sent Musa Shafiq, the senior mullah of the royal family's palace mosque to debate these clerics on Quran's injunctions. Shafiq, who held a law degree from Columbia University and had also graduated from al-Azhar University in Cairo, was regarded as one of the country's experts on Islam. When he met with the imprisoned clerics, he—per Daoud's request—asked them to provide Quranic texts in support of their demand that women's faces should be covered. When they failed to do so, Daoud felt vindicated, and his "modernization" plan continued unabated.[29]

Under Daoud's administration, women in the urban areas experienced rapid transformation. Women were admitted into areas of public society and the workforce. By 1962, women participated in international conferences and women's delegations were allowed to go abroad. Yet, opposition to Daoud's modernization program continued to grow despite the state's brutal suppression of dissent and this led to his removal by Zahir Shah in 1963 following a power struggle within the ruling family.

AFGHANISTAN'S POLICIES DURING THE 1960S: EMPOWERMENT OF WOMEN

The 1960s ushered in a period of rapid emancipation and activism of women in the urban areas. It was a time when women emboldened by the stipulations of the new constitution, moved to organize into groups and became involved in the political process through membership in political parties. Women's organizations consisted of two types: liberals and leftists. The liberals were represented by the state-sponsored *Muassisa-e-Khayria-e-Zanan*, Women's Welfare Association (WWA). Founded in 1946, the WWA included ex-king Amanullah's sister, Bibi Jan, as one of its long term members. In 1975, the WWA became an independent institution called *Muassisa-e-Zanan*, the Women's Institute. As it expanded with branches throughout the country, it claimed to represent the interests of Afghan women regardless of class background or ideological position. It advocated gender equality, elimination of sex discrimination in employment, and increased participation of women in the state apparatus. Through its monthly journal, *Merman* ("Women"), which was founded in 1953, it advocated the improvement of women's status in the country. Articles published in *Merman* challenged the patriarchal traditions of the Afghan society.[30]

WWA worked to combat illiteracy and it also founded the *Anjuman-e-Rahnuma-e-Khanawada-e-Afghan*, or the Afghan Family Guidance Association (AFGA), on July 22, 1968, to address women's health concerns. By 1973, the AFGA had six clinics in Kabul and thirteen branches in provincial towns. WWA considered the high fertility rates to be an impediment to women's status in society. In their clinics the WWA encouraged family planning through contraception. To avoid antagonizing the conservative and religious elements, female personnel of WWA would go door-to-door to educate women on fertility matters and to offer them birth control.[31]

The "progressive" birth control policies of WWA (exclusively belonging to the elite) did not appeal to the majority of Afghan women because of ingrained social mores and religious beliefs.[32] In Afghan society having many children, especially boys, was the only way for a woman to enhance her social position, especially as she grew older. Most women in the rural areas believed that the number of children they had was determined by God alone and must not be tampered with. Children were a source of income and labor for poor families, and with high infant mortality rates, more births, not less, were considered desirable as well as an economic necessity. Furthermore, most Afghan men did not permit their women to practice birth control measures or family planning.

While liberals from the urban areas did try to initiate social programs for women in the rural areas, they met with resistance as the leftists and conservative elements challenged their initiatives. Thus their role remained limited to celebrating Mother's Day on June 14 of every year by organizing meetings and publishing articles on the role of women in raising children in a society where the overwhelming majority could neither read nor write.[33]

The other group of female activists was the leftists who advocated a revolutionary transformation of the socioeconomic system and its ideology as the only means to ensure gender equality. The two groups that espoused such a transformation consisted of the *Hizb-e-Demokratik-e-Khalq-e-Af-*

ghanistan (the People's Democratic Party of Afghanistan, PDPA) and the *Sazman-e-Jawanan-e-Mutaraqi* (the Progressive Youth Organization, PYO). The PDPA, founded in 1965, wanted an evolutionary and peaceful transition to socialism and claimed to be reformists not revolutionaries. While the PYO—also established in 1965—stressed class struggle and revolutionary armed uprising as a means of ending class oppression and creating a socialist society.[34]

When the PDPA split into two factions (the *Parcham* or banner and the *Khalq* or masses), the Parcham faction established *Sazman-e-Dmokratik-e-Zanan-e-Afghanistan* (the Women's Democratic Organization of Afghanistan or WDOA) and headed by Anahita Ratibzad. WDOA's primary objective was to expand the social base of the Parcham among women in both the private and public sectors.[35]

The 1964 Constitution and Its Impact on Women's Status

The 1964 Constitution, which had been requested by Zahir Shah and who appointed a committee for this purpose, was a progressive document in that it gave legal equality to men and women. Debate at the constitutional convention included discussion regarding the role of women and exactly how equality should be spelled out in this new constitution. According to Dupree:

> Some of the female delegates wanted to be certain that women would be clearly and explicitly granted rights, but finally a woman member withdrew her proposal for the special mention after a most meaningful discussion where the constitutional committee assured her that the word "Afghan" embraced both sexes. . . . The emphasis on the legal equality of women is one of the most important aspects of the 1964 Constitution.[36]

The finalized document, in comparison to the 1923 Constitution, was a relatively secular document but with caveats to appease the religious elements: Article 69 established the supremacy of secular law over religious law but caveats this with the provision that when no law exists on a subject, the Sunni Hanafi jurisprudence will be utilized. Article 102 stipulated the supremacy of secular over religious courts with the same caveat as stipulated in Article 69. Article 1 identified the locus of sovereignty in the nation "composed of all those individuals who possess the citizenship of the state of Afghanistan in accordance with the provisions of the law"; and Article 6 proclaimed that the king personified sovereignty in Afghanistan. Omission of any mention of an Islamic "umma" was deliberate and reflected the increased capacity of the state to exert social control over the religious and traditional elements.[37]

The 1964 Constitution allowed for freedom of association, press, and the formation of independent political parties which led to the emergence of a number of private newspapers and political parties. Both the state-owned and private papers declared the constitution to be a progressive document that protected women's liberties and granted them equal rights. In the *Wahdat*, a private newspaper, the Constitution was described as a document that treated men and women equally with regards to civil and political rights. Since the new constitution had declared that women were now equal to men in all walks of life, *Wahdat* promised to campaign for the amendment or replacement of all discriminatory or undemocratic laws and regulations that did not serve the interests of the people.[38] Other newspapers followed suit in their declarations of support for women's rights. The 1964 Constitution mandated compulsory education for all children.[39]

The problem with this new constitution was that it reflected what the king and his Western educated advisors considered feasible in terms of their political needs and aspirations, rather than corresponding to the realities of Afghanistan.[40] In its recommendations the constitution, while commendable, was hardly indigenous as it was based on ideas and concepts borrowed from different Western documents which were presented, with some contradictory modifications, as applicable to Afghanistan. For example the principle of legality adopted from the 1791 French Constitution and the 1948 Universal Declaration of Human Rights was asserted in Afghanistan's new constitution:

> at a time when statutory law had remained underdeveloped and legal practice in the country largely governed by Sharia law. . . . It soon became evident that the constitutional principle of legality could not be implemented without the existence of a body of statutes to guide the legal practice and the on-going activities of the courts.[41]

Although the 1964 Constitution has been heralded as a major step forward in improving the status of Afghan women in the legislative and judicial systems, the reality remained that even a decade later, traditional courts based on Hanafi *fiqh* continued to dominate Afghanistan, although in appearance they may have become statutory courts.[42] The reality was a written constitution relevant to a very limited segment of the Afghan populace: the ruling branch of the royal family; senior government officials; and the politically active segments of the small urbanized intelligentsia.[43] The fact that the constitution had essentially, but not specifically, declared women to have equal rights as Afghan citizens was a huge step forward, but it remained a *symbolic* move particularly in the rural areas where the stipulations of this document had little, if any, impact on the daily lives of women who lived there.

Women's Involvement in the Parliamentary Elections of 1965

Armed with the new constitution, upper-middle-class women in the urban areas moved from seclusion to public involvement overnight. They participated in the new political system and a number of women from privileged backgrounds were appointed to cabinet posts. From 1965 to 1972, two women served as ministers in government: Kubra Noorzayi was Minister of Health (1965–69) and Shafiqa Ziaya served as political advisor to Abdul Zahir (1971–72). The unwritten rules required a ruling class background, wealth and association with a political-economic organization or the state in order for women to run for a seat in the House of the People and the House of the Elder.[44]

In the first parliamentary election of 1965, several women from prominent families ran for a seat in the House of the People. Two of these women were from Kabul, one from Herat and one from Kandahar province. All four were elected as *wakil* (representatives) to the House of the People. There were also two women in the Senate. Majority of the voters in the 1965 election were men. Most of the women who voted were from the urban areas where very few working class women voted. The only women who went to the polls in the rural areas were in the Doshi district of Baghlan province, where Nasir Naderi, a chieftain of the Ismaili sect, contested the parliamentary election. He encouraged women there to go to the polls and vote for him. He was elected *wakil* from that district in the 1965 election. Unlike the urban areas, women in the rural areas deferred to their men. The tribal chiefs and landowners were the local arbiters and had traditionally acted as the spokespeople for the people of their community.[45]

Although women of the elite in the urban areas experienced a sea change in their roles and rights during this decade, for the majority of women things remained the same notwithstanding legislative, judicial, and executive actions on behalf of the state that aimed to ameliorate women's position in society. For example, in the area of education, while the state had made elementary education mandatory and free for all children, girls in rural areas were unable to take advantage of this opportunity because of tribal traditions and restrictions, as well as economic considerations which hampered their ability to attend school. Children in urban areas who belonged to the working classes were also unable to benefit from state policy on education due to economic necessity which required them to obtain work at a young age. Overall, for Afghan women living outside the urban centers, significant improvements in their lives were generally absent. For example, by the early 1970s, around 42 percent of Kabul's females were educated and an estimated 40 percent were working outside the home. A World Bank study revealed that only 8 percent of Afghan girls were attending primary school, another 2 percent were in secondary school, and only 4 percent of Afghan women were in the labor force.[46] One of the flaws of such studies by World Bank and other international organizations (such as the United Nations) is their definition of "labor force" (defined strictly as comprising of "work for pay" beyond family confines), which lends itself to an inaccurate assessment. Historically, although Afghan women have rarely worked outside their familial village or neighborhood boundaries for strangers, their involvement in the family livelihood has been an important—albeit unpaid—one. It is Afghan women and girls who have traditionally contributed much of the back-breaking work in the fields or with the livestock, run households, gathered wood for fuel and water for households needs. They have sought various ways to increase the family income through cottage industries at home involving weaving or sewing handicrafts and carpets to be sold at the bazaar by their male folk. The inherent limitations of such external studies lie in their reliance on benchmarks which only convey part of the picture on the economic health of such developing countries as Afghanistan. In short, female economic contribution to their communities has historically been a vital one.

DAOUD'S REPUBLICAN PERIOD, 1973–1977: WOMEN'S STATUS AND SOCIAL CHANGE

Consolidation concerns limited Daoud's ability to implement state measures aimed at ending gender inequality in Afghan society.[47] It was not until 1975, when the state moved to enact a new constitution which stipulated gender equality: Article 27 of the new constitution stated that "all the people of Afghanistan, both women and men, without discrimination and privilege, have equal rights and obligations under the law." Article 29 gave every Afghan, who had attained the age of eighteen, the right to vote.[48]

The new constitution allowed for the creation of a *Milli Jirga*, the NA (formerly known as the Loya Jirga) as the only institution with the power to amend this constitution and to elect or remove the head of state. Daoud appointed eight women to this body, while four additional women were elected to it. All of these women were college graduates and did not reflect the overwhelming majority of Afghan women who were illiterate and lived in poverty. Although Daoud had no women in his cabinet, women were hired to work in junior level positions within the state apparatus, which included ninety-one women in the Office of Minister of the State, fifty-four in the Presidential Secretariat and three at the Ministry of Foreign Affairs.[49]

Later Daoud's administration began to formulate social development programs aimed to improve women's status. In 1977, a civil code was enacted which included several articles addressing relations between men and women. It defined a minimum marriage age (sixteen for females and eighteen for males), allowed men and women to freely choose their marriage partners (reminiscent of Amanullah's time), permitted a couple to marry despite family opposition, and set rules for divorce. While men had the exclusive right to divorce, women were allowed to seek one under certain circumstances and, as part of their marriage contract, they could demand the right to a divorce if the husband took a second wife.[50]

In divorce cases, the new laws also gave mothers custody of boys (up to the age of seven) and girls (up to the age of nine). This period could also be extended if the court deemed such action to be in the best interests of the child. If a mother had acted improperly, however, she could not seek custody or she could lose custody in the case of remarriage. Although remarriage would improve the economic situation of a divorced woman, many chose to remain single simply to retain custody of their children. Most women who desired a divorce chose not to seek one for economic and social reasons and continued to tolerate harsh conditions at home.[51] It must also be emphasized that most of these new civil laws had a very limited impact on the daily lives and conditions under which most Afghan women lived. Matters involving divorce and custody, marital choices and age, and remarriage were the purview of the small elite primarily located in the capital of Kabul and some of the other cities. While on the surface these state-imposed changes appear to be significant in terms of their impact on women's status in society, the reality was that they had minimal impact on the lives of most women since implementation across the board was nonexistent and tribal customs and traditions continued to dictate how women were to conduct themselves and how they were to be treated in a conservative society.

By 1977, Daoud's administration was beginning to focus more on improving women's status through provision of educational programs geared to help women. *Kumita-e-Ensijam-e-Zanan*, the Women's Coordinating Committee, was established to promote the women's issues and to encourage their participation in public affairs. The committee sponsored a series of educational programs via Radio Afghanistan, which included programs on family affairs, short dramas, discussions of family issues, etc. During the annual celebration of Mother's Day on June 14, 1977, Daoud initiated a program that honored outstanding women who had been abandoned or widowed, yet had managed to support and educate several children. Again, such public displays of state support for women were not reflective of the conditions for most women.[52]

When the state established a family court in Kabul, it appointed a woman, Soraya Parwiz, to head this court which was mandated to resolve family-related issues. Similar courts were established in other provinces such as Herat, Kandahar, and Kunduz. The state also recruited a number of women into the police and armed forces. In 1978, the government introduced family health plans for mothers and children.[53]

The Founding of RAWA and Its Original Agenda

Although Daoud's government took some steps to help improve women's status, women's groups were not satisfied with the pace of these reforms. While members of WDOA and other liberal women's organizations were critical of the state's attempts to implement gender equality, they did not take concrete steps to challenge this state inaction. It was the women who ideologically identified with leftist groups that took a more activist approach to challenging the state apparatus.

Jamiat-e-Enqilabi-e-Zanan-e-Afghanistan, the Revolutionary Association of Women of Afghanistan (RAWA) was founded in 1977 as an independent political and social organization of Afghan women striving for human rights and social justice in Afghanistan. The founders of RAWA were a group of intellectuals under the leadership of Meena who would be assassinated in Quetta, Pakistan, in 1987.[54]

RAWA—which would evolve once the Soviets occupied the country—aimed to increase the number of women in social and political activities which sought to acquire basic human rights for women and contributed to the struggle for the establishment of a government based on democratic and secular values. It was not long before RAWA became involved in a variety of activities in a number of areas: education, health, income-generating activities for women and political organization.[55]

THE SOVIET-MONITORED STATE AND WOMEN'S STATUS, 1978–1992

Daoud's government was overthrown on April 27, 1978 in a military coup orchestrated by army officers who were supporters of PDPA. Noor Mohammad Taraki, head of the Khalq faction of PDPA, became president, prime minister and chairman of the Revolutionary Council, and Babrak Karmal, head of the Parcham faction, became vice chairman and deputy prime minister. Under the auspices of PDPA rule, the state accelerated the process of female emancipation begun under Daoud's rule. Just prior to the coup which ousted Daoud's regime, women could be found employed within the government, in the civil service and, on a lesser scale, in the military and police. By the end of the Daoud period, the social changes experienced by the elite women in Kabul had begun to filter down into the urban middle class and were slowly influencing changes in the rural communities as well. But Daoud's efforts on behalf of women were dismissed by the PDPA as merely "cosmetic gestures."[56]

The PDPA regime and its Soviet patron viewed social reform as critical to legitimacy.[57] The Taraki regime declared that in all social and political spheres of society women were equal to men. Anahita Ratibzad, a woman, was appointed Minister of Social Affairs to promote women's emancipation. She would later be sent to Yugoslavia as Afghanistan's ambassador. It was Ratibzad, the first female doctor in Afghanistan, who formed the Parcham's Women's Democratic Organization of Afghanistan (WDOA) in 1964, renamed the Khalq Organization of Afghan Women (KOAW) under Taraki's rule. It was the only women's group that supported the Soviet invasion.[58] First led by Delara Mahak and later by Aziza Azizi, the KOAW organized meetings and rallies and forced women to attend them in support of state policies. The KOAW employed approximately 510 teachers and 60 supervisors and stated its goal was to use these employees to train approximately 6,000 army soldiers to read and write within a year.[59]

The state, under the leadership of Taraki and the *Khalq* faction of the PDPA, outlawed arranged marriages, limited amounts of dowry, and campaigned against illiteracy by opening night schools with the intent of indoctrinating women.[60] When the PDPA government promised freedom of choice in marriage, this was seen as a threat to rural economic relations which were based in part on bride price payments for daughters and the dowries that accompanied the brides which were a form of social security for the brides. Also since arranged marriages, generally between first cousins, was what preserved social relations and helped to retain clan identity, the PDPA's decree on marriage was seen as the state's attempt to destroy the social fabric of close clan interactions. When PDPA tried to bring girls into new schools in rural areas, this was perceived to be a move to destroy the traditional customs of rural Afghan society. The decree that encouraged the establishment of girls' schools in rural areas was not welcomed because the process involved girls being taught alongside boys by teachers who were not from the area and were instructed to inculcate party propaganda into their curriculum, which was an anathema as far as the local villagers were concerned.[61]

During this period of Soviet occupation, women and men were declared equal "in social, economic, political, cultural and civil aspects." In 1979, under pressure from the Soviets, the state instituted Decree No. 7 that aimed at improving the status of Afghan women. This decree forbade forced marriages and required a minimum age to marry, with punishment of imprisonment of up to three years for violators. Through the promulgation of Decree No. 7, the state sought women's support in its quest for legitimacy and consolidation. In its efforts to seek legitimacy, the state catered to that segment of society (women) which traditionally was on the sidelines and whose support had historically been considered by state actors to be inconsequential. Decree No. 7 contained six articles that outlined marriage practices and ceremonies. No one could marry a girl in *nikah*, marriage, in exchange for cash money or commodities. Nor could the bridegroom be forced to pay cash or commodity, the *toyana*, marriage expenses, at the time of marriage. The bridegroom was no longer required to provide clothing for festivals to the bride and her family. The decree limited to Afs. 300 (US$6 in 1978) the amount of cash or value a girl and her family could legally accept as *mahr*. Engagements and marriages required the full consent of both parties; while a widow could no longer be forced into marriage with one of her husband's male relatives.[62]

In the rural communities villagers were opposed to literacy classes and the communists used force to compel them to attend. Some of the refugees who fled to Pakistan cited the communists' repressive tactics to compel them to have their women attend literacy classes as the reason for leaving Afghanistan. In the rural areas where tribal custom dictated social mores and women's status, educating women was regarded as a dishonorable act, while others perceived this as an "unbearable interference in domestic life." From a purely economic perspective, abolishing the tradition of "bride price" (the payment given from the groom to the bride's father to compensate for the loss of her labor) had a detrimental effect on households that needed the bride price as a convertible capital in the future.[63]

The Labor Law of 1984 provided equal job opportunities for all Afghans. Afghan women served in the police and the army and constituted 50 percent of the labor force.[64] By the late 1980s and early 1990s women held senior positions such as Deans of universities. Women worked in factories, were pilots, diplomats and army generals. In short, women occupied prominent positions in society which had no precedent in Afghanistan.[65]

Before the Taliban gained control of the country in 1996, women became the critical part of the workforce in the urban centers. In Kabul, for example, 70 percent of teachers were women; 40 percent of doctors were women; over half the university students were women; schools at all levels were coeducational. Women held jobs as lawyers, judges, engineers, and nurses; and the burqa or chador was not required to be worn in public.[66] This reality also had to do with the fact that the men were either conscripted into the army or had fled abroad or had joined the resistance movement (*mujahidin*).

WOMEN PARTICIPATE IN SOCIAL RESISTANCE TO THE PDPA REGIME

Although educated women in Kabul who were affiliated with the PDPA regime greatly benefitted during the period of Soviet occupation, there were other equally educated women who—irrespective of the overt social and economic benefits that women were offered by the new state (read: communist) actors—were opposed to occupation and to the puppet regimes of PDPA. They resisted the state's often repressive, and enforced, attempts at "modernization" through the creation of informal gatherings of small groups of women. These women used traditional female activities, such as knitting, sewing, and tea parties to disguise their meetings and discussions. Through these informal networks they were able to share information about the whereabouts of loved ones and to support each other. They held protest rallies in front of the Ministry of Interior, demanding information on their missing loved ones. It was through their continued efforts through protest that the state released a list of the dead that numbered in the thousands.[67] When the women asked about their missing husbands, the official answer was: "They were reactionary and were killed. You are now free to marry another man of your choice."[68]

After the April 1978 coup, RAWA, notwithstanding its leftist leanings and secular agenda, moved from its founding goals of gender equality in a democratic setting to being actively involved in the war of resistance against the Soviet supported regimes of PDPA's Khalq and Parcham factions.[69] RAWA's objective was to mobilize women and girls to support the war of liberation. RAWA envisioned an Afghanistan where

> men and women unite and fight for the independence of our beloved country, to establish an Islamic republic, and to build a society in which oppression, torture, execution and injustices must be replaced by democracy and social justice. . . . RAWA which is comprised of progressive women, fights for women's equality, and maintains that the liberation of oppressed women is inseparable from the liberation of our oppressed nation . . . RAWA will continue its principled struggle for women's rights and liberation after the restoration of the country's independence and freedom from the superpowers and other imperialist powers.[70]

Unlike the Islamic fundamentalists (*mujahidin*) groups fighting the Soviets, RAWA advocated for a country based on democratic and secular principles where women would be granted equal status and opportunities. RAWA's influence grew as more women joined it and were sent to work among refugee women in Pakistan. RAWA worked to address the needs of refugee women and their families through the establishment of schools with hostels for boys and girls and a hospital with mobile teams for refugee women and children in Quetta. It also conducted courses in nursing, literacy, and vocational training for women.[71]

Political indoctrination in compulsory classes in both the urban and rural areas led to the bombing of some of these schools. During this period, women were jailed and tortured for the first time for ties with political groups opposed to the PDPA regime.[72] Women's role in resistance movement was not limited to rallies, demonstrations, and refusal to cooperate. Women actively participated in activities like abduction and assassination of the supporters of the government and the Soviets. Many of the disappearances and assassinations of Soviet soldiers and personnel of the government in Kabul have been linked to women's efforts. Tajwar Kakar, also known as Tajwar

Sultan, was a prominent female resistance fighter who actively participated in various antigovernment activities and was instrumental in organizing women in various resistance activities. In 1982, Kakar was arrested on charges of anti-state agitation and activities. She was tortured in prison and later released after signing a written confession. She fled to Pakistan where the authorities restricted her movement.[73] Another woman, Nur Bibi of Paghman, is credited with killing several Soviets. She had watched her entire family killed and in her despair picked up a pistol and killed three Soviets. She was seriously injured in the incident and left for dead. A group of men carried her across the border to Pakistan where she was treated. During her stay in hospital, Nur Bibi expressed a desire to return to the resistance movement when she was better.[74]

The state during this period enacted laws that aimed to significantly improve women's status in society through provision of economic and social opportunities. The reality, however, was that through its autocratic and repressive implementation methods these efforts ended in failure especially in the rural communities.[75] Furthermore, the state's attempts to improve women's status were cited by the conservative and resistance elements as proof that the real aim was to convert Afghanistan into a godless, communist country as had been done before in various Central Asian Republics.

FAILING STATE AND WOMEN'S STATUS, 1992–1996

Following Najibullah's removal from office in March 1992, the PDPA collapsed and the various mujahidin factions began to resort to violent means in their efforts to gain power. During this four-year period, the people of Afghanistan witnessed a brutal civil war that left thousands dead and millions homeless. They saw the destruction of their capital city, Kabul, as various mujahidin factions battled over the city. It was in this milieu that urban women, particularly those of Kabul, found their realized status and freedoms threatened by these mujahidin groups who pillaged, murdered, and raped with complete abandon. The Jihadi Islamic fundamentalists (mujahidin) bands that fought the Soviets now targeted women in horrifying ways.[76] Amnesty international reported that

> armed groups beat, raped, and murdered women in their homes. Young women were kidnapped as wives of the commanders or sold into prostitution. Some committed suicide to avoid this fate. . . . In March of 1994, a fifteen-year-old girl was repeatedly raped after soldiers killed her father for allowing her to go to school.[77]

Robert Fisk, a journalist wrote: "it remains a fact that from 1992 to 1996, the Northern Alliance was a symbol of massacre, systematic rape and pillage."[78]

The most horrific period for women began in 1992, when the use of sexual violence against Afghan women became widespread: "The rape and abduction of women by armed forces appeared to be condoned by leaders as a method of intimidating vanquished populations and of rewarding soldiers."[79] The mujahidin would try to legitimize their behavior (rape of Afghan women) by going to the girls families and demanding them for "marriage" at gunpoint. If the women refused they were shot or if their male family members refused, they were shot and the women (or girls) were taken away never to be seen again by their families.[80] The mujahidin's behavior made many of the urban residents wish for the days of Soviet occupation and control. It also exposed their human rights record to greater scrutiny than before, particularly as it pertained to women.[81]

Shortly after the mujahidin seized power, they began to institute programs designed to Islamize an already conservative society. Their policies on women's status challenged the state's position on women during the Soviet occupation. For example, on August 27, 1993, the Rabbani-led government's Office of Research and Decrees of the Supreme Court issued an order to government agencies and state functionaries to dismiss all female employees from their posts and issued further guidelines concerning women's societal obligations. The decree read:

> Women need not leave their homes at all, unless absolutely necessary, in which case, they are to cover themselves completely; are not to wear attractive clothing and decorative accessories; do not wear perfume; their jewelry must not make any noise; they are not to walk gracefully or with pride and in the middle of the sidewalk; are not to talk to strangers; are not to speak loudly or laugh in public; and they must always ask their husbands' permission to leave home.[82]

Zoya (an Afghan woman who lived through this period in Kabul) wrote:

> Far from rejoicing that the Russians had been defeated, Grandmother told me that a new worse Devil had come to my country. There was a popular saying around this time: Rid us of these seven donkeys and give us back our cow. The donkeys were the seven factions of the Mujahideen and the cow was the puppet regime . . . the Mujahideen entered Kabul and burnt down the university, library and schools. Women were forced to wear the burqa and fewer women were visible on television and in professional jobs.[83]

As Ahmedi writes about her experiences during the mujahidin period:

> in the days of the mujahedin, we women had the legal right to go out, go to school, and to go to work, even if it was sometimes too dangerous to do these things . . . the mujahedin disapproved of Western dress, and most of them had

conservative standards; but within those limits, they allowed women to choose their own style of dress.[84]

In February 1994, the UN special rapporteur informed UN General Assembly of the massive civilian casualties incurred in Kabul as a result of rocket and air attacks, including the use of cluster bombs. A few months later, the rapporteur noted that the Rabbani-led government had introduced a decree stipulating various restrictions on female dress and mobility and noted that women should not wear "sound-producing garments" or go outside their homes "without their husband's permission.[85]

In 1995 the Rabbani government canceled the participation of its representatives in the Fourth World Conference on Women in Beijing on the grounds that the prepared statement of the delegation was not in line with Islamic principles. That same year, Amnesty International reported that armed groups "have massacred defenseless women in their homes, or have brutally beaten and raped them. Scores of young women have been abducted and then raped, taken as wives by commanders or sold into prostitution. Some have committed suicide to avoid such a fate. Scores of women have reportedly disappeared and several have been stoned to death."[86]

The RAWA was concerned over the reports it received regarding the law and order situation and the horrible treatment of women by the various mujahidin factions. On July 16, 1996, just two months prior to the fall of Kabul to the Taliban, representatives of RAWA had a meeting with a delegation of Amnesty International in Peshawar. In the meeting RAWA told Amnesty International that it needed to inform the world about the barbaric and savage nature of the Afghan fundamentalists. It presented its report to Amnesty International that cited numerous incidents of mass killing, kidnapping, rape, torture, and arbitrary execution. This period (1992–1996) was characterized by large-scale violence against women and severe restrictions placed upon urban women by a failed state[87] and by the outbreak of a violent civil war between the mujahedin factions.

CONCLUSION

The Afghan state's gender policies since independence (1919) to the failed-state period (1994) reflected the whims of those in power. Historically, the absence of a vibrant civil society and the fragmentary nature of this state (limited central control over the periphery) encouraged state autonomy in the policy-making process but also limited the state's capacity, or ability, to implement controversial measures which involved female status in a hypersensitive culture. King Amanullah's ambitious gender policies—largely influenced by his urban familial ties—led to outright rebellion in the provinces. It is important to point out that although it appears that this rebellion primarily involved a reaction to the state's enunciated goals for Afghanistan's females (its "modernization" plan); the reality was that this (rebellion) had more to do with the pocketbooks of the tribal chieftains: Amanullah had stated that in order to pay for his modernization program he intended to gradually phase out the traditional state stipends to the tribal chiefs. This was the straw that broke the camel's back and not the bewildering gender policies per se. Historically, pragmatic chieftains have always looked the other way and accepted certain conditions if there were generous financial inducements and appearances could be maintained (i.e., their *nang* or honor remained intact).

Amanullah quickly abandoned his modernization program in order to stabilize the volatile situation and to restore state legitimacy in the eyes of the powerful regional tribal chieftains. But his actions were too little too late and led to his overthrow. This spoke volumes however, on the social and economic dichotomy: Amanullah and his immediate entourage appeared to live in a cocoon far removed from the social reality that constituted day-to-day life in the provinces. The fact that Amanullah barely survived being assassinated suggests that the state while free to enact controversial social measures, faced an uphill and often violent social resistance when it comes to the implementation of gender-related policies that traditionally were the purview of the periphery. As a result of Amanullah's overthrow, the kings (Nadir and Zahir) that followed in Amanullah's footsteps adopted a more cautionary style on the subject of gender relations, although this led to the assassination of Nadir Shah by a pro-Abdullah (and pro-modernization) supporter in Kabul.

The PDPA's gender policies, which were primarily a legitimizing tool of an illegitimate regime, were not only resisted by the periphery, but they also encountered opposition from urban women's organizations such as RAWA, due to the perception that PDPA was a puppet regime of the Soviets. This suggests that even an authoritarian state is concerned about its legitimacy in the eyes of its populace and is influenced by social reaction and concerns.

The post-PDPA period reflected the breakdown of civil order in a brutal civil war as vying social forces competing for control of the state. As mujahidin factions battled it out, it was women (the weakest group) who bore the brunt of this power struggle. The complete breakdown of law and order, coupled with a criminal element within these militias, exposed women, especially those in the urban areas, to extreme danger and their status in society was reduced to that of an abused victim.

NOTES

1. Vartan Gregorian, *Emergence of Modern Afghanistan: Politics of Reform and Modernization, 1880–1946* (Stanford: Stanford University Press, 1969); Shireen Burki, "The Politics of

Zan from Amanullah to Karzai: Lessons for Improving Afghan Women's Status," in *The Land of the Unconquerable: The Lives of Contemporary Afghan Women,* eds. Jennifer Heath and Ashraf Zahedi (Berkeley: University of California Press, 2011), 45–50.

2. Lowell Thomas, *Beyond Khyber Pass: Into Forbidden Afghanistan* (New York: Grosset and Dunlap, 1925), 181–182.

3. Hafizullah Emadi, *Repression, Resistance and Women in Afghanistan* (Westport, CT: Praeger Publishers, 2002), 60.

4. Ibid.

5. Emadi, 63.

6. Rosemarie Skaine, *The Women of Afghanistan under the Taliban* (NC **[AQ: city?]**: McFarland & Co. Inc., 2002), 14.

7. Emadi, 62.

8. Emadi, 62.

9. Helena Malikyar, "Development of Family Law in Afghanistan: The Roles of the Hanafi Madhhab, Customary Practices, and Power Politics," *Central Asian Survey* 16: 3 (1997), 393.

10. Zohra Yusuf Daoud, "Miss Afghanistan: A Story of a Nation," in *Women for Afghan Women: Shattering Myths and Claiming the Future,* ed. Sunita Mehta (New York: Palgrave, 2002), 107.

11. Emadi, 63; Huma Ahmed-Ghosh, "A History of Women in Afghanistan: Lessons Learnt for the Future or Yesterday and Tomorrow: Women in Afghanistan," *Journal of International Women's Studies* 4 (May 2003), 4–6.

12. Skaine, 14.

13. Emadi, 64.

14. Martin Ewans, *Afghanistan: A New History.* Surrey, UK: Curzon Press, 2001, 95.

15. Emadi, 65.

16. For more on the uprising see R. D. McChesney, *Kabul under Siege: Fayz Muhammad's Account of the 1929 Uprising* (Princeton, NJ: Marcus Weiner Publishers), 1999.

17. Gregorian, 293.

18. Emadi, 68.

19. Emadi, 68.

20. Emadi, 68–69.

21. Emadi, 69.

22. For more on the politics of gradualism under Nadir Shah, refer to Amin Saikal's *Modern Afghanistan: A History of Struggle and Survival* (London: I.B. Tauris, 2004), 99–101.

23. Anne E. Brodsky, *With All Our Strength: The Revolutionary Association of the Women of Afghanistan* (New York: Routledge, 2003), 35–36.

24. Emadi, 69.

25. Fahima Rahimi, *Women in Afghanistan* (Liestal: Stiftung Foundation, Stiftung Bibliotheca Afghanica), 1986, 74.

26. Rahimi, 74.

27. Fahima Vorgetts, "A Vision of Justice, Equality and Peace," in *Women for Afghan Women: Shattering Myths and Claiming the Future,* 94–95.

28. Emadi, 71.

29. Jan Goodwin, *Price of Honor: Muslim Women Lift the Veil of Silence on the Islamic World.* (Boston: Little Brown, 1994), 89.

30. Emadi, 91.

31. Emadi, 93.

32. Emadi, 93.

33. Emadi, 91–95.

34. Emadi, 95.

35. Emadi, 95.

36. Louis Dupree, *History of Afghanistan* (Princeton, NJ: Princeton University Press, 1980), 578.

37. Saikal, 145.

38. Emadi, 84.

39. Nancy Hatch Dupree, "Revolutionary Rhetoric and Afghan Women," in *Revolutions and Rebellions in Afghanistan: Anthropological Perspectives,* eds. M. Nazif Shahrani and Robert L. Canfield (Berkeley: Institute of International Studies, University of California, 1984).
40. Saikal, 149.
41. M. H. Kamali, *Law in Afghanistan* (Leiden: E.J. Brill, 1985), 44–45.
42. Saikal, 149; see also Valentine Moghadam, "A Tale of Two Countries: State, Society and Gender Politics in Iran and Afghanistan," *The Muslim World* 94, no. 4 (October 2004), 452.
43. Saikal, 149.
44. Emadi, 85.
45. Emadi, 86.
46. Brodsky, 37.
47. For more details on Daoud's rule, see Martin Ewans, *Afghanistan: A New History* (Surrey, UK: Curzon Press, 2001), 128–137.
48. Emadi, 97.
49. Emadi, 98.
50. Mohammad Hashim Kamali, *Law in Afghanistan: A Study of the Constitutions, Matrimonial Law, and the Judiciary* (Leiden: E.J. Brill, 1985), 153–154.
51. Emadi, 98.
52. Emadi, 98–99.
53. Emadi, 99.
54. Michael Dartnell, "Post-Territorial Insurgency: The Online Activism of the Revolutionary Association of Women of Afghanistan (RAWA), *Small Wars and Insurgencies* 14 (Summer 2003), 159–160; Weeda Mansoor, "The Mission of RAWA: Freedom, Democracy, Human Rights," *Women for Afghan Women,* 76.
55. Mansoor, 77.
56. Sippi Azarbaijani-Moghaddam, "Afghan Women on the Margins of the Twenty-first Century," in *Nation-Building Unraveled: Aid, Peace and Justice in Afghanistan,* eds. Antonio Donini, Norah Niland, and Karin Wermester (West Hartford, CT: Kumarian Press, 2004), 98.
57. Antonio Giustozzi, *War, Politics and Society in Afghanistan, 1978–1992* (Washington, DC: Georgetown University Press, 2000), 20.
58. Skaine, 17.
59. Emadi, 100.
60. Goodwin, 88.
61. Henry Bradsher, *Afghanistan and the Soviet Union* (Durham, NC: Duke Press Policy Studies, 1983), 93–94.
62. Emadi, 100–101.
63. Skaine, 18.
64. Musa Khan Jalalzai. *Women Trafficking and Prostitution in Pakistan and Afghanistan* (Lahore: Dua Publications, 2002), 146.
65. Skaine, 20–21.
66. See Mavis Leno's testimony in front of the U.S. Senate as cited in Skaine's book, 21.
67. Emadi, 104.
68. Mansoor's article in *Women for Afghan Women*, 70.
69. Brodsky, 49–51.
70. As cited in Emadi, 109.
71. Mansoor, 77.
72. Sippi Azarbaijani-Moghaddam, 98.
73. Emadi, 113.
74. Emadi, 114. As cited from Wilhelm Dietl, *Bridgehead Afghanistan* (New Delhi: Lancer International, 1986), 262–263.
75. For more details on the difficulties encountered by the Saur revolution in implementing its modernization policies refer to Giustozzi (2000), 20–32.
76. Mansoor, 71.

77. Kathleen Richter, "Revolutionary Afghan Women," *Z Magazine,* November 2000 as cited in Mansoor, 71.

78. Robert Fisk, "What Will the Northern Alliance Do in Our Name? I Dread to Think," *London Independent,* November 14, 2001, as cited in Mansoor's "The Mission of RAWA," 71.

79. Hardy, 15. Hardy is citing Amnesty International's 1995 Human Rights Catastrophe, Section 5. The 1995 Amnesty International report on human rights abuses and its follow-up installments have constituted the primary source material for the world's realization of the treatment of women under the Taliban. The AI 1995 report that was based on interviews in refugee camps in Pakistan and Iran, attracted the attention of the UN which, after AI's follow up report, assigned a "Special Rapporteur" to investigate the situation of women and girls in Afghanistan, which was released in July 2000.

80. Hardy, 15–16.

81. Norah Niland, "Justice Postponed: The Marginalization of Human Rights in Afghanistan," in *Nation-Building Unraveled: Aid, Peace and Justice in Afghanistan,* 64.

82. H. Malikyar, "Development of Family Law in Afghanistan: The Roles of Hanafi Madhab, Customary Practices, and Power Politics," *Central Asian Survey* 16: 3 (1997), 58.

83. Ahmed-Ghosh, 1–13.

84. Farah Ahmedi with Tamim Ansary, *The Story of My Life: An Afghan Girl on the Other Side of the Sky* (New York: Simon Spotlight Entertainment, 2005), 97.

85. Niland, 65.

86. Niland, 65.

87. Amalendu Misra cites the definition of a "failed state" as one which cannot or will not safeguard minimal civil conditions, such as peace, order, and security domestically.

Chapter Five

Rise of the Taliban and Female Practice

The Politics of Repression, 1996–2001

> It's like having a flower, or a rose. You water it and keep it at home for yourself, to look at it and smell it. It [a woman] is not supposed to be taken out of the house to be smelled.
> —Syed Ghaisuddin, Taliban Minister of Education, on why women had to be confined at home

> If we are to ask Afghan women, their problems have been solved.
> —Qudratullah Jamal, Taliban Minister of Culture

> Because of the Taliban, Afghanistan has become a jail for women. We haven't got any human rights. We haven't the right to go outside, to go to work, to look after our children.
> —Faranoos Nazir, a thirty-four-year-old woman in Kabul

> Indignity is our destination.
> —Seema, thirty, a former health care worker forced to beg on the streets of Kabul to support her children

The emergence of the Taliban in 1994 and their rapid physical takeover of most of the Afghan state by September 1996 were both unprecedented and unexpected. The leadership[1] of this group of religious students (Taliban) did not play a prominent role during the Afghan resistance to Soviet occupation (1979–1989). What Mullah Omar (a Hotaki Ghilzai from Uruzgan) and most of the Taliban's leadership had in common with most of the Pushtun mujahidin leadership selected by Pakistan's Army was that none of their *qaums* (tribes) belonged to the Durrani Confederacy. Rather, their qaums belonged to the Ghilzai Confederacy which hadn't played a prominent leadership role in Afghan politics since Ghilzai Mirwais Hotaki established the short lived Hotaki dynasty in 1709.

Although the Taliban (with clandestine help from the Pakistani army) managed to restore law and order, it came at a steep price: draconian—Shariah compliant—decrees which sought to institute a truly "Islamic" society in the "Islamic Emirate of Afghanistan." Afghans of all ethnicities witnessed or experienced a degree of intolerance and punishment at the hands of the Taliban state which was harsh even by historical standards. Those who didn't fit the "ideal" of what a citizen of the Emirate should comprise of endured brutal treatment from the Taliban's foot soldiers. The Shia Hazaras, and the urban elite in the cities, were prime targets of the Taliban's wrath. So too were the Tajiks, Uzbeks, Baluch, Farsiwan, and homosexuals. But it was the *zan* (women) in general who were singled out for the harshest measures to include stoning to death, hangings, whippings, and beheadings for the flimsiest of charges.

INTRODUCTION

The Taliban began their takeover of the Afghan state in 1994 but were never able to consolidate their rule over the entire country. The rise of the Taliban can be directly attributed to the violence and chaos that accompanied the civil war period.[2] By 1994, life in Afghanistan was characterized by unrelenting violence against the populace thanks to vying warlords and criminals. It was within these anarchical conditions that the Taliban (a creation of Pakistan's Inter Services Intelligence Directorate-ISI) found a weary population which sought the restoration of law and order. The Taliban stepped into this power vacuum with an agenda which emphasized the restoration of women's dignity and safety. The mujahidin groups, local warlords and bandits had wreaked havoc upon the lives of women for their own sadistic interests because dishonoring women by rape, or other violent means, brought dishonor to the entire rival group and was also a method of intimidation/control. Initially, the Taliban were welcomed by women, both urban and rural, as they moved quickly to restore law and order and to protect women from various physical dangers they encountered on a daily basis from the warring factions of the mujahedin.

The Taliban viewed themselves as "purists" with a mandate for establishing a state that reflected real Islamic values and principles *as interpreted by them*. They were a product of a compilation of factors: the ongoing civil war, the Pushtun culture and a *madrassa* education where they were schooled in the *Deobandi* tradition.[3] The Taliban, many of whom were orphans raised in the madrassas, had never really come into contact with females of any kind. Second, most of the Taliban were tribal Pushtuns mostly from the east and southeast portion of Afghanistan and the northwest region of Pakistan, which even by local standards was considered the backwoods where the Pushtunwali code was strictly adhered to. Third, the Taliban had been taught in the madrassa milieu that control over females and their virtual exclusion was a powerful symbol of manhood and a reaffirmation of the students' commitment to jihad. The Taliban believed that denial of a public role for women would help to legitimize their rule with their internal or external audiences.[4] This was particularly true in that their primary audience was the rural, conservative, Pushtun belt where women's role was strictly limited to the private sphere.

The Taliban embodied religious traditionalism *and* a Pushtun tribal ethos, a combination which gave the movement

> an exceptionally vigorous dynamic . . . [which] enabled it to prevail not only against the secular tendencies in Afghan society, but also against the adherents of an Islamic ideology which calls for a Muslim internationalism and the radical restructuring of government and society in the context of the contemporary world, rather than a return to traditional values.[5]

The Taliban's first objective was to again place women under the responsibility of their male family members. This was to be accomplished using four elements that bolstered the primary objective. First, women were required to wear the *burkha* or *burqa* (Pashto/Dari: head to toe cloak); second, women were prohibited from working outside of their homes; third, education was placed off limits to females; and fourth, women's freedom of movement was restricted by a mandatory requirement that a close male family member accompany a woman whenever she leaves her home.[6] What these four elements had in common was that they all aimed to restrict women's access to the outside world.

Although the Taliban's conservative agenda elicited little in the way of a negative response in their own conservative tribal belt of Kandahar and the southern Pushtun heartland, their policies and worldview were not appreciated by the rest of the population, particularly in the urban centers of Kabul, Mazar-e-Sharif and Herat, as well as in Hazara, Uzbek, and Tajik populated regions. In these non-Pushtun areas, such an agenda was regarded as unnecessarily extreme since the inhabitants of these regions did not subscribe to such draconian levels of gender control.

TALIBAN AND WOMEN'S STATUS: SOCIAL PROHIBITIONS AND RESTRICTIONS

The Taliban moved quickly to establish their credentials as "Islamist purists," and to build the Islamic Emirate of Afghanistan, a state which would expect society to embrace a strict adherence to an austere lifestyle. Within hours after taking over Kabul, the Taliban's "High Council" announced the following over Radio Kabul: women were to stop working and were to restrict their movements outside their homes to emergencies and then in a burqa (a tent-like garment) with a familial male escort (*mahram*). Schools were closed.[7]

One Western journalist, Jack Hardy, described the Taliban as practicing "gender-based terrorism" which he writes is not a novel concept.[8] According to Hardy, the Taliban created an environment of complete domination of women in society, effectively removing them from all social contact: "In general terms, the Taliban demonstrate how populations can be effectively manipulated through deliberate acts of political violence without necessarily resorting to the more mainstream conceptions of terrorism."[9]

While the Taliban have been viewed by outsiders as having been the architects of draconian state measures and policies involving women, the reality is less clear cut. The Taliban in many respects took over where the mujahidin left off in their repressive policies toward women. Like the previous governments of Rabbani and Hikmatyar, the Taliban moved to seclude women and to restrict their access to education. The Taliban governor of Herat stated:

> It is a matter of pride for all Afghanistan that we have kept our women at home. . . . The Sharia has described everyone's way of conduct. I mean that the Sharia allows for a woman to see a male doctor when she becomes ill. The fact of the matter is that no other country has given women the rights we have given them. We have given women the rights that God and his Messenger have instructed, that are to stay in their homes and to gain religious instructions in hijab (seclusion).[10]

The Taliban's conduct reflected their Pushtun and rural roots and was greatly influenced by *Pushtunwali* (the code of honor by which Pushtuns were supposed to live their lives).[11] The Taliban believed that the only way to recoup the essence of Pushtunwali *as they interpreted it* (emphasis added) was to eliminate all social changes that had been implemented not only during the PDPA rule but going all the way back to 1950s. According to the Taliban, the communist regime had exploited women for the purpose of advancing their own political and social agendas. They merely wanted to revive the traditional Afghan family and way of life.

Once the Taliban consolidated their power as they gained control of most of the regions of the country, they issued a number of decrees that involved a comprehensive pattern of social restriction on its citizens, especially women. Some of the restrictions imposed by the Taliban on women included:

1. Complete ban on women's work outside the home, which applied to female teachers and engineers. Only a few female doctors and nurses were allowed to work in some hospitals in Kabul.
2. Complete ban on women's activity outside the home unless accompanied by a *mahram* (close male relative such as a father, brother, or husband).
3. Ban on women dealing with male shopkeepers.
4. Ban on women being treated by male doctors.
5. Ban on women studying at schools, universities, or any other educational institution.
6. Requirement that women wear a long veil (burqa), which covers them from head to toe.
7. Whipping, beating and verbal abuse of women not clothed in accordance with Taliban rules, or of women unaccompanied by a mahram.
8. Whipping women in public for having non-covered ankles.
9. Public stoning of women accused of having sex outside marriage.
10. Ban on the use of cosmetics.
11. Ban on women talking or shaking hands with non-mahram males.
12. Ban on women laughing loudly. No stranger should be able to hear a women's voice.
13. Ban on women wearing high-heeled shoes, which would produce sound while walking: A man must not hear women's footsteps.
14. Ban on women riding in a taxi without a mahram.
15. Ban on women's presence in radio, television or public gatherings of any kind.
16. Ban on women playing sports or entering a sports center or club.
17. Ban on women riding bicycles or motorcycles, even with their mahrams.
18. Ban on women's wearing brightly colored clothes. In Taliban terms these are "sexually attracting colors."
19. Ban on women gathering for festive occasions such as Eid, or for any recreational purpose.
20. Ban on women washing clothes next to rivers or in a public place.
21. Modifications of all place names including the word "women." For example, "women's garden" had been renamed "spring garden."
22. Ban on women appearing on the balconies of their apartments or houses.
23. Compulsory painting of all windows, so women cannot be seen from outside their homes.
24. Ban on male tailors taking women's measurements or sewing women's clothes.
25. Ban on female public baths.

26. Ban on males and females traveling on the same bus. Public buses have now been designated "males only" ("females only").
27. Ban on flared (wide) pant-legs, even under a burqa.
28. Ban on the photographing or filming of women.
29. Ban on women's pictures printed in newspapers and books, or hung on walls of houses or shops.
30. Ban on listening to music.
31. Ban on watching movies, television, and video.
32. Ban on celebrating the traditional New Year (Nowroz) since it is "un-Islamic."
33. Disavowal of Labor Day as it is deemed a "communist" holiday.
34. People with "non-Islamic" names are required to change their names to "Islamic" ones.[12]

These restrictions imposed by the new Taliban government were an extreme version of the gradual restrictions enacted by the mujahidin led governments that preceded the Taliban. The main difference between Rabbani's government and the Taliban was that, initially, the Taliban had put an end to the slave trade, rape, kidnapping, and pillaging which took place in chaotic conditions and served to reduce women's status to one dictated by fear and shame.[13] It was only after the Taliban consolidated their rule, that some of their commanders began to replicate the behavior of their predecessors, like forcible marriages of underage girls to Taliban officials.

The new restrictions imposed life-threatening conditions upon females all in the name of Islam and the Afghan tradition of "family honor." For example, restrictions number two and four jeopardized a woman's chance of seeking medical help for a serious medical condition. Under number two, if a woman did not have an appropriate *mahram* (male escort) to take her outside to get medical treatment, she was forbidden to leave her home; and, second, under number four, she was only allowed to seek the medical care from a female healthcare provider. Given the limited number of healthcare providers and the rarity of female healthcare providers since most women were forbidden employment in public health facilities, this decree amounted to a death sentence for women with life-threatening medical conditions.

In 1998, the executive director of Physicians for Human Rights, Leonard Rubenstein, stated: "We are not aware of any place in the world in recent history where women have so systematically been deprived of every opportunity to survive in society—from working to getting an education to walking on the street to getting health care."[14]

According to a Physicians for Human Rights study, Taliban restrictions on women received wide media coverage but very little was actually known about the personal experiences of Afghan women. This report argued that their study invalidated the Taliban's assertion that gender segregation is based on Afghan history and culture. The study highlighted women's participation in Afghan society through history. Almost all 160 women interviewed by the Physicians for Human Rights agreed that women should be allowed to regain their freedom.[15]

TALIBAN AND WOMEN'S STATUS: URBAN VERSUS RURAL DIVIDE

The Taliban believed that the loose morals of Afghan women in the cities were a result of Western influence which was related to the abandonment of Afghan values.[16] Taliban concentrated their wrath toward women primarily on the urban, Dari-speaking (a variant of Persian) elite, most of whom had fled the country:

> that the Taliban targeted the minority Persian-speaking, including non-Pushtun elite women, over their counterparts is a little known fact. Indeed, the Taliban were especially cruel to women in the cities, whereas those in the rural areas were left to live a normal life, as they conformed to the pre-modern moral order envisioned by the former.[17]

Pre-Taliban urban Afghanistan was influenced, and controlled, primarily by the non-Pushtun elite of Tajiks in Kabul, Uzbeks in Mazar-e-Sharif and the Farsiwan of Herat. Even the Pushtuns who belonged to the urban elite of Kabul, and elsewhere, often did not speak their own mother tongue of Pashto, but spoke in Dari, French, and/or English. It was a known fact in the countryside that the urban elite lived a life that was alien (even dishonorable in the eyes of many rural dwellers) to the majority of Afghans and that they looked down upon their rural brethren with contempt and disdain. The Taliban, who consisted of rural peasants, mountain folk, or nomads, were aware of this dichotomy even among their own Pushtun brethren, and were determined to restructure urban society in accordance with their worldview.[18]

The women of Kabul were initially terrified of these zealous "mujahidin" (in reality they were a separate entity from the mujahidin). But as the new regime proved incompetent, and inconsistent, in enforcement of its stated rules, urban women were emboldened and they began to act more assertively as they moved about the city as they had in the past.

Nancy Dupree, a well-respected Afghanistan scholar, writes:

> The change was rapid and extraordinary. At first, they were so terrified they dared not leave their homes; a scant four months later, women walked the streets with confidence, returning measure for measure when young men deigned to question the appropriateness of their apparel. At the same time, the Taliban lost their fervor, became weak, gave in to the lures of women and succumbed to corrupt city ways.[19]

Dupree, while correct in her assessment of the situation, does not provide the complete picture in that while women in Kabul were emboldened when they witnessed the inconsistencies of the Taliban's enactment machine—the Taliban's foot soldiers of young men from the madrassas—they (the women) were often harshly punished when caught in an act of defiance of the Taliban's new edicts. For example, in December 1996, the Taliban controlled radio announced that a group of 225 women had been arrested and punished in Kabul for violating Taliban rules on clothing. Their punishment consisted of being lashed on the back and legs after the sentence was handed down by a tribunal.[20]

In March 1997, the Taliban ordered Kabul residents to cover the windows on the ground and first floor of their homes with paper or other materials to ensure that the women in the house would not be visible from the street. A Taliban representative speaking from the attorney general's office in Kabul explained the edict to journalists, "The face of a woman is a source of corruption for men who are not related to them."[21]

Rural and nomadic women, who had traditionally gone about their daily lives unveiled, unless they traveled out of their village or region, were now also required to wear the *chadari* or *burka*. In the past, only those rural women whose families had prospered to the point where they could now be secluded and not be required to perform menial labor in the fields, wore the *chadar* as a symbol of "having arrived" socially and economically. The lives of the vast majority of rural women both prior to, and during, the Taliban rule remained unchanged. These lives involved back breaking work in the fields (which the Taliban did not prohibit), gathering material to be used as fuel, or carrying water from the closest available source. The burka was not conducive to such tasks and traditionally women in these areas did not bother to cover up, especially since most of the members of their community were either extended family or belonged to the same tribal *khel* (clan).

Rural women have not been actively involved in any of the female emancipation programs dating back to the 1920s, nor had the urban "experiments" with female emancipation trickled down to directly have an impact on their rural lives. It was precisely because of this reality that the Taliban were not particularly concerned with intruding in rural areas to the extent they did in the urban ones, where they felt compelled to reverse the "evil influences" of all that came before them since King Amanullah's rule.

While the Taliban did require women in rural areas to cover up in public with a *chadar*, enforcement was sporadic. But in urban centers, particularly Kabul, the Taliban not only required women to cover up but tried to impose a measure of standardization by insisting on the burka. Women, as a method of defiance, chose a variety of colors rather than the standard white that the Taliban would have preferred. Although purchase of a burka could amount to more than an average month's salary for a family, women chose to buy burkas made from expensive fabrics. In Kabul women preferred various clear shades of blue and one would see the occasional canary yellow on the streets of Kabul. Burnt orange and forest green were fashionable in Jalalabad. Black was never the color of choice, except among certain groups in Herat. The fabric of choice was soft artificial silk. This was, however, not the intent of the Taliban authorities but since the women were abiding by their edict requiring that they be fully covered up they chose to ignore the challenge.[22]

TALIBAN ATTITUDES TOWARD THE NON-PASHTUN WOMEN IN URBAN AREAS

The Taliban targeted not only educated women in the urban areas but also women from other ethnic groups besides Pushtuns, especially the Shia Hazaras. One thirty-five-year-old women confided to Human Rights Watch that there was a great fear among Hazara women of having their daughters abducted and raped by Taliban forces. Due to this anxiety many Hazara families were eager to marry off their daughters at a young age. Another woman who formerly lived in Ali Chapan, a Hazara neighborhood, and witnessed the Taliban capture of Mazar-i-Sharif in August 1998, said many Hazara families had hidden their daughters to protect them:

> We knew that if the Taliban came they would kidnap our daughters, and so we sent them to safe places. I sent my daughters to my sister's house, in the Tajik neighborhood away from the Hazara area. The aim of the Taliban was to attack Hazara places, not the Tajik areas of the city.[23]

Uzbek and Hazara women from rural areas, who had fled conflict zones in northern Afghanistan during the Taliban era, reported to Human Rights Watch that when the Taliban controlled their region, they ordered women to stay indoors. Zhora Gul, a Tajik from Shomali, was removed from her home by force when the Taliban invaded her village between September and December of 1999. She told Human Rights Watch, that the Taliban on the pretext of making sure that we were not men hiding in *chadaris* (a long sheet used to completely cover up including the face), tore them away from us but it was really to get a look at the women. The Taliban took the young girls away with them and they were never seen again by their families.[24]

TALIBAN AND WOMEN'S STATUS: IDENTITY POLITICS

According to the Taliban, women did enjoy the right to a civil identity, it was just not one envisioned by Western ideals and norms. For the Taliban, women's civil identity was non-negotiable and involved women being restricted to the confines of their homes.[25] The Taliban argued:

> the world should know that the United Nations and all the other foreign welfare organizations in the name of women's rights are but destroying the society, the culture of the Muslims. Under the veil of "rights" they want to take away their purdah, their veil, and thus dishonor the Muslim women. Their intention is to destroy completely all the Islamic values.[26]

In Afghan society, as in the rest of the Middle East, the family is paramount and the religious institutions consider themselves to be the guardians of family integrity and in turn they hold families responsible for safeguarding religious sanctity.[27] In addition to religious influences on the Taliban's definition of "women's identity," the (Pushtun code of conduct) also provided the guidelines as the Pushtun dominated Taliban moved to establish what they considered to be an "Afghan woman's identity."

TALIBAN AND FEMALE EDUCATION

The Taliban closed down all the schools on the pretext of making them "Islam compliant" institutions when they took over Kabul in September 1996. Although they would later reopen the boys' schools, girls' schools never resumed full functioning, and the only public girls' schools that were reluctantly reopened were for girls till the age of eight, and the curriculum consisted of reading and studying the Quran.

As a result of the forcible closures of girls' schools, some Afghans desperate to educate their daughters relied on a private network of schools which were operating in defiance of the Taliban ban. The Taliban shut down over one hundred private schools on June 16, 1998. These schools had provided thousands of girls with an education in violation of the Taliban's ban on education for girls.[28] Human Rights Watch reported examples of Taliban treatment of teachers secretly teaching girls in private homes, such as:

> Nikba Shah, a former teacher in Samangan's Lycee Ajani for girls, worked secretly in a home school, soon after the Taliban took over her area in 1998. She said, "I was beaten on the way to school. Our papers were torn up. I had books and papers hidden under my arm. I dropped some, and when they fell three Taliban started to beat me. They were Afghans and had black turbans. We had started to organize schools elsewhere. We were hiding materials under our chadari and wore dirty clothes so that we did not attract attention. They realized because as soon as two or three women got together, they would become suspicious.[29]

According to Human Rights Watch, another teacher working for an international aid organization that ran primary schools for girls in a number of provinces and also secretly helped home-based schools described the situation in Nangarhar province in eastern Afghanistan as typical of what was transpiring in the rest of the country:

> Girls schools were only home-based schools, and some girls attend schools up to the age of eight or ten. Until recently, it worked fine, but now there are more restrictions. The Taliban go to the teacher's husband and ask him to guarantee that she will not teach anymore. It is the same all over Afghanistan. Only very few women can teach.[30]

In another case, as reported by Human Rights Watch, a teacher states:

> I was teaching. They (Taliban) came in. They did not knock. We all tried to hide in the house. There were six of them from the Religious Police. They were quite young, thirty to thirty-five years old. We hid our fourteen and fifteen-year-old students because teaching them is prohibited. Only up to twelve years old is tolerated. They told us, "we will not do anything to you but send us your husband." My husband went to the office of the Religious Police, and they made him sign a paper saying that I would not teach anymore.[31]

Taliban's attitude toward schools wasn't a consistent one. The Taliban's attitude toward girls' schools outside the urban centers was more lax and they often chose not to contest a local community's wish to maintain a girls' school.[32] In some rural areas, NGOs were successful in negotiating with the Taliban to allow their girls' schools to remain open, at least at the primary level. In general, the NGOs had difficulty in convincing the Taliban to allow privately funded girls' schools to operate. Human Rights Watch cites an example of a school that the Taliban ordered closed in 1999. After protracted negotiations, the Taliban authorities agreed that the school could remain operational but after it reopened, the staff was under greater scrutiny.

Anwar Shah, an employee of an international NGO involved in education, identified similarities between the mujahidin and the Taliban attitude toward girls' education, and charged that these stem from the way in which girls' and women's education historically has been politically exploited:

> In one district of eastern Afghanistan, there is one high school and one middle school, but no girls' school. This is because there is a religious leader there who does not allow girls' schools. During the communist regime, the girls' schools started and girls were forced to go to school. Then the opposition to this started, and after one or two years that district was taken over by mujahedin. Both the boys and girls schools closed because of the fighting . . . the propaganda stated that the schools were where the communists bred. The situation now is almost the same or worse. The Taliban government is not in

favor of secular and modern education, only religious education, so there is no support for schools.[33]

Many of the rural women that were interviewed during the Taliban period by Human Rights Watch were denied access to education both because of the distances involved in traveling to school and the conservative attitudes of their men that limited women's role to the domestic sphere of daily chores and child bearing. What Human Rights Watch discovered in the rural areas among illiterate women was the desire to send their own daughters to school.[34]

TALIBAN AND FEMALE EMPLOYMENT

The Taliban believed that women working in the public are, by definition, women of questionable character. They believed "good women stay home; bad women expose their faces and mingle with men in public."[35] Immediately after seizing power the Taliban prohibited women from working outside their homes on the basis that conditions were not conducive for women to be employed as they did not meet "Islamic standards" as envisioned by the Taliban. Overnight it has been estimated that between 40,000 to 150,000 women, including doctors, nurses, teachers, administrators, and others in the urban centers were affected by the Taliban's ban on female employment. In Kabul alone, around 30,000 women, mostly widows, found themselves unable to support their families, leading some of them to resort to begging and in some cases prostitution at the risk of being stoned to death. Physicians for Human Rights reported that in 1998 one of its researchers observed "a city of beggars—women who had once been teachers and nurses now moving in the streets like ghosts under their enveloping *burqas*, selling every possession and begging to feed their children."[36] The PHR concluded that the restrictions on employment, education, mobility, and health care are life-threatening to women and their children.[37]

After the Taliban government realized the harsh consequences of their decision, they made some modifications to their gender policy. In November 1996, facing continued pressure due to the misery caused by the prohibition of women from working in the medical field; women were once again permitted to work in the medical sector. Employment was contingent on obedience to a set of eleven rules that were provided by the Minister of Public Health which dictated how female medical personnel would conduct themselves.[38]

While changes in policy toward women regarding employment in the medical field led to the resumption of work by thousands of women in the urban areas on various humanitarian projects involving women's health concerns, the continued absence of clear enactment standards and the arbitrary nature of general enforcement of the Taliban edicts, led to a number of serious incidents. In May 1997, for example, five CARE International female employees, duly armed with written authorization from the Ministry of Interior to conduct monitoring and survey work for emergency feeding programs for widow-headed households were forcibly ordered from their car by members of the *Amar Bil-Maroof Wa Nahi An al-Munkar* (the Department of the Promotion of Virtue and Prevention of Vice). Summarily dismissing the letters of authorization, the guards publicly insulted the women over a loudspeaker, calling them prostitutes because they worked for foreigners, and proceeded to strike them several times with whips made of metal and leather. The women escaped unhurt but badly humiliated, the driver was arrested, and apologies were eventually extended by the deputy director of the Religious Police, with the explanation that the action had not been authorized. When the women resumed their work, they carried yet another letter of authorization with them from the *Amr bil-Maroof wa Nahi An il-Munkir* itself.[39]

This incident reflected the realities on the ground which were: (1) women worked at the risk of physical harm even if they had official sanction to do so; (2) the country was filled with individuals who considered themselves "unpaid servants" of the Taliban who were willing, in their self righteous rage, to indiscriminately punish women for perceived violations of what they personally interpreted was appropriate behavior; (3) the religious police, in their official capacity, were notorious for being undisciplined and ill informed on Taliban edicts and policies which they randomly enforced.[40]

When the Taliban informed the World Food Program (WFP) that its female staff could no longer go to office, the organization responded by adjusting its modus operandi so that its female Afghan staff could operate from their own homes. The only way these women could stay in touch with their WFP office was through the phone and radio. When their female staff traveled away from their home in UN vehicles, they risked the real possibility of harassment and beatings by the religious police simply for appearing in public. The Afghan women who worked for the World Food Program were also aware that their work also jeopardized the safety of their families. Given the food shortages that had gripped Afghanistan during this period, the WFP considered recruiting Pashto-speaking women from neighboring Pakistan to do the job. The Taliban responded by issuing a new edict that *any* Muslim woman working anywhere in Afghanistan must be accompanied by her family and since Afghanistan was a unaccompanied posting for WFP workers, this prohibited WFP from implementing this idea. This edict only exacerbated the food shortages and food distribution difficulties within the country. Daniela Owens, who was in charge of WFP's sub-office in Herat, said that the Taliban would not allow their staff to monitor their projects.[41]

As a result of the Taliban edicts, Oxfam pulled out from working in Afghanistan, with the exception one project which did not involve the issue of women: an urban water supply project in Kabul. This decision only exacerbated the suffering of Afghan women, most of whom were war widows, and prevented the provision of food and health aid to families in need.[42]

Within the Taliban ranks there was dissension on the subject of allowing Afghan women to work in international relief agencies. After an internal battle in the Taliban hierarchy, the hard liners prevailed and an edict was issued in July 2000 that banned women from working for international relief agencies. The head of the United Nations' Afghan operations at that time, Mr. Erick de Mul, tried to negotiate with the Taliban Foreign Minister, Wakil Ahmed Muttawakil, who agreed to reverse the edict. Instead the hard liners, particularly those in the Ministry of Vice and Virtue under Mullah Muhammad Turabi, prevailed and women were forbidden to work for aid organizations.[43]

TALIBAN AND WOMEN'S MEDICAL CARE

Although the Taliban had banned women from employment, female doctors were allowed to resume work in 1997 because of their stringent requirement which stipulated that women could only be attended to by female doctors for medical treatment. The female doctors and nurses who resumed work found themselves in danger of incurring the wrath of the Taliban regime and were often a witness to the beatings of their female colleagues for real or perceived transgressions. A Kabul health worker reported that even though she had permission from the Ministry of Health to work, it was still a great risk:

> One day the religious police may stop me on the street and ask where I am going. At that point the fact that I have "permission" may mean nothing to him; he can beat me or harass me or arrest me at his whim. Every day I leave my house and I pray that I might get back home safely at the end of the day.[44]

Christiane Amanpour stated in a CNN report on September 30, 1997:

> The latest crisis, say aid agencies, is in health care, women now get practically none. The Taliban had banned women from the main hospitals and dumped them in a crumbling building with no window panes, no running water, no proper operating theater or the electricity to power the equipment as a basic sterilizer.[45]

The Taliban established specific rules for the medical system which they argued were based on Shariah principles. According to Mufti Mohammad Masoom Afghani, acting minister of public health, these regulations were as follows:

1. Female patients should go to female physicians. In case a male physician is needed, the female patient should be accompanied by her close relatives (*mahram*). During examination, the female patients and male physicians should be dressed with Islamic hijab.
2. Male physicians should not touch or see the other parts of female patients except the affected part.
3. Waiting rooms for female patients should be safely covered.
4. The person who regulates turns for female patients should be female.
5. During night duty, in the rooms where female patients are hospitalized, a male doctor without the call of patient is not allowed to enter the room.
6. Sitting and speaking between male and female doctors is not allowed. If there be need for discussion, it should be done with hijab on.
7. Female doctors should wear simple clothes; they are not allowed to wear stylish clothes or use cosmetics and makeup.
8. Female doctors and nurses are not allowed to enter the rooms where male patients are hospitalized.
9. Hospital staff should pray in the mosque on time. The director of hospital is bound to assign a place and appoint a priest (mullah) for prayer.
10. Staff of (Amri Bel Maroof Wa Nai Az Munkar) Department are allowed to go for control at any time and nobody can prevent them. Anybody who violates the order will be punished as per Islamic regulations.[46]

These draconian restrictions imposed in 1997 regarding the "appropriate" medical treatment of women caused such misery that by 1999 the Taliban were forced to ease up on some of these restrictions, which included segregation of men and women in hospitals. The Taliban moved to construct one single hospital to centralize women's health care. Because the one "hospital" that the Taliban reserved for the half million women of Kabul had never been used as a hospital and did not have electricity nor running water; this edict meant a cessation of medical services for women. Besides this ban preventing women from using other hospitals, the Taliban also forbade female hospital personnel, including physicians, nurses, pharmacists, and technicians, from working in any of Kabul's twenty two hospitals. As a result of these edicts, many women and young girls died from preventable illnesses and traumas.[47]

Due to international pressure, the Taliban reopened a few hospitals for women and female medical personnel were allowed to return to their jobs. By 1998, women were allowed to be treated by male physicians given the acute shortage of physicians, especially female doctors, as long as they were accompanied by a male relative. The reality remained that under the Taliban women were excluded from most hospitals and Kabul's war widows found it difficult to obtain medical services.[48]

In 1998, the Physicians for Human Rights did a survey of 160 Afghan women and found high levels of poor health, multiple specific symptoms, and a significant decline (71 percent) in their physical condition since the beginning of the Taliban takeover. Seventy-seven percent reported poor access to services in Kabul, while an additional 20 percent reported no access at all. Access (62 percent) and quality (58 percent) were worse than the previous year. Fifty-three percent experienced a serious illness and had been unable to obtain any medical care.[49]

TALIBAN VIOLENCE AND WOMEN'S RESISTANCE

Under the Taliban regime from 1996 to 2001, women were regularly stoned to death for adultery.[50] By 1999, Human Rights Watch encountered widespread fear and rumors of the abduction, forced marriage, and rape of women by Taliban forces, but they found it difficult to document individual cases. One reason: such brutal acts resulted in shame for the victim and her family; others victims feared their family and/or community might ostracize them as a woman who was raped and thus had brought dishonor upon her family. Layla Shah, a twenty-five-year-old Hazara woman, still remembers what happened to her neighbor in Mazar-i-Sharif:

> Two Taliban did bad things to her. Now she has a bad name and no one will marry her. She told me that they came to search the house and she was alone. That was the first time when the Taliban took over Mazar. They did not tell her anything. They just raped her. She said she screamed but they did not say anything.[51]

In one case of enforcement, the religious police in the Khair-Khana area of Kabul cut off the end of a woman's thumb for wearing nail polish.[52]

During the Taliban period women did demonstrate in the urban areas but these protests were few and far between. For example, in early 1996, before the fall of Kabul, 150 women demonstrated in front of the Governor's office in Kandahar. These poor beggar women were objecting to shopkeepers who refused to accept bank notes of small denominations. That night the Governor announced over the radio that shopkeepers would accept the notes or be closed down. On October 23, 1996, women encouraged by a female judge from General Dostum's former administration, rallied for five hours in Mazar-i-Sharif raising slogans such as "Taliban law is not Islamic law." In Herat, a demonstration on December 21, 1996, by fifty women protesting the closing of women's bath houses turned ugly. Twenty were arrested and several others were hospitalized after being beaten.[53]

RAWA continued to be active in trying to bring the crimes committed against women by both the Taliban and the other mujahidin factions to the attention of the International Court of Justice.[54] On November 9, 1996, some members of RAWA were invited by Pakistan's Women's Action Forum (WAF) to participate in a seminar which was organized by WAF to discuss the question of women's rights with a focus on the issue of consent of patron for marriage. During the meeting all participants emphasized that full rights should be extended to women to decide themselves about their marriage. Representatives of RAWA informed the attendees of the miseries, the unbearable and inhuman conditions which Afghan women face in their daily lives because of the ongoing civil war between the Taliban and fundamentalist "gangs."[55] A representative of RAWA opined that "the Pakistani women were enjoying relatively more freedom. They could even occupy the post of Prime Minister. But in Afghanistan the situation was different. There women could not go outside their homes without a male relative nor could they go to school or have jobs outside." This RAWA representative asked that WAF and the other participating women's groups to help Afghan women by exposing the criminal acts of Afghan fundamentalists and to support the Afghan people to pave the way for the establishment of a democratic broad-based government in Afghanistan.[56]

On December 10, 1996, RAWA staged a demonstration in Peshawar, Pakistan, in observance of Human Rights Day. They asked the "freedom-loving and democratic organization of Pakistan and other countries to raise their voices against the disastrous situation in Afghanistan." Hundreds of Afghan women and children attended the rally and kept chanting slogans against the Taliban, Rabbani, Hikmatyar, Dostum, and Sayyaf.[57]

CONCLUSION

The Taliban never consolidated their hold over the entire country. At the time of the U.S. invasion in 2001, the Taliban controlled 93 percent of the country. In 2000, the Taliban controlled 90 percent of the country.[58] Once they took over Kabul in 1996, the Taliban had petitioned the UN for official recognition of their rule as the legitimate government of Afghanistan which was not forthcoming. Instead the UN offered a degree of accommodation in order to be able to send in the UNHCR (United Nations High Commission for Refugees) to help with the ongoing refugee crisis there. But the UN withheld its recognition of the Taliban regime pending resolution of human rights issues, particularly those involving the status and rights of women.[59]

The Taliban's initial raison d'être was the reestablishment of law and order and to restore women's dignity and the sanctity of the home which had been trampled upon by their predecessors (the mujahidin). The Taliban came to base their legitimacy on protection of women's sexual *nang* (honor) and thus protecting the male *nang* (honor) which was the cornerstone of Pushtun culture. Pushtun nang is based on the protection of one's material wealth in the form of *zar* (gold), *zan* (women), and *zamin* (land). Many Pushtun tribals will fight to the death to protect his share of said items, especially the honor of his *zan* (women).

The central government in Kabul never functioned as is required, or expected, of such a state entity. Furthermore, its power base lay in the hands of vulnerable young men who were products of Pakistani madrassas with limited, if any, exposure to women. The leadership of the Taliban realized that without controls over the female populace via strict segregation, they would face the same issues (on rape and slavery of women) which led to the chaos of the mujahidin years, and to the ultimate demise of that government. The Taliban's muscle (the young talib from the madrassas) had been indoctrinated along the Salafist traditions that viewed unveiled and emancipated women with grave suspicion as being morally bankrupt. It was with this worldview that the Taliban's foot soldiers conquered Kabul and which led them to quickly act upon their beliefs that suggested that the cosmopolitan women of Kabul represented the *shaitan* (satan).[60]

For the Taliban, denial of specific rights to women was a legitimacy tool in order to consolidate their power and to retain control over their impressionable, and in a way, vulnerable, rank and file as well as future recruits from the madrassa system. As journalist and writer Ahmed Rashid writes:

> The gender issue became the main platform of the Taliban's resistance to UN and Western governments' attempts to make them compromise and moderate their policies. Compromise with the West would signal defeat that they were wrong all along, defiance would signal victory.[61]

Governance under the Taliban state ensured that half of Afghanistan's population would not only be severely discriminated against and oppressed but would be invisible to the outside world.

NOTES

1. Most of the Taliban leadership had attended for various lengths of time the Haqqania madrassa at Akora Khattak in Pakistan's Khyber Pukhtunkhwa (formerly the North West Frontier) province. Mullah Omar had even been awarded an honorary doctorate from the institution. See Jeffrey Goldberg, "Inside Jihad U: The Education of a Holy Warrior," *New York Times Magazine*, June 25, 2000. Accessed at: http://www.nytimes.com/2000/06/25/magazine/inside-jihad-u-the-education-of-a-holy-warrior.html

2. Hafizullah Emadi, *Repression, Resistance and Women in Afghanistan* (Westport, CT: Praeger Publishers, 2002), 125. Although Emadi and other scholars have literally defined "Taliban" as "students of religion," in Arabic and Urdu, "Taliban" is actually plural for "student" and the term does not connote what kind of student (i.e., religion).

3. The Taliban religious roots go back to the establishment of a School of Islamic Studies at Deoband in northern India in 1867. When the influence of the great madrassas of Central Asia waned with the incorporation of Bokhara, Samarkand, and Tashkent into the Czarist Russian Empire, Afghan ulama began to look east for religious direction and in the early twentieth century, a number of prominent Afghan ulama made their way to Deoband to train at this school under the inspirational maulvi, Mahmud al-Hassan. There were also regular visits from Deobandi maulvis to Afghanistan which established the framework, and influence, of this orthodox school of Islamic thought. While madrassas (religious schools) were set up in Afghanistan since the early twentieth century, it was not until the Soviet invasion, and with large Saudi funding, that many madrassas sprouted up on the Pakistan side of the Durand Line (border). Their influence increased significantly following the Soviet departure from the area due to continued funding from Pakistan and Saudi Arabia, and to a lesser degree, from other Gulf states.

4. Jack Hardy, "Everything Old is New Again: The Use of Gender-based Terrorism against Women," *Minerva Quarterly Report on Women and the Military* 19 (2001), 3.

5. Martin Ewans, "The Taliban and the Future," in *Afghanistan: A New History* (Surrey, England: Curzon Press, 2001), 205.

6. Hardy (2001), 3.

7. Nancy Hatch Dupree, "Afghan Women under the Taliban," in *Fundamentalism Reborn? Afghanistan and the Taliban*, ed. William Maley (New York: New York University Press), 1998, 148.

8. Hardy (2001), 3. Hardy credits Amy Ray for coining the phrase "gender-based terrorism."

9. Hardy (2001), 4.

10. Peter Marsden, *The Taliban: War, Religion, and the New Order in Afghanistan* (Karachi: Oxford University Press, 1998), 98. See also Emadi, 126.

11. Marsden, 98–99.

12. Skaine, 156–158. Cited from RAWA's *Some of the Restrictions Imposed by Taliban on Women in Afghanistan,* at http://rawa.htm, April 3, 2000.

13. For a brief synopsis of Taliban misogyny within a historical context see Shireen Khan Burki, "The Politics of *Zan* From Amanullah to Karzai: Lessons for Improving Afghan Women's Status," in *Land of the Unconquerable: The Lives of Contemporary Afghan Women.* Jennifer Heath and Ashraf Zahedi, eds (Berkeley: University of California Press, 2011), 54–55.

14. Skaine, 22.

15. Skaine, 23. Skaine is citing Vincent Iacopino et al., *The Taliban's War on Women: A Health and Human Rights Crisis in Afghanistan: A Report* (Boston: Physicians for Human Rights, 1998), 5, 10.

16. Hardy (2001), 3.

17. Misra, 72.

18. Misra, 74.

19. Misra, 151.

20. M. J. Gohari, *The Taliban Ascent to Power* (New York: Oxford University Press, 2002), 108.

21. Gohari, 108.

22. Dupree (1998), 160.

23. "Afghanistan: Humanity Denied, Systematic Violations of Women's Rights in Afghanistan," Human Rights Watch (October 2001). Accessed at: http://www.hrw.org/reports/2001/afghan3/

24. Human Rights Watch (October, 2001).

25. Misra, 72.

26. Gohari, 109.

27. Joseph Suad and Susan Slyomovics, eds., *Women and Power in the Middle East* (Philadelphia: University of Philadelphia Press, 2001), 1.

28. Suad and Slyomovics, 98.

29. *Human Rights Watch* (October 2001).

30. Human Rights Watch (October, 2001).

31. Human Rights Watch (October, 2001).
32. Ewans, 207.
33. Human Rights Watch (October 2001), see # 23.
34. Human Rights Watch (October 2001).
35. Hardy (2001), 3.
36. Vincent Iacopino et al., *The Taliban's War on Women: A Health and Human Rights Crisis in Afghanistan*, Report (Boston: Physicians for Human Rights), 1998, 76.
37. Iacopino, 76.
38. For these medical rules, refer to the Taliban and Women's Medical Care section of this chapter.
39. Dupree (1998), 157.
40. Dupree (1998), 158.
41. Dipankar De Sarkar, "Women: Taleban Discrimination Blocks U.N. Aid Work in Afghanistan," *Interpress Service*, March 13, 1998.
42. De Sarkar.
43. "Afghan Women Again Banned from Working," *New York Times*, July 21, 2000. Accessed at: http://topics.nytimes.com/top/news/international/countriesandterritories/afghanistan/index.html
44. Iacopino, 66.
45. As reported in Skaine, 73.
46. Human Rights Watch (October 2001).
47. Zohra Rasekh, "Public Health: A Reconstruction Priority in Afghanistan," in *Women for Afghan Women*, ed. Sunita Mehta (NY: Palgrave MacMillan, 2002), 177.
48. Skaine, 29.
49. Iacopino, 6.
50. "Afghan Police Arrest Six Men in Fatal Shooting of Woman for Adultery," *FBIS*, April 29, 2005.
51. Human Rights Watch (October 2001).
52. Gohari, 107.
53. Mr. Choong-Hyun Paik, Special Rapporteur, United Nations, Report on the Situation of Human Rights in Afghanistan, February 20, 1997, 16, as cited in Dupree (1998), 161–162.
54. For the most comprehensive examination of RAWA see Ann Brodsky, *With All Our Strength: The Revolutionary Association of the Women in Afghanistan* (London: Routledge, 2003).
55. "RAWA: The Voice of Afghan Women," in *The Burst of the Islamic Government Bubble in Afghanistan*, no. 2 (1997), 79. Accessed at: http://www.afghandata.org:8080/xmlui/bitstream/handle/123456789/2509/azu_acku_serial_jc599_a34_c33_v4_n2_w.pdf?sequence=1
56. "RAWA."
57. "RAWA."
58. Hardy (2001), 13.
59. Hardy, 13–14.
60. Dupree (1998), 150.
61. Ahmed Rashid, *Taliban: Militant Islam, Oil and Fundamentalism in Central Asia* (New Haven, CT: Yale University Press, 2000), 111.

Chapter Six

Gender Politics in the Post–Taliban Afghan State

The Politics of Accommodation?

> I don't fear death; I fear remaining silent in the face of injustice. You can cut down the flower, but nothing can stop the coming of the spring.
> —Malalai Joya, Afghan women's rights activist and former parliamentarian

Since the ouster of the Taliban and due to the continued presence of NATO forces to bolster a weak central government, Afghan women and girls (primarily in urban areas) have experienced a dramatic improvement in their daily lives. Although self-imposed dress restrictions remain due to security concerns and traditional mores, Afghan females are able to publicly attend school without risking the wrath of the religious police. Improved access to health care and better employment prospects have translated into tangible improvements in the lives of many Afghan families, especially for the non-Pushtun. The traditionally oppressed Hazaras have enthusiastically embraced the unprecedented educational and entrepreneurial opportunities now available to them under the state's tutelage. They have the highest high school graduation rates of any ethnic group.[1]

Afghan women now participate in various occupations previously off limits to them such as in the Afghan military and the police forces. Women are working as journalists, doctors, nurses, teachers, actresses, and in other positions outside their homes. Afghan women now vote and run for public office. They serve in the Loya Jirga as elected members of the Afghan Parliament and in the Karzai government, which would never have been possible during Taliban rule. Yet notwithstanding all the indicators or metrics of success, many of these social and economic improvements in women's lives seem fragile, even superficial, because they are not deeply embedded, or evenly spread across the social landscape irrespective of ethnicity, socioeconomic status, or locale. Worse, females seeking nontraditional opportunities often pay a steep price. For example, those who've bravely sought to join the police or military forces, or work in the entertainment industry, either out of necessity or to break down traditional social barriers, have faced sexual harassment and assault which is rampant as many Afghan men perceive such women to be "fair game."[2] Furthermore, despite improvements in the socioeconomic situation, cases of domestic violence continue to rise leading to public protests by female activists demanding the government protect them.[3] This indicator or metric is worrisome and cause for concern vis-à-vis the future for Afghan females.

INTRODUCTION

One of the justifications cited by the Bush administration for overthrowing the Taliban involved their misogynistic treatment, dire even by Afghan standards, of their own female populace. Five weeks after the United States began bombing Afghanistan on October 7, 2001, America's First Lady, Laura Bush, stated triumphantly: "Because of our recent military gains in much of Afghanistan, women are no longer imprisoned in their homes. The fight against terrorism is also a fight for the rights and dignity of women."[4]

Over a decade since the overthrow of the Taliban, there have been some tangible improvements in the status and lives of many Afghan women, especially for urban dwellers who were particularly targeted by the Taliban. But for the majority of Afghan women, not to mention the general populace, the situation remains dire. This has much to do with the fact that despite the presence of NATO forces and efforts to develop a professional Afghan army and effective local police forces, the security situation remains appalling. The absence of security, coupled with high unemployment in a deeply conservative society, has had an adverse impact on the female populace's quality of life. The improved conditions for females in general are threatened by state and social forces. For example, Gulnaz, a rape victim incarcerated for having a child out of wedlock, was forced to marry her rapist in February 2013 in order to be set free.[5] In March 2012, President Karzai approved the influential council of clerics' restrictive "code of conduct" which recognized a husband's right to beat his wife and defended the need for the segregation of females as being congruent with Shariah law.[6] Furthermore, the Taliban have become emboldened in their harassment of females as NATO continues its troop withdrawal, and the Karzai government attempts reconciliation measures with the Taliban.[7]

AFGHAN WOMEN IN THE POST-TALIBAN POLITICAL PROCESS

Afghan Women and the Bonn Agreement[8]

Afghanistan's current political process is based on the December 2001 Bonn Agreement; an accord signed by representatives of the militia forces who fought with the U.S.-led coalition against the Taliban, representatives of the former king of Afghanistan, Zahir Shah, and representatives of other exiled Afghan groups. Often described as a peace agreement, the Bonn Agreement was a deal brokered by the victorious factions in the wake of a war won largely by an external power.[9]

The terms of the Bonn agreement pledged to foster the political participation of women in the upcoming loya jirgas and the interim administration.[10] Two women, Sima Wali and Rona Mansuri, participated as full delegates of the Rome process; while other Afghan women participated as representatives of particular groups: Amena Afzali was a full delegate of the United Front, Sediqa Balkhi as advisor to the Cyprus Group, and Fatima Gailani as advisor to the Peshawar Group.[11]

The Bonn Agreement made provisional arrangements for Afghanistan, pending the reestablishment of permanent government institutions and was signed on December 5, 2001. It called for the establishment of a "broad based, gender-sensitive, multi-ethnic and fully representative government."[12] The interim authority that was set up to run Afghanistan pending the convening of the Loya Jirga, followed by presidential and Parliamentary elections, included two ministries that would be run by women as per the terms of the Bonn Agreement: the Ministry of Public Health and Ministry of Women's Affairs, a body which had never existed before in Afghanistan. The Minister of Public Health was headed by Suhaila Seddiqi. She was a former army surgeon and a surgeon who had continued to practice medicine during Taliban rule. Sima Samar, also a physician who had run a network of hospitals, clinics and schools in Pakistan and central Afghanistan, was chosen to lead the Ministry of Women's Affairs.[13]

In a remarkably short period of time following the removal of the Taliban regime, Afghan women mobilized to ensure that their voices would be heard in the reconstruction of their state and society. First, on December 4, 2001, in response to numerous requests from Afghan women, a number of NGOs convened the Afghan Women's Summit for Democracy in Brussels. Around forty Afghan women from different ethnic, linguistic, and religious backgrounds participated, including three who had also attended the UN negotiations in Bonn. The Brussels Proclamation was the outcome of this summit and it included specific demands in order ensure recovery of Afghan society:

1. The right of women to vote and to receive pay.

2. The right to equal access to healthcare, education and employment.
3. An emergency plan for reopening schools by March 2002 for both girls and boys.
4. The training of teachers.
5. The inclusion of Afghan female lawyers in the development of a new constitution.
6. The rebuilding of hospitals.
7. Provision for healthcare, including psychological counseling.
8. The inclusion of women in the Emergency Loya Jirga.
9. The protection of women from forced underage marriages and sexual harassment.[14]

Second, on December 27, 2001, for the first time in the history of Afghanistan, more than seven hundred Afghan women gathered in a Loya Jirga (traditional assembly) in Pakistan to discuss ways in which to ensure that the newly installed interim government of Hamid Karzai would provide for equal representation of women under a future constitution. These delegates, led by Shafiqa Siraj, sister of the former Afghan King, Amanullah Khan, discussed the various issues involving their country and promised to hold future women's "jirgas" in the Afghan capital of Kabul. As one participant, Dr. Malali Salimi of the Afghan Women Council put it: "We are here to voice our grievances and seek a better place in the future set-up of the country, which has been ravaged by the twenty three year war and interference of external powers."[15]

This early activism on part of Afghan women reflected a deep seated concern that, as in the past, women's status and rights would be something the state would either fail to address or choose to regulate in a manner which would relegate their status to the mercy of both state and social actors. Historically nonexistent when it came to matters involving *their* status or rights and, in the more recent past, having been oppressed in ways that involved more than just their "social status," these female activists sought to ensure that their voices would be heard in the upcoming political processes of reestablishing the Afghan state.

Afghan Women's Participation in the Emergency Loya Jirga

The convening of the Emergency Loya Jirga (ELJ) in June 2002 as per the terms of the Bonn Agreement was significant in that approximately 12 percent of the delegates were women. About 1,600 delegates participated in the ELJ and 160 seats were reserved for women. Some two hundred women participated in the process having been elected or appointed.[16] The experience was, however, marred by the fact that female delegates faced intimidation, threats, and were forced to participate in a process that included their former aggressors, the various mujahedin commanders and warlords.[17] Many of the women felt that their efforts to fully participate in the process were hampered by the other male delegates who limited their ability to speak at the forum and, at times, would shut off the women's microphones after a mere five minutes. In contrast, powerful mujahedin leaders, some of whom were alleged war criminals, were allowed to ramble on for half an hour or so. Massouda Jalal, the sole women candidate for president at the ELJ, refused to cave into pressure to withdraw her candidacy and went on to win 171 votes, second to Karzai's 1,295.[18]

The purpose of the ELJ was to: (a) elect a head of state for the transitional administration; (b) approve proposals for the structure of the administration; and (c) approve appointment of key personnel. It, however, soon became apparent to many that most of the decisions would be made behind closed doors and victorious warlords would have significant influence over the proceedings notwithstanding their history of human rights abuses.[19] This was seen as a serious setback to the process of establishing a semblance of equality and justice for Afghan women, particularly in rural areas who remained at the mercy of various warlords and factions. Furthermore, it was a harbinger of things to come.

Afghan Women and the Constitutional Loya Jirga of 2003

The Constitutional Loya Jirga convened to debate and approve a new constitution for Afghanistan. On December 14, 2003, 502 delegates arrived in Kabul to review and approve the proposed Afghan Constitution.[20] Although it was scheduled to last ten days, the assembly did not endorse the Charter until January 4, 2004. The process was characterized by a lot of wrangling, arm twisting and even threats as the approval process was by way of consensus rather than majority vote. Due to the level of strife and bickering (even by Afghan standards), this Loya Jirga was mockingly called by some Afghans, the "*loya jagra*" ("big fight"). As in the previous ELJ, women delegates continued to face harassment, threats and intimidation but they actively participated in the drafting of Afghanistan's new constitution. These female delegates accused militia factions of preventing some from being candidates, buying votes, and unfairly influencing the election of delegates.[21] Many female delegates experienced various forms of harassment which led some of them to censor themselves out of fear of retaliation once they returned to their homes.

Human Rights Watch followed up with some of the women participants after the Constitutional Loya Jirga and found that a number of women who attended the jirga later experienced various forms of retaliation: dismissals from jobs, harassment and transfers to less desirable positions. Because only a few women attended from each province, they all asked Human Rights

Watch not to publish their names or locations for fear of retaliation. One delegate from northern Afghanistan reported: "After I participated in the Loya Jirga, I did not receive my salary for six months. Other former delegates reported harassment from local warlords and authorities via phone calls or face to face meetings."[22]

Women's Legal Status under the New Afghanistan Constitution of 2004

On January 4, 2004, 502 delegates to the Constitutional Loya Jirga (CLJ) agreed on a new constitution for Afghanistan.[23] Despite the various degrees of intimidation and harassment encountered by the female delegates to the CLJ, the end result mirrored most of the stipulations of the 1964 Constitution when it came to the status of Afghan women. The Afghan Constitution of 2004 contained specific provisions which guarantee certain rights for women. Under Article 22, women are entitled to equal rights and duties before the law. Article 52 enshrines the right to health care; while Article 44 states:

> The state shall devise and implement effective programs for balancing and promoting of education for women, improving of education of nomads and elimination of illiteracy in the country.[24]

Articles 83 and 84 guaranteed women a specific number of seats in Afghanistan's bicameral National Assembly. Approximately 25 percent of the seats in the *Wolesi Jirga* (House of the People) were reserved for women, while one-sixth of the seats in the *Meshrano Jirga* (House of the Elders) have been set aside for women through Presidential appointments. In addition, the 2004 Constitution states that the government is required to "protect human rights and to create a prosperous and progressive society based on social justice." Article 7 stipulated "the state respects the UN Charter and the Universal Declaration of Human Rights." Prior to the enactment of this constitution, Afghanistan had acceded to the CEDAW without any reservations on March 5, 2003.[25]

Women's organizations like RAWA, while pleased that this document made reference to the issue of human rights, were disappointed when they failed to get a special declaration on women's rights inserted to protect them against possible atrocities in the future which replicated the Taliban template. Some women delegates also expressed concern regarding certain provisions that involved barring any laws that were contrary to Islamic jurisprudence. This, they argued, could potentially be used in an effort to block or restrict measures designed to protect women's equal rights in divorce or inheritance.[26]

Their fears proved justified when a controversial law called the *Shia Personal Status Law* was passed by parliament and signed off into law by President Hamid Karzai in early 2009. It was a consequence of a loophole in the 2004 Afghan Constitution which made special provisions for Shias (who constitute around 10 percent of the population) to have a separate family law based on traditional Shia jurisprudence. Despite the fact that the 2004 Constitution and various international treaties signed by Afghanistan guarantee equal rights for women, this law essentially legalized marital rape within the Shia community.[27] The original bill had stipulated that the age of marriage for girls would be nine. This was later changed to sixteen. It also allowed for temporary Shia marriages (*mu'ta*) before this was also removed. Mothers were able to retain child custody if their child was under the age of nine from the previous seven years of age.[28]

Shinkai Zahine Karokhail, like other female parliamentarians, complained that after an initial deal, the law was passed with unprecedented speed and limited debate: "They wanted to pass it almost like a secret negotiation," she said. "There were lots of things that we wanted to change, but they didn't want to discuss it because Karzai wants to please the Shia before the election."[29] This piece of legislation—which was in violation of Article 22 of the 2004 Constitution—was eerily reminiscent of the Taliban period in that it sought once again to restrict and control female behavior in the name of Islam. According to the United Nations High Commission for Human Rights, the legislation stipulated that Afghan Shia women would not have the right to leave their homes except for "legitimate" purposes and it forbid women from working or seeking an education outside their homes without their husbands' or fathers' express permission.[30] The legislation explicitly permitted marital rape by specifying the wife is duty-bound to submit to the sexual desires of her husband.

The UN High Commissioner for Human Rights, Navi Pillay, immediately called on President Hamid Karzai to rescind the law saying that it was reminiscent of the decrees passed by the Taliban in the 1990s. In Kabul, on April 15, 2009, around two hundred women (Shia, Sunni, and some Hindus), held a public demonstration to protest this restrictive law. They were quickly surrounded by over a thousand men and women, some of whom threw small stones at them and spat at them while shouting that they were "enemies of Islam and infidels." On April 12, 2009, a prominent women's rights advocate and politician, Sitara Achakzai,[31] was killed in Kandahar.[32]

The Shia Personal Status Law of 2009 was amended after strong domestic and international pressure.[33] "The first version [of the law] was totally intolerable," said Najia Zewari, a women's rights expert with the UN Fund for Women (UNIFEM). "Despite positive changes in the final version, there are articles that still need to be discussed and reviewed further," she said.[34] The problem with the enactment of this law (even in its modified form) is that it creates a regressive precedent for a specific group of Afghan women (the Shia Hazaras) who have historically enjoyed greater privileges and "status" than Afghan females from the other ethnic groups, especially the Pushtun. It also violates the spirit of the 2004 Constitution and creates "legal space" for future regressive laws that may have a detrimental impact on all Afghan women. Legal action involving women's concerns by Karzai's government can be characterized as schizophrenic, conflicting, discriminatory, *and* emancipating. Karzai has been known to contradict himself on the subject of gender issues and women's status as he tries to be conciliatory toward various interests. In March 2008, on the occasion of International Women's Day, Karzai publicly told several hundred women packed into a high school auditorium in Kabul of the need to "stop violence against women, to stop child marriages and forced marriages as well."[35] Yet less than a year later Karzai signed the extremely regressive Shia Personal Status Law bill without consultations with women who would bear the effects of its passage.

Presidential Elections (2004 and 2009) and the Provincial Council Elections of 2009: Afghan Women's Participation

On October 9, 2004, Afghans went to the polls to vote for a president. According to official tallies, 41 percent of the 10.5 million registered voters in Afghanistan were women. Upon closer examination it was discovered that there were multiple registrations that had inflated the figures. In certain regions the fear of violence prevented mobile registration teams from going door to door prior to the election, which prevented many women from registering, especially in the rural or conservative areas. This contributed to very low female registration in the Pushtun belt in the South (Uruzgan: 9 percent; Zabul: 10 percent; Helmand: 16 percent).[36]

While the Election Day was fairly uneventful, inadequate monitoring and staffing problems, as well as security threats appeared to limit Afghan women's ability to vote, according to Human Rights Watch. The very low turnout in the South and South East of women voters was attributed not only to the difficulty in getting women registered prior to the election, but also was based on the fact that many women there were afraid to go to the polls, while some feared the wrath of their extended families if they did so. As Human Rights Watch reported, election officials failed to recruit enough women to oversee the polling stations established for women, and instead had to rely on mullahs and respected male elders, which still appeared to act as a deterrent in terms of bringing women out to the polls.[37]

A female civics educator told Human Rights Watch: "There are a lot of security problems. When we sent civic educators to the districts, there was no one to protect us and we were afraid." One female election worker from Kandahar told HRW: "Because we don't have enough women teams, a lot of women can't register even if they want to." In one of the more violent incidents during that election campaign, on June 25, 2004, a bomb targeting a bus filled with election workers near the eastern city of Jalalabad killed three and injured twelve.[38]

The sole female presidential candidate, Massouda Jalal, also encountered a campaign of opposition. For example, Ms. Jalal was barred from speaking at an Afghan New Year celebration at the central shrine in Mazar-e-Sharif, the Rowza Hazrat Ali, while other government officials as well as other potential political candidates spoke. She also received death threats.[39] Yet, by and large, the 2004 presidential election results were widely accepted by the Afghan populace who hoped president-elect, Hamid Karzai, with the backing of the United States, would improve the internal situation.

The 2009 presidential election could be characterized as a sham exercise that enabled an unpopular government, led by President Hamid Karzai, to remain in office.[40] On August 20, 2009, Afghans went to the polls to elect their President.[41] This time there were two female presidential candidates running for office.[42] Shahla Ata, a Pushtun from Kandahar, ran on a socialist platform à la Daoud Khan (1973–1978);[43] while Frozan Fana, the wife of the assassinated Afghan Aviation Minister Abdur Rahman, also contested the election but restricted her public campaigning.[44] Numerous problems were reported prior to the local elections which included female candidates being threatened. This impeded their ability to campaign freely. In many parts of the south and east, female candidates for the provincial councils' seats[45] found the conditions not conducive to public campaign appearances and they also faced pressure from conservative elements.[46] Almost all female candidates reported that they only contested in the provincial elections after receiving the blessing of their tribal elders or senior male family members.

Female candidates for the provincial councils also had difficulty funding their campaigns. Several organizations told NDI about women who decided not to run because of the transportation costs and the $80 registration fee which they could not afford. In Kabul Province, of the 524 candidates who competed for places on Kabul's provincial council, 65 were women. These female candidates felt additional pressure to campaign and cited a lack of funds to create posters to compete with the better funded males. UNIFEM decided to provide the female contestants with a place located in Kabul where they could photocopy up to 1,000 posters. Approximately 170 women from various provinces made 680 visits to this facility in Kabul to take advantage of this offer and to also obtain other support from UNIFEM, such as on how to better design their posters and business cards.[47] The International Election Commission's difficulty in recruiting sufficient numbers of women to administer the polling stations deterred women from casting their votes. Also, because a picture on their voting cards was optional, widespread identity fraud was a real possibility.[48]

The decision ended weeks of political drift since a first presidential poll in August was declared invalid due to massive fraud. Most Afghans heaved a sigh of relief when, on November 3, 2009, election officials declared Afghan President Hamid Karzai the winner of a new five-year term despite widespread fraud at the ballot box.[49] However, many Afghans, especially women, feared Karzai, without a clear mandate from his people, would face numerous public challenges and would also be vulnerable to various influences that could bring pressure to bear on his administration on "controversial" policies, such as those related to women.[50]

Since the 2009 presidential election, due to the perception of illegitimacy, coupled with its growing unpopularity among the general public, Karzai's government found itself compelled to backtrack on many of its campaign promises to Afghan's female populace in order to appease its social critics, especially those in the conservative Pushtun belt, as well as prominent clerics, as it tries to seek a truce with the Taliban, an anathema for women.

The 2005 Parliamentary and Provincial Council Elections and the 2010 Parliamentary Elections and Women's Status

By May 2005, Afghanistan faced the prospect of not having enough women to fill parliamentary seats reserved for them due to lack of candidates. On May 22, 2005, two days before registration closed for most candidates, Electoral Commission Chairman Bismillah Bismil told reporters in Kabul:

> Countrywide, we are short of 18 female candidates for provincial councils ... we hope that in the one and a half remaining days this problem will be solved. In Afghanistan there must be 68 female representatives (for provincial councils). We hope this problem is solved. If it is not solved these seats will remain vacant.[51]

Although enough women did register to run for the allocated seats in the Wolesi Jirga (298 women registered for the 68 reserved seats), registration for the provincial council elections (124 seats) was skewed. Enough women registered in the country's more liberal cities and northern provinces; but not a single woman ran in the provincial council election in the eastern province of Kunar. Most of the 172 women who registered were from the cities and the north, but there were not enough candidates to fill seats in eleven provinces mostly in the conservative Pushtun south and east of the country. One notable exception was Malalai Joya,[52] who would become the youngest member to be elected in 2005 to the Loya Jirga from Farah province.[53] President Karzai had urged Afghan women to stand for the provincial and district councils in 2005.[54]

The reluctance of women in the Pushtun areas to run for provincial council seats that would require participation on one's own home turf, suggests an entrenched fear of local hardline militias and remnants of the Taliban, which remained in control in some of these areas. One Afghan woman, Safia Siddiqi, campaigning for the parliamentary election survived an assassination attempt after gunmen opened fire on her convoy in Nangarhar province.[55] Women also faced stiff opposition from extended family and community in seeking public office. In fact none ran without the explicit permission from their male folk and elders. Running in provincial council elections without one's family or tribal support would have meant failure or worse, possible death or ostracism.

The day of the parliamentary election witnessed many veiled women queuing at polling stations throughout Afghanistan, notwithstanding the Taliban's threats to disrupt the process. A female voter in Kailak said: "I will look at the photos of the candidate and will choose a woman, any woman in the list. I want to vote for a woman because I am a woman."[56]

In Kandahar, the former stronghold of the Taliban, women crowded polling stations in greater numbers than in the country's first presidential election. One of the city's female candidates, Shahida Hussein, was ecstatic with the turnout of women: "I am so happy to see all these women coming out of their homes to vote."[57]

The relatively peaceful parliamentary election, coupled with a strong female participation in running for office, as well as in voting, was perceived as a victory for Afghan women. The local and parliamentary elections on September 18, 2005, were an important test for women's rights—and for Afghanistan itself. Unlike the presidential election, women participated in greater numbers and they challenged the power base of the local warlords. These elections involved greater incidents of violence toward women who chose to run for office or vote against the warlords. As expected, there were more attempts at intimidation and vote buying during this process than in the presidential election as the stakes were higher at the local level.

In order to run for office, candidates were required to collect five hundred copies of voter registration cards—the equivalent of signatures. Given continued intimidation and harassment in the form of death threats and attacks, many potential female candidates decided not to run for office because they feared for their safety as well as doubted whether the process would be tamper free. Human Rights Watch interviewed dozens of Afghan women who considered running for office in the 2005 parliamentary elections. Almost all of them expected warlords and dominant political factions to intimidate them if they decided to run for office. Since the interviews, some women did commit to becoming candidates. Others did not want to run for office due to safety concerns. One women's rights activist from Mazar-e-Sharif said: "I have to sit quiet. I think the conditions are not good for me (to run). . . . Maybe there will be a problem for me, or for my friends, because they would help me campaign."[58]

Human Rights Watch reported that many women who had planned to run as independent candidates faced continued harassment from dominant military factions. One potential candidate said: "My brother-in-law collected a few cards (voter registration) for me. The police harassed him. . . . They arrested him at his shop."[59] Another said: "I'm not hopeful that an independent woman will be successful. In the provinces, all the commanders have collected votes. . . . Every Friday they kill lots of animals and feed people, they offer this much money, and land to build a house—even if it is government land. They promised to send children abroad to study."[60]

Afghan women activists repeatedly emphasized their concern over the overall security environment and the need to disarm the armed factions which they believed impeded the ability of Afghan women to participate in these political processes, to advocate freely for their rights and to vote without fear of retaliation and violence. As long as these armed factions retain control of the countryside, women have to risk their safety in order to participate in the reconstruction of the country and in order to take part in various elections including local and parliamentary ones.[61]

When one female delegate from Farah province, Malalai Joya, bravely demanded at the Loya Jirga that the former warlords, many of whom were delegates themselves, be tried in national and international courts for war crimes, the chairman of the Jirga, Sebghatollah Mojadedi, prevented her from continuing to address the Jirga; while other participants tried to expel her. She soon received death threats.[62] In 2007, she was forced out of the Parliament and received numerous death threats for speaking out against both the warlords in power and the NATO occupation of her country. In an interview in 2009 with *The Independent*, Malalai said:

> Dust has been thrown into the eyes of the world by your governments. You have not been told the truth. The situation now is as catastrophic as it was under the Taliban for women. Your governments have replaced the fundamentalist rule of the Taliban with another fundamentalist regime of warlords.[63]

On September 18, 2010, Afghanistan held its second parliamentary elections after a four-month delay to elect members to the Wolesi Jirga. There were 2,584 candidates on the ballots for 249 seats of which 68 were allocated for women. Approximately 406 of the candidates were women. Violence and fraud characterized the day of the election with Afghan officials reporting some 33 bomb explosions, 63 rocket attacks, and 93 attacks on polling stations which killed at least 21 voters and wounded 46 others. Only 3.6 million votes were cast, the lowest number of all four elections held in Afghanistan since the Taliban were routed in 2001.[64] The highly respected former parliamentarian and women's activist, Malalai Joya, best summed up the reasons why she decided not to run in the 2010 Parliamentary election:

> We had another so-called parliamentary election in September, but I chose not to run. Any hope I had for using the ballot box to achieve change in Afghanistan is gone. Like last year's presidential vote, September's election was full of the buying and selling of votes—one province, Paktika, reported a turnout of 626 percent. This sort of thing is the reason elections in Afghanistan long ago became a bad joke. The only change that can make us hopeful about the future is the strengthening and expansion of a national anti-fundamentalist and democracy-loving movement. Such a movement can be built only by Afghans. And while we want the world's support and solidarity, we neither need nor want Nato's occupying forces.[65]

President Karzai's increasingly erratic behavior—reaching out to societal and foreign elements traditionally hostile toward Afghan women and/or society in general—was reflected in his nomination in January 2011 of Abdul Rab Rasul Sayyaf as his favorite candidate for the important slot of Speaker of the Parliament.[66] Sayyaf is widely considered, along with Gulbuddin Hikmatyar, to be one of the most misogynistic and intolerant of the mujahidin and is a close confidant of both the Saudi regime and Osama bin Laden. Thus, Karzai's nomination of Sayyaf was regarded by women's organizations and the non-Pushtun representatives in parliament as proof of Karzai's "true loyalties." The Hazaras especially saw this as a huge step backward for them since it was Sayyaf's militant faction which murdered thousands of Hazaras in Kabul in 1993. Shukria Paikan, a female parliamentarian from the northern province of Kunduz, expressed her views on many of her fellow parliamentarians: "The hands of these people [mujahidin] are red with the blood of the Afghan people . . . Taliban and mujahideen are the same for me. . . . It's very obvious that Karzai is supporting Sayyaf."[67] Despite Karzai's public support for his candidacy, Sayyaf was unable to secure enough votes and to the relief of many Afghan women, a more "neutral" candidate, Abdul Rauf Ebrahimi, an Uzbek from Kunduz was chosen as speaker.

State Action and Societal Violence against Afghan Women

Since the Taliban's overthrow, an ongoing concern of Afghan women, especially in the urban areas, has been over the character and motivations of those running their central and provincial governments. Increasingly Afghan women voice their reservations over the fact that many of those in charge of running the Karzai government were indeed the *same* people who had repressed Afghan women between 1992 and 1996.[68] Over a decade since the removal of the Taliban's misogynistic regime, most Afghan women outside of Kabul (and many within) continue to lead lives dictated by fear, repression and violence.[69] Violence—especially within domestic confines—is endemic. It is estimated that 90 percent of Afghan women are victims of some form of domestic abuse according to the United Nations Development Fund for

Women.[70] Some of this unacceptable violence is cultural, but it is also reflective of the dysfunctional society Afghanistan has become thanks to decades of upheaval and war.

Since 1978, the people of Afghanistan have been both victims and perpetrators of violence. The psychological scars of an intentionally scorched land—thanks to ten years of a brutal Soviet occupation—are deep; worsened by the violence and mayhem later inflicted on the populace by their own kin and countrymen vying to gain the reins of power at all cost. Numerous cases of violence toward women have been unreported, while others make the headlines. These included cases of women and girls having acid thrown in their faces; being stoned to death; set on fire or being murdered for working for NGOs or television stations.[71]

Despite the state's best efforts to protect women in Afghanistan from this endemic violence, Special Rapporteur of the United Nations Commission on Human Rights Professor Yakin Erturk announced in a press conference on July 18, 2005, that violence against Afghan women remains a significant concern.[72] Following a ten-day visit to Afghanistan, where she met with judges, prosecutors, aid workers, and women living in shelters and prisons, Erturk announced that of all the countries she had visited, Afghanistan faces the most daunting challenges in terms of women's rights. She cited poverty, lack of education, and the damage left from decades of conflict were often cited as the prime causes of women's plight. Erturk blamed the situation on the fact that Afghanistan still did not have a working system within which to address these concerns. She was also informed by Afghans that one of the primary sources of violence against women was forced marriages and child marriages.[73] It is not uncommon for young girls, who are forcibly married at a very young age, to commit suicide. Afghan newspapers began reporting growing cases of suicide since 2005 and the numbers continue to grow.[74] The term "Opium Brides" has become commonplace to describe widespread desperation in the poppy growing provinces where poppy crops are eradicated just prior to harvest by the Afghan government. The government's failure to provide some sort of financial compensation for the destruction of these illicit crops forces the farmers to give their daughters in marriage to drug traffickers who provided the seed money.[75]

On the widespread prevalence of rape, United Nations Assistance Mission in Afghanistan's (UNAMA) research found that this underreported and concealed crime is a problem of "profound proportions." It stressed that women and girls of all ethnicities and socioeconomic backgrounds are at risk of being raped. Furthermore, it found that often the perpetrators are influential members of society and are protected from being prosecuted. For example, in the northern areas, UNAMA's findings reveal that 39 percent of rape cases are committed by local powerbrokers that, more often than not, enjoy immunity from the law.[76] Worse, frequently the female victims are punished or even jailed for the crime. Colonel Ghulam Ali, a high-ranking regional security officer in Lashkar Gah, explained sternly in 2008 that he supported the authorities' right *to convict victims of rape*, arguing that such acts cause the spread of disease:

> In Afghanistan whether it is forced or not forced it is a crime because the Islamic rules say that it is, he claimed. I think it is good. There are many diseases that can be created in today's world, such as HIV, through illegal sexual relations.[77]

Karzai's government has decried, and even criminalized, the widespread discrimination and violence against women.[78] When the Taliban stoned a couple to death in the northeastern province of Kunduz on August 15, 2010, for adultery, Karzai joined other Afghans in publicly condemning the brutal execution.[79] The continued ability of certain social elements to defy the laws related to gender matters brings into question the government's enforcement capacities. Females remain vulnerable to exploitation and abuse, with over 50 percent married off before the legal age of sixteen.[80] In a society where honor and shame dictate courses of action, courts often decide cases not on the best interests of the child/girl/female but on the grounds of "respecting Afghan culture." In one case, a ten-year-old girl, who sought refuge in a female shelter (she had been forcibly married off without her consent at the age of six), was returned to her family when a senior justice official pressured by the girl's family implored the woman in charge of this shelter to return the girl to her husband out of "respect for Afghan culture and customs."[81]

While the evidence suggests that social forces, particularly those in the isolated regions of the country, continue to adhere to strict versions of Islamic law and tribal customs on the subject of female status within their respective communities; the same cannot be said for the state, at least on paper. Under the watchful eye of international actors, the Afghan state in fits and starts has generally made a significant departure from the social environment of the mujahidin and Taliban periods. The state's attempts—through its central and provincial infrastructure—to uphold the stipulations of the 2004 Constitution through enforcement are sporadic at best for varied reasons. This is likely to remain the state of affairs especially since the Karzai government has failed to create the appropriate law and order conditions. Nonetheless, some of the new laws and provisions do represent steps in the right direction, in stark contrast to the period of mujahidin and Taliban rule when such protections under the law were nonexistent. For example, immediately after being informed on April 21, 2005, of the first stoning to death case for adultery in Afghanistan since the ouster of the Taliban, the deputy governor of Badakhshan was quick to distance his provincial officials from this incident. He argued that contrary to initial reports, this had been the conduct of independent social elements and was not ordered by a provincial court. He vowed to have a delegation investigate the issue and ordered security forces to arrest the girl's father and others involved in the crime.[82]

President Karzai did move to make several positive changes in the judicial system. One positive development—in the summer of 2006—was the appointment of the new chief justice of the Supreme Court, Abdul Salam Azimi. Azimi, widely perceived as a modern thinker sympathetic to women's rights, said in an interview that Afghan civil laws and Islamic principles do provide ample protection to women. It is the conservative culture that is powerful, and social and psychological barriers preclude women from seeking legal help.[83]

Given the limited state resources and lack of a functioning state apparatus, especially in the provinces, the state has not yet been able to appropriately, or adequately, address violence against women, which remains endemic. Advocates for women's rights argue that the limited legal protections women have are only enforced in Kabul and several other large cities. But even here, the courts rarely grant women divorces. Custody of minor children goes to the fathers irrespective of the facts, which more often than not involve severe domestic violence and abuse. In a culture where concepts such as honor, shame, and reputation are paramount, women never seek court intervention unless they are experiencing horrible—even by Afghan standards—conditions. Yet both state and social institutions are reluctant or dismissive of the overwhelmingly legitimate complaints of females. This is a direct consequence of a culture in which females are generally regarded as being the property of their husbands, fathers, or brothers, whose honor still takes precedence over their own physical safety and general well-being.

MOBILIZATION OF URBAN AFGHAN WOMEN IN THE POST-TALIBAN STATE

Since 2001, Afghan women in the urban centers have mobilized to challenge the repressive policies they had been forced to live under in the Taliban controlled state. In stark contrast, women in the rural areas by and large have remained silent. On November 27, 2001, one of Afghanistan's prominent women's rights advocate, Soraya Parlika, held a *burqa*-removing ceremony outside her Kabul apartment. Approximately two hundred Afghan women gathered outside her building and all removed their *burqas* at the same time. Parlika stated that "it was a very emotional moment. After years, the women of Afghanistan came out in the open. Under the Taliban we all wore *burqas* and did not know each other. Now we all know each other's faces."[84] Sima Samar, the former Women's Affairs Minister told a Canadian newspaper that she did not believe in *Shariah* (Islamic law) leading to her receiving a summons to appear in court to face a blasphemy charge (which was later dropped after President Karzai intervened).[85]

Since the overthrow of the Taliban, women in the urban areas have petitioned the Karzai government, as well as international aid organizations, to provide resources for the re-establishment of education facilities for women. As a result of their efforts, the Medical College of the University of Nangarhar in eastern Afghanistan graduated the first class of sixty-one midwives and about two hundred other students in 2005. The class of midwives came from Nangarhar, Kunar, Laghman, and Nuristan provinces. The only childbirth resource available to rural women is the local midwife, who is the only professional healthcare provider for pregnant women. The return of these women to their villages means an improvement in the survivability rate of Afghan infants and their mothers in a country with one of the world's highest infant mortality rates.[86]

In the urban centers, women have returned to working in hospitals, schools, government departments, and as entrepreneurs. Women are taking driving lessons, martial arts courses, and joining the military. Girls no longer have to secretly attend classes but attend public schools even in isolated villages in the Hindu Kush. Cases of individual gestures of generosity such as fourteen-year-old Rima Nuri's decision to donate her share of adjacent farmland her family had inherited in the village of Nemla in Nangarhar Province, ensured the expansion of the village's girls' school. Attitudes toward girls' education are slowly changing as more families in places like Nemla are increasingly supportive of female education and employment in schools, hospitals, and nongovernmental organizations.[87] Women are also back attending universities and colleges in the urban areas. The booming private sector has provided entrepreneurial women with limited opportunities that allow them to engage in businesses involving cottage industries that can employ women involving weaving carpets, sewing handicrafts, and so on. For example, Zolaykha Sherzad launched Zarif Design in Kabul in 2005 which created job opportunities for women in traditional Afghan textiles and handstitched embroidery. Currently, she employs fifty-two people in Afghanistan, of whom 60 percent are women. Many Afghan women have returned from abroad to head or work in NGOs involved in humanitarian assistance, as well as run for Parliament.[88]

In addition to cultural roadblocks, the security situation for women remains dire in the provinces as long as the warlords and their militias retain control in certain areas and hold public office. As early as 2006, a report by the UNIFEM warned in its main conclusion of a disturbing trend reminiscent of the civil war period of the 1990s in that women and girls are being subjected to physical and psychological violence, often at an early age, and that neither employment, education levels, or marital status determines who will be victimized.[89] The problem is that the abusers are often intimate partners who act "with impunity" as there are few repercussions, either legally or within families. Furthermore, Afghan women often have nowhere to go and suffer in silence. The UN report recommends that while more research is needed to understand the full extent of the violence against women, the state must step in immediately to provide support to those against whom acts of violence are committed.[90]

Elimination of Violence against Women (EVAW) Decree of 2009

Afghanistan's president issued a Presidential Decree in August 2009 titled "Elimination of Violence against Women (EVAW)." This measure was an enormous *symbolic* victory for Afghan females living in perilous times. For the first time in the country's history, certain embedded, and widely prevalent, cultural norms which relegated females to the status of property or chattel and/or permitted outright cruelty were officially criminalized. The forms of violence and norms outlawed included child marriage, forced marriage, the selling and buying of females for the purpose of marriage, the traditional practice of *ba'ad* (which requires giving away of a woman or a girl to settle a dispute), forced self-immolation, and nineteen other acts of violence including rape and physical abuse. This decree also specified punishment for the perpetrators.[91]

Predictably, the implementation of this decree has been problematic and sporadic due to a myriad of factors, including limited governmental enforcement capacity and entrenched social stigma which precludes effective enforcement measures. Thus, according to the recent UN study, enforcement of the EVAW is frequently hampered by substantial underreporting of violence, as well as a lack of investigations into most of the reported incidents.

According to the UNAMA's 2012 report: "Incidents of violence against women are under-reported due to cultural restraints, social norms and taboos, customary and religious beliefs, discrimination against women that leads to wider acceptance of violence against women, fear of social stigma and exclusion, and at times threat to life."[92] Such cases that do reach law enforcement and judicial authorities or receive public attention through the media due to their egregious nature, however, represent the tip of the iceberg of incidents of violence against women throughout the country.

The latest UNAMA study noted that the number of violent incidents against females reported to certain organizations and entities increased over the reporting period which is an encouraging development. The Afghanistan Independent Human Rights Commission recorded 4,010 cases of violence against women from March 21 to October 21, 2012, throughout Afghanistan compared to 2,299 cases it recorded for the entire year in 2011 (from March 21, 2010, to March 21, 2011). This trend toward reporting violence may be the result of increased public awareness and sensitization to violence against women and its harmful and criminal consequences, and to women's rights generally through efforts of civil society organizations, the government and international actors. Some of the stigma associated with reporting such cases has eroded due to increased public awareness and the possibility of prosecution. The increase in reported cases does suggest a greater willingness to come forward and bring such violence to the attention of the authorities. Other reports, however, do indicate a disturbing trend toward increased levels of domestic and other forms of violence leading to a number of public protests in Kabul demanding greater protection of females.[93]

During a news conference in Kabul, UNAMA's Human Rights Director, Georgette Gagnon, suggested that the underreporting of incidences of violence against women was not only due to cultural restraints, social norms, and taboos: "Prevailing insecurity and weak rule of law have further hampered women's access to formal justice institutions." According to Gagnon, in 163 of the 470 reported cases of violence against women, prosecutors had filed indictments resulting in the conviction at trial of 100 cases—a 61 percent success rate. She stressed: "This shows that in the small number of cases of violence against women that were investigated and prosecuted, use of EVAW law was more likely to result in justice for the women." At the launch of the latest UNAMA report, the Secretary-General's Special Representative for Afghanistan and head of UNAMA, Ján Kubiš, agreed with Gagnon: "If the advances identified in implementing the EVAW law are expanded and built upon, Afghan women can be empowered to take a more active part in peacekeeping and political life."[94]

The UNAMA report erroneously describes the EVAW as a "law" and not a "decree," as certain Afghan politicians and activists battle their conservative counterparts to get the EVAW passed into law by the Loya Jirga (parliament) to give it permanence that a presidential decree does not.[95] The crux of the disagreement between vying social factions reflects the chasm that exists between those in government who view such "secular laws" as antithetical to Shariah (Islamic law) versus those who don't view such legislation as being in violation of Islamic precepts. Masooda Karokhi, a female member of parliament, who has been pushing to get the proposal through the male-dominated legislature sees this as one struggle Afghan women can't afford to lose. Along with some of her colleagues, Karokhi has tried to appease the hardliners by suggesting some changes to the EVAW.

However, because the Afghan Constitution contains a clause which states that all laws must be in compliance with Shariah, the hardliners and others in the Loya Jirga have argued that really at issue are a range of provisions involving a female's "appropriate role" in an Islamic republic and that, under Shariah, a man is entitled to beat his wife if she disobeys him. One parliamentarian, Hossein Balkhi, agrees that while such a law might be necessary, most of its proposed provisions violate Islam and need to be changed. He says Shariah is stricter in many of its punishments than the proposed law: "In this law, it proposes that if a man commits a sexual assault, he will be sentenced to 16 years in jail, while in Islam, that man should be executed." Enayatullah Balegh, an adviser to the president and a member of Afghanistan's Council of Religious Scholars argues that "the interpretation and definition of violence against women is very different from here and the West."[96]

Balkhi, the legislator, believes the parliament needs to form a committee of religious scholars to evaluate the provisions of the EVAW and issue a majority decision. Shukria Barakzai, a prominent female parliamentarian, agrees in principle, but worries there are few legitimate Shariah scholars in the legislature: "If we have religious scholars in the parliament who are interpreting all these religious issues for the benefit of [Afghans], that's different," she says. "Right now, we don't have it."[97] Given the sensitivity of this issue (females' role in a Muslim society) and the determined pushback from the hardliners in the Loya Jirga, passage of the EVAW is an uphill battle. This struggle to ensure that this landmark decree becomes permanently embedded and implemented encapsulates the perilous fight ahead for those who wish to protect and expand the gains females, and society as a whole, have made since the Taliban's removal from power.[98]

The Future for Afghan Females: Progression or Regression?

The future for Afghan females appears to be grim once NATO completes its drawdown in 2014 and foreign aid is drastically cut as the world's attention turns away from the domestic issues that continue to bedevil the Afghan state (security and economy). At present, thanks to the generous external aid (primarily from the West) and the presence of foreign troops, the Afghan government whose ranks are filled with war criminals, warlords, and Islamists (such as Abdul Rasul Sayyaf, Abdul Dostum, and Ismail Khan as examples) has been amenable to external "advice" on its gender policies. It has humored its Western paymasters and donors by going through the motions vis-à-vis "gender justice" and all the other pet issues of these donor states, who seem to exhibit little appreciation/comprehension of Afghan history, culture, and mores.

Afghan women from all ethnicities and socioeconomic backgrounds are worried that, yet again, they will be pawns in the various power struggles and conflicts that unfold after 2014. Furthermore, the unpredictable nature of Karzai's government, as it desperately seeks to hold onto the reins of power by trying to co-opt certain Taliban elements, does not bode well for Afghan females. As in the past, the Hazaras (who have worked the hardest and made tremendous gains) will pay the heaviest price should open conflict break out if the Afghan National Army disintegrates into well-armed militias. In a land where memories are long and often bitter, many have good reason to worry once foreign oversight is removed.

All indications, within the larger regional context, suggest a real possibility for dramatic regression in the quality of life (starting with physical security) for all citizens without the robust support through the sheer presence of some sort of NATO or UN-led quick reaction force. Furthermore, meddling by both the Pakistanis and the Iranians, coupled with the influx of vast sums of petro-dollars from the Saudis to build mosques[99] and madrassas (that would preach the most draconian version of Shariah law), would contribute to instability and strife, with females bearing the greatest brunt.

Afghanistan society *has* made enormous gains over the last twelve years thanks to social activism and external assistance. Girls' enrollment in school went from 5,000 to nearly 3 million. The number of total midwives increased from less than 500 to nearly 3,000—an important boost in a country where giving birth is the leading cause of death among women. Women regained the right to vote and hold public office in 2004. Women comprise 27 percent of parliamentarians and Fawzia Koofi has boldly announced her intention to run for president in 2014. These have been tremendous victories despite the rampant corruption and violence. But advocates fear that these newfound rights of Afghan women will be the first casualty without the protection and support from the international community. There is much ambivalence among the populace now despite the clamoring for the complete removal of foreign forces from Afghan soil. According to the humanitarian organization, Action Aid, in a 2011 poll 86 percent of the 1,000 Afghan women polled were worried that a Taliban-style government could return. To say this would be "a bitter pill to swallow" would be a gross understatement after over three decades of war and sacrifice.[100]

CONCLUSION

As in the past, certain incendiary efforts to promote women's status that rapidly push acceptable social boundaries in a deeply traditional Muslim milieu only serve to incite stiff social opposition. Worse, they tend to backfire and ultimately lead to detrimental results which impact *all* Afghan females. This has especially been the case in the Pushtun belt where rumors of real or imagined female behavior in Kabul, Herat, or elsewhere inevitably provide the propaganda fodder for those conservative elements who wish to see a return to a Taliban-style regime. Furthermore, the removal of the Taliban hasn't lead to significant improvements in female security as various forms of domestic violence remain rampant. For example, Herat is plagued by rising incidences of self immolation in acts of suicide by mostly Farsiwan women and girls who are desperate to end their domestic misery by setting themselves on fire.[101] The situation for all Afghans is a precipitous and uncertain one as they remain vulnerable to the fickleness of those in power, many of whom have close ties to the warlords and the drug mafia.

While certain enacted laws have legislatively protected and promoted better conditions and opportunities for Afghans in general; actual implementation has been problematic and limited in scope. Whether or not Afghan women throughout the country will actually see a marked improvement in their social status is contingent on a number of factors, both social and structural. In 2013, two disturbing trends give reason for pause: The Taliban gains in both strength and support because of the widespread corruption; and the incompetence of the government at both the central and provincial levels to deliver security and improve economic conditions for the populace. The Taliban and the criminal warlords have been emboldened enough to threaten to carry out targeted attacks against females who defy their edicts and dare to go to school or work in order to help feed their families. Increasingly, they burn girls' schools, poison water supplies, throw acid, and/or threaten women who do not behave according to their "Islamic" norms.[102] Widows remain especially vulnerable and are still often forced into prostitution. Acid attacks are on the rise against girls who go to school. For example, in November 2008, acid was thrown on fifteen girls in Kandahar on their way to school by two men on motorcycles. Leaflets distributed in villages at night warning families against sending their daughters to school have led to the closure of over six hundred schools.[103]

Afghan scholar, Nancy Dupree, views Afghan women as comprising a socioeconomic pyramid. The base of the pyramid represents the majority of Afghan women and consists of women who live in the rural areas. These women's aspirations focus almost exclusively on the family. At the tip of the pyramid are the women who bore the full brunt of the Taliban ire: assertive working women who led the women's movement since 1959, and who advocate for equal participation in all decision making. The center of the pyramid consists of the growing middle class that is composed of professional teachers, medical practitioners, engineers, judges, administrators, businesswomen, social workers, and civil servants. Dupree argues that Afghanistan's recovery is contingent on the core of the pyramid, which consists of *women who believe that Afghan women can function in society without compromising tradition* (emphasis added).[104] Dupree's assessment, which argues for a more pragmatic approach to gender policy, is a wise one. Afghanistan's history has repeatedly shown that rapid introduction of measures designed to improve the status of Afghan women have always failed due to stiff social resistance to such drastic changes that appear to be out of sync with the Afghan interpretation of what constitutes "a Muslim state and society."[105]

However, given the level of violence toward women and girls in Afghan society in general, what is needed is a more proactive approach at the grassroots level "encouraged" by the central government to create a social climate that does not tolerate such abusive action. Engaged in a cultural clash with stubborn repressive norms, a robust educational/public awareness campaign funded by Kabul is needed that invokes a culturally derivative narrative which resonates and serves to shame (if this is possible) those who insist on tormenting and abusing their female family members as being culturally (and religiously) sanctioned. religiously) sanctioned. Local/regional homegrown narratives are required to counter the Islamists' literalist (and medieval) tendencies as they seek ultimate control over society. This endeavor must seek legitimacy through comparison: existing customs need to be compared to cherry-picked Quranic *ayats* (verses) in order to delegitimize such abusive behavior such as the sale of daughters to settle opium debts and other forms of violence against females. Enactment of laws to address this endemic menace are not enough; the security apparatus (whether an *arbaki* [tribal militia], the ANP, and/or ANA) must be willing to take action against those who transgress and violate established protections against women and children, particularly in rural areas. Given the continued pervasiveness of violence toward women and children, safety issues should be one of the important policy concerns of the Karzai government. A complete restoration of law and order throughout Afghanistan takes precedence, accompanied by provision of essential services to families such as basic health care, education, and income opportunities. None of these goals contradict or challenge embedded customs, nor are they controversial. But they constitute the essential first steps toward restoring and improving women's status in all of Afghanistan and not just in the urban centers. However, due to the precariousness of the current security and economic situation as external support (economic and military) begins to recede, Afghan females have good reason to be anxious and concerned about their future.

NOTES

1. Richard A. Oppel and Abdul Waheed Wafa, "Hazara Hustle to Head of Class in Afghanistan," *New York Times,* January 3, 2010. Accessed at: http://www.nytimes.com/2010/01/04/world/asia/04hazaras.html?_r=1

2. Quil Lawrence, "For Afghan Policewomen, Sex Abuse Is a Job Hazard," *NPR,* March 8, 2012. Accessed at: http://www.wbur.org/npr/148041305/for-afghan-policewomen-sex-abuse-is-a-job-hazard.

3. "Dozens of Afghan Women, Activists Mark Valentine's Day By Marching against Violence," *Associated Press,* February 14, 2013. Accessed at: http://www.foxnews.com/world/2013/02/14/dozens-afghan-women-and-activists-mark-valentine-day-by-marching-against-rising/.

4. Mariam Rawi, "Rule of the Rapists," *The Guardian,* February 12, 2004. Accessed at: http://www.guardian.co.uk/world/2004/feb/12/afghanistan.gender.

5. Jeremy Kelly, "Afghan Rape Victim Gulnaz Forced to Marry Her Attacker," *The Times,* March 4, 2013. Accessed at: http://www.thetimes.co.uk/tto/news/world/asia/afghanistan/article3677718.ece.

6. "Hamid Karzai Backs Restrictive Code for Women," *The Guardian*, March 6, 2012. Accessed at http://www.guardian.co.uk/world/2012/mar/06/hamid-karzai-restricive-code-women-afghanistan.

7. Golnar Motevalli, "Afghan Taliban Target Women," *DAWN*, February 21, 2013. Accessed at: http://dawn.com/2013/02/21/afghan-taliban-target-women/.

8. Access the Bonn Agreement at: http://www.afghangovernment.com/AfghanAgreementBonn.htm.

9. Chris Johnson, *Afghanistan*, UK: Oxfam, Second Edition, 2004, 31.

10. "Between Hope and Fear: Intimidation and Attacks against Women in Public Life in Afghanistan," *Human Rights Watch Briefing Paper*, NY: Human Rights Watch, October 2004, 8-9.

11. Angela King, "United Nations and Afghanistan," in *Women for Afghan Women: Shattering Myths and Changing the Future*, ed. Sunita Mehta (New York: Palgrave MacMillan, 2002), 147.

12. For a copy of the Bonn Agreement go to: www.uno.de/frieden/Afghanistan/talks/agreement.htm.

13. King, 148.

14. See the Bonn Agreement: www.uno.de/frieden/Afghanistan/talks/agreement.htm

15. Nadeem Iqbal, "Afghanistan: Women Meet to Demand Role in Reconstruction," Interpress Service, December 27, 2001. Accessed at: http://www.ipsnews.net/

16. "Between Hope and Fear: Intimidation and Attacks against Women in Public Life in Afghanistan," *Human Rights Watch Briefing Paper*, October 2004, 9.

17. Johnson, 32.

18. *Human Rights Watch Briefing Paper* (October 2004), 9.

19. Johnson, 32.

20. "Constitutional Loya Jirga Begins in Afghanistan," *NATO*. December 17, 2003. Accessed at: http://www.nato.int/docu/update/2003/12-december/e1217a.htm.

21. *Human Rights Watch Briefing Paper* (October 2004), 9.

22. *Human Rights Watch Briefing Paper*, 10.

23. For more on this event see James Ingalls, "The New Afghan Constitution: A Step Backwards for Democracy," *Foreign Policy in Focus*, March 13, 2004. Accessed at: www.fpif.org.

24. *Human Rights Watch Briefing Paper* (October 2004), 10.

25. *Human Rights Watch Briefing Paper*, 10-11.

26. *Human Rights Watch Briefing Paper*, 10.

27. "Worse Than the Taliban—New Law Rolls Back Rights for Afghan Women," *The Guardian*, March 31, 2009. Accessed at: http://www.guardian.co.uk/world/2009/mar/31/hamid-karzai-afghanistan-law.

28. "U.S., U.N. Concerned about Afghan Shia Law," *Khaleej Times*. April 2, 2009. Accessed at: http://www.khaleejtimes.com/DisplayArticle08.asp?xfile=data/international/2009/April/international_April163.xml&section=international.

29. "Worse than the Taliban—new law rolls back rights for Afghan women," *The Guardian*, March 31, 2009. Accessed at: http://www.guardian.co.uk/world/2009/mar/31/hamid-karzai-afghanistan-law.

30. Golnaz Esfandiari, "New Law Seen as Setback for Afghan Women's Rights," *RFE/RL*, April 4, 2009. Accessed at: http://www.rferl.org/content/New_Law_Seen_As_Setback_For_Afghan_Womens_Rights/1601618.html.

31. Paula Lerner, "The Life and Death of Sitara Achakzai," *PRI's The World*, July 29, 2009. Accessed at: http://www.theworld.org/2009/07/29/the-life-and-death-of-sitara-achekzai/

32. Lerner, "The Life." See also Golnaz Esfandiari, "Afghan Protest against Discriminatory Law," *RFE/RL*. April 16, 2009.

33. Ben Farmer, "Afghanistan Revises Marriage Law But Women Still Required to Submit to Sexual Intercourse," *The Telegraph*, July 9, 2009. Accessed at: http://www.telegraph.co.uk/news/worldnews/asia/afghanistan/5790702/Afghanistan-revises-marriage-law-but-women-still-required-to-submit-to-sexual-intercourse.html.

34. "Women Rights Trampled Despite New Law," *IRIN Asia*, March 8, 2010. Accessed at: http://www.irinnews.org/Report.aspx?ReportId=88349.
35. Rahim Faiez, "Karzai Urges More Freedom for Women," *Newsvine*, March 8, 2008. See also "Karzai Called on Parents not to Give Away Daughters into Early Marriages," *Afghan News Service*, March 8, 2008. Accessed at: http://www.afghan-press.com/release/karzai-called-on-parents-not-to-give-away-daughters-into-early-marriages/.
36. "Women and Elections in Afghanistan," *Human Rights Watch*, October 2004. Accessed at: http://img.static.reliefweb.int/report/afghanistan/special-report-women-and-elections-afghanistan.
37. Human Rights Watch (October 2004).
38. Human Rights Watch (October 2004).
39. Human Rights Watch (October 2004).
40. Pamela Constable and Joshua Partlow, "In Kabul, A Collective Sigh of Relief," *Washington Post*, November 3, 2009. Accessed at: http://www.washingtonpost.com/wp-dyn/content/article/2009/11/02/AR2009110203455.html.
41. For complete details on the 2009 presidential and provincial council elections, please see "The 2009 Presidential and Provincial Councils Elections in Afghanistan," *National Defense Institute*, 2010. Accessed at: http://www.ndi.org/files/Elections_in_Afghanistan_2009.pdf.
42. Heidi Vogt, "Shahla Ata and Frozan Fana: Two Women among Those Vying For Afghan Presidency," *Huffington Post*, August 5, 2009. Accessed at: http://www.huffingtonpost.com/2009/08/05/shahla-atta-frozan-fana-2_n_252001.html.
43. For more on Shahla Ata see "Afghanistan's Elections: Presidential Biographies," *Washington Post*, 2009. Accessed at: http://www.washingtonpost.com/wp-srv/special/world/afghanistan-election/biographies.html.
44. Zarghuna Kargar, "Afghan Women Strive to be Heard," *BBC News*, August 13, 2009. Accessed at: http://news.bbc.co.uk/2/hi/8198126.stm.
45. The Provincial councils nominate members of the upper house or Meshrano Jirga which rules on legislation.
46. "The 2009 Presidential and Provincial Councils Elections in Afghanistan," 27.
47. "The 2009 Presidential and Provincial Councils Elections in Afghanistan," 28.
48. "The 2009 Presidential and Provincial Councils Elections in Afghanistan," 27.
49. Jon Boone and Mark Tran, "Hamid Karzai Declared Winner of Afghanistan's Presidential Election," *The Guardian*, Novemeber 2, 2009. Accessed at: http://www.guardian.co.uk/world/2009/nov/02/hamid-karzai-afghanistan-winner-election.
50. Amber Raz, "Hamid Karzai Is Failing Afghan Women," *The Guardian*, May 10, 2010. Accessed at: http://www.guardian.co.uk/commentisfree/2010/may/10/karzai-failing-afghan-women.
51. "Afghanistan Faces Shortage of Women in New Parliament," *AFP*, May 22, 2005 Accessed at: http://www.dailynews.lk/2005/05/23/wld03.htm.
52. Malalai Joya, *A Woman among Warlords: The Extraordinary Story of an Afghan Who Dared to Raise Her Voice* (New York: Scribner, 2009).
53. "Profile: Malalai Joya," *BBC News*, November 12, 2005. Accessed at: http://news.bbc.co.uk/2/hi/south_asia/4420832.stm.
54. "Afghanistan Faces Shortage of Women in New Parliament," *AFP*, May 22nd, 2005.
55. "Afghan Woman on Vote Campaign Trail Escapes Assassination Bid," *FBIS*, September 7, 2005.
56. Sardar Ahmed, "Joy, and Some Confusion, as Afghans Vote," *Reuters*, September 19, 2005.
57. Ahmed, "Joy, and Some Confusion."
58. Ahmed, "Joy, and Some Confusion."
59. Ahmed, "Joy, and Some Confusion."
60. Ahmed, "Joy, and Some Confusion."
61. Ahmed, "Joy, and Some Confusion." Human Rights Watch continues to actively monitor human rights and women's rights concerns on the ground in Afghanistan. Their website is www.hrw.org.

62. "Afghanistan: Threats of Violence and Expulsion against Female Loya Jirga Delegate Condemned," *Amnesty International News Release*, December 17, 2003. Also refer to: "Afghan Rights Advocate Expects Death," *BBC*, August 9, 2004. For more on this also refer to Kathy Gannon, "Afghanistan Unbound," *Foreign Affairs* 83 (2004), 40. Accessed at: http://www.foreignaffairs.com/articles/59891/kathy-gannon/afghanistan-unbound.

63. "Malalai Joya: The Woman Who Will Not Be Silenced," *The Independent*, July 28, 2009. Accessed at: http://www.amazon.com/Land-Unconquerable-Lives-Contemporary-Afghan/dp/0520261860/ref=sr_1_1?ie=UTF8&s=books&qid=1295661216&sr=1-1.

64. Dana Chivvis, "Afghanistan's 2010 Parliamentary Elections: Baby Steps or Step Backwards?" *AOL News*, September 20, 2010. Accessed at: http://www.aolnews.com/2010/09/20/afghanistans-2010-parliamentary-elections-baby-steps-or-backwa/.

65. Malalai Joya, "Any Hope I Had in the Ballot Box Bringing Change in Afghanistan Is Gone," *The Guardian*, November 2nd, 2010. Accessed at: http://www.guardian.co.uk/commentisfree/cifamerica/2010/nov/02/hope-ballot-box-afghanistan-gone.

66. Accessed at: http://www.rawa.org/temp/runews/2011/01/29/karzai-backs-infamous-warlord-to-be-speaker.html.

67. http://www.rawa.org/temp/runews/2011/01/29/karzai-backs-infamous-warlord-to-be-speaker.html.

68. Philip Smucker, "Rights Still Lag for Afghan Women," *Christian Science Monitor*, June 14, 2002.

69. Valerie M. Hudson and Patricia Leidl, "Betrayed," *Foreign Policy*, May 10, 2010. Accessed at: http://www.foreignpolicy.com/articles/2010/05/07/the_us_is_abandoning_afghanistan_s_women

70. Atia Abawi, "Afghan Women Hiding For Their Lives," *CNN.com*, September 23, 2009. Accessed at: http://articles.cnn.com/2009-09-23/world/afghanistan.women.abuse_1_afghan-women-safe-house-afghan-society?_s=PM:WORLD.

71. For more on post–Taliban violence toward women see: "Taking Cover: Women in Post-Taliban Afghanistan," *Human Rights Watch Briefing Paper*, May 2002; N. C. Aizenmen, "A Killing Commanded by Tradition," *Washington Post*, May 6, 2005. Accessed at: http://www.washingtonpost.com/wp-dyn/content/article/2005/05/05/AR2005050501563.html; "3 Women Found Dead with Warning Note," *Washington Times*, May 3, 2005, 10.

72. "Violence against Afghan Women Remains Dramatic," *Kabul Times*, August 4, 2005, 1.

73. "Violence against Afghan Women."

74. "Young Girl Drowned Herself in Kokchah River," *Daily Outlook Afghanistan*, August 2, 2005, 1.

75. Sami Yousafzai, "The Opium Brides of Afghanistan," *Newsweek*, March 29, 2008. Accessed at: http://www.newsweek.com/2008/03/29/the-opium-brides-of-afghanistan.html.

76. "Silence Is Violence: End the Abuse of Women in Afghanistan," *UNAMA Report*, July 9, 2009. Accessed at UNHCR site: http://www.unhcr.org/refworld/country,,UNAMA,,AFG,,4a548f532,0.html.

77. "The Afghan Women Jailed for Being Victims of Rape," *The Independent*, August 18, 2008. Accessed at: http://www.independent.co.uk/news/world/asia/the-afghan-women-jailed-for-being-victims-of-rape-900658.html.

78. "Women's Rights Trampled Despite New Law," *IRIN*, March 8, 2010. Accessed at: http://www.irinnews.org/Report.aspx?ReportId=88349.

79. Abubakar Siddique, "Stoning of Afghan Couple for Adultery Sparks Debate on Sharia Law," *RFE/RL*, August 17, 2010. Accessed at: http://www.rferl.org/content/Stoning_Of_Afghan_Couple_For_Adultery_Sparks_Debate_On_Sharia_Law/2130407.html.

80. Farangis Najibullah, "Afghan Bill Aims to Criminalize Discrimination Against Women," *RFE/RL*, July 20, 2009. Accessed at: http://www.rferl.org/content/Afghan_Bill_Aims_To_Criminalize_Discrimination_Against_Women/1781098.html.

81. Pamela Constable, "A Precarious Shelter in Afghanistan," *Washington Post*, December 5, 2006. Accessed at: http://www.washingtonpost.com/wpdyn/content/article/2006/12/04/AR2006120401148.html

82. "Afghan Deputy Governor: Woman Not Stoned by Public Order or Court Order; Blames Father," FBIS, in Pashto, April 24, 2005. See also, "Afghan Paper Details Circumstances of Stoning Woman for Adultery," FBIS, in Dari, April 24, 2005.
83. Pamela Constable, "A Precarious Shelter in Afghanistan." *Washington Post* (December 2006).
84. "Latest on Women in Afghanistan," *Off Our Backs*, December 2001, 8.
85. "Afghanistan: Former Women's Minister Intimidated," *Human Rights Watch Report*, June 26, 2002.
86. Curtis Matsushige, "Midwives Graduate from Nangarhar University," *Afghanistan Freedom Watch*, August 1, 2005, 5.
87. Farangis Najibullah, "Teen Donation Forms Cornerstone for Girls' Education in Afghan Village," *RFE/RL*, February 8, 2009. Accessed at: http://www.rferl.org/content/Teens_Donation_Forms_Cornerstone_For_Girls_Education_In_Afghan_Village/1377847.html
88. Tanya Goudsouzian and Helena Malikyar, "For Afghan Women, Some Hard Won Successes and an Ongoing Struggle," *RFE/RL*, March 8, 2010. Accessed at: http://www.rferl.org/content/Struggle_And_Success_For_Afghan_Women/1977529.html
89. "UN Study Declares Violence Against Women a Widespread Problem in Afghanistan," *Feminist Daily Wire*, August 17, 2006.
90. "UN Study Declares Violence."
91. "Still a Long Way to Go: Implementation of the Law on Elimination of Violence against Women in Afghanistan," *United Nations Assistance Mission in Afghanistan*, December 2012. Accessed at: http://unama.unmissions.org/LinkClick.aspx?fileticket=Qy9mDiEa5Rw%3D&ta. For earlier reports on the endemic violence against females by UNAMA see "Silence is Violence—End Violence against Women in Afghanistan," *UNAMA*, July 2009. Accessed at: http://unama.unmissions.org/Portals/UNAMA/human%20rights/vaw-english.pdf; "Harmful Traditional Practices and Implementation of the Law on Elimination of Violence against Women in Afghanistan," *UNAMA*, December 2010. Accessed at: http://unama.unmissions.org/Portals/UNAMA/Publication/Harmful%20Traditional%20Practices_English.pdf
92. UNAMA (2012), 3.
93. "Insurgent Violence against Women, Girls in Afghanistan Jumps 20%-UN," *RAWA News*, February 20, 2013. Accessed at: http://www.rawa.org/temp/runews/2013/02/20/insurgent-violence-against-women-girls-in-afghanistan-jumps-20-un.html; "Dozens of Afghan Women, Activists Mark Valentine's Day By Marching against Violence," *Fox News*, February 14, 2013. Accessed at: http://www.foxnews.com/world/2013/02/14/dozens-afghan-women-and-activists-mark-valentine-day-by-marching-against-rising/
94. "UN Report Urges Greater Implementation of Law Protecting Women's Rights in Afghanistan," *UN News Centre*, December 12, 2012. Accessed at: http://www.un.org/apps/news/story.asp?NewsID=43742
95. Sean Carberry, "The Afghan Battle Over a Law to Protect Women," *NPR*, February 20, 2013. Accessed at: http://www.npr.org/2013/02/20/172491435/the-afghan-battle-over-a-law-to-protect-women See also Ali M. Latifi, "Afghan Women in Fight over Rights Law," *Al Jazeera*, May 30, 2013; Sajda Khan, "Conflating Cultural Practices and Islam," *Gulf News*, June 4, 2013.
96. Sean Carberry, "The Afghan Battle over a Law to Protect Women," *HPPR*, February 20, 2013.
97. Carberry, "The Afghan Battle."
98. Lauryn Oates, "Demonstration Planned to Oppose Violence against Women in Afghanistan," *The Propagandist*, June 5, 2013.
99. Emma Graham-Harrison, "Saudi Arabia funding $100m mosque and education centre," *The Guardian*, November 2, 2012. Accessed at: http://www.guardian.co.uk/world/2012/nov/02/saudi-arabia-funding-kabul-mosque
100. A gem of a book on the plight of Afghan women is the edited volume of essays by Jennifer Heath and Ashraf Zahedi, eds. *Land of the Unconquerable: The Lives of Contemporary Afghan Women*. (Berkeley: University of California Press, 2011).
101. "Afghanistan: Women's Rights Trampled Despite New Law," *RAWA News*, March 8, 2010. Accessed at: http://www.irinnews.org/Report.aspx?ReportId=88349; Ahmed Quraishi,

"94 Self Immolation Cases Registered in Western Afghanistan," *RAWA News,* March 28, 2012. Accessed at: http://www.rawa.org/temp/runews/2012/03/28/94-self-immolation-cases-registered-in-western-afghanistan.html

102. Farangis Najibullah, "In Afghanistan, Traditional Values Still Threaten Women's Rights," *RFE/RL.* March 8, 2009. Accessed at: http://www.rferl.org/content/In_Afghanistan_Traditional_Values_Still_Threaten_Womens_Rights_/1506146.html

103. Carolyn Tytler, "Women's Rights in Afghanistan Today," *Associated Content.* February 3, 2009. Accessed at: http://www.helium.com/items/1325024-women-in-afghanistan

104. Skaine, 25; Nancy Hatch Dupree, "Afghan Women under the Taliban," 165–166.

105. For an excellent overview of Afghanistan's "Islamic identity," refer to Thomas Barfield's "Radical Political Islam in an Afghan Context," *Political Transition in Afghanistan,* Asia Program Special Report (Washington, DC: Woodrow Wilson Center), April 2004, 15–18.

III

Iran

Chapter Seven

The Politics of Gender in Iran, 1906–1941

From Constitutional Revolution to Monarchical "Modernization"

> I am extremely delighted that women have become aware of their rights and entitlement. . . . Now women are on their way to gain other rights in addition to the great privilege of motherhood.
> —Reza Shah (1878–1944) speech in 1936 to civil servants upon his return from Turkey

At the start of the twentieth century, Persia[1] was in the throes of social and political turmoil exacerbated by foreign meddling (Great Britain and Russia). The weak Qajar dynasty rule (1794–1925),[2] coupled with its inability to rein in disparate, vying social groups (the tribes, ulema, petty bourgeoisie and bazaaris[3]) all contributed to growing instability and economic hardship for the populace.[4] The widespread social discontent and the perceived "selling out" of Persia to foreign interests exacerbated the growing rift between the Qajar-led state and Persian society.[5] Reza Khan's ascendency from a mere foot soldier in the Qajar Shah's Cossack Brigade in the late nineteenth century to the Royal throne in 1925 was due in no small part to his successful leveraging of the extreme discontent of the population over perceived injustices at the hands of their Qajar rulers. Reza Khan's success in seeking power was also directly attributable to his manipulation of the ulema, whom he skillfully won over with his "Islamic" and nationalist convictions as publicly enunciated to a desperate audience.[6]

The reality—as revealed vis-à-vis state policy once Reza Khan consolidated his hold on power—was a bitter pill for the ulema and others to swallow. Reza Khan's successful deceit of critical social elements as to his real political and social agenda (à la Mustafa Kamal Ataturk of neighboring Turkey[7]) did reflect the self-titled Pahlavi Shah's brilliant diplomatic and political skills in a culture wherein scheming, double dealing, and *taqiyyah* (deception) were an art form. It was the formidable clerical establishment's critical role in the Constitutional Revolution of 1906–1911 which had compelled Reza Khan to woo the ulema. Reza Khan knew that he would need their support if he was to succeed in overthrowing the unpopular Qajar rule. Once in power, now known as Reza Shah, as the self-appointed Pahlavi King (1925–1941), would embark on an ambitious social policy that included the improvement of female status in society often at the expense of the conservative elements such as the ulema, whom he quickly sidelined. In a land where people have long memories, Reza Shah's approach in dealing with the ulema and the conservative bazaaris and landlords (deception, betrayal, and persecution), would come back to haunt his son, Muhammad Reza Pahlavi. Worse, it would lead to his son's overthrow by a "Revolution" led by a charismatic Ayatullah named Ruhollah Khomeini who, like Reza Shah, also deceived the Iranian populace as to his intentions.[8] Throughout the twentieth century, "nationalism" provided the context within which the "appropriate" female position in society would be determined by either the Pahlavi Dynasty or by Khomeini's Fiqh-e-Jafaria theocracy.

WOMEN'S STATUS IN THE LATE QAJAR PERIOD (1890–1925)

The Qajar[9] dynasty's rule was characterized by a weak central administration (the Royal Court), with no real standing army and a heterogeneous warring populace comprised of vying social groups such as the ulema and the tribal elements with their own militias. What is striking is how little power the Qajar Shah was able to exert in the late nineteenth century outside Tehran, the capital. Lacking a significant standing army or bureaucracy (the two pillars of a centralized state), heavily dependent on unreliable tribal levies, and without any means to reach the provinces, the shah was forced to delegate authority to provincial governors, tribal leaders, and other power brokers. Playing an elaborate game of divide and rule just to retain the reins of power, they were unable to have much influence in social and local matters outside of Tehran.

In short, social decision making at the local level remained in the hands of conservative elements that comprised of the ulema and the tribal leadership.[10] It has been written that nineteenth-century Persia witnessed some basic reforms and greater centralized control[11] in order to create a strong state (i.e., royal rule) which could embark on social reforms to overcome Iranian "backwardness."[12] Women, slaves, and minorities continued to be victims of subjugation with limited rights. While slaves and minorities (male) could hope for an improvement of their condition if they were (a) freed (in the case of the slave) or (b) converted to Islam (if a non-Muslim); female status was contingent on a number of factors such as ethnicity, physical location and socioeconomic background.

Societal Diversity and Women's Status in the Late Qajar Period (1896–1925)

Like its neighboring Muslim states, Persian society was diverse in both its socioeconomic and female status spheres. Perceptions, views, and ideals of what constituted the "ideal woman" varied from region to region, ethnic group, religious affiliation, physical occupation, social position, and even between urban and rural dwellers. Throughout its history, Persia's social diversity has meant that its female population never universally enjoyed the tangible benefits from social reforms meant to improve their lives; nor did they—as some sort of monolithic group—equally experience the atrocities, prejudices, hardships, and suffering that were more the norm than any tangible privileges.

Thus the social position of females was not a uniform one in this patriarchal society. There had always existed significant variation in female status. The key determinant of female status across ethnicities and regions lay in their socioeconomic background. There was a direct correlation between social position and individual rights and protections for females. For example, although there were known cases of Kurdish and Baluchi families selling their daughters off due to extreme poverty and desperation; the more affluent Persian families in the urban areas generally ensured that their daughters, wives, sisters, and mothers inherited their share of property as enunciated in Islamic law (Shariah). Daughters from affluent families were often not forced into marriage at a young age, in stark comparison to girls from peasant or nomadic backgrounds. Furthermore, their male kin often ensured that their marriage contracts included favorable provisions for their daughters or sisters. Women affiliated with the local nobility or to powerful tribal groups often exercised enormous power and influence from behind the curtains or walls of the *harem* or women's quarters. For example, Nasir-ud-Din Shah's (1848–1896)[13] mother, Mahde Aliya, played an influential role behind the scenes in her son's political affairs when he was young but lost much of her influence once he matured.[14] Women of the Royal Court—a minority—did not have to endure backbreaking labor in the fields or within the family compounds. But they did experience being confined and guarded by the eunuchs within the walls of their *mahals* (palaces). Although the less affluent females enjoyed greater mobility; they also endured lives of constant misery and hardship characterized by unrelenting workloads.[15] A deep social chasm existed between these two groups as it always had.

Most women in Persia were second-class citizens with limited, if any, rights such as to inheritance or to obtain a basic education. There, however, were some notable distinctions even among those living in poverty. For example, tribal and nomadic groups (like the Kurds, Bakhtiari, Qashqai) allowed their women to interact with men to a certain extent and even some considered polygamy and *mu'ta* (Shia temporary marriage) as undesirable.[16] Yet within these same tribes, child marriage was not uncommon, with girls younger than the age of puberty being married off. As mentioned earlier, some young girls in certain communities were even sold off in acts of financial desperation by their families. Furthermore, most of the tribes in Persia did not honor Islam's position on inheritance which stipulated that females had the right to half of what her brother inherited. Therefore, although females living in tribal communities were not forced into strict veiling and segregation by their male folk, in stark contrast to the more affluent urban court affiliated females; they were at an economic disadvantage vis-à-vis inheritance and the ability to own property.[17] In some rural areas, especially along the Caspian Sea regions of Mazandaran and Gilan, rural women moved around freely in bright clothes and no black chadors in comparison to rural women in other regions such as Yazd and Qom, where they had to wear headscarves at a minimum or the all-enveloping black chador and led secluded lives engaged in carpet weaving and handicrafts.

Enforcement of Shariah was also sporadic and uneven across social groups when it came to gender issues. Polygamy was pervasive in the more affluent communities. Women's right to inheritance according to Shariah were unevenly enforced in the more affluent groups; while social prestige was determined by placement in the social hierarchy of one's family. For example, in a census carried out in Tehran during the reign of Nasir-ud-Din (1848–1896), Tehrani women ranked (from highest to lowest) as follows: royal women, respectable women, wives of merchants, wives of shopkeepers, nannies, maids, and black concubines.[18]

Even women who occupied the highest social strata as members of the royal—Qajar—family did not enjoy identical rights. Their status within their relatively small social circle was not only determined by the status of their father or husband or even brothers, but also by their "social skills" and intellect to navigate the social complexities of daily harem life. A life often characterized by scheming, machinations, and even diplomacy among the wives and other family members. The favorite wife or mother of a powerful figure (generally male) was effectively able to navigate the politics of harem life with her sharp intellect, cunning, and social ability and often enjoyed significant influence to include matters involving the affairs of the state. For example, Fatemeh, also known as Anis ud-Dawleh, who was Nasir ud-Din's favorite wife, exerted a lot of influence over the shah and also within the Royal Court to the extent that she indirectly influenced matters of the state.[19] Fath Ali Shah, the second Qajar ruler (1794–1834), relied on two of his daughters, Khazen ud-Dawleh and Anis ud-Dawleh, as his trusted secretaries and advisors. Women of the royal harem often were highly educated for their times through private tutoring within the palace in religious studies, literature, and music.

Women who belonged to the working classes generally worked at home as seamstresses, spinners, and weavers or were employed as maids, nannies, servants, healers, preachers, matchmakers. Some women worked in public baths; while others played music and sang in mostly female gatherings. Prostitution was widespread as a source of income for many impoverished females.[20]

Some social norms universally shared by all social groups irrespective of ethnicity or locale vis-à-vis female status within her community, included the local politics of one's village or town. The placement of one's family in the village or town's pecking order also determined female status. As in the broader Middle East, the number of sons a woman gave birth to was an important determinant as to her power or status within the family and/or tribe. The more sons a woman produced, the greater her influence and power within her family/community. Women who failed to produce any sons—or worse, those who produced no offspring at all—were often divorced or mistreated and ridiculed.

The Role of the Ulema in the Anti-Qajar Movement and Women's Status

The Qajar rulers—unlike the Safavids (1502–1736)—were less conciliatory toward the ulema as they sought to "Westernize" Persian society, and limit the power and influence of the clergy, who then sought and established new centers of power outside the boundaries of the Persian state in Najaf and Karbala in present-day Iraq.[21] Furthermore, the increased meddling of competing Western powers (Russia and Great Britain) in the nineteenth century served to exacerbate the growing conflict between the Qajar Shah, Nasir-ud-Din (1848–1896), and the clerics. The clerical establishment grew increasingly alarmed by both the weakness and willingness of Nasir-ud-Din to make major economic and trade concessions to infidel powers at the expense of fellow Persians and mother Persia.

The clergy's patience came to an end when the Qajar state granted a generous tobacco concession to one British company in 1890 in return for cash. Nasir ud-Din had secretly granted a monopoly over the production, sale, and export of a key cash crop, tobacco, which affected the livelihoods of a large number of landlords, merchants, and shopkeepers.[22] When this deal was exposed, Muslim activists like Jamal al Din al Afghani[23] (1838–1897) expressed that he "reserved his strongest hatred for the Shah," whom he accused of weakening Islam by granting concessions to Europeans and squandering the money earned thereby. His agitation against the shah is thought to have been one of the "fountain-heads" of the successful 1891 public protest against the granting a tobacco monopoly to a British company.[24]

What is significant about the social opposition to the Tobacco Concessions of 1890 is (a) the dominant social forces on an economic matter were the *ulema* and not the *bazaaris*; (b) the level of social congruence on the issue, and (c) the shah reversed himself on social reforms to appease the ulema. During this rebellion, the clerics took center stage in instigating and promoting the rebellion and pressuring social groups to comply with the "voluntary" abstinence from tobacco products. Even women in the urban areas, who were traditionally wary or hostile toward the clergy, enthusiastically supported the ulema's lead role in this social rebellion. The shutdown of the bazaar in Shiraz in April 1891 after the British company personnel arrived was quickly and voluntarily followed by other similar closures in the bazaars of other major cities thanks to the new telegraph system. This general strike was legitimized with the issuance of a fatwa from the clerics that prohibited the use of any tobacco by the citizens. This boycott was widely supported by women from all socioeconomic walks of life and, importantly, even members of the shah's own harem supported this boycott. It was the women of the harem who eventually convinced Nasir-ud-Din to annul the foreign concession and to revise certain social programs in order to placate his furious ulema.[25]

As a consequence of this major public humiliation and due to the growing discontent of the powerful ulema and bazaaris, Nasir-ud-Din reversed some of his reformist policies to appease these forces. Previously he had been a proponent for the establishment of schools; now he forbade the opening of new schools and even turned a blind eye when a religious mob burned down a modern teaching establishment in Tabriz. The reformist Malkum Khan's famous newspaper *Qanun* was outlawed. Nasir-ud-Din restricted government scholarships for study abroad and even prohibited his citizens, to include his own family members, from visiting Europe as he boasted that he wanted his ministers to not know whether Brussels was a place or a cabbage. He also sought to shut down many teahouses in Tehran on the pretext that these were dens of "idleness and storytellers."[26]

The Impact of the 1906–1911 Constitutional Revolution on Women's Social Position

The Constitutional Movement, which ultimately became the Constitutional Revolution of 1906–1911, led to institutional limits on Qajar rule by effectively curtailing power under a Constitutional Monarchical System.[27] The main struggle between the shah and the *Majlis* (Parliament) evolved around the future structure of the government. The deputies in the majlis, working with a translation of the Belgian Constitution, formulated a document called "The Supplementary Fundamental Laws" which contained two sections. The first was a "Bill of Rights" which guaranteed citizens equality before the law, protection of life, property and honor, safeguards from arbitrary arrest, and freedom to publish newspapers and to organize associations. The second section concentrated power in the legislative branch (the Majlis) at the expense of the Executive Branch (the shah, his prime minister, and his ministers).[28]

The Constitutional Revolution of 1906 had introduced new (Western) concepts to the people of Persia such as freedom, social justice, equality, and popular sovereignty in stark contrast to their traditional religio-patriarchic social structure. Ironically, although this movement shared a vision of Iran which was independent of meddling by foreign powers (Russia and Britain), it encompassed values, norms, and ideas borrowed from these detested foreign entities. The ulema—threatened by the propagation of such "un-Islamic" ideas—worked behind the scenes to temper their influence on the written constitution by successfully demanding the inclusion of a Supplementary Basic Law which required that legislation issued by the Majlis must conform to *Shariah* (Islamic) law.[29] This supplementary law to placate the ulema was not implemented but its mere presence within the written constitution ensured a certain degree of caution by the Majlis in enacting laws (especially on controversial subjects that included female roles and status in a Muslim society) that were not perceived by the ulema as being "un-Islamic." Thus, more often than not, women became the sacrificial lamb in order to appease the ulema.[30]

This civil society based process, though led by the well-connected and influential ulema, was broad based and represented an alliance of strange urban bedfellows which included the Shia clergy, the bazaaris, and the secular intelligentsia. Participation in this movement included women who, for the first time, were able to actively participate as political activists against state entities. This involvement by women's groups led to the emergence of the women's movement which was supported by the Constitutionalists.[31] Despite varying degrees of clerical opposition, the social efforts to bring the monarchy under constitutional control included an ongoing discussion on the subject of women's emancipation as being an intrinsic component of this march toward democracy and a greater voice for the people in the political affairs of the state. Women from the lower and middle classes took part in street demonstrations and riots and enthusiastically supported the clergy; while women from more affluent backgrounds focused on educational activities, founded and joined secret societies, as well as wrote and presented speeches and lectured on constitutionalism and female emancipation. Their support of the clergy was more tactical and circumstantial.[32] While at this stage the women's movement was indistinguishable from the struggle of the Constitutionalists, their involvement (even though the numbers were small) in the process marked the beginning of a new era for women and opened the way to broader activism as females sought greater educational opportunities, the right to vote and so on.

The Women's Movement and Female Status at the End of Qajar Rule, 1911–1925

Emboldened and energized by the perceived political gains made during the Constitutional Revolution, women mobilized in establishing their own media networks rather than remaining mere contributors to liberal journals owned and managed by men. In 1910, the first women's newspaper *Danesh* (Knowledge) was published by Mrs Kahal. It was an eight-page weekly that addressed various women's issues.[33] In 1913, Mrs. Maryam Amid Mozayen-ol-Saltaneh founded *Shokufeh* (Blossom) newspaper as well as a women's organization called *Anjoman Khavatin Irani* (Iranian Women's Society). Its objective was "the promotion of Iranian goods, promotion of art, industry, education, science and art among women." Membership in the Iranian Women's Society reached 5,000 within a few weeks of its founding; while *Shokufeh* continued to be published until Mrs Saltaneh's death in 1919. This journal covered a range of topics of interest to women: literature, education, female attitudes, child marriage, housekeeping, childrearing and "elevating women's moral standards."[34] In 1920, *Nameye Banovan* (Women's Letter) was established by Shahnaz Azad to publish on subjects that were of interest to women and its slogan was: "Women are men's first teachers." It published for a year before being banned for advocating abolishment of the veil.

Two more newspapers for women were established in 1921. Fakhr Afagh Parsa founded *Jahan Zanan* (Women's World) in Mashad with the support of her husband. While it tried to be careful not to offend the clergy, the publication of a letter from a Kermani woman led to it being banned. The letter implied that the clergy had a vested interest in keeping females ignorant. This led to Mrs Parsa being exiled to the more liberal Tehran, where she tried to publish this paper only to have it banned. *Alam Nesvan* (Women's Universe) was founded in 1921 by the Associated of the Graduates of the American Girls' School. Approximately forty pages in length it explained its objective: Assisting the elevation and progress of women; encouraging them to serve their country and family, and improve their education.[35]

In its thirteen years of existence, *Alam Nesvan* printed many articles on the plight of women in Iran and the detrimental impact of seclusion and purdah on women's status and rights as productive members of society. During the period of turmoil and political repression (1911–1917), women's activists made previously unimaginable gains which served to embolden them to seek more concessions from the state. Their contribution—whether in joining public protest marches against foreign meddling or publishing newspapers or journals—gave them a confidence and optimism (for the future). It inspired woman like Sedigheh Doulatabadi to become a political activist. Doulatabadi first affiliated with the National Ladies' Society in 1911 and would continue to work for social reforms to improve female status until her death in 1961. She established women's organization and published newspapers like *Zaban Zanan* (Women's Language) which were quickly banned, reopened, and banned again. Returning from France after obtaining a degree in Psychology in 1927, Doulatabadi refused to wear the veil and walked around Tehran in European clothes and a hat.[36]

One of the most significant outcomes from the drafting of the Constitution was Article 19 of the Supplementary Fundamental Law, which was liberally interpreted by Prime Minister Vosugh ud-Douleh to require the implementation of public education for females. Naser ud-Douleh, the Cabinet Minister for Cultural Affairs, announced the decision to open public (state) schools for girls. Ten public schools were opened and this was quickly followed by the establishment of the first Teachers' Training College for Women. Predictably, these actions by the state were opposed by some clergy who condemned this meddling. Despite clerical opposition to female access to a secular (state established) education, many public schools for girls were first opened in Tehran. By the 1920s, thousands of girls were attending public and private schools in Tehran. However, this was not the case in the more conservative provinces where the clergy and the tribal elements often had more sway as to whether or not girls could attend such (secular) schools.

The activism of women and their support base during the last days of Qajar rule can be characterized as one primarily driven by urban elites and middle classes. The rise of the labor movement in Persia, plus the establishment and influence of socialist and communist elements in the political process, led to participation by the working (primarily urban) poor in the fledgling women's movement. Studies on the backgrounds of the leaders of both the Communist and Socialist parties, however, reveal that they overwhelmingly represented the urban professional middle class.[37] While a study on the socioeconomic composition of the leaders/founders of women's organizations and publications shows that all came from upper and middle class backgrounds, were educated and had educated fathers and husbands.[38]

Reza Khan's Social Views and His Co-option of the Ulema, 1921–1925

Although the ulema helped pave the way for Reza Shah's assumption of power as he first tried to consolidate his position as Prime Minister and Minister of War of an "Iranian Republic," he was never comfortable with this relationship. Personally, Reza Shah was not a religious man and was in fact hostile toward the ulema and suspicious of their constant meddling in the affairs of state and viewed them as an obstacle to "modernization." But cognizant of the crucial role they played in "king making" and also in legitimizing political entities, he displayed an obedient, even at times subservient, manner toward them. Once convinced that the ulema would never support the establishment of a republic in lieu of monarchical rule; he encouraged them to remove the Qajar dynasty via the Majlis, but to retain a constitutional monarchy with himself as the shah of a new Pahlavi dynasty. Reza Shah astutely couched all his actions in Islamic and nationalistic terms. He honored the ulema at religious festivals and made pilgrimages to holy Shia shrines in order to curry favor and gain the Persian throne.[39] As soon as the Majlis deputies passed a bill that deposed the Qajars and entrusted the state to Reza (now called Reza Pahlavi), he banned all sale of alcohol, reduced bread prices, outlawed gambling, exhorted women to uphold "national honor," and promised to enforce moral conduct. He also proclaimed that his two ambitions in life were to attain peace for his people and implement the true laws of "sacred Islam."[40] Once crowned "shah," Reza Shah would quickly shift gears and move to break the powerful hold of the clergy and other social entities that threatened his power and consolidation efforts as he sought to move Persia into the twentieth century a la Mustafa Kemal's model (known as Ataturk or Father of Turkey) in neighboring Turkey.

EMERGENCE OF THE PAHLAVI DYNASTY AND WOMEN'S STATUS (1925–1941)

With the assumption of power by Reza Khan in 1925 as the first Pahlavi Shah, the emancipation of women became one of the cornerstones of his "modernization" program to bring Persia into the twentieth century by embarking on an ambitious program of social, cultural and economic reforms.[41] In order to replicate Mustafa Kamal's (Ataturk) bold modernization schemes in Turkey, Reza Shah knew he would have to co-opt both the ulema and the conservative landed aristocracy, not to mention the tribal elements, through the creation of a strong centralized state structure. He believed that lasting reforms were impossible even if implemented by the state, unless it had the mechanisms in place to implement comprehensive reforms. Reza Shah moved to build a strong army while simultaneously putting down socialist revolts in Gilan and Azerbaijan. Tribal rebellions too were militarily crushed and these actions won him the critical support of the Majlis. As Reza Shah accelerated the process of secularizing state institutions (education and the judiciary), he encountered resistance from the clerical establishment who rightly viewed his efforts as an attempt to encroach on turf that was traditionally within their sphere of influence. The increasingly vocal women's movement became more structured and organized during Reza Shah's reign. Their demands, however, were not opposed by the secular political parties (socialists, communists and the revivalists). These included a right to an education, abolition of child marriages, segregation and polygamy. Their primary opposition came from the ulema and the traditional elements (bazaaris, landed class and tribal segments). During this period, all of these hot button issues would be addressed, but female education would be the arena in which most progress would be made.

STATE INITIATED SOCIAL REFORM: "MODERNIZATION" POLITICS AND SOCIAL RESPONSE

Once Reza Shah Pahlavi consolidated his position at the helm of the Persian state (which he would rename "Iran" in 1935), he initiated a number of social reforms but never developed some sort of blueprint or roadmap on how the state would proceed on gender relations/matters. But his long-term goal—undoubtedly influenced by Ataturk next door—was to rebuild Iran in the image of the West which was ironic given his strong animosity toward the West and anger at perceived Western meddling and intrigue in Iran's internal affairs. He waged his secularization war on many fronts: secularization of the judicial process (modified versions of French and Italian Penal Codes); prohibition of Shia demonstrations on Ashura (to include self-flagellation processions) in the holy month of Muharram; opening up of mosques to foreign tourists; denying exit visas to Iranians wishing to make the Haj pilgrimage to Mecca or even pilgrimage to Shia holy sites like Karbela and Najaf; and banning of the veil.[42] Reza Shah's assault on the clergy did not exclude junior clerics like Ruhollah Khomeini who was content to go along with the passive attitude of much of the clergy, which included adoption of the Shia process of *taqiyya* or dissimulation in times of danger or threat.[43]

Reza Shah's efforts to raise the status of women accelerated following his visit to Turkey in 1934, where Mustafa Kemal was busy implementing drastic social changes over the protestations of many conservative Turks, especially in the rural areas. Fascinated by what he had heard of Turkey's progress under Ataturk, his visit only confirmed his favorable impressions. Upon his return at the bordertown of Maku, Reza Shah stated: "We have been to meet a very great man. We must bring our people to the same level of development and progress as his."[44]

By the 1930s—and especially following his trip to Turkey in 1934—Reza Shah's about-turn behavior completely bewildered the clergy who had been his steadfast supporters in ensuring him the throne in 1925. In their eyes, he had not only betrayed their and the Iranian peoples' trust, but had insulted Allah and Islam. Under constant assault by the Pahlavi state, clerics like Khomeini moderated their sermons and Khomeini moved his lectures to more obscure sites to avoid the wrath of the Shah's police. The mullahs not only witnessed the wrestling away of their traditional sources of power and influence (family and social affairs such as marriage registration, divorce, etc.) but were forced to be "re-trained" if they wanted to practice shariah jurisprudence now supervised by the Ministry of Justice. To them it seemed that Reza Shah had turned completely against the clerical establishment and, worse, he seemed to be against Islam itself. Over time they became convinced that he was out to both destroy and humiliate them as well: Reza Shah decreed that all men (including the mullahs) had to wear European hats and clothes.[45] Only those clergy who were qualified as mojtaheds were allowed to wear their traditional attire. Educational institutions like Tehran University were now required to be coeducational (a hot button issue for the clerics). Any public site caught discriminating against women such as cafes, hotels, or movie theatres were slapped a heavy fine. But it was the outlawing of the veil that really shocked the clerical establishment and other conservative elements of society such as the traditional bazaaris, etc. Officially, the ban on the veil (especially the traditional chador, which covered a woman from head to toe) went into effect on February 1, 1936. After this date, any officials of the Ministry of Finance were subject to dismissal if their wives were caught wearing the chador. Women wearing the chador were no longer allowed into movie theaters or public baths and taxi cabs and bus drivers were liable to be fined if they accepted veiled women as passengers.[46]

Reza Shah's first wife, Tadj ol-Molouk, was the first queen of Persia to seek a public role for herself, and to have performed an official position out in public. She was instrumental in the abolition of the veil in Iran during the reign of her husband. At Nowruz (New Year) 1928, the Queen Mother visited the shrine at Qom wearing only a light chador instead of the traditional black one and was criticized by the one of the ulema present. When he heard about the incident, an enraged Reza Shah immediately went to Qom, strode into the shrine without removing his boots, and beat the offender with his riding crop.[47] In the winter of 1934, Reza Shah demanded the presence of the Queen and his two daughters in an official ceremony at the Teheran Teacher's College. All three were present at this ceremony and were dressed in Western clothes, without a veil. This was the first time an Iranian queen had showed herself in public unveiled and in foreign attire. Afterward, the Shah had pictures of his wife and daughters published, much to the horror of the traditional aristocracy.

On January 8, 1936, Reza Shah arrived at the Normal School, where the Queen Mother was to distribute the diplomas to female graduates of the Faculty of Medicine and other schools. Neither the Queen Mother nor the princesses wore the chador. Reza Shah delivered a speech to an invited audience of unveiled teachers and wives of civil servants:

> I am extremely delighted to see that women have become aware of their rights and entitlement. . . . Women of this country not only could not (before unveiling) demonstrate their talents and inherent qualities because of being separated from society. . . . We must never forget that one-half of the population of our country has not been taken into account, that is to say, one-half of the country's working force has been idle. Future prosperity is in your hands (because you) train the future generations. You can be good teachers to train good individuals.[48]

But state pressure to "unveil" began to be applied from 1934 onward to various members of society: high-ranking officials risked being removed from office unless they brought their wives unveiled to office parties. Even low-ranking government employees like drivers, road sweepers, risked fines unless they paraded their unveiled wives through the main streets and bazaars.[49] In 1934, women teachers and female students were first allowed, and then ordered, to appear in school without the chador. Worse, in the clergy eyes, women were forced to leave their homes without their veils and those caught wearing one in public were made to discard them or pay a heavy fine by the police who strictly enforced these laws in the streets.[50] A European wife of an Iranian man witnessed police on the streets of Tehran "tearing scarves from the women's heads and handing them back in ribbons to their owners."[51] After 1936, cinema houses and public baths were closed to women who wore the veil. The law forbade bus and taxi drivers to accept veiled women as passengers. While educated women belonging to the urban elite rejoiced as such measures, the majority of women felt disgraced and humiliated.[52] Enforcement, however, was sporadic at times or halfhearted (especially in the conservative regions) at best. In such a conservative Muslim society, where veiling (especially among the elites and nobility) had been enforced for centuries, this decree to most Iranians who were traditionally conservative was the equivalent of asking their women to walk around naked. It violated personal and family honor and was so unpopular (until mandatory veiling was abolished in 1941 when Reza Shah went into exile) that many older women chose to remain within the confines of their home than risk humiliation and embarrassment. Sattareh Farman Farmaian writes in her memoir on the impact Reza Shah's outlawing of the veil had on the women of the old Persian aristocracy: "For a Persian aristocrat to allow strange men to gape at his wives in public was shameful in the extreme. To my mother, it was exactly as if he (Reza Shah) had insisted that she parade naked in the street."[53]

In some homes women decided to remain confined to their homes for years, while prominent clerics prevented their daughters from attending school as a result. Reza Baraheni recalls the crisis in his family when unveiling became law: "Since there were no showers in Iranian homes, women had to go to a public bath. The husband would put his wife in a large sack and carry her like a bale of cotton to the bath. I remember from my childhood, when my father would carry his mother in a sack, empty his load at the bath, then come back for his wife. He once told me that Reza Shah's policeman had asked him what it was that he was carrying. He had improvised an answer: pistachio nuts. The policeman said, 'let me have some,' and started tickling Granny. First she laughed, and then she wiggled her way out of the sack and took to her heels. My father was arrested."[54]

Reza Shah's precipitous social reforms lead to a crisis of identity for his people, especially women. On the one hand, he advocated a nationalist agenda free of foreign (read: Western) interference and an emphasis on Iran's pre-Islamic glory; while on the other he pushed to enforce Western dress styles and social customs. In addition to forced unveiling, the state expected urban women to conform to a Western aesthetics of the body. Unveiled women could have been allowed to wear loose and colorful clothes worn in provinces like Gilan. Instead, they were ordered in cities like Tehran to wear Western dress. Many impoverished women did not have the resources to buy such clothes nor the skills to make them and were placed in a desperate situation which they resented. Even stranger, in a place trying to emphasize its uniqueness and great past, these newly unveiled women were also expected to replicate the walk, talk and interaction of modern Western life, which was especially enforced by the elite who resorted to social ostracism of those who failed to comply within their social circle. Overnight, men and women began to pay closer attention to women's gestures, height, and bodily dimensions, which was applied to scrutinize an unmarried girl's eligibility for marriage.[55]

The mullahs were incensed but felt outgunned and out maneuvered by the shah for whenever one of their members publicly complained or objected to women walking around unveiled as being contrary to the teachings of their beloved faith, they were humiliated and/or even punished. For example, when one mullah condemned the shah for allowing his female members to appear in public unveiled, he was publicly humiliated by having his turban forcibly removed in public and the shaving of his head and beard.[56] The ulema's response to the unpopular unveiling measures was best summed up as follows: "Bloodied and bruised in its battles with Reza Shah, the ulema essentially retreated from politics."[57]

Reza Shah's best, and least controversial, policies involved developing Iran's educational system and improving access to educational institutions for its female populace.[58] His educational reforms were impressive and opened up equal access to education for girls as education became compulsory for both boys and girls. Although determined to purge Iran of Arab and European influences in the Persian language, he did not go as far as Ataturk did in Turkey and retained the use of the Arabic script for the traditional alphabet and spelling. He even decreed that Latin lettering not be publicly displayed, for example, on movie posters, store signs, and in schools.

Between 1925 and 1941, the annual allocations for education increased in real terms by as much as twelvefold. The budget allocated to education was 2 to 5 percent of the national budget during the period 1927–1941.[59] In 1925, there were around 55,960 children enrolled in 648 modern primary schools administered by state officials, private boards, religious communities, or foreign missionaries. By 1941, there were more than 287,245 children in 2,336 modern primary schools, almost all administered by the Ministry of Education. Meanwhile, the enrollment in the traditional maktabs rose slightly from 28,949 to 37,287. In 1925, 14,488 studied in 74 modern secondary schools, 16 of which were missionary institutions. By 1941, 28,194 studied in 110 private and 241 in state secondary schools, modeled after the French lycee system. In 1930, the number of state schools for girls in the entire country was 73 and there were 145 private schools for girls. A total of 16,328 girls were being educated in schools and 9,732 were learning to read and write in the maktabs. The Ministry of Education expected girls to enroll in physical education classes and school girls marched en masse in public parades.[60]

During this same period, the number of theology students in the traditional madrassas declined sharply from 5,984 to 785.[61] This decline in enrollment in what had traditionally been a sought after stepping stone to a coveted clerical position was indicative of how quickly and precipitously the clerical establishment's traditionally powerful social position had fallen. It suggests that pragmatic (read: economic) interests had been a powerful incentive in a poverty stricken region when it came to seeking a religious education. How did these declining numbers in the cleric producing industry (the madrassas) impact female status? The decline in influence of the clerics on society correlated with the relaxation of the more draconian stipulations of shariah and a more permissible atmosphere vis-à-vis a number of female issues like access to education and "respectable" work opportunities. Traditional home environments, and the need to "maintain honor," still acted as restraints on female behavior irrespective of the mullahs' power.

During Reza Shah's reign there was an unprecedented increase in higher education. In 1925, there were fewer than six hundred students in the country's six institutions of higher learning: in the Colleges of Medicine, Agriculture, Teacher's Training, Law, Literature, and Political Science. In 1934, these six were consolidated to form Tehran University. When Tehran University was consolidated, the shah insisted—against the expectations of the university officials—that female students should be admitted to all classes. Of the twelve women who took up this offer, almost all went on to hold important positions in education, medicine, and public affairs.[62] In the late 1930s, five new colleges were added: Dentistry, Pharmacology, Veterinary Medicine, Fine Arts, and Science and Technology. By 1941, there were over 3,300 enrolled in the eleven colleges of Tehran University and there were also thirty-six Teachers' Training Colleges. The numbers of Iranians sent overseas for higher education were impressive as well as unprecedented: prior to 1929, only a small number of affluent Persians went abroad for education. In 1929, the government decided to finance one hundred new scholarships each year to Europe. By 1940, over 500 of these graduates had returned and another 450 students were completing their studies. By 1941, ministers were training almost 3,200 employees in technical schools and the Education Ministry was teaching 173,907 adults in evening literacy classes. Yet, despite these improvements in the educational system, the vast majority (over 90 percent) of the rural population remained illiterate.[63]

Women found employment opportunities in the civil service open to them but contingent on mandatory unveiling. These government opportunities were concentrated in the fields of teaching and midwifery.[64] Under the Ministry of Health, a three-year training course was set up in the newly established government hospital. Female teachers were paid half as much as men. Some women managed to gain access to new middle class professions as foreign companies were the first to employ women as clerks and typists, a trend which replicated by other firms and later government departments.[65]

WOMEN'S LEGAL STATUS DURING REZA SHAH'S REIGN

If one examines Reza Shah's actions divorced from the social realities of Iran in the 1920s and 1930s, it can be argued that Reza Shah's approach to female empowerment seemed to be more show than substance. According to Paidar: "Reza Shah fell short of introducing comprehensive legal rights for women not because he feared the clergy, but because he faced consensus in preserving the fundamental aspects of patriarchy rather than its overthrow . . . the project . . . *was to bring modernity to Iran through the establishment of a secular nation state based on 'Iranian culture' rather than Islam.* Within this project, the familial position of women as advocated in the 'Iranian culture' and 'Islam' happened to be more or less the same. Social conservatism coincided perfectly with the Shii shariat."[66]

Given Reza Shah's intimate understanding of Persian culture and his willingness to leverage it to further his interests (and by extension the interests of Persia as *he* saw them), it can also be postulated that he was working toward female empowerment by limiting controversial measures involving family law which would have lead to extensive social blowback. Thus, in the legal realm—the arena that counted the most vis-à-vis female empowerment and protection under the law—the pre-Reza Shah status quo prevailed in matters pertaining to the family.

The secularization of the judicial system did not include matters related to family law. Existing customs and traditions on family matters such as inheritance, marriage, and divorce remained in place based on Shariah law as interpreted by religious judges (qadis) overseen by the Ministry of Justice.[67] Reza Shah dissolved the religious courts and had family law codified between 1928 and 1935 as part of the Iranian Civil Code, but polygamy was not legally abolished. Men could take up to four wives (Reza Shah was a polygamist) and could divorce at will which in essence contradicted Reza Shah's public enunciations on the need for gender equality.[68]

The new Civil Code of 1931 contained 1,335 articles of which 100 were devoted to the family. These articles covered wills, marriage and divorce, legitimacy and custody, guardianship and child maintenance.[69] On the subject of marriage, the Civil Code specified a number of rules within the framework of a polygamous family. Article 1091 involved women's dowries: a woman's social worth was assessed by her family background, status, personal qualities and the local traditions of the area in which she was raised. The minimum age of marriage was specified as fifteen for females and eighteen for males. Article 1062 required both parties to give their consent to marriage. Articles 1042–1043 required the woman to obtain her father or grandfather's permission before contracting her first marriage. Article 1040 gave both parties the right to request a medical certificate from the other. Articles 1059–1060 prohibited Muslim women from marrying non-Muslim men and made marriage of women to other nationals conditional on government approval. Article 1105 recognized the husband as head of the household and put responsibility for the wife's maintenance on him. Articles 1075–1077 on *sigheh* (temporary) marriages permitted the husband to take an unlimited number of temporary wives, each for a period of one hour to ninety-nine years.[70]

On the dissolution of marriage, Article 1133 stipulated that divorce is the right of the husband. Article 1134 specified that the husband could divorce his wife at will without having to give a reason. Divorce could take place either in the presence of two male witnesses or by proxy. The woman was not required to be present when divorce was taking place or have any knowledge of it. Article 1139 stated that a husband could renounce the unexpired period of sigheh. Articles 1121–1132 provided grounds for women to seek divorce from their spouses. These included the failure of the husband to maintain his wife and perform his (unspecified) duties and if he is insane. If a husband has a venereal disease, the wife could not be granted a divorce but was entitled to refuse to have sexual relations with him (Article 1127). Articles 1146–1147 detailed how a woman could buy her divorce by forfeiting her *mehrieh* (dowry).[71]

The new laws on child custody, guardianship, and maintenance stipulated that the custody of the child belonged to the father after a daughter reached the age of seven and a son the age of two. Until then custody belonged to the mother on behalf of the father (Article 1169). Financial responsibility for the children remained with the father or paternal grandfather and uncles (Articles 1199–1203). Article 860 stipulated if a mother remarried during the period she was not allowed to keep the children, custody would immediately transfer to the father. In inheritance matters (mirroring Shariah stipulations), the Civil Code specified that daughters should inherit half of what sons did (Article 907), mother would inherit one-third of their child's estate and fathers' two-thirds (Article 906). Article 940 prohibited a sigheh wife from inheriting from her husband but her children had the same rights as those of the permanent wife. Articles 927–938 stated that a permanent wife received one-eighth of the husband's estate if she was the only wife and had children. But if she had no children, she only received a quarter of the one-eighth. Co-wives received a proportion of one-eighth if they had children and a quarter if they did not. Articles 1197–1200 placed the burden of caring for elderly and/or destitute parents on the children.[72]

The Civil Code articles on family matters were supplemented in 1937 by the Marriage Act of Iran. The most significant impact of this provision was that it protected a woman's marital status in writing and placed it under civil jurisdiction in the event of a divorce or potential inheritance disputes. It did this by making the registration of all marriages, divorces, and deaths in the state notary offices mandatory. This function traditionally had been under the jurisdiction of the powerful Shia clergy and gave them enormous influence in familial matters. The 1937 Marriage Act also stipulated punishment for failure to comply with the minimum age of marriage for women. In 1933, an act had been passed that allowed religious minorities to abide by their own personal laws on matters concerning family and personal issues. Thus, women from these minorities were not mandated to observe the stipulations of the 1937 act.[73]

SOCIAL RESISTANCE TO GENDER POLICIES AND THE STATE'S RESPONSE

One could argue that by moving precipitously in banning the veil (a protection against predatory males for many women which allowed them greater physical mobility), Reza Shah inadvertently limited a more active female participation in national programs and institutions. Although the demand for banning the veil was raised by male and female reformers during the Constitutional Revolution, and in the late 1920s educated women found ways to challenge the practice of veiling in a variety of ways, the fact remained that for the overwhelmingly majority of women in a predominantly conservative agrarian rural society, this was an unnecessary hot button issue. In their minds, it was a pet project of tainted (i.e., Westernized) influential individuals in Tehran.

The mullahs and ulema who had been co-opted—and were furious at their handpicked "shah" and themselves for having fallen for his deceit—by and large remained quietly subservient or disengaged from events involving controversial "modernization" (read: Westernization/un-Islamic) pet projects that—in their minds—included the public humiliation and enticement to "immoral" behavior of Iran's female populace in a traditional Muslim society. Iranian culture regarded the protection of females' dignity and virtue as the cornerstone of a family's reputation. Thus, as important implementers/overseers of public behavior, the clerics believed that a society which allowed what was perceived as a loss of this gender "status" equaled a failure to preserve family honor. It can be surmised that the reason for the muted response by this historically influential (and vocal) social group had much to do with Reza Shah's willingness to leave no stone unturned in order to humiliate, punish, and diminish the status of members of the clerical establishment who dared to challenge his vision of what a "modern" Iran should look like: one in which women would play an important public role.

The traditional middle classes and rural populace also resisted this controversial intrusion by Reza Shah's state into matters involving a sensitive subject: behavior of their female members. The bazaaris, landowners, traditional aristocracy, and tribal chiefs, all more or less, despised the Shah's meddling to force their women to unveil, work outside the homes and so on. In the educational sphere, however, most went along with the mandatory education of their daughters but resisted the idea of co-educational facilities. Most of those opposing the Shah's gender policies were not encumbered or directly impacted as implementation of these "female emancipation" measures were sporadically and selectively implemented and thus had no direct bearing on the lives of most Iranian women during the sixteen-year reign of Reza Shah.

Even the (almost exclusively urban based) reformists, the communists, the socialists, and many feminists in Iran were not pleased that Reza Shah's gender-related "modernization" measures did not go far enough. To many of them, Reza Shah seemed to be trying to have the best of both worlds at the expense of women and their societal supporters when he continued to support (and practice) polygamy and temporary marriages even when it was increasingly unpopular among those segments of society that could afford such measures. Some argue that his own marital habits reflected a man who was determined (through consequent marriages) to improve his social position and felt no need to limit such privileges of Iranian men who sought to increase their power at home and in society.[74]

CONCLUSION

Although Reza Shah encouraged female education and employment outside the home in the fields of nursing and education, he did not give them the right to vote, run for public office, have custody of their children in the event of a divorce, or even obtain a passport without their husbands' permission. As Sattareh Farman Farmaian observes, Reza Shah's public enunciations and efforts to "emancipate" women was more about appearances than any meaningful substance.[75] His policies, it can be argued, ended up hurting Iranian women's status rather than improving it as they covered areas/issues which were controversial and/or inflammatory (such as dress code) and even humiliating to many women (ban on veiling). Worse, they failed to offer women genuine protections from injustice of say a cruel marriage or women's access to their children in the event they were divorced. According to one Persian scholar (Afary): "The regime scrapped laws and customs that violated its new modernist concept of a housewife and mother, but reaffirmed women's sexual subordination."[76] Although some scholars have argued that Reza Shah's controversial and precipitous introduction of a Western dress code helped build a cohesive sense of national identity,[77] as the new dress requirements undermined social, religious, and tribal distinctions based on appearance; one could also argue that it created large-scale simmering discontent which would ultimately blowback on the Pahlavi state and have dire consequences that would make the subject of "dress code" pale in comparison.

While certain urban women commended such "modernization" steps as forcible unveiling of the female populace, notwithstanding the reality that Iran was still a deeply conservative Muslim society; for other less "modern" women, the state's prerequisite of being unveiled in order to reap the so-called modernization benefits of education and female employment opportunities, was a bitter pill to swallow. Often it was the key obstacle in their desire to improve their status because their conservative male folk would rather they remain illiterate and not reap the benefits of new economic opportunities that dishonor the family by abandoning the veil. Thus, economic opportunities and higher education were often intricately tied to the controversial unveiling measures which in effect limited access of many women outside the key cities like Tehran to opportunities meant to improve their daily lives.

NOTES

1. Historically, the region now occupied by the state of Iran, was known as "the Persian Empire," "Persia," as well as "Iran" which was the indigenous name for the whole area in pre-Islamic times. Persia was primarily the region in what is now South Western Iran and Persia was the spoken language there. The name "Persia" was used by ancient Greeks, and later other Europeans for the Achaemenian Empire whose most famous rulers were Cyrus the Great and Darius. Reza Shah sought to place an emphasis on Persia pre-Islamic roots/grandeur as a land of an "Aryan" race by officially changing the country's name from Persia to Iran in 1935. It can be postulated that this change in lexicon at such a time may have had something to do with Reza Shah's growing sympathies with Nazi Germany much to the alarm of his British allies.

2. For more on the Qajar Dynasty see Ann K. S. Lambton, *Qajar Persia* (Austin: University of Texas Press, 1987); Abdollah Mostofi, *The Administrative and Social History of the Qajar Period* (Costa Mesa, CA: Mazda Publishers, 1997).

3. The bazaaris were the influential shopkeepers in the crowded bazaars in the cities and towns, who often had a good sense of which way the wind was blowing vis-à-vis people's sentiments as they pertained to both the state and other social actors.

4. By the early nineteenth century, one-third to one-half of the population belonged to individual tribes; while urban classes made up around 20 percent of the population; with nontribal agriculturalists constituting the rest. See Nikkie R. Keddie, *Qajar Iran and the Rise of Reza Khan, 1796–1925* (Costa Mesa, CA: Mazda Publishers, 1999), 10.

5. For a comprehensive look at Persian foreign policy from 1500 to 1914 see R. K. Ramazani, *The Foreign Policy of Iran, 1500–1914* (Charlottesville: University of Virginia Press, 1966).

6. Ervand Abrahamian, *Iran Between Two Revolutions* (Princeton, NJ: Princeton University Press, 1982), 134–135.

7. Abrahamian, 144. Reza Shah's 1934 state visit to Turkey where he witnessed Mustafa Kemal's own "modernization" campaign undoubtedly influenced and/or reinforced his own convictions on the necessity of transforming Persia into a modern "nation-state."

8. For more on Khomeni's life see Baqer Moin's *Khomeini: Life of the Ayatollah* (New York: St. Martin's Press, 1999). During Reza Shah's rule Khomeini was adamant that he continue his popular lectures about the "degeneration of Persia" even though the authorities tried to dissuade him (p. 54).

9. The Qajars (also Anglicized as Ghajar or Kadjar) was a Persian royal family of Turkmen origin who ruled Persia (later renamed Iran in 1935) from 1794 to 1925. What is noteworthy is that from the eleventh through twentieth centuries most of the ruling dynasties (to include the most famous, the Safavids) came from a nomadic Turkish speaking background. The Safavids, although non-nomadic, were brought to power with the help of Turkish nomadic tribes.

10. Nikki R. Keddie, "The Iranian Power Structure and Social Change, 1800–1969: An Overview," *International Journal of Middle Eastern Studies* 2, no. 1 (January 1971), 4.

11. Shaul Bakhash, *Iran: Monarchy, Bureaucracy, and Reform under the Qajars, 1858–1896* (London: Ithaca Press, 1978).

12. Keddie (1999), 15.

13. For more on Reza Shah's rule see Sandra Mackey, *The Iranians: Persia, Islam and the Soul of a Nation* (New York: Penguin Group, 1996), 136–143.

14. Gholam Reza Afkhami, *The Life and Times of the Shah* (Berkeley: University of California Press, 2009), 238.

15. For more on the lives of rural "traditional" women see Mary Elaine Hegland, "Traditional Iranian Women: How They Cope," *Middle East Journal* 36, no. 4 (Autumn 1982), 483–501.

16. Morteza Ravandi, *Tarikh Ejtemai Iran (The Social History of Iran).* (Tehran: Amir Kabir, 1978), 723.

17. For more on the socioeconomic diversity of Persia's women see Michael M.J. Fischer, "On Changing the Concept and Position of Women," in *Women in the Muslim World*, ed. Lois Beck and Nikki Keddie (Cambridge, MA: Harvard University Press, 1978), 189–215.

18. Ravandi, 4.

19. For more on women's status during the late nineteenth century Qajar period see Parvin Paidar's seminal work on the subject titled: *Women and the Political Process in Twentieth Century Iran* (Cambridge: Cambridge University Press, 1995), 30–49.

20. Paidar, 41.

21. Nikki R. Keddie, "Religion and Irreligion in Early Iranian Nationalism," *Comparative Studies in Society and History* 4, no. 3 (April 1962), 290.

22. For more on the tobacco crisis see Nikki R. Keddie, *Religion and Rebellion in Iran: The Tobacco Protest of 1891–1892* (London: Frank Cass, 1966).

23. For more on Afghani's views and writings see Nikki R. Keddie, *An Islamic Response to Imperialism: Political and Religious Writings of Sayyid Jamal ad Din "al Afghani."* (Berkeley: University of California Press, 1968). For Afghani's biography see Nikki R. Keddie, *Sayyid Jamal ad Din "al-Afghani:" A Political Biography* (Berkeley: University of California Press, 1972).

24. Roy Mottahedeh, *The Mantle of the Prophet: Religion and Politics in Iran* (Oxford: One World, 2000), 183–184.

25. Keddie (1999), 46–47; Keddie (1966).

26. Abrahamian, 74.

27. Mackey, 143–156.

28. Abrahamian, 89.

29. Afkhami, 239.

30. Afkhami, 239.

31. Nahid Yeganeh, "Women, Nationalism and Islam in Contemporary Political Discourse in Iran," *Feminist Review,* no. 44 (Summer 1993), 4.

32. Paidar, 73.

33. Paidar, 92.

34. Paidar.

35. Paidar, 94.

36. Paidar.

37. Abrahamian, 132–133, 158–161. On page 133, what is striking is Abrahamian's column on "ethnic origin" of early members of the communist movement (fourteen in total): Only two were "Persian." The majority (ten) were "Azeri;" the other two were "Armenian." On pages 158–161, Abrahamian lists the details of the social and political backgrounds of forty eight of the "Fifty-Three" who were put on trial in 1938 and jailed. Many of these leaders in 1941 would form the nucleus of the *Hezb-e-Tudeh Iran* (Iranian Party of the Masses). Interestingly, the majority are Persians (36), followed by Azeri (7), Qajar (2), and Turkmen (1).

38. Eliz Sanasarian, *Women's Rights Movement in Iran* (New York: Praeger, 1982), 40–44.

39. Mohammad H. Faghfoory, "The Ulama-State Relations in Iran, 1921–1941," *International Journal of Middle Eastern Studies* 19, no. 4 (November 1987), 414.

40. Abrahamian, 135.

41. For a more comprehensive examination of Reza Shah's "modernization" program see Amin Banani, *The Modernization of Iran: 1921–1941* (Stanford: Stanford University Press, 1961).

42. Azadeh Namakydoust, "Covered in Messages: The Veil as a Political Tool," *The Iranian,* May 3, 2003. Accessed at: http://www.iranian.com/Women/2003/May/Veil/p.html; see also Hamideh Sedghi, *Women and Politics in Iran: Veiling, Unveiling, and Reveiling* (Cambridge: Cambridge University Press, 2007).

43. Moin, 56.

44. Moin, 55.

45. Reza Shah's incendiary dress codes, to varying degrees, mirrored those of his counterparts in Turkey (Ataturk) and Afghanistan (during the tail end of King Amanullah's rule in 1928) and were unpopular with the majority of the populace.
46. George Lenczowski, *Iran under the Pahlavis* (Stanford, CA: Hoover Institute Press, 1978), 98.
47. Janet Afary, *Sexual Politics in Modern Iran* (Cambridge: Cambridge University Press, 2009), 155; Lenczowski, 97; Mackey, 181.
48. Ibid, 34; Paidar, 106–107, 135–139.
49. Abrahamian, 144.
50. Abrahamian, 144; Mackey, 181.
51. Paidar,132,
52. Mackey, 182. Olive Hepburn Suratgar, *I Sing in the Wilderness: An Intimate Account of Persia and Persians* (London: Stanford Press, 1951).
53. Sattareh Farman Farmaian, *Daughter of Persia: A Woman's Journey from Her Father's Harem through the Islamic Revolution* (New York: Crown Publishers Inc, 1992), 95.
54. Reza Baraheni, *The Crowned Cannibals: Writings on Repression in Iran* (New York: Vintage Press, 1977), 52.
55. Afary, 157.
56. Paidar, 107.
57. Mackey, 182.
58. Paidar, 90–91.
59. Paidar, 108.
60. Paidar.
61. Abrahamian, 144–145.
62. Lenczowski, 34.
63. Abrahamian,145.
64. For more on the history of Iranian women in the workforce during Reza Shah's rule see Valentine M. Moghadam, "Hidden from History? Women Workers in Modern Iran," *Iranian Studies* 33 (Summer–Autumn 2000), 387–389.
65. Laurence Paul Elwell-Sutton, *Modern Iran* (London: G. Routledge and Sons. Ltd, 1941), 126.
66. Paidar, 113–114.
67. Afary, 153.
68. Suad Joseph and Afsaneh Najmabadi, *Encyclopedia of Women and Islamic Culture: Family Law and Politics* (Leiden: Brill Academic Publishers, 2005), 392. See also Nahid Yeganeh, "Women, Nationalism and Islam in Contemporary Political Discourse in Iran," *Feminist Review* 44, Nationalisms and National Identities (Summer 1993), 5.
69. Paidar, 109.
70. Paidar, 109–110.
71. Paidar, 110.
72. Paidar, 110–111.
73. Paidar, 111.
74. Afary, 154–155.
75. Sattareh Farman Farmaian, 95.
76. Afary, 154.
77. Houchang E. Chehabi, "Staging the Emperor's New Clothes: Dress Codes and Nation Building Under Reza Shah," *Iranian Studies* 26 (3–4), 1993: 209–229.

Chapter Eight

Modernization and Female Status

Life under the Second Pahlavi Shah, 1941–1979

> Justice and common sense required that women enjoy the same political rights as men ... we who wanted to place the nation on the path to progress could not relegate our mothers, sisters, wives and daughters to the same category as the insane and the criminal.
> —Muhammad Reza Pahlavi (1919–1980)

Muhammad Reza Pahlavi's assumption of the Pahlavi throne in 1941 following the forced exile of his father by the British due to his Nazi sympathies, made him more malleable, and vulnerable, to external and internal interests. Unlike his father, the new shah was willing to back down on controversial social policies instituted during his father's arbitrary sixteen-year rule.[1] Muhammad Reza Pahlavi's primary concern was survival on the throne and consolidation of his rule during the early days of his reign. The ulema and the conservative elements of Iranian society sensing his vulnerability immediately began to clamor for a relaxation, or complete abolition, of controversial policies such as mandatory unveiling. Initially, the shah was forced to accede to many of these social demands given his weak position due to a widespread perception that he was a mere toady of the detested foreign powers (especially the British) and commanded a much weakened military due to large-scale desertions.

It was only after Muhammad Reza Pahlavi consolidated his rule and began to replicate his father's authoritarian style in the late 1950s that he was able to embark on "modernization" schemes that involved the female populace much to the dismay/chagrin of the clerics and other conservative social elements. One of the most significant and lasting reforms of this period was the enfranchisement of women in 1963. His concurrent land reforms introduced under the "White Revolution," however, were deeply unpopular and helped to unify disparate social groups, with clerics such as Ayatullah Khomeini (1900–1989) leading this opposition. As a result of this rising social discontent, the subject of women's rights became an incendiary issue. In a society with long memories, it was a combination of perceived injustices at the hands of this Pahlavi dynasty by the conservative elements (to include the clerical establishment) going back to its founder's authoritarian rule, and the increasingly autocratic modernization schemes of Muhammad Reza Pahlavi that seemed mostly to consist of window dressing without addressing deep-seated socioeconomic concerns of the populace, that imperiled social gains made by Iranian women. Furthermore, increasing social dichotomies would ignite large scale unrest, encouraged and abetted by the ulema and the mullahs, which would lead to an outright revolution and, ultimately, the overthrow of the short-lived Pahlavi dynasty (1925–1979).

VYING SOCIAL GROUPS AND WOMEN'S STATUS, 1941–1963

The forced abdication of the new shah's autocratic father enabled competing social groups to attempt to re-exert themselves after sixteen years of suppression. Emboldened by the weakened position of Muhammad Reza Pahlavi, vying members of various groups (majlis, ulema, tribal chieftains, politicians, etc.) all fought each other to gain control over the center.[2] Even within these groups there were competing factions (for example, within the majlis, the conservatives, liberals, and radical factions fought within and between each other).[3] Under Reza Khan, the primary battleground between the ulema and the shah had involved the state's controversial "modernization" policies, whose cornerstone was a reinvention of Iranian female identity along more Westernized (read: infidel) lines at the expense of an "Islamic" one as propagated by these ulema and their conservative social allies. While with the leftist and nationalist political parties, the shah had to contend with more secular demands (such as greater women's rights; equal pay for equal work) that were polar opposites to the demands made by a restive clergy and conservative bazaaris, leading to inevitable clashes between the supporters of these groups. These competing groups and their conflicting demands placed the new shah in an unenviable position of having to navigate between two dedicated and passionate entities as he consolidated his rule: the religious hardliners and the secularists. This situation inevitably led to much backtracking on his father's stated policies, especially when it came to female matters even though Muhammad Reza Shah was a chip off the old block when it came to his ideas on what twentieth century Iranian society would look like: modern, developed, and prosperous.

BACK TO THE FUTURE: THE SHAH VERSUS THE ULEMA ON WOMEN'S ROLE IN IRANIAN SOCIETY

Cognizant of his weak position, and reminiscent of his father's premonarchic strategy, the second Pahlavi Shah initially moved to acquiesce to the demands of the ulema, and the landed class interests, on a number of issues, foremost of which involved women's status/role in a Pahlavi ruled Iran and reinstatement/protection of certain traditional practices.[4] The ending of the highly unpopular mandatory ban on veiling—which was never to be restored—helped mollify the ulema and the conservative social elements.[5] It can be surmised that it was no accident that a cleric with Ruhollah Khomeini's ambitious drive did not speak out more publicly against Pahlavi rule, which seemed determined to promote a more secular, Persian identity over an "Islamic" one, until Reza Shah's overthrow. Khomeini anonymously wrote a short book in 1942 after the abdication of Reza Shah titled *Kashf-al-Asrar* (The Discovery of Secrets), which attacked secularism and Reza Shah.[6] In it Khomeini bemoans the loss of prestige traditionally held by the mullahs in the eyes of their people, and attributes the poor treatment of many mullahs by the populace to Reza Shah's "anti-clerical propaganda."[7] In *Kashr al-Asrar*, he provides examples of such "mistreatment" during Reza Shah's rule:

> During his reign the mollahs had lost their influence over the people to such an extent that no one was prepared to give them a lift in their car. If a mullah was by any chance given a lift, any fault that developed in their car was promptly attributed to his "evil presence."[8]

On the social impact of Reza Shah's "dictatorship," Khomeini warned:

> When his dark dictatorship was over . . . the people who have taken over are still asleep and have forgotten their darkest days of exploitation . . . it is they who are subduing the clergy, challenging religion and belief itself and trampling the rule of the Qur'an so that they can get on with the implementation of their corrupt and poisonous intentions.[9]

Khomeini's *Kashf al-Asrar* was a template on how a future Islamist regime could coexist with the monarchy. Written almost as a warning shot, he criticized the orders issued by the previous shah and also wrote that the laws passed by the Majlis had no value and must be abolished. Khomeini also criticized Reza Khan and Ataturk (Kemal Mustafa of Turkey) as "idiotic dictators" who forced programs upon the populace which prevented "real progress of the country" from taking place by repressing the role of the clergy; by "spreading means of pleasure"; and by "preoccupying people with unveiling, European clothes, cinema, theatre, music and dance."[10] Khomeini proposed archaic laws of retribution (flogging adulterers, cutting off hands of thieves) and stressed the need to support a muscular/militant interpretation of *jihad* to achieve this goal. Khomeini condemned Reza Shah's modernization schemes and propaganda as "corrupt Westernization." On gender matters, Khomeini made few allowances with modernity. He opposed unveiling, co-education, women's employment outside the home and socializing between men and women.[11] But it was the mandatory unveiling that in particular irked Khomeini who believed that it symbolized all the evils committed by the ousted Shah. Khomeini warned: "The unveiling of women has caused the ruin of female honor, the destruction of the family, and untold corruption and prostitution."[12]

Khomeini argues in *Kashf ol-Asrar*:

> The dishonorable act of unveiling, or better call it, the movement of bayonets, inflicted moral and material damage on our country and is forbidden by the law of God and the Prophet. . . . The coeducational schools which have destroyed the chastity of girls and the masculine powers of boys are forbidden by God. . . . The wine shops and drug businesses which exhausted the minds of our youth and damaged the health and sanity of the masses are against the shariat. . . . Music which encourages the spirit of passion and love among the youth is forbidden in the shariat and should be taken out of school programs.[13]

Khomeini in his *Resaleh Tawzih al Masail* (1946) discussed family law and the duties and responsibilities of a husband and wife. According to him, the rights and duties of both were completely different:

> A woman who has entered into a permanent marriage is not allowed to leave the house without her husband's permission. She must submit herself to any pleasure he desires. She may not refuse herself on any grounds other than religiously accepted ones . . . if a woman does not obey her husband according to the manner set out . . . she is then sinful and is not entitled to food, clothes, housing and intercourse. But she is entitled to her mehr (dowry).[14]

In *Resaleh Tawzih al Masail*, Khomeini devotes a whole section to *mu'ta* (temporary marriages) arguing in support of such unions; while he also allocates ten sections to discussing the *hijab* (veil) and rules on who may look at whom and which parts of the body may be viewed by whom. He wrote that the only parts of a woman's body that can be viewed is the oval of her face and her hands and even this permission is qualified as the onlooker must not regard them with sexual desire. The section on *talaq* (divorce) specifies that men have complete power to divorce their wives at will without having to provide an explanation, with the only time restrictions imposed by the last date of sexual intercourse and the woman's menstrual period. No restrictions were necessary in the case of a menopausal woman and wives below the age of nine.[15]

Khomeini's views were widely shared within the clerical establishment and the *bazaari* (merchant) families, many of whom backed him in his opposition to unveiling and other social concerns.[16] The ulema justified their stance on women's role in a *Muslim* society by emphasizing that, while women in the ancient world had no rights, Islam had provided them with certain legal rights. But this did not equate with the version of "rights" that certain Iranian women clamored for such as the demand for "liberation," which the clerics regarded as merely a "corrupting influence" of the infidel west. Since there were specific biological differences between men and women, and men's unbridled passion had to be held in check, this reality in their minds necessitated the need for veiling, polygamy and *mu'ta* (temporary) marriages.[17] In 1948, a group of fifteen mujtehids had signed a fatwa which banned unveiled women from shopping in the bazaar and markets.[18] Khomeini admired and maintained ties to Ayatullah Sayyed Abolqassem Kashani (1882–1962), who was closely aligned with the *Feda'iyan-e-Islam* (Crusaders of Islam), a group of militant clerics with close ties to Egypt's *Ikhwan al Muslimin* (Muslim Brotherhood).[19]

On the surface Khomeini's pronouncements—based on Shariah law—seemed to be polar opposites to the tenor of the Pahlavi dynasty vis-à-vis women's role in Iranian society. Closer examination reveals that, in fact, Khomeini's views on how family law needed to be implemented in order to fulfill the stipulations of Islamic laws did not significantly differ from those held by the founder of the Pahlavi dynasty, Reza Khan. Reza Khan did not abolish polygamy or *mu'ta* and practiced it himself; while, ironically enough, Khomeini—also an advocate of polygamy, was married to one woman, Khadije Saghafi (m: 1926), his entire life. Where the two men parted company was on the subject of the hijab and the minimum marriageable age. The shah and his successor, Muhammad Reza Pahlavi, both believed the hijab limited women's empowerment and that marriage at a very young age was also detrimental to females; while Khomeini argued that the hijab was vital to protect the honor of the female and her family and was a fundamental precept of Islamic law on women. Furthermore, on the subject of early marriage, Khomeini argued that Prophet Muhammad—the perfect man—married a six-year-old and consummated the marriage when she was nine. Since in Islam Muslims are reminded to replicate the behavior of the Prophet, similar unions were thus *halal* (legitimate) under Shariah was Khomeini's rebuttal to Pahlavi laws establishing a minimum marriageable age.

In 1940, Navab Safavi[20]—a theology student at Tehran University who in 1946 founded and lead the *Feda'iyan-e-Islam*—published a manifesto that stated: "Flames of passion rise from the naked bodies of immoral women and burn humanity into ashes . . . cinemas, theatres, novels and songs teach crime and arouse passion and therefore must be banned."[21] Navab Safavi's *Feda'iyan-e-Islam* was the first systematic cultural defense of Islam and advertised itself as the first Islamic political organization with a comprehensive political program for Iran. It pledged to rid society of its immoral (read: un-Islamic) ways and resorted to assassinating select political (secular) opponents as a legitimate means to its desired ends with the killing of Ahmed Kasravi as its first political action.[22]

Mirroring the views of most clerics, the *Feda'iyan-e-Islam* was obsessed with what it perceived was the embedded "moral decadence" and the "rise of passion" in Iranian society. Echoing the views of the clerics and conservative elements of Iranian society, the organization in its writings condemned coeducation and demanded that it cease at all levels. Although not averse to females being educated, it believed that women should have access to education that bolsters their familial efforts within the confines of the family. On the volatile subject of unveiling, the *Feda'iyan e-Islam* argued:

> Day and night, men and women face each other in the streets, offices, schools and in other public places and their senses are stimulated at all times without control. The continual stimulation of the sexual sense gradually paralyzes the nervous system . . . gradually all the organs of society get paralyzed and society's affairs remain unattended to . . . yes, yes, passion kills the wisdom and culture of society and when it is stimulated in a man by all those naked women around him, he becomes inattentive to his own family and divorce and separation between husbands and wives take place and increase every day.[23]

ERA OF NATIONALISM AND WOMEN'S ISSUES: PROLIFERATION OF POLITICAL PARTIES AND ORGANIZATIONS

Notwithstanding the weakness of the shah's government as it concerned itself with consolidation/survival concerns and with appeasing defiant social groups like the landed aristocracy, tribal leaders, and an emboldened clerical establishment, this period witnessed an expansion of vying secular political organizations representing not just the vested interests of the old families and landed classes but also those of the working poor and the growing middle class.[24] Between 1941 and 1953 over seventy political parties and a dozen women's organizations were formed. These entities included "progressives" (read: communists and socialists) like the Tudeh Party (established in 1941), Mohammad Mossadeq's National Front (socialists/nationalists/Islamists) and the Women's Party (*Hezb-e-Zanan*), which changed its name to the Women's Council (*Showra-ye-Zanan*) in 1945–1946, which was an umbrella organization of several women's groups.[25]

The Tudeh Party quickly became the country's largest and best-organized party despite its publicly known connections to the Soviet Union. It had a "progressive" social agenda that managed to attract Iranians from all walks of life. Tudeh's women's branch was established in 1943 and advocated for greater educational and employment opportunities for women, better working conditions, vacation time, childcare centers, equal pay, and colleges for women.[26] The Tudeh Association of Women became a member of the International Democratic Federation of Women in 1947 and sent representatives to international conferences. When it was banned in 1949, it was replaced two years later with the *Tashkilat Democratic Zanan* (Democratic Association of Women). The Democratic Association of Women (DAW) organized a celebration of the forty-fifth anniversary of the Constitution by demanding women's suffrage and criticizing the Pahlavi government for its failure to extend the vote to include women.[27] The goals of DAW—which were quite ambitious for both the times and locale—included:

1. To struggle toward the attainment of social and political rights for women via conferences and speeches.
2. Cultural development—the struggle against illiteracy.
3. Mobilization of women.
4. The struggle against prostitution and moral decadence.
5. The struggle against the exploitation of women and young girls in factories; the establishment of working hours for women workers; the right to paid leave on weekends and public and annual holidays; equality of pay for men and women workers.
6. Prohibition of work for children below the age of fourteen.
7. Paid maternity leave of at least two months for women workers and servants.
8. Free kindergarten for the children of women workers and servants.
9. The establishment of training workshops for young girls from poor families.
10. The establishment of clubs, reading centers and libraries for women.
11. The establishment of women's newspapers and journals.[28]

These aims and objectives of DAW vis-a-vis civil society—with the exception of goal #4—inevitably placed them in direct conflict with the clerics and their supporters to whom such goals were ample proof that the communists and socialists were out to destroy their traditional (read: Islamic) way of life in order to create a society that reflected the values of the *kuffar*.

The Democratic Party of Azerbaijan (DPA), which demanded autonomy for Azerbaijan within Iran, elected a short-lived provincial government in 1945. The DPA had formed a women's section called the Women's Organization of Azerbaijan and organized a conference in Tabriz in 1946 in which three hundred women participated. This conference passed a resolution which stated: "We will struggle until the last breath for the emancipation of the oppressed women of Iran who live under the chains of injustice and captivity."[29] The Provincial Government of Azerbaijan gave women the right to vote in provincial elections for the first time in Iran's history in 1945. It also established equal pay for equal work for men and women and paid maternity leave for women workers.[30]

Although most of the women's organizations during this era were independent of the shah's government, with the exception of the Women's Party, most operated as auxiliary branches of leftist or nationalist political parties. While women's demands were important to these female members, they understood that their aspirations would have to take a back seat to the primary demands of the parties as enunciated by its male members in the hopes that, in time, their aspirations would be realized.[31]

In what has been described as the "radical nationalist atmosphere" of the 1940s and 1950s,[32] some pro-establishment organizations like the Ladies Centre (set up by Reza Shah) became training centers for women who could not afford to pursue further education. Publications like *Zaban Zanan* (Women's Language) resumed publication in 1942. The first issue focused on topics such as housekeeping, childrearing, health, and education. When the second issue published an editorial on "women and the bread shop" which protested over the shortage of bread and also reported on the women-led riots over this, the government banned the journal. The publisher, Sedigheh Douletabadi, succeeded in getting the ban removed, and managed to publish ten more issues until she published an article inviting the Allies to leave Iran.[33] Douletabadi regarded herself as a pro-monarchy nationalist who was opposed to the concepts of "women's rights" as they were espoused by the communists and socialists. She believed that it was possible for Iranian women to improve their lot in life through reforms carried out within the established order. In addition to the short-lived *Zaban Zanan,* there were many other women's magazines that were published during the late 1940s and early 1950s. Most contained "progressive" (i.e., those affiliated with the communists and socialists) material on social and political matters. Some like *Zanan Pishrow* (Progressive Women) was a weekly magazine published by Sedigheh Ganjeh in 1949 which stated that its aim was to defend social justice and women's rights. *Ghiyam Zanan* (Women's Revolt) was published in 1949 by Soghra Aliabadi and concentrated on social issues and literature.[34]

WOMEN'S STATUS DURING THE CONSOLIDATION PERIOD: 1941–1963

Despite an emboldened clergy with the ouster of Reza Shah and the weaker personality of his successor (Muhammad Reza Pahlavi) in the eyes of Iranians; their impact on progress made on behalf of Iranian females was limited. The 1950s and early 1960s, characterized by successful consolidation (of power) measures by Muhammad Reza Pahlavi, also involved attempts to co-opt the women's movement. Thousands of women brought up under Reza Shah and exposed to unprecedented opportunities were not about to retreat without a good fight. Still there was a palpable fear among the intelligentsia, the urban elite and the growing middle class, that the clock would be turned back and hard won concessions for women in the workforce, in education, and in family law would be lost due to a resurgent ulema, an ambivalent shah and their respective supporters.[35]

Many Iranian women who sought what were considered controversial changes, however, understood that there was a fine line in the eyes of most Iranians between demands for more economic and political rights by women on the one hand, and sexual and personal ones on the other. Even the secular leftist and nationalist parties intuitively understood the difference and took care to emphasize that their demands were strictly concerning employment opportunities, pay equity, health and education access, and the right to vote. Furthermore, they took great pains—which still did not help assuage the clerical establishment nor their supporters—to stress that none of their objectives concerning women's rights in Iranian society would upset the social balance or, more importantly, would conflict with Islamic stipulations on women's role in a Muslim country. Thus they avoided promoting goals that might (or did) appear to grant women greater individual rights or that would in any way challenge the existing status quo of the traditional family and marriage structure which led to some of the leftists labeling such political entities as representing the "bourgeois" interests.[36]

The Battle over Iranian Women's Suffrage 1944–1963

One controversial issue that activist Iranian women pursued in the early days of Muhammad Reza Pahlavi's rule was women's suffrage. In the summer of 1944, the Democratic Union of Women introduced a Women's Suffrage Bill with the assistance of Tudeh deputies in the fourteenth Parliament (Majlis). Female leaders of the Tudeh Party, such as Fatimeh Sayyah and Maryam Firouz, later continued to pursue these demands by writing letters to the prime minister in which they insisted that women be treated equally to men by being given equal representation in the legislature and judiciary. They also demanded gender equality in academic institutions. In the spring of 1946, Minister Mozaffar Firuz suggested the need for reforming the electoral laws that would grant women the right to vote according to the United Nations Charter. But the clerics vociferously opposed such measures and they were shelved.[37]

In 1951, the subject of women's right to vote in general elections re-emerged. Thousands of Iranian women in Tehran and other major cities, many of whom sympathized with the communist/socialist leftist parties like the Tudeh, participated in various public demonstrations to demand the right to vote. This was unprecedented and was reflective of how powerful new social entities with foreign connections had become within the country's urban areas. When Mohammad Mossadegh (1882–1967)[38] became prime minister in 1951, some measures were instituted toward providing women with limited franchise. In September 1951, women were granted the right to vote and hold office in trade unions. In November of the same year, they were permitted the same rights in district and village council elections. In August 1952, Ayatollah Abu al-Qasem Kashani,[39] as a leading member of Mossadegh's National Front, became the Speaker of the Parliament. He warned the *Showra-ye Zanan* (Women's Council) that their calls for women's suffrage were divisive to the country's interests at a time when it was facing imperialist threats. When Mossadegh's government presented its draft electoral law to the Parliament in December 1952, women's suffrage was not included in the proposal, leading to weeks of passionate debate on suffrage. On December 30, 1952, MP Mahmoud Nariman, one of Mossadegh's strong supporters, argued on the floor:

> Article 8 of the Supplementary Constitutional Law states: "The people of the Iranian state are to enjoy equal rights before the law, and since Iranian women are citizens of this nation, they therefore must be included in this article and should have equal rights in the electoral law." Furthermore, Article 2 of the Constitution states: "the National Consultative Assembly represents the whole of the people of Persia, who participate in the economic and political affairs of the country. Therefore, women should be able to take part in the affairs of the nation through the election of deputies."[40]

The battle over women's suffrage was revelatory: it disclosed some very deep social—ideological—schisms. Those opposed to women's suffrage came from diverse backgrounds contrary to popular imagination that it was solely the clerical establishment that fought this measure. The majority of the opponents belonged to the old middle classes who included clerics, merchants and artisans. The head of the Bureau of Islamic Propaganda submitted a petition with four hundred signatures to the leading newspaper, *Ettela'at*, which quoted the Quran (4:34): "Men have authority over women." Furthermore, it argued that "the *Umma* (Muslim nation) of Iran opposes the participation of any woman in the elections. We thereby express our contempt for such a measure." A second petition signed by *bazaaris* (merchants) and artisans and which was addressed to Kashani, took this a step further by demanding that all female employees from government positions must be expelled.[41]

Despite the strong push back, women's organizations like the *Jamiyat Rah Now* (New Path League), which was founded by Mehrangiz Doulatabadi in 1955 to pursue suffrage and other women's rights, and the *Jamiyat Irani Zanan* (Iranian Women's League) continued their efforts toward attaining suffrage for women. The Association of Women Lawyers also joined their suffrage campaign as they also wrestled with the Pahlavi state in seeking additional rights for women in order to raise their status in society (these included equality in employment matters, referral of divorce cases to court, abolition of polygamy and sigheh). Together these women's organizations formed an independent Federation of Iranian Women's Organizations, which coordinated the activities of fourteen member organizations. Most of the members of these groups were from affluent backgrounds and they were few in numbers in comparison to their conservative opponents.[42] In 1956, the Women's Council succeeded in getting an audience with the shah in order to submit a request for specific political rights. Their list of demands to the shah included "banning polygamy and temporary marriage; removing all inequalities between men and women under civil law; granting women the right to vote in the Majlis and Senate elections."[43]

In 1959, the subject of women's enfranchisement was broached in the nineteenth Majlis. Predictably, the clergy objected strongly to this. Abdolghasem Falsafi, a popular Imam, condemned the recommendation and the issue was dropped from debate in the Majlis. But it quickly reappeared as women continued to lobby for enfranchisement; while the shah remained noncommittal on the subject even after having consolidated his hold on power. The Prime Minister Ali Amini was publicly opposed to it as he tried to woo the nationalist and religious elements who would be alienated if he took a pro-suffrage position.[44]

Despite pressure from the Kennedy administration, and with an economic crisis at home, the shah continued to ignore the subject of women's franchise. Caught between two increasingly vocal social groups, he was hesitant to rock the boat by capitulating to women's demands well aware of the power of both the clerics and bazaaris in their respective constituencies. Moving toward increasing accommodation of women's demands vis-à-vis their political rights, the state moved to take control of the women's movement. Toward this end, in 1961 the Federation of Iranian Women's Organizations was dissolved. In its stead, the *Shoraye Aliye Jamiyat Zanan Iran* (High Council of Women's Organizations of Iran) was established under the direct tutelage of the shah's twin sister, Princess Ashraf. In addition, Prime Minister Amini was forced to resign in May and was replaced by Asadollah Alam in July 1962. Within weeks of Amini's resignation, the new cabinet announced that local elections would be held under the new law which did not ban women from voting.[45]

There was immediate criticism from the clergy. For Ayatollah Khomeini, as well as the rest of the clergy, women's right to vote was the final straw after some twenty years of a relatively peaceful truce between the crown and the clergy. Khomeini sent Prime Minister Alam a long telegram in which warned him not to ignore the advice of the clergy: "your illegal bill (on local elections) is contrary to Islamic (Shariah) Law, the Constitution and the laws of the Majlis. The ulama have publicly stated that the franchise for women and the abrogation of the condition that one must be a Muslim in order to be allowed to vote or to run in an election is contrary to Islam and the Constitution."[46] Khomeini confided to one of his colleagues: "the son of Reza Khan has embarked on the destruction of Islam in Iran. I will oppose this as long as the blood circulates in my veins."[47]

And with the passage of this local council election bill—which was announced in the Tehran press on the afternoon of October 8, 1962—the battle of wills between the shah and Khomeini began. Government newspapers presented a public mood of impatience with "meddlesome" mullahs and sought to appeal to women and the educated middle class by portraying the clergy as a reactionary force which lived in the Dark Ages. In response the clergy used their own large circulation religious monthly, *Maktab-e-Islam,* to galvanize their flock over the question of women's franchise. *Maktab-e-Islam* condemned Iranian women's participation in social and political affairs as "blindly aping the West," arguing that even in Europe there were countries like Switzerland where women did not have the right to vote. Protests against this bill spread to other opponents of the shah's government with the bazaaris jumping on the bandwagon.[48] The Second National Front also supported the clerics' condemnation but for different reasons: they wanted to delay the drafting of such an electoral law until free and fair elections were held for the Majlis.[49]

After growing civil unrest over the matter, and large scale clergy-led demonstrations, in December 1962 Prime Minister Alam announced the cancellation of the new Electoral Law. On December 10, 1962, the Association of Women Lawyers issued a statement on Human Rights Day, complaining about the government's retreat:

> Whenever there is talk of progress in this country, there are certain circles which try to make sure that this progress does not apply to one half of the population—the women. We pride ourselves on being Muslims. Islam is the religion of logic and reason. In the Muslim world today, many Islamic countries have given suffrage to their women and none has been ex-communicated for it . . . the policy of demagogy should not force the government to act against the interests of the country by withdrawing the Local Election Law . . . The Government, to compensate for its improper act, should not only reiterate the Law, but should also repeal Section I of Article 10 and Section 2 of Article 13 of the Majlis Election Law which prohibits women from participating in elections.[50]

The Battle to Abolish Mandatory Unveiling

Another battleground issue between the conservative social elements like the ulema and female activists involved the veil. The abolishment of the veil in 1936 was widely unpopular throughout the country and had forced some women to be confined to their homes rather than dishonor their families and religion by leaving their homes unveiled. In the eyes of the clerics, however, this ban was proof that Reza Shah was a *kafir* (unbeliever). With his ouster, the clerical establishment and their supporters immediately clamored for a return of the *chador*. In 1944, Ayatullah Tabataba'i Qomi issued a fatwa calling for the lifting of government restrictions on veiling. A significant number of women who had not left the confines of their homes since 1936 to avoid public unveiling decided to appear veiled in public.[51] Many Iranian women decided to resume wearing the *chador* after being persuaded by their husbands, fathers, or other family members; or by wishing to listen to the pleas of the clerics to do so on moral grounds or because without it they faced a hostile neighborhood or because it made them feel safer as they moved about outside the safe confines of their homes. Despite this reversal in attire, many middle class women continued to refuse to return to veiling.[52] According to Afary, women from the old middle class backgrounds of Tehran and other northern cities continued to wear a modified form of chador or a large headscarf. Without the face covering (*rubandeh*), the veil no longer provided the anonymity, and the neighbors and community could monitor the comings and goings of a "veiled" woman.[53] Michael Fischer made the observation that "the veil now served as a complex moral device on several levels": (a) the chador provided religious women the ability to move freely in public areas; (b) the chador was a social and class marker, reflecting a woman's place of origin and social status; (c) the veil or chador served many practical needs (protection from the elements; as a blanket; towel; or cover to breastfeed a baby.[54] In this way, the chador became a cultural and class identifying marker that helped onlookers gauge their socioeconomic standing and their views on "modernity."

Women's Expanding Role in the Workplace, 1941–1963

Women's role in the workplace grew as Iran continued to expand its economic base from consisting primarily of an agricultural sector to widening its industrial base. Although Iranian women had traditionally played an important role in subsistence agriculture in a primarily rural agrarian society; their numbers in the industrial sector continued to grow during Muhammad Reza Pahlavi's reign. The 1956 census counted 573,000 women involved in economic activity. It also revealed that half the country's population lived in rural areas and child labor, especially involving young girls, was commonplace. Official statistics showed a high concentration of women in cottage industries, mainly in rural areas. Women were mostly employed in carpet weaving, textile, and spinning factories; in factories making matches, glass and cardboard boxes; in tea factories, cotton cleaning, and gunny sack factories; and in the embroidery industries. In the service sector they were at the bottom rungs and worked at cleaning and catering, where they were categorized as unskilled laborers and received wages that were lower than men.[55] Between 1956 and 1966, women working in the manufacturing sector rose from 36 percent to 40 percent. Moghadam, however, points out in her study that these statistics are probably an undercount as home based productive work in rural areas often went unaccounted for even though it was an important source of income for the family.[56] Historically, in the economic sphere, females have always been an important labor force in cottage industry.[57]

Militant Islamic political organizations like the *Feda'iyan e-Islam* disapproved of working women except in cases where the survival of the family was at stake thus necessitating a woman to leave the safe confines of her home in order to seek work to provide for her family. According to them, a woman's primary job was to nurture and rear the children and keep the home fires burning. According to *Feda'iyan e-Islam:*

> Do women want to stop legal and moral sexual relationships with their husbands and cease to menstruate and bear children, so that they can share social duties with men? In that case, fifty years from now when this generation is dead, there won't be any more people in existence . . . or (do women want) the men to menstruate and become pregnant and bear children so that they can share responsibilities with women? Damn the logic and wisdom that presents this idea . . . the best thing for a woman is to be the manager of the house and a mother and wife who will be the producer and teacher of children at home. Is there any more basic duty than this for a woman in the world?[58]

The ethos of *Feda'iyan e-Islam* was not a social anomaly, however. Rather, it was a widely shared view (on "modernity") that captured the imagination of a broad segment of Iranian society, as well as Middle Eastern society as a whole, on the subject of "women's empowerment" and what this would mean for society in general. The fear of such change was palpable especially when it came to permitting the female members of the family to work unveiled outside the home among unrelated males. The threat to the female's reputation, and thus to the family's honor, in a society that was in the process of reinventing itself socially and culturally along the lines of neighboring states such as Turkey, in order to "progress" and join the twentieth century.

WOMEN'S STATUS FROM THE "WHITE" TO "ISLAMIC" REVOLUTIONS: 1963–1979

The "White Revolution" of 1963: Women's Suffrage and the Clerics Response

After the repeal of the Local Council Election Bill, a fragile peace seemed to exist between the government and clergy, although the media continued their propaganda against what they called were "the retrogressive and reactionary elements of society."[59] As Moin writes in his biography of Khomeini, the success of forcing the shah's government to shelve the bill advocating suffrage for Iranian women served to embolden Khomeini who became confident as he emerged from the semi-shadows to take a more prominent public position against the Shah's policies. When Khomeini gave his post-crisis speech on December 2, 1962, less than two months from when he had begun his public career, he tried to justify his twenty-year stance of political quiescence citing the example of Ali cooperating with the illegitimate Caliphs "because they appeared to be acting according to the rule of religion."[60]

The shah frustrated in his attempts at social and land reforms, decided to take drastic measures by dissolving the Majlis and removing Ali Amini as Prime Minister on May 9, 1961. During this period the Shah promulgated and began implementation of a Six Point Reform that marked the beginning of what came to be called "the White Revolution."[61] This Six-Point Reform was overwhelmingly approved by a national referendum on January 26, 1963.[62]

The original six principles were:

1. Land reform.
2. Nationalization of forests and pastures.
3. Sale of state owned factories to the private sector as security for land reform.
4. A profit sharing scheme for employees in industry.
5. Reform of the Electoral Laws to include female suffrage.
6. Creation of the Literary Corps to combat illiteracy.[63]

These reforms meant a sea change in Iranian society, especially as it concerned the status of women. Women activists were delighted that, finally, after an almost twenty-year struggle they would gain the right to be heard via the ballot box. It was an enormous victory for them, although immediately there was the expected backlash from the ulema and other conservative constituencies who especially opposed the land reforms and women's suffrage. The public demonstrations organized by the clergy, especially Ayatollah Khomeini, in Tehran and elsewhere led to violence as the police tried to disperse the crowds. The clergy argued that such laws not only violated the Constitution but, more importantly, defied the stipulation of Shariah (Islamic) law and thus were a danger to Islam itself.[64] On January 23, many people left work in protest. Shops and offices in Tehran's covered bazaar were closed as people marched toward apolitical Ayatollah Khonsari's house to ask him to lead their procession to the Seyyed Azizollah mosque. The mistreatment of this seventy-five-year-old well-respected Ayatollah at the hands of the shah's police only solidified the visible public schism that had emerged between the Crown and the clerics.[65] The shah, unlike his father, in taking on the clerics had failed to frighten them into submission and the situation only deteriorated vis-à-vis relations between the two. This lead the shah to verbally attack the clergy in public at Qom where he went to distribute lands and gave a speech defending his Six-Point Plan:

> Six Points (White Revolution) is an idea suited to everybody. What we are doing is not behind other nations. If anything, it is more advanced. . . . But who is opposing it? Black reaction, stupid men who don't understand and are ill intentioned. The Red subversives [communists] have clear decisions . . . and I have less hatred for them. They openly say they want to hand over the country to foreigners, without lying and hypocrisy. But those who lie about being patriotic and in practice turn their backs on the country are what I mean by black reaction . . . it is they who formed a small and ludicrous gathering from a handful of bearded, stupid bazaaris to make noises . . .[66]

Arguing that Articles 2 and 27 of the Supplementary Constitutional Laws were being violated by these reforms, most of the high-ranking clerics especially were not in favor of women holding leadership positions. Some, however, were not opposed to women's right to vote in elections. By leveraging the Constitution in their stated opposition to the "White Revolution," the clergy cleverly cloaked themselves as "constitutionalists" in order to enhance their nationalist credentials and to broaden their social base of support. They also resorted to spreading rumors in order to rile up the public against the Electoral Bill by making claims that women would be called up for military service.[67] For many clerics, giving women the right to vote equaled giving them a greater voice in sensitive matters which were vital to the fabric of society. Women, they believed, were more emotional and less rational than men; hence they would be more likely to be influenced by frivolous and/or sentimental concerns in making important decisions. It was such perceptions, as enunciated by the ulema, which led them to initially oppose the provision of suffrage to women. They argued that women's mental inferiority made them unfit to be involved in the affairs of the state or to attain the position of lawmaker or military leader which should only be the special province of men.[68]

On August 11, 1963, undaunted by the attempts at intimidation and public humiliation by the clerics and their conservative supporters, the High Council of Women's various member organizations announced their preparedness to participate in the upcoming parliamentary elections following the passage of the electoral reforms which had granted women suffrage in January. The next day they organized a procession in Tehran despite the threats and occasional violence stoked by the clerics. On the seventeenth, a meeting was held which included women, farmers, guilds and local council members who declared that a national congress would be convened in Tehran to choose candidates that would represent them in the Majlis election. On the twenty-seventh, a Congress of Free Men and Free Women convened in Tehran and choose candidates to stand for the Majlis, and pledged them their support. This was the first time in Iran's constitutional history that women ran for seats in the Majlis. Six women were elected to the Majlis and two were appointed to the Senate. A majority of the women elected had been active in the women's movement. Hajar Tarbiat, elected from Tehran, had founded the Women's Center in 1935, the first organization of its kind in Iran. Showkat-Malek Jahanbani was a pioneer in girls' education and a founder of several educational institutions. Farrokhroo Parsa was the daughter of a female activist who had been the editor of one of the first "feminist" magazines in Iran, *Jahan-e-Zanan* (Women's World). Nayyereh Ebtehaj-Samii, a graduate of the American Missionary School in Tehran, was a teacher and female activist. Mehrangiz Doulatshahi had a doctorate in sociology of journalism from Heidelberg University. Nezhat Naficy was the youngest and least experienced female activist. Of the two female senators, Mehrangiz Manuchehrian was a doctor of law and founder and president of the Iranian Federation of Women Lawyers. Shams-ul-Mulk Mosahab, with a Ph.D. in pedagogy, had been a teacher and principal of a girls' school. These women in the Majlis would actively lobby for the proposed family law.[69]

The 1967 and 1975 Family Protection Law: Implications for Female Status under the Law

By the mid-1960s, the only component of women's lives that remain untouched by the state involved the family. This had traditionally been an "off limits" area for the Crown and its supporters, as well as the conservative elements. The understanding had been that the Pahlavi state sought to improve women's status economically and politically, and would leave social and personal matters alone. In short, the private sphere was an incendiary subject, akin to walking in a mine field, and the Pahlavis had no intention of tipping over the boat as they sought to refurbish its contents. Emboldened female members of Muhammad Reza Pahlavi's family such as Princess Ashraf, who had jumped onto the "women's empowerment" bandwagon by co-opting the women's movement in the mid-1960s, pressed the Majlis toward passage of bills aimed at "family reform."

In 1967, a bill was presented to the Majlis by the New Iran Party which proposed to reform the Iranian family structure, much to the growing alarm of the ulema. The bill had significant input from the Women Organization of Iran (WOI) which had been founded in 1966 under the direct tutelage of Princess Ashraf. This bill became known as the Family Protection Law.[70] It was widely publicized that the stipulations of this bill meant to preserve and protect family life by limiting, or making illegal, certain prevalent practices which were detrimental to the family unit. These practices were identified as follows: arbitrary divorce, polygamy based on pleasure, and the man's right to child custody. The Family Protection Law of 1967 did not seek to replace the Civil Code of 1931 nor the Marriage Act of 1937. Rather, it sought to make amendments to the current legal structure as it pertained to "the requirements of a modern society." The old laws remained in effect until, and unless, they conflicted with the Family Protection Law. In such cases, the courts were required to enforce the latter.[71]

The Family Protection Law of 1967 consisted of 24 Articles. Articles 1–7 reintroduced the secular control (the courts) of marriage and divorce registrations which had—notwithstanding the enactment of the Civil Code of 1931—reverted to clerical control. Article 8 held that divorce could only be initiated through submission of an application to a family protection court. These courts were then to attempt reconciliation between the parties involved and, if this failed, to issue a certificate of irreconcilability, following which the divorce could be registered in divorce registry offices. Article 9 placed the responsibility for reaching agreement of maintenance and child custody in the hands of the couple who jointly sought a divorce. It mandated court intervention only if this arrangement failed to achieve a mutual agreement. Article 13 placed the responsibility of setting maintenance and child custody in the hands of the courts in cases where only one party sought a divorce. Decisions would be made that took into account the best interests of the child. Article 14 specified that if a husband or wife was imprisoned for over five years and/or disappeared, this time frame would constitute legitimate grounds for awarding the aggrieved party a divorce in addition to the other grounds specified in Articles 1121–1132 of the Civil Code. Women were also given permission to initiate divorce if her husband to another wife without her consent. Article 15 stipulated that the husband must seek permission from the court if he wanted to take a second wife and specified punishment if he failed to do so. When he sought such permission, the court was required to decide on a case by case basis based on evidence provided and through enquiries, including the testimony of the first wife. The remainder of the Family Protection Law of 1967 endorsed relevant article of the Civil Code and Marriage Act.[72]

The Family Protection Law of 1967, on the heels of women's suffrage, primarily provided middle class women in the urban areas much greater control over their lives in matters such as marriage, divorce and child custody and, concomitantly diminished the power of men. In 1972, the Association of Women Lawyers criticized the Family Protection Law of 1967 for legally permitting polygamy, even if the first wife gave her written consent. It also criticized the bill for failing to allow women to divorce their husbands should he suffer from a contagious disease. It also set up a special committee to examine this bill and to recommend specific amendments in order to bolster women's status in Iranian society.

In 1975, the Majlis passed a bill proposing specific amendments to the Family Protection Law of 1967. The amended bill, the Family Protection Law of 1975, had twenty-eight articles.[73] It raised the age of marriage to twenty for men and eighteen for women, but asked the Family Protection Courts to consider marital applications from girls over the age of fifteen (Article 23). Article 18 gave both spouses equal right to contest in court the right of their spouses to seek employment that would be detrimental to the family but the court could not stop a man from working if this interfered with the financial affairs of the family. Article 16 and 17 clarified Article 15 of the 1967 Law specifying the conditions under which the courts can allow a man to take a second wife. These included permission of the first wife. Although the earlier bill had required court determination, if a man was financially able to provide for a second wife it had generally granted this permission to the husband. The amendment made permission contingent on the agreement of the first wife or her lack of consent to sex, mental illness, barrenness, or disappearance.[74]

The impact of these laws on the institution of marriage was primarily felt in the urban middle and upper classes, while their rural sisters carried on with their lives based on tradition and religious mores under the watchful eyes of their local mullahs and imams. For many women activists, the primary limitation of these family laws was that they failed to specify financial support for divorced wives. Nor did either the Civil Code or the Family Protection Law give women any share in the property that the couple had acquired during their marriage. Nonetheless, the impact on urban women's psyche was immediate. Many were emboldened in all areas of their lives and pursued options like work and dress styles that had been unthinkable at the turn of the century. The social response to these reforms was mixed with the conservative elements and the clerical establishment complaining that "uppity," educated urban women were no longer behaving like loyal and subservient wives. The clerics seethed in private due to the pervasive security apparatus—SAVAK—keeping a watchful eye over their words and actions after Khomeini had been forced into exile in 1963.

Divorces skyrocketed in the urban areas following the passage of these laws as more and more women chose to initiate divorce proceedings. Mothers-in-law complained that their daughters-in-law, although educated, were not the docile wives they preferred for their sons. The ulema and bazaaris were incensed that divorced women were living independently. Between 1966 and 1976, the number of female headed households increased from 6.4 percent to 7.3 percent. In earlier Persian society, young divorcees would become second aqdi or sigheh of a more well to do man or would be absorbed into the larger family network.[75]

Impact of State-Initiated Gender Policy: Women's Identity and Social Response 1977–1979

Beginning in the 1960s, Iranian society found itself in the throes of a crisis of identity as the traditional—religiously inspired—boundaries became unclear due to a variety of factors, not least of which was direct state intervention vis-à-vis specific policies and legal measures. The so-called White Revolution of 1963, which challenged the traditional socioeconomic status quo, with the clerics and the landed classes at the top of the social pyramid, created the conditions that increased—not decreased—social divisions. In such an environment which was reinforced by an increasingly intrusive state that no longer satisfied itself with "regulating" the political and economic realms of the Pahlavi Monarchy, the social rifts widened once the state decided to meddle in the most sensitive arena of civil society: the family. The schism between the "modernized" Iranian women/family and the traditional women/family became pronounced as evident in their dress preferences. One could visibly see this social and cultural dichotomy on the streets of Tehran or Tabriz, with young women in miniskirts walking past women in chadors.

Unlike their more secular (read: modern) sisters, women who joined the Islamist movement in the 1960s and 1970s were ambitious women from lower middle class families with little formal education. Furthermore, they came from patriarchal backgrounds with very limited opportunities to pursue higher education or employment. Many joined the Islamic leftist Muhahidin-e-Khalq (People's Mujahidin)[76] which emerged in 1965 as the religious wing of the Mossadegh movement.[77] Others joined the Marxist-Leninist Fedayeen-e-Khalq (People's Fedayeen), which was formed in 1971, with activists who had belonged to the Tudeh Party and the Marxist wing of the National Front.[78] These groups would play an instrumental role in the "Revolution" which would be the culmination of the growing opposition to state instituted measures begun under the "White Revolution" in 1963. The women activists who belonged to the Mujahedin-e-Khalq wore the hijab, which during this period consisted of a long sleeved shirt, a scarf and pants. Those who belonged to the Fedayeen-e-Khalq did not wear the hijab but dressed in T-shirts or Maoist shirts and jeans. Women in both groups avoided wearing makeup, perfume, or jewelry.[79] In short, there was much diversity in the outlook and lifestyles of women who participated in the increasingly violent opposition to the shah. What united them was their shared desire to remove "a tyrant" but most were unclear on what, or who, would replace him. As Nashat observes, the vast majority of the more traditional women who responded to the call of revolutionary leaders, especially Ayatollah Khomeini, took to the streets without espousing a specific program for women. The familiar image of this revolution was of the chador clad woman carrying a child in one arm and raising the other in protest or carrying a machine gun. Furthermore, the seemingly spontaneous enthusiasm of these women was propelled not by any specific ideas or concerns related to their circumstances in society; rather, it was an internal rage and anger triggered by external elements such as fiery speeches of Ayatollah Khomeini in exile against the despotism of Pahlavi rule, that led to this sort of activism.[80]

From the mid-1960s until the overthrow of the Pahlavi monarchy, the WOI which had been approved by the shah when it was formed in 1966 and chaired by his twin sister Princess Ashraf, opened 400 branches, with a total membership of approximately 70,000.[81] It set up literary and vocational training centers, provided health care and legal counseling on marriage, divorce and inheritance, as well as day care facilities for urban lower-income women. Due to pressure from WOI, the state required three months' of maternity leave which could be extended to seven months, and part-time employment for new mothers. The WOI also sponsored research on gender issues, such as critical studies of the sexist and demeaning portrayals of women in the media and in textbooks, which recommended reforms.[82] American-educated social activists such as Sattareh Farman Farmaian returned to Iran in the late 1950s to set up civil institutions to train fellow Iranians in skills needed to improve the welfare of ordinary Iranians. In Farman Farmaian's case, she set up the Tehran School of Social Work which, for two decades, made enormous contributions to civil society by training thousands of social workers to go into the provinces to work in Health and Family Planning clinics and dispensaries, schools, and prisons.[83]

Although the WOI was a social institution created by an increasingly unpopular Pahlavi state, it quickly became very popular among Iranian women. WOI's members were a diverse group with the village and factory workers especially engaged and demanding from WOI's leadership what they needed. Interestingly, it was the elite members who espoused the status quo and showed reluctance toward reforms, while professional women were somewhere in the middle. WOI showed flexibility in how it treated its diverse membership. In some of its classes, all the women attended veiled; while in other areas some would be veiled, others "half unveiled" or unveiled.[84] Its flexibility and inclusiveness made WOI popular, with some prominent clerics, like Ayatollah Shariatmadari, allowing their daughters to participate in its activities.

As a result of state policies, women for the first time were not only enfranchised but—at least on paper—they were able to pursue a variety of employment opportunities which was unprecedented. Yet, in reality, while women did indeed have access to more options, they were "encouraged" to pursue so-called feminine professions like teaching and nursing. They continued to face discrimination, harassment, and low wages in their professions.[85] On the eve of the revolution, women earning wages and salaries in public and private sector manufacturing made up between 20 and 27 percent of the total workforce.[86] Just before the revolution there were two female cabinet ministers (Farrokhroo Parsa,[87] Minister of Education and Mahnaz Afkhami,[88] Minister of Women's Affairs).[89] By 1978, in addition to two women holding cabinet positions, two were senators, nineteen were Majlis deputies, three deputy ministers, and one was an ambassador. There were around 1,800 women employed as teachers in institutes of higher education and universities; 793 worked as engineers, and 316 as judges.[90]

The Pahlavi state was able to affect tangible results in the expansion of female literacy levels. It had placed an unprecedented emphasis on female education with the net result that between 1970 and 1975, the number of girls attending schools increased from 80,000 to 1.5 million. A sizeable increase but still small given that the total population of Iran was around 40 million. In 1974, half of all girls between six and ten were not attending school. The ratio of boys to girls was three to one in secondary school. However, to put this record in its proper context, it is important to disclose that in 1959 only 8 percent of all females over seven years of age were literate; by 1971 this had increased to about 26 percent. In 1971, 49 percent of urban women had some education, whereas only 9 percent of rural women were literate.[91] In 1976, women constituted 30 percent of students in higher education.[92]

Although WOI did play a role in the revolution, it was one that would have surprised its founding members who were secular feminists. Given the diversity and growth in its membership since its founding, across all socio-income strata, many of its members participated in the Islamist demonstrations in 1978 and openly supported the return of Ayatollah Ruhollah Khomeini from exile. One of the earliest demonstrations against the Pahlavi regime, and pro-Khomeini, in the province of Kerman included veiled women who were members of WOI. The WOI leadership had wanted to "mobilize their members" without specifying for what purpose, only to discover that some of their members had indeed mobilized themselves and against the shah. An outcome they had clearly not expected.[93]

Ironically, one of the impacts of state-initiated gender policies, which constituted the central feature, or core, of the shah's "modernization" policies was that it provided women whose lives it sought to improve with the opportunity to mobilize *against* the state during the so-called revolutionary mobilization against the shah in 1977–1979. Much to the chagrin of those closely affiliated with the Pahlavi state's gender-related programs, a large number of educated—in other words, empowered—women accepted the cleric-led revolutionaries' view on veiling and had openly rejected the shah's reforms on women. They also adopted the veil in public as they demonstrated against the shah. Even the shah weighed in when he wondered why Iranian women did not respond to such reactionary demands like gender segregation in the university cafeterias: "Where are the liberated women we hear so much about?" he demanded. The shah, like many other members of the Iranian urban elite, was genuinely surprised at the degree of support expressed for Khomeini and his ilk by all segments of Iranian society (to include women).[94] By mid-1978, gender politics were in full swing as the "Iranian Revolution" unfolded in that veiling quickly came to be viewed by many *not as a sign of women's oppression but as a symbol of resistance to the shah's rule.*[95] Women's groups who quickly rejected the changes introduced by the state vis-à-vis their status in society included the "Islamic modernists." Begun in the 1960s as a religious reform movement by educated laymen, it became widely popular among the educated urban middle and lower classes, especially in Tehran. The leading advocate of "Islamic modernism" was Western-educated Dr. Ali Shariati (deceased 1977), who was a Sorbonne educated intellectual and professor. Dr. Shariati called for a return to the teachings and principles of Islam of the time of the Prophet Muhammad in order to cleanse society of its moral decadence and political corruption. He blamed the current problems on people turning away from the *real* Islam as embodied in Shi'ism. He placed the blame of the decline of Shi'ism on the ulema.

Dr Shariati's worldview resonated with many young women who wished to emulate Fatima's example (the Prophet Muhammad's daughter) of combining feminine virtues and competence. The emergence of the large beige scarf, the Islamic scarf, and even the chador on university campuses, was a response to Shariati's message.[96]

CONCLUSION

Women were active participants in the Iranian Revolution that overthrew the shah. This fact alone, in light of the shah's government's efforts to provide females with a more level playing field, should pique one's curiosity as to why would females bite the hand that seeks to help them? The reasons are varied: effective propaganda, economic deprivation, political repression, identification with Islamism.[97] Notwithstanding the evident tangible improvement in the overall quality of life for many Iranians—and especially for of its womenfolk—the widespread perception bandied about during Friday

Mosque sermons, among the petty bourgeoisie, the bazaaris and certain rural entities, was one of shame and the corrupting decadence of an increasingly "un-Islamic" society thanks to the shah's policies. For others, like the so-called secularist urban dwellers, the fixation appeared to be on a "glass half empty" and a misplaced hope—thanks in no small part to Khomeini's deceptive assurances that he did not seek power nor radical social change—in a better future without a monarch.

NOTES

1. Homa Katouzian, "Arbitrary Rule: a Comparative Theory of State, Politics and Society in Iran," *British Journal of Middle Eastern Studies* 24 (May 1997), 71.
2. Roger M. Savory, "Social Development in Iran During the Pahlavi Era," in *Iran under the Pahlavis,* ed. George Lenczowski (Stanford, CA: Hoover Institute Press, 1978), 100.
3. Ervand Abrahamian, *Iran Between Two Revolutions* (Princeton, NJ: Princeton University Press), 169–224.
4. Hammed Shahidian, "The Iranian Left and the 'Women Question' in the Revolution of 1978–79," *International Journal of Middle East Studies* 26, no. 2 (May 1994), 225.
5. Janet Afary, *Sexual Politics in Modern Iran* (Cambridge: Cambridge University Press), 2009, 187–188.
6. Baqer Moin, *Khomeini: Life of the Ayatollah* (New York: St. Martin's Press, 1999), 60–61; Afary, 191.
7. Moin, 61.
8. Moin, 61.
9. Moin, 61.
10. Parvin Paidar, *Women and the Political Process in the Twentieth Century* (Cambridge: Cambridge University Press, 1997), 121.
11. Afary, 192.
12. Afary, 192. For more on the veil see Ashraf Zahedi, "Contested Meaning of the Veil and Political Ideologies of Iranian Regimes," *Journal of Middle East Women's Studies* vol. 3, no. 3 (fall 2007), 84.
13. Kashf ol-Asrar, 313–314 as cited in Paidar, 121.
14. Shireen Mahdavi, "Women and the Shi'i Ulama in Iran," *Middle Eastern Studies* 19 (January 1983), 23.
15. Mahdavi, 23.
16. Paidar, 120.
17. Mahdavi, 18.
18. Shahrough Akhavi, *Religion and Politics in Contemporary Iran* (Albany: State University of New York Press, 1980), 63.
19. Moin, 63.
20. In 1956, when the increasingly autocratic shah clamped down on the activities of his opponents, the Feda'iyan e-Islam was banned and its leader Navab Safavi executed. But the ideas upon which Safavi based his party lived on and would be reflected down the road in the post-Islamic revolution era under Khomeini.
21. Afary, 192.
22. Paidar, 121–122.
23. Paidar, 122.
24. Nikki R. Keddie, "The Iranian Power Structure and Social Change 1800–1969: An Overview," *International Journal of Middle Eastern Studies* 2 (January 1971), 11; Afary, 177.
25. The national front comprised of a mélange of characters and groups from across the political and social spectrum.
26. Afary, 176
27. Abrahamian, 322.

28. Paidar, 125
29. Paidar, 123.
30. Paidar, 123.
31. Afary, 176–177.
32. Paidar, 125.
33. Paidar, 125–126.
34. Paidar.
35. Moin, 58.
36. Afary, 178.
37. Afary, 192–193.
38. For more on Mossadegh's political life and times see Stephen Kinzer, *All the President's Men: An American Coup and the Roots of Middle East Terror* (Hoboken, NJ: John Wiley and Sons, 2008); Farhad Diba, *Mohammad Mossadegh: Political Biography* (Kent, UK: Croom Helm, 1986); Sepehr Zabih, *The Mossadegh Era* (Chicago: Lake View Press, 1982).
39. Ayatollah Kashani was a strong supporter of the *Feda'iyan e-Islam* and a rival for the leadership of the National Front.
40. Afary, 194.
41. Afary, 194.
42. Paidar, 137–138.
43. Leonard Binder, *Iran: Political Development in a Changing Society* (Berkeley: University of California Press, 1962), 198.
44. Paidar, 141.
45. Moin, 75; Paidar, 141.
46. Paidar, 142; Moin, 76.
47. Moin, 75.
48. Moin, 76–77.
49. Paidar, 143.
50. Iran Almanac, 1963, 411 (as quoted in Paidar, 144).
51. Shahidian, 225.
52. Moin, 58.
53. Afary, 208–209.
54. Afary, 209–210; Michael M. J. Fischer, "On Changing the Concept and Position of Persian Women," in *Women in the Muslim World*, eds. Lois Beck and Nikki Keddie (Cambridge, MA: Harvard University Press, 1978), 207–208.
55. Valentine M. Moghadam, "Hidden From History? Women Workers in Modern Iran," *Iranian Studies*, 33, no. 3–4 (Summer–Autumn 2000), 389.
56. Moghadam, 389.
57. Michael M. J. Fischer, "On Changing the Concept and Position of Persian Women," in *Women in the Muslim World*, eds. Lois Beck and Nikki Keddie (Cambridge, MA: Harvard University Press, 1978), 192.
58. *Feda'iyan e Islam*'s publication titled *Rahnamay Haghaegh* (The Guide to the truths), 11–12, as quoted in Paidar (1997), 122.
59. For more on the tenuous relationship between the Pahlavi state and the clerics see Dariush Zahedi, *The Iranian Revolution, Then and Now: The Indicators of Regime Instability* (Boulder, CO: Westview Press, 2001), 71–79.
60. Moin, 81–82.
61. For a detailed examination of the White Revolution see Gholam Reza Afkhami, *The Life and Times of the Shah* (Berkeley: University of California Press, 2009), 208–237.
62. Paidar, 144.
63. Savory, 104.
64. For a detailed examination of the clerics response following the public unveiling of the Six-Points Program in January of 1963, see Moin, 82–91.
65. Moin, 86.
66. Moin, 88; Paidar, 145.
67. William M. Floor, "The Revolutionary Character of the Iranian Ulama," *International Journal of Middle Eastern Studies* 12 (Spring 1980), 503.

68. Guity Nashat, "Women in the Islamic Republic of Iran," *Iranian Studies* 13 (1980), 169–170.

69. Gholam R. Afkhami, *The Life and Times of the Shah.* Berkeley (Berkeley: University of California Press, 2009), 243–244.

70. Doreen Hinchcliffe, "The Iranian Family Protection Act," *The International and Comparative Law Quarterly* 17 (April, 1968): 516–521.

71. Paidar, 153.

72. Paidar, 154; Afary, 216–219.

73. For more details on this bill see "Family Protection Act (1975)," *Foundation for Iranian Studies.* Accessed at: http://fis-iran.org/en/women/laws/family

74. Paidar, 155.

75. Afary, 218.

76. For more on Iranian women who joined the Mujahedin-e-Khalq see Rokhsareh S. Shoaee, "The Mujahid Women of Iran: Reconciling 'Culture' and 'Gender'," *Middle East Journal* 41, no. 4 (Autumn 1987): 519–537.

77. Abrahamian (1982), 483–495.

78. Afary, 245.

79. Ervand Abrahamian, *Iranian Mojahedin* (New Haven, CT: Yale University Press, 1989), 224.

80. Nashat, 174.

81. For more on the Women's Organization of Iran see G. R. Afkhami (2009), 249–253.

82. Afary, 211.

83. For more on Farman Farmaian's early contribution to the welfare of her people see Sattareh Farman Farmaian and Dona Munker, *Daughter of Persia: A Woman's Journey from Her Father's Harem through the Islamic Revolution* (New York: Crown Publishers, 1992), 205–231.

84. Afary, 212.

85. Nahid Yeganeh, "Women, Nationalism and Islam in Contemporary Political Discourse in Iran," *Feminist Review*, no. 44 (Summer 1993): 6.

86. Valentine M. Moghadam, *Modernizing Women: Gender and Social Change in the Middle East* (Cairo: The American University in Cairo Press, 1993), 189.

87. Farrokhroo Parsa (1922–1980) was one of the most prominent female activists during the shah's rule. Parsa was executed by Khomeini's regime on alleged charges of corruption in 1980. She was appointed Iran's first female Minister of Education in 1968. She was a mentor to many young women and an inspiration for her courage shown at the time of her execution.

88. For more on Mahnaz Afkhami's background see Afkhami (2009), 251–252.

89. Fischer, 192.

90. Nashat, 168.

91. Shahidian, 225.

92. Yeganeh, 6.

93. Afary, 215.

94. Afkhami (2009), 261.

95. Mansoor Moaddel, "Religion and Women: Islamic Modernism versus Fundamentalism," *Journal for the Scientific Study of Religion* 37 (March 1998), 126.

96. Nashat, 172–173.

97. Valentine M. Moghadam, "A Tale of Two Countries: State, Society, and Gender Politics in Iran and Afghanistan," *The Muslim World* 94 (October 2004), 449.

Chapter Nine

Trials and Tribulations in Iran

Gender Politics in a Theocracy

> Women are free in the Islamic Republic in their selection of their activities, their future and their clothing.
> —Ayatollah Khomeini (in an interview with *The Guardian*, November 6, 1978)

> It is a crime to be a woman in Iran.
> —Maryam Namazie, Iranian Human Rights Activist [1]

The *Jamhuri-ye-Eslami-ye-Iran* (Islamic Republic of Iran) officially replaced the *Imperial State of Iran* on April 1, 1979. The implications of this official name change for Iranian women quickly became apparent in the draconian measures implemented with the threat, or use of force by Khomeini's fledgling theocracy. Promises made to the Iranian people by a certain segment of the Shia ulema during "the Revolution" quickly rang hollow as this theocracy moved to silence dissent within the Islamist camp (expressed by the Fedayeen-e-Islam [2] and the Mujahidin-e-Khalq) and the secular opposition (the National Democratic Front, the Tudeh Party, and the pro-shah elements). The immediate impact on women's lives in Iran was the annulment of the social reforms implemented under the Pahlavi Shah's tutelage. The "White Revolution" (with its emphasis on "modernization" and "progress" as determined through the lens of the shah) of the 1960s was replaced with the "Islamic Revolution" with its emphasis on protecting women's honor and in its enunciated concerns with female modesty as the bulwark of a truly Islamic society. [3]

The Islamic Republican Party (IRP)—founded by clerics aligned with Khomeini such as Ayatollah Mohammad Beheshti, Hojatoleslam Hashemi

Rafsanjani, and Hojatoleslam Javad Bahonar—quickly muscled its way to prominence and domination with the help of a grassroots army formally established by Ayatollah Khomeini in May of 1979: the Revolutionary Guards Corps. The opposition within the clerical establishment to Khomeini's *Velayat-e-Faqih* (rule of the jurisprudent)[4] was suppressed by exile or house arrest of clerics opposed to this new Khomeini-inspired version of Shi'ism that renounced the notion based on the acceptance of temporal rule and which limited clerical influence solely to spiritual matters.[5]

REGIME CONSOLIDATION AND SOCIAL POLICY: WOMEN'S STATUS IN A THEOCRACY, 1979–1985

Regime consolidation concerns of the Provisional Government under the auspices of Ayatollah Khomeini, following his triumphant return from exile in February 1979, rather than tempering the hand of the Islamist revolutionaries only seemed to exacerbate the situation for women, especially for urban "modernized" (read: secular) women. During two years of transitional upheaval (1979–1981), in which the various Islamist, nationalist and leftist groups battled it out for state control, women became the pawns of this violent cycle.[6] The Khomeinists abandoned the façade of respecting the broader wishes of the Iranian people who had struggled to liberate themselves from the increasingly authoritarian rule of the Pahlavi-led monarchy, when they formed the IRP led by Ayatollah Mohammad Beheshti.[7]

The intent of the Khomeinists quickly became clear: to create an Islamic state governed by *Shariah* (Islamic) law. Early supporters of Khomeini's quest included Akbar Hashemi Rafsanjani and Ali Khamenei. They were, however, opposed by certain clerics in the seminaries who stressed the importance of the clergy remaining aloof from matters of governance as had historically been the case. These "quietist" were led by Ayatollah Kazem Shariatmadari whose supporters founded the Islamic People's Republican Party (IPRP) to challenge the IRP.[8] Many of the Iranian clergy, including Iran's senior ayatollahs—the *marjas* Shariatmadari, Golpaygani, and Najafi-Marashi—thought Khomeini's ideas were beyond the pale and dangerous.[9]

This power struggle—which would determine how women would be expected to live their lives in the public realm—was won by Ayatollah Khomeini's henchmen thus ensuring the absolute supremacy of his clerical rule under *Fiqh-e-Jafaria*.[10] Regime consolidation was not completed until 1985 due to a myriad of factors such as a bitter struggle between the proponents of liberal democracy and those supporting Islamic theocracy; and the ongoing Iran-Iraq War which threatened Iran's sovereignty.[11]

Ayatollah Khomeini's return to Iran from exile marked the beginning of the Islamization of women's status in Iranian society through the immediate abrogation of the Family Courts and the Family Protection Law.[12] With these measures women's legal status within the family reverted back to that prescribed by the Family Laws of the 1930s, which Ayatollah Khomeini actually supported as being "proper" and "Islamic" notwithstanding the fact that they had been instituted by a man he despised: Reza Shah. Family planning policies were discontinued and abortion was made illegal; while large families were encouraged by the clerics in charge.[13]

Khomeini's consolidation measures included the establishment of local *komitehs* (supporters of the Islamic revolution) who acted as informal police and informants.[14] In this capacity they would take opponents of "shariah" to closed hearings where secret verdicts and mass executions resulted as the hard line clerics under Khomeini consolidated their hold on power. Khomeinist vigilante groups sprouted up and, in addition to "modern" women, they targeted members of the Mujahedin-e-Khalq, Baha'is, and others who increasingly resisted Khomeini's tyrannical consolidation efforts.[15]

One of the most conspicuous measures vis-à-vis Khomeini's regime was the immediate institution of the *hijab* (veil),[16] which came to symbolize for the Khomeini's revolutionaries as being an emphasis on their women's unique and superior identity over that of Western "imperialist" societies. The veil, in the minds of "Muslim feminists," was a sign of resistance to Western values which were "immoral" and made women into "sex objects."[17] Yet prior to the overthrow of the shah, the majority of Iranian women covered their heads in public in some fashion albeit not to the extent advocated by the Khomeinists. The symbolism of mandatory veiling was to promote "the Islamic Revolution" as one which sought to protect the honor and dignity of the family by ensuring the chastity (in appearance) of their womenfolk in public.[18]

Back to the Future: Khomeini's Position on Women's Role in an Islamic Society

Upon his return Ayatollah Khomeini chose to be called *Imam*, a title previously used by Shia only for the twelve direct descendants of the Prophet Muhammad, and *Valayi-e-Faqih*, the religious and political leader who could implement the "sublime ideals of Islam" based on religious laws as interpreted by him.[19] Khomeini liked to stress that although women were equal to men according to Allah, the creator; their importance to society lay in their role as "mother." Thus for Khomeini "motherhood" was the epitome of a woman's life. Khomeini denounced the Family Protection Laws of 1967 and 1975 as attempts by an illegitimate ruler (Pahlavi) to destroy the social fabric of an Islamic society. To Khomeini this was "unacceptable and encouraged home wrecking." He saw such secular laws—which gave women automatic custody in divorce—as being "irreligious" attempts to destroy Muslim families and condemned all who had supported or voted for them.[20] Khomeini, who had opposed the enfranchisement of Iranian women in 1963, now supported women's right to vote but urged them to contribute to the "revolution" by being good mothers and wives.

In Khomeini's postrevolutionary Iran, women could be the pillars of the nation by being "strong forts of virtue and chastity" and by "raising brave and enlightened men and meek and united women." In May 1979, Khomeini said:

> Women have the responsibility of motherhood and raising the children. The mother is the child's first class, a good mother is a good class. . . . If you bring up a child correctly, and one day that child is a leader of society, then the country will be prosperous and yours will be the credit.[21]

Some Iranian scholars like Halah Afshar have compared Khomeini's views of women's role in society with that of Hitler's in that both placed great import on women's role in defending the nation. Like Hitler before him, Khomeini stressed that mothers were invaluable as educators, who could raise martyrs and played an important role in their education and in turning them into dedicated soldiers.[22]

On the subject of marriage, Khomeini—although a monogamist himself—was a strong advocate of both polygamy and *sigheh/mu'ta* (temporary marriage).[23] He believed that men were unable to control their natural urges as they were highly sexed predators. Thus the minimum marriage age, as stipulated by the Family Protection Act, was reduced to the age of menstruation or younger for females. This was considered one of many setbacks by Iranian women who had fought hard to get the age of consent for marriage raised from fourteen (Iranian Civil Code) to eighteen (Family Protection Act). Khomeini gave fathers the right to marry off their children at birth and thus permitted the violation of the Islamic requirement of consent by allowing fathers to do so.[24]

Khomeini restored the institution of temporary marriages which had been banned by the Pahlavis. Khomeini believed that men, as highly sexed beings, were easily lured by the opposite sex of all ages and thus were entitled to have sexual relations with females in marriages that could last as long as an hour to a lifetime. Furthermore, men were not—under Shariah Law as interpreted by Khomeinists—obliged to inform their wives and Khomeini encouraged temporary unions for men in order that they may satisfy their natural sexual urges. The permanent wife had to submit to her husband's every desire and wish. Khomeini wrote that it was the wife's religious duty to always be subjugated to her husband.

Due to the high casualties during the Iran-Iraq War (1980–1988), the Khomeini regime began to encourage polygamy and high birth rates for "martyrdom." War widows were urged to celebrate, not mourn, the loss of their loved one.[25] Adultery was especially frowned upon and sex outside of marriage was made an offense punishable by death. While homosexuality and adultery had always been regarded as punishable offenses in Iran, the manner of punishment proscribed for these two offenses (death by hanging or stoning) by the Islamic Republic reflected a much harsher worldview in action by an Islamic theocracy. This had much to do with the importance subscribed to "Islamic gender relations" as the foundation of an authentic "Islamic society" and therefore the requirement to ensure compliance with "Islamic norms," in other words, Shariah law as interpreted by these ruling clerics by implementing harsh punishments on transgressors.[26]

Khomeini in his writings went to extraordinary lengths to discuss some of the most intimate aspects of women's lives when he opined in some detail on topics such as women and menstruation, vaginal discharges, etc., in order to declare them "impure" and thus should refrain from religious activity. For example, he goes into some graphic detail on the subject of menstruation and how to distinguish it from an abscess, etc. He even deemed it important to make pronouncements on the normal duration of the menstruation cycle (three to no more than ten days). Khomeini did, however, state that this period of the month gave a woman the right to refuse her husband's sexual advances and still be considered "obedient" by the husband and his family.[27] Khomeini, like other Muslim scholars, prohibited sexual intercourse during menstruation but legitimized sodomy for men with their wives in "cases of great need."[28] Khomeini, however, contradicts himself when he also wrote that men could insist on sexual relations during menstruation provided they pay a specified *kofareh*, a sum of gold to the needy, despite having stated that women during this time could refuse their husband's advances.[29]

Khomeini's strongest social support base was among the poorest women[30] who were delighted with his emphasis that it was the husband who was obligated to care (feed, house, and clothe) his obedient wife and family regardless of his circumstances.[31] The Khomeinist's IRP set up the Committee for the Celebration of Women's Day which organized mass rallies every year to mark the birthday of the Prophet Muhammad's daughter, Fatima, which was named the official Women's Day by Khomeini. In these rallies, the supporters of the hardline clerics (aka Khomeinists) carried placards and shouted slogans in support of the "Islamic Republic." The IRP mobilized its female supporters in the early days of the postrevolutionary period against secular, and later the Islamic, opposition. Some of these IRP supporters became well known in disrupting antigovernment rallies such as Zahra Khanum, who became famous in Tehran for leading a group of female thugs against peaceful female demonstrators in order to disrupt their anti-*hijab* demonstrations in March 1979. Khomeini and other officials praised the efforts of these IRP affiliated women and publicly stressed how critical their support was to the survival of the Islamic Republic.[32]

Interestingly, Khomeini's stance vis-à-vis women was contrary to traditionalist clergy views in that he encouraged women to participate in the public sphere (wearing the *hijab*) and criticized the traditional clerics' opposition. This move by Khomeini at a critical juncture was brilliant as it ensured a much broader base of support among Iranian women from all walks of life at a time when the Islamist regime had not yet consolidated its iron grip hold on the reins of power. It could be argued that his stance was a crucial one for "the Islamic Revolution" given the historical activism of Iranian women since the Constitutional Revolution of 1906. Khomeini it appears was astute to believe that by endorsing women's right *within* an *Islamic* context, he would be able to gain their unfettered allegiance. During the referendum held to declare Iran an "Islamic Republic," he encouraged women to vote for the "Islamic Republic." This was the same cleric who in 1964 had opposed women's suffrage on the grounds that it was "un-Islamic." In 1984, the *basij* (paramilitary forces), on Khomeini's orders, even began to recruit women for military training in order to "double the strength of men already fighting."[33]

Impact of the 1979 Constitution on Iranian Women's Status

Khomeini and his supporters, aware of the divisions among the various "revolutionary forces," sought to dominate and consolidate their power through the quick enactment of a new Constitution without any meaningful debate and under politically charged and tense circumstances.[34] From the perspective of many educated and/or secular women, the 1979 Constitution—ratified in December of that year—embodied a blatant attempt of an illegitimate regime toward regression in social, cultural, and even economic affairs of the Iranian state. The Constitution of the Islamic Republic of Iran was indeed a byproduct of the ongoing power struggle during the consolidation phase of the clerical regime.[35] But it also reflected unresolved tensions; thus Mir-Hosseini describes it as a "compromise document."[36] Interestingly enough, this document gave women a prominent place in its description of women as the *key* factor in the establishment of an "Islamic nation." It stressed that only with the "Islamization of women's position" can there be the creation of a successful "Islamic nation" called the Islamic Republic of Iran. This document sought to provide a general framework for the Islamization of gender policies. The document that was ratified, unsurprisingly, reflected the formulation of gender policies that closely aligned with the political and economic development of the Islamic Republic and, specifically with the ideological vision of Khomeini and the *nahzat* (movement) that had both sustained and assisted him in his ascent to power. The dominant conception of gender was based on "*Islamic modernization* or *Islamization*," and mirrored the context of its times within Iran prior to consolidation by the Khomeinists.[37]

The 1979 Constitution, consisting of 175 articles, is a contradictory document. On the one hand, it represents secular principles of rights, equality, and justice; while on the other, it places emphasis on the supremacy of restrictive Islamic views on what constitutes rights, justice and equality. Furthermore, it pushes the envelope vis-à-vis traditional Islamist views on governance by emphasizing the undisputed right of the clergy to rule and by giving such a regime priority over civilian interests.[38]

According to the Constitution of 1979, the ideal woman is not a caricature of the "immoral Western woman" who was to be pitied not replicated. Rather, it stressed that the ideal Muslim woman in a patriarchal conservative society like Iran's recognized the dominance of her males and thus their control over her. Article 10 of the Constitution states: "Since the family is the most basic unit of Islamic society, all rules and regulations regarding family should serve the purpose of preservation of family and its relations based on Islamic rights and morals." Women's role in the "struggle" is acknowledged and their rights affirmed (preamble and Article 21) but the family (not the individual) is to be the fundamental unit in society, pivotal to the development of human beings and the area where women would have the greatest responsibility.[39]

The 1979 Iranian Constitution legitimized the "Islamic state" which subordinated the people's will to that of the clerics through the establishment of institutions of guardianship of the jurist (*velayet-e-faqih*) or leadership (*rahbari*) and the Guardian Council (*shura-ye negahban*), composed of twelve male members, six of whom were to be jurists appointed by the leader; while the other six being laymen nominated by the head of the judiciary and approved by parliament, with a tenure of six years. Khomeini was named "leader for life" and this constitution created an Assembly of Experts (*Majlis-e Khebregan-e Rahbari*) to choose his successor. The governance infrastructure established based on its stipulations reflected a form of "democratic governance" which facilitated the rule of the clerics and the implementation of Shariah as defined by those in power.[40]

Impact of Islamization on the Legal System: Legal Reforms and Women's Status, 1979–1985

The first legal setback to women's status occurred when Ayatollah Khomeini ordered the immediate suspension of the Family Protection Laws of 1967 and 1975, a few days after his return from exile.[41] To most Iranian clerics, the Family Protection Laws had symbolized an illegal usurpation of a traditionally clerical role in determining societal and familial norms and mores. They had been vehemently opposed to the enactment of such laws. Second, these secular laws enacted by the Pahlavi state challenged Islam's Shariah laws and advocated Western conceptions of societal behavior, which were anathema to the traditional societal elements and the clerical establishment.

Khomeini declared the Family Protection Law "non-Islamic" and announced its suspension and the restitution of "the Shariah." The problem was that there were no specific "Shariah laws" to implement. Thus, ironically, Reza Shah's 1935 Civil Code was implemented as "Shariah." Suspension of the Family Protection Laws was not immediately implemented due to a strong public backlash even though its suspension had meant a return to the Civil Code of 1935 drafted under Reza Shah which was based on a rather liberal interpretation of "Shariah." In April 1979, Ayatollah Mahdavi Kani, a member of the Council of Revolution, publicly declared that since Islam grants men the right to divorce, they should not be required to go through the courts. This public announcement, in essence, was an open invitation to men to circumvent the Family Protection Courts established to deal with cases involving divorce, custody and other family matters. Under the Family Protection Law, a divorce could only be issued by the courts and the decision registered in a notary's public office. Ayatollah Kani recommended that men who divorce their wives could simply register their verbal divorces in the notary public offices without producing a court order.[42] Ayatollah's Kani's stance (on divorce) was a harbinger of things to come for the more liberal elements of Iranian society and certain political parties (especially the National Front and Liberation Movement).

In August 1979, under pressure from the Khomeinists, the Provisional Government capitulated to all the demands of the hardline supporters of Khomeini. The Minister of Justice in the Provisional Government, Sadr Haj-Seyyed-Javadi, formally announced that the Family Protection Laws had been abrogated and while the family courts would not be closed, they were prohibited from issuing verdicts that were against (Shia) Shariah laws. This forced the Family Protection Courts to rely on the old Civil Code enacted under Reza Shah. Following this period of uncertainty and confusion, new Special Civil Courts were established by law and were ratified by the Revolutionary Council in September 1979. These courts were presided over by clerical judges free from the provisions of the Civil Procedure Code, hence the use of the term "Special." Through the creation of these Special Civil Courts, the clerical establishment took what was the first step toward the application of "Shariah" in the most critical sphere of social life: the family. Furthermore, this outcome reflected a compromise between the hardliners who wanted immediate implementation of "Shariah" and those who argued for a gradual approach.[43]

By October 1979, the Special Civil Courts presided over by clerics, replaced the family courts and were given a very limited mandate: they were authorized to only deal with contested divorce cases. In cases where there was mutual consent and both parties agreed to the divorce, the husband could register it, in the presence of two male witnesses, in notary offices without permission from the court.[44]

The jurisdiction of these Special Civil Courts also included disputes related to marriage, annulment, dowry, child custody, wills, and inheritance. Soon branches of Special Civil Courts were established all over Iran. Although these courts were headed by a cleric, a lay attorney assisted, along with a secretary. By 1981, there were eighty-one branches throughout Iran. In March 1981, the Civil Code ceased to be the primary family law when hardline Prime Minister Mohammad Ali Rajai presented a bill which amended the Special Civil Courts Act of 1979, which was passed by the Council of Revolutions. The bill specified that "in cases where there is no guidance on family matters either from the Council of Revolution or the Majlis, the special civil courts would base their judgments in relation to family disputes on Ayatollah Khomeini's *fatavi* (Arabic: fatwas; English: edicts/resolutions). This bill, however, failed to assuage Khomeini due to its diversity of legitimate sources for the purposes of decision making, even though it gave the clergy in charge of the Special Civil Courts a menu of options (family laws) to interpret and select from. Apparently not satisfied, Khomeini angrily intervened in August 1982, complaining about the persistence of what he called "*taghuti* laws,"[45] Khomeini ordered the "purification" of what he perceived was still a corrupted legal process that included remnants of Pahlavi era laws and demanded strict conformity with "Shariah."[46]

Khomeini's influence in the so-called Islamic judicial system which struggled to find its way was reflected in the insistence of his subordinate clerics that when certain sections of the Civil Code appeared to interpret Shariah differently than Khomeini intended, Khomeini's *Tawzih al-Masa'el*[47] would determine the decision. One example of this "conflict" between the Civil Code of the 1930s and Khomeini's views involved the age of consent for marriage. While the Civil Code recommended the age of fifteen for girls and eighteen for boys, Khomeini's book—which was far stricter in its interpretation of Shariah than the Civil Code—prescribed a minimum age of nine for girls and fifteen for boys.[48] Thus Khomeini's views prevailed in such marital matters.[49] On the subject of jurisdiction vis-à-vis non-Muslims, Khomeini's views were that the Islamization of the law did not apply to them and they were free to adhere to their religious traditions and practices in matters related to family law.

Despite the best efforts of Khomeini's new clerical establishment, the intent of the Khomeinists was not strictly adhered to when it came to implementation of "Shariah." Take the case of polygamy: according to Hojatoleslam Kermani in November 1984, there still existed a multiplicity of sources of legal guidance on family matters such as polygamy. According to him, the

Council of Guardians considered it a man's unconditional right; while those who administered the law (the Special Civil Courts) required that the first wife's permission be obtained. It was this duality in the law which prevented the courts ability to enforce sanctions against those who took second wives without the court's permission. As a result, it led to many illegal marriages and meant that sections of the Family Protection Law were still being referred to in the court system.[50]

The confusion surrounding the whole legal edifice was further exacerbated by the multiplicity of administrative centers. In its dismantlement of the Family Protection Law and the confusion surrounding interpretation and implementation, inevitably created a backlog of cases. To deal with this backlog, the High Council of the Judiciary announced its strategy of dealing with over 80,000 outstanding cases from the Family Protection Courts, as well as with new applications by creating a network of smaller and nimble "Shariat Courts." These "informal" courts were set up within the revolutionary committees and were given a remit to resolve family disputes within a week. With not enough branches of Special Civil Courts to cover the entire country, the High Council of the Judiciary instructed the public courts to take on cases involving family disputes in areas where such courts did not exist. The result of this ad hoc, quick fix, and arbitrary due process was poor coordination which led to contradictory verdicts that resulted in public displeasure and complaints. Azam Taleghani, a female member of the Majlis complained on behalf of her constituents that the verdicts of the Family Courts were uncoordinated and demanded something be done about this. She also recommended that a female consultant should be placed in every court.[51] Although seminars were conducted in which Special Court judges attended to discuss how to better coordinate their work in order to resolve increasing complaints by women over the resolution of family disputes in their courts; women continued to bear the brunt of a schizophrenic judicial system which generally failed to protect women's rights in family cases.[52]

Many recognized the problem for what it was: the precipitous abrogation of the Family Protection Law had not been complemented with the enactment of laws to address all the areas of family law covered by the abrogated law. Thus due to lack of clarity and insufficient legislation, many cases such as those involving kidnapping of a child under the custody of one parent by the other parent, required the application of the abrogated Family Protection Law which provided the only guidance on the matter.

It would take the government of the Islamic Republic of Iran until 1989 to compile an authoritative collection of the Islamic Republic's "family laws." These laws were a compilation of a number of sources on family matters including the Civil Code of 1931, the Family Protection Law (1967 and 1975), the Special Civil Courts Act of 1979, and other related legislation which had been passed by the Majlis and the Council of Guardians, regulations and opinions of the High Council of the Judiciary and General Board of Supreme Court, as well as various *fatavi* (fatwas or opinions) issued by Ayatollah Khomeini and Ayatollah Montazeri.[53]

The *Majlis-e-Shoray-e-Islami* (Islamic Consultative Assembly or Parliament), known as the Majlis (it replaced the shah's own elected Majlis), convened in the Summer of 1980. After the Iranian revolution, the Senate was abolished and the Majlis became a unicameral body. Following the March 14, 1980 parliamentary election, the IRP dominance was obvious in that it won 131 of the 216 seats; while a total of 137 seats were won by clerics. This ideological transformation meant that it was a very different majlis from previous ones in its homogeneity: it comprised of elected officials who were from similar, conservative religious, and socioeconomic backgrounds. Thus the theocratic aspirations of the Khomeinists were closer to being fulfilled in that now they could move to enact legislation that reflected their theocratic (Shia) ethos and create a truly "Islamic" society.

Women were allowed to run for office. The four women who were elected and joined the Islamic Republic's first majlis in 1980 were from conservative religious backgrounds: Gohar-al Sharia Dasteghayb, Atefeh Rajai, Maryam Behruzi and Azam Taleqani all belonged to the IRP. The credentials of the women who were elected to the Majlis reflected their religious schooling: like the male members, they all agreed that in following the teachings of Islam, the Islamic Republic had been attentive to women's rights.

The dominant state ideology of the Khomeinists was largely shared by the male parliamentarians of the first, second, and third majlis, convened respectively in 1980, 1984, and 1988. The women parliamentarians who tried to defend women's rights under the rubric of "Islamic needs and rights" were outnumbered. Marziyyeh Dabbagh (a member of the second, third and fifth majlis), who was head of women's volunteers (*basij*) and the Commander of the Pasdaran in Western Iran during the Iran-Iraq War, expressed her frustration:

> in the second and third Majlis, each time we (women) wished to present motions (concerning the condition of women), we had to first talk to and persuade every single male member that we had to take the motion to the general assembly. But even those who had already agreed with our propositions in a given commission would, as a rule, vehemently oppose it once in the general assembly.[54]

The only female parliamentarian in the first Majlis who differed somewhat from her female counterparts was Azam Taliqani (also spelled "Talaghani"), the daughter of the radical cleric Ayatollah Taliqani. Unlike the other female parliamentarians, Taliqani was a well-educated political activist who had been a political prisoner during the shah's rule. Her quest, however, was a broader one than matters involving women's issues in that she wanted to address social injustice in general which included the plight of women.[55] Azam Taliqani also publicly opposed polygamy on the grounds that it was not allowed unless based on specific criteria and that no man should be allowed more than one wife unless the needs of an "Islamic society" required such an action.[56]

Less than a month after returning from exile, Khomeini announced on March 3, 1979, that females could no longer preside over courts as judges. Shirin Ebadi, the first Iranian women to become a judge and a staunch supporter of the "Islamic Revolution," was forced to take an administrative position instead.[57]

Introduction of the 1982 Laws of Retribution (Layeh-ye-Qisas): Impact on Iranian Women

The Retribution (*Qisas*) Law was first proposed in 1980 when Ayatollah Beheshti was head of the Supreme Court, on the basis of Article 158(b) of the Constitution which instructed "preparation of bills on judicial matters appropriate to . . . the Islamic Republic." This law, however, was not fully ratified until July 1982 and it took another two years to overcome certain legal impediments to its implementation. Prior to its passage in the Majlis in 1982, it was implemented by the Revolutionary Courts and later by the Anti-Corruption Courts. The Retribution Law of 1982 replaced sections of the Public Punishment Law (1924). The Retribution Law involved two types of offenses: (1) murder and bodily harm caused by one person on another; and (2) sex related offenses.

The first segment of the law involved resolving cases of murder and bodily harm through reliance on the concept of "an eye for an eye." The aggrieved party—or his or her relatives if deceased—could request the identical punishment for the perpetrators. This was a major departure from the secular laws it replaced. Unlike the Public Punishment Law, the concept of punishment under the Retribution Law was not to be based on "society" versus "individual" but rather on that of "individuals and families" versus "individuals and families."[58] This was based on historical tradition under Shariah in which the murder or injury done to one person or family should be prosecuted through retaliation in the exact same manner ("an eye for an eye") by the aggrieved party or parties or their representatives. In addition, there could be an exchange of *Diyat* (blood money). As Kazemi observes on this law which served to relegate women to second class status:

> entailed extensive and elaborate procedures for restitution and depends heavily on the testimony of witnesses. Article 33 of the law, which elaborates on testimony in murder trials, proclaims unequivocally that a woman's testimony is equivalent to no more than half of a man's: a) Intentional murder is proven only with the testimony of two just male witnesses; b) Quasi-intentional or

accidental murder is proven with the testimony of two just males and/or one just male and two just females and/or one just male and the plaintiff's oath.[59]

The most well-known *qisas* case in Iran involved Ameneh Bahrami and Majid Movahedi, two university students in Tehran: Majid threw acid at Ameneh's face in 2004 when she refused his marriage proposal. The acid left her blind in both eyes and severely disfigured her face. It was Bahrami who demanded, per the stipulations of the Retribution Law of 1982, that she be allowed to blind Movahedi using acid, thus literally applying the "eye for an eye" intent of this law. Bahrami said: "I've suffered so much in these years but now I am really happy. . . . The verdict is completely legal and I would like to carry it out."[60]

By saying that "the verdict is completely legal," Ameneh Bahrami was referring to the Islamic Shariah law (of *Qisas*) in Iran that allows for the "eye for an eye"–style judicial punishment. Generally in Iran, *qisas*-type punishments are meted out to murderers and to those convicted of causing intentional physical injury. There have, however, been a number of cases of acid attacks reported in Iran in recent years. Ameneh Bahrami stated she wanted the *qisas* punishment to be implemented on Majid Movahedi in order to deter other acid throwers. However, when it came time to implement the court's decision in Bahrami's favor on July 31, 2011, she pardoned Movahedi just as the doctor was about to apply five drops of acid in a live broadcast on Iranian state television.[61] In another famous case which involved the sigheh wife, Shahla Jahed, of a well-known football player, Nasser Mohammadkhani; Jahed was found guilty of killing Mohammadkhani's wife and condemned to death by hanging based on the Qisas law. This sentence was carried out on December 1, 2010, in the presence of the judges, Mohammadkhani and the relatives of his wife. Asked to forgive Jahed for her sins just before the hanging, the family refused and forgave her only after she was executed.[62] Many Iranians believe that Jahed was framed by her temporary "husband" Mohammadkhani who sought to get rid of his wife.[63]

REFORMS AND HOPE: WOMEN'S LIVES IN AN EVOLVING IRANIAN THEOCRACY, 1985–2005

Once the Khomeini-led regime had largely purged the country of rivals (religious and secular), dealt with various growing pains, and consolidated its hold on power, it was forced to consider a more pragmatic approach vis-à-vis its "Islamization" program. Furthermore, the end of the Iran-Iraq War in 1988 accelerated this reexamination, as the survival narrative to consolidate the Khomeinists hold on power, and incorporate divergent interests, was no longer applicable or justifiable. A new age began which Kian calls "the period of reconstruction." It forced the power elite and their allies to acknowledge the economic, social, and demographic realities within this "Islamic state" in order to adopt new strategies.[64] For example, there had been an explosive population growth as the 1986 census revealed a net gain of about 15 million people. This led the Iranian government to do an about face notwithstanding its publicly enunciated pro-birth traditions of Islam and Iranian culture, and the traditionalist *ulema*'s disapproval of birth control and abortion: it reintroduced family planning and birth control from 1988 onward.[65]

The death of Ayatollah Khomeini seemed to create a more receptive climate in the country on issues affecting women. Many of the harsher policies of the early years were overturned by the Majlis, while others coexisted with new policies, which led to an appearance of an Islamic Republic embroiled in some sort of "identity crisis."[66] For example, on the one hand, women could serve in the military; while on the other, they were restricted in what they could study in school; women had been elected to the Majlis, but were forced to wear chadors; and women won the right to claim "wages in cash" from husbands who filed for divorce, but they were still required to ride in the back of the bus, segregated from men.[67]

Ironically it was the paradoxical behavior of the Khomeinists that emboldened women of all political leanings to demand better conditions in the workplace, at home or in educational institutions.[68] Due to the demands of a long war with Iraq (1980–1988), the theocracy had been forced to recruit women for both the war effort and to perform in traditionally male professions (in factories, for example) in order to free up able-bodied men for the war front. The number of women employed in government positions also grew.[69] Women from all walks of life were hopeful that their aspirations and demands would be heard and addressed in light of their sacrifices made during the war with Iraq. Things certainly seemed to suggest that the Islamic Republic was amenable to reasonable gender-based reforms once Ali Akbar Hashemi Rafsanjani became the president in 1989. The reforms that followed were all cloaked in "Islamic norms" and women were urged to contribute to the economic development of Iran "without the corruption of Western societies." Rafsanjani encouraged women to join the military but to retain their "Islamic morality." He supported greater female roles in the social milieu which he lauded as the "progressive Islamic code of ethics that sanctions the complete social participation of women."[70]

The Iranian state seemed to be moving toward some sort of "*glasnost*"[71] and those segments of civil society—like the intellectuals and the more secular urban dwellers—who had felt betrayed and/or repressed began to hope that, in the post-Khomeini period, perhaps civil society would now be allowed greater freedoms and opportunities as the theocracy moved away from the repressive actions of the 1980s presumably conducted in the name of state survival and regime consolidation.

MOBILIZED WOMEN AND THE PERSONAL STATUS LAW IN IRAN, 1986–2005

For many women, the advent of theocratic rule represented a dramatic overnight reversal in the slow gains women had made in civil society. Even conservative (i.e., religious) women, who had disapproved of the shah's "modernization" efforts as reflected in liberal dress codes and coeducational interaction between the sexes, came to view the Khomeinists' interpretation of female rights as constituting a very restricted—and patriarchal—reading of what constitutes women's "rights" in Islam. Initially supportive of the efforts to overthrow what they viewed was a degenerate and corrupt monarchy, such women realized much to their horror that the removal of key protections afforded to them in the Family Protection Laws had all but ensured that they would no longer experience even a bearable version of second class status in society. Rather, this new social paradigm, reinforced by Shariah-inspired laws as interpreted by clerics who supported the ethos—Velayat-e-Fiqh—of the Khomeinist government seemed to infringe upon their personal lives in a detrimental fashion. Thus, it also served to galvanize Iranian women to "gender activism."

The Iranian female realized that, for example, unless a bride explicitly specified in her marriage contract her *mehr* (dowry)[72] where the family would live after marriage, or whether or not she would be allowed to pursue a career, she would have to obey the wishes of her husband. A woman could no longer legally select her first husband and this marriage would only be legal if endorsed by her father or other paternal male kin.[73] Furthermore, the father or any other male guardian retained significant rights: girls as young as nine—some even at birth—could be betrothed without their consent before puberty; a custodial mother could not take the children out of the country without permission from the father or the courts; worse, the limited visiting rights for a noncustodial mother, as outlined in the Family Protection Act, were no longer stipulated by the courts and many mothers were unable to visit or see their children following a divorce.[74]

The long and costly Iran-Iraq War forced the Iranian government to reexamine its Shariah-based family laws due to the high casualties suffered, which left many young women as widows. With the abrogation of the Family Protection Law, these widows who had lost their husbands in combat were often forced to give up custody of their children to the paternal grandfathers or father's male kin. For these paternal male relatives, one of the attractions or incentives in acquiring custody was a financial one: the custodian of a "martyred" soldier's children would receive his government pension and not the wife per se. The plight of these war widows galvanized female activists and the media to take up their cause. Women argued that for a regime which emphasized the need to create a *just* Islamic society as its official slogan and which had stressed the need for females to be active participants in this "revolution"; the treatment meted out to women was abysmal. This concerted effort by the media and female activists to bring attention to bear on the apparent disconnect between the regime's enunciated claims and its actions certainly embarrassed segments of the Iranian theocracy. More importantly, it was the government's emphasis on motherhood as the highest and most desirable status for women, which galvanized female opposition to force a reexamination of governmental policy vis-à-vis the war widows and their children.[75]

Women from all walks of life who initially had supported the overthrow of the shah and his monarchy now became political activists (such as Shirin Ebadi, Shahla Lahiji, Faezeh Hashemi, Mahboubeh Ummi, Shahla Sherkat, Goharolsharieh Dastgheib, and Mehranguiz Kar) who demanded "justice" for women as an "Islamic right." The Martyrs (*Shohada*) Foundation,[76] which also acted as an advocate for the families, widows, and children of those who perished during the war with Iraq, pushed for amendments to the law. The social pressure forced Ayatollah Khomeini to issue a statement which returned custody (though not guardianship) to the martyrs' widows, even in the event of remarriage.[77] This action did set an important precedent as it indicated a significant change in the Khomeinists' position vis-à-vis family matters and was a huge step forward for the more moderate conservative elements within the clergy and society. This victory helped embolden Iranian women as it meant that the so-called Shariah-based interpretations of the regime were not carved in stone and, with sufficient support, they could influence gender policies in favor of female rights in the name of Islam and family well-being. More importantly, this specific redirection helped to strengthen the recognition that the mother-child relationship took precedence over those with the paternal kin of a deceased father. Lastly, it sent a signal to the family court judges, who enjoyed considerable discretionary power, that they could "interpret" such custody cases in favor of the mother without worrying about any adverse reaction from the theocracy.[78]

When the Family Protection Act was abrogated by the Khomeinists in 1979, men were able to reassert their "right" to an arbitrary divorce and assert that under "Shariah" they weren't even required to register their divorces (verbally stating three times to the wife "I divorce thee" would suffice). Middle-aged women suddenly found themselves without any legal protection from the whims of husbands who might suddenly decide to divorce them. Without marketable skills and financial means, such women were forced to rely on the kindness of extended family or of their grown children for survival. Worse, without the mechanism of registration, women who remarried could be accused of bigamy if the husband denied he had verbally granted a *talaq* and meanwhile she had remarried. Men's arbitrary divorce rights would remain a major source of dissatisfaction for women.[79]

In response to the alarming trends in society vis-à-vis the implementation of Shariah law that was adversely affecting women's lives regardless of socioeconomic background, women mobilized. They began to inundate newspapers and magazines with stories of personal injustices suffered by them due to these "interpretations" of Shariah which presumably were supposed to create an environment characterized by family stability but, instead, had made their lives a living hell in that many wives, after years of marriage, now had no legal protections from the whims of husbands should they decide to divorce them and remarry without their wives' permission.

Interestingly enough, it was the Special Civil Court judges who came to the rescue of Iranian women. Specifically it was the head of this court, Hojatoleslam Mahadvi Kermani, who announced that Shariah would apply to the custody of children under twelve. But for children older than twelve, if they demonstrated maturity, the court would allow the child to choose which parent to live with. Financial responsibility, however, would remain with the father regardless of the child's residence. The right of a martyr's paternal family to custody of a young child was challenged in the Majlis. Mrs. Goharolsharieh Dastgheib, a member of the Majlis, brought up the subject in the Parliament regarding the fate of the offspring of "martyrs" of the Iran-Iraq War:

> Many of the children of our martyrs not only lose their father but also become victims of a custody law which separates them from their mothers . . . are forcibly separated to live with paternal relatives who claim custody because of some old family grudge against the mother of the child in order to ruin her. This is a misuse of the Islamic law of custody. The Islamic law of custody cannot be implemented in spirit until this un-Islamic behavior is eliminated.[80]

Thanks to the initiative of the few female deputies in the Majlis, the Majlis Committee on Legal Matters prepared a proposal on the right of mothers to custody as early as 1981. After the final reading in the Majlis in December 1981, it was referred to the Council of Guardians for approval. In March 1982, after discussion this bill was rejected by the Council of Guardians which had the authority to reject a bill if it was determined that its stipulations were incompatible with Shariah. The content of the bill were not made public and it would take another three years for the custody bill to be reintroduced in the Majlis. In February 1985, it was reintroduced by the Majlis Committee on Revolutionary Institutions who made a number of suggestions on how to amend the original bill to make it "Shariah compliant" in the eyes of the Council of Guardians. During the discussion on the bill on Mothers' Right to Foster Minor and Forlorn Children on the Majlis floor, some deputies spoke of the importance of granting the right of custody to men on two grounds. First, they stressed the dangers of having "unsuitable" mothers raising children; second, they argued that burdening a widow with raising children would limit her chances of remarriage by placing such a burden on her. Furthermore, this bill gave the Special Civil Courts the power to punish the father or paternal family by imprisonment, flogging or fines, if they did not abide by the decision of the court to place the child with the mother. But it ignored the critical issue of specifying to whom the right of custody would actually belong to overcome the objections of the Council of Guardians.[81]

The Majlis deputy Dastgheib argued that the judgments of the Special Civil Courts were often legally inconsistent and hampered by procedural difficulties and needed to be streamlined in a manner that takes into account the emotional needs of a child rather than treating a child like a stone to be shifted around. She stressed that such measures had led to increased juvenile delinquency because fathers often sought custody as a matter of right and then placed them in the care of "unqualified" relatives. Since the Council of Guardians had already ruled on the subject and refused to back down from its earlier interpretation of custodial matters according to Shariah, *the only face saving way around this impasse was to allow the Special Civil Courts to avoid relying on a strict interpretation of Shariah*. Thus, the *Majlis* and the Council of Guardians informally reached a compromise when it was agreed that the matter would be left in the hands of the judges of the Special Civil Courts on a case by case basis and the judge's personal interpretation of the Shariah.[82]

By 1986, pragmatic considerations also seemed to force the hand of the hard core supporters of the "Islamic Revolution" in the Majlis. That year, the Majlis passed a twelve-article law on marriage and divorce which appeared—at least on the books—to ameliorate the conditions for women in marital affairs. All marriage contracts now allowed for prenuptial agreements and women were urged to protect their interests. The law also recognized a divorced woman's right to a share of the property the couple had acquired during their marriage and were given alimony rights (Article 1). Article 12 of the 1986 law offered women some protection on polygamy. It, in essence, reinstated the provision of the 1975 Family Protection Law which had granted a wife the right to divorce her husband if he marries a second woman without her consent, or if a husband does not treat his wives fairly and equally as required by Islamic law.[83]

Another huge legal victory for women occurred in December 1991, when the Iranian government finally passed the *ujrat-e-mesel* (wages for housework) laws. It stipulated that while men and women must get the court's permission before pronouncing and registering their divorce, the law did not limit men's right to divorce: a man who wanted to divorce had to be permitted by the court to do so. The passage of the *ujrat-e-mesel* law was meant to discourage men from pursuing arbitrary divorces with no financial consequences for them and dire ones for their former wives.[84] In order to make the divorce proceedings less draconian for women (i.e., fairer), the court could decide to award the wife monetary compensation for all her household labor undertaken during their years of marriage if she had performed her wifely duties and she made this request of the court. The husband then was mandated by law to pay her the specified sum for her labor and fulfill any other financial obligations before he could obtain a divorce from the court. Since no guidelines were established for the judges to determine these "wages," individual judges were authorized to determine the compensation on a case-by-case basis which took into consideration the financial position of the husband and the duration of the marriage. Because judges are exclusively male, women are still vulnerable to the whims of a male dominated legal system as they seek "justice."[85]

The successful passage of this law reflected the years of lobbying by female activists and their increasing support within society. They had successfully argued that wages for housework laws are in conformance with Islamic program of the regime since according to Shariah, women do not have to work in their husband's home. Furthermore, they argued that women are even entitled to receive compensation for breastfeeding their children and that all women who work and manage their homes should be entitled to the fruits of their labor in a just Islamic society. This legal victory was more symbolic than tangible in that enforcement mechanisms in the judiciary continued to favor the males irrespective of the laws on the books.

In the fall of 1991, the minimum age for marriage was raised to fifteen for females and eighteen for males, with marriage below the legal age allowed with a court's consent.[86] Historically, the average age at marriage in Iran was a factor influenced by region, ethnicity, and socioeconomic status and implementation of state-instituted measures had a limited success especially in the more rural and isolated regions.

PRAGMATIC ACTIVISM IN A THEOCRACY: SOCIAL ALLIANCES TO INFLUENCE GENDER POLICY

As early as 1982, even the conservative female supporters of Khomeini's "Islamic Revolution" realized how dire circumstances had become for *all* Iranian women thanks to the rigid interpretations of "Shariah" by the clerics ruling the country. But it wasn't until the latter part of the 1980s that these female regime supporters would acknowledge that they had, in essence, become advocates for the *same* fundamental rights as their more secularized (read: "modernized") sisters, who had worked so hard since the 1906 Constitutional Revolution to assure Iranian women some basic legal protections.

In many ways it was back to the future in that now it was the female deputies of the Islamic Republic—vice those who served in the Majlis during the Pahlavi Monarchy—who were applying the same arguments as their more secular "Westernized" sisters did during the shah's period when they pressed for improved custodial rights.

Mahbubeh Ummi, the editor of *Farzaneh* (an Islamist women's magazine), acknowledged the need for collaboration with other Iranian women who did not share their views:

> Although secular women do not share our convictions, we can collaborate because we all work to promote women's status. We (Islamist women) no longer consider ourselves to be the sole heirs of the revolution. We have realized that our sectarian views of the first post-revolutionary years led to the isolation of many competent seculars, which was to the detriment of all women. We now hope to compensate for our errors.[87]

Shahla Shirkat (also spelled "Sherkat"), the editor of the *Zanan* (another Islamist women's magazine) shared Ummi's view which were based on pragmatic considerations superseding narrow ideological lanes in order to unite and galvanize Iranian women to seek better social conditions in a "just Islamic State."[88] The aim of magazines such as *Zanan* was to reach the widest possible female audience, as well as male sympathizers, in order to promote the importance of women's status in a truly Islamic society. This was accomplished through the publication of articles that emphasized legal, social and economic shortcomings and which proposed concrete changes in civil and penal laws, in employment legislation and constitutional law.[89] For example, since its inauguration in 1993, the Islamist women's journal *Farzaneh* focused its coverage on depicting the Prophet Muhammad's treatment of his wives and also by citing specific Quranic *ayats* (verses) which hold women in high esteem. They have highlighted the prominent roles Khadijah, Muhammad's first wife, and Aisha (his favorite wife after Khadijah's death) played in his lifetime.[90]

In November–December 1992, soon after its inception, *Zanan*[91] published a series of articles which examined the real or potential roadblocks to women's participation in religious and judicial institutions. The author of one piece titled "*Qizavat-i-Zan*" (Women's Religious Authority), Mina Yadigar Azadi, argued that based on the evidence "a man has no natural privilege over a woman. If a man can become a judge, so can a woman, and if a man can become a source of imitation, so can a woman."[92]

Unlike *Zanan*, *Farzaneh* and other popular women's magazines targeted the intelligentsia and the political elite. *Zan-i-Ruz* (Women Today) became a popular magazine among the less-educated women. Thanks to its cooking recipes, stories on health care, fashion, and sewing, it was transformed into a vocal magazine on issues concerning a wider spectrum of Iranian society. Under Tayyibeh Iskandari's tutelage, it raised certain fundamental questions regarding the condition of women. One approach to solving "women's problems," according to Iskandari, was "to reach men who are the main decision makers." The activism of these women who were strong supporters of the theocracy did not go unnoticed by the senior clerics running the show. Furthermore, many of their articles inspired even some of the more hard line elements of Iranian society to question the interpretations of this *Velayet-e-Fiqh*. The debates initiated by such female magazines even influenced women political activists like Faizeh Rafsanjani who argued that "it is not Islam but the clergy's interpretations of its precepts which led to the prohibition of women's access to the judiciary."[93]

The success of such magazines in influencing public debate on the legitimate role (and rights) of females in an "Islamic society" was evident in the—often violent—response by the traditionalist press, including *Keyhan* and *Subh*, and the physical attacks by the *Hizballah* mobs, backed by the traditionalist clergy. These traditionalist supporters of the Islamic state viewed the attempts of such women as "an attempt to annihilate Islam from within by increasingly demanding accommodations they view as antithetical to an "Islamic way of life." What incurred, and continues to incur, their wrath is that in addition to demanding legal changes, often in anonymously published articles, these female activists published reports on spousal abuse suffered at the hands of husbands; stories of women who have been forcibly divorced and of those women who were denied custody of their children; and the salary and status disparities between men and women. Such exposure of "dirty social laundry" was an anathema for the "traditionalists" who,—rightly as it turns out—feared how such magazines increased women's awareness and encouraged some to become activists to the detriment of the traditional fabric of their "Islamic society." Furthermore, it led to a reassessment of some of the "traditionalists" such as Munireh Nawbakht, who became receptive to reform measures:

> the increasing social activity of women . . . necessitates radical reforms in the existing laws to determine women's rights and their social responsibilities. . . . These issues should be discussed by the majority of the deputies and this will only be possible if women are members of different commissions.[94]

There were, however, still enough critics among the females who were traditionalists. For example, Maryam Behruzi harshly criticized Faizeh Rafsanjani in public for promoting such female outdoor activities as cycling and horseback. Behruzi believed that should Iranian females engage in such activities they could be adopting Western habits. Furthermore, *zanan* continued to incur the anger of the traditionalists—male and female—notwithstanding the fact that it was an advocate for "Islamic ideals and society."

Opponents of the "Muslim feminists," however, had a harder time trying to smear the reputations of women who were devout in both dress and behavior. Trying to label these women as "Westernized feminists" backfired and only served to increase social support for their efforts to ensure Iranian women some semblance of basic human rights. The efforts of these Muslim feminists certainly came to be appreciated, and even assisted where possible, by their more "Westernized" (read: secularized) sisters who recognized the value of their female opponents' work to restore women's hard earned position in Iranian society.

State-Societal Compromises and Conflicts: Women's Lives in Iranian Society, 1985–2005

By the late 1980s, with the end of the Iran-Iraq War and the death of Ayatollah Khomeini; coupled with the increased, and effective, activism of Muslim feminists and their growing allies in society, conditions began to slowly improve for women thanks to certain state initiated measures. In 1988, the High Council of Cultural Revolution, chaired by President Rafsanjani, founded the Social and Cultural Council of Women to promote women's economic and social activity; and in 1992, the Office of Women's Affairs was established to "detect problems and shortcomings and to propose solutions to ameliorate women's status and their economic, social, cultural and political role. In 1990, President Rafsanjani stated that women needed to play a larger role in Iranian arts, sports, politics and religion: "We are in need of a women's labor force."[95] In this period of increasing openness, various types of female social and political activists emerged who were willing to push the envelope of change in women's favor.

The reformist movement (1997–2003) under President Khatami, however, proved illusionary, characterized by superficial reforms that were only "skin deep" according to Shahra Razavi, a gender rights researcher of Iranian descent at the United Nations.[96] The Iranian regime on gender matters did not often practice what it preached notwithstanding the fact that even prominent Ayatollahs and Hojjat ul-Islamis were now advocating equal rights for women. Ayatollah Mohammad Yazdi argued that in Islam "women enjoy the same rights as men."[97] Another leading cleric in the popular movement for the reform of family law in Iran was Hojjat ul-Islam Seyyed Mohsin Saidzadeh.[98] A prolific writer, Saidzadeh began to research women's issues in 1988 and wrote extensively on the subject, with some of his work published in *Zanan* (the Islamic feminists' journal). He also published in *Payam-e-Zan,* another women's journal published by seminaries in Qom. As Mir-Hosseini highlights, Saidzadeh did not shy away from obvious gender inequalities that were embedded in the orthodox interpretations of the Shariah. He called this approach "the Equality Perspective." His arguments shocked many of his clerical counterparts (especially the Khomeinists) because he wrote that, with the exception of some minor religious rules related to obvious biological differences between males and females, Islam regards men and women in the same way . . . as equals. Thus his views bolstered the cause of the feminists. Saidzadeh defined "feminism" as "a social movement whose agenda is the establishment of women's human rights . . . it recognizes that women are independent and complete beings and instead *places emphasis on common humanity of sexes and not on their differences*." Unlike many of his religious counterparts, Saidzadeh believed that gender inequality in Shariah law was due to a mistaken construction by male jurists and that this went against divine will.[99]

Saidzadeh's views were seen as being incendiary and harmful to the interests of the state by the Khomeinists. It is, however, noteworthy that though the so-called moderate reformers were in power, Saidzadeh was arrested on June 30, 1998, and jailed. Released from prison in 1999, Saidzadeh was banned from performing any clerical duties for five years and he was banned for life from publishing his works.[100]

Another widely regarded religious intellectual who was forced into exile was Abdolkarim Soroush who belonged to a group of clerical and seminary intellectuals who wanted—via *ijtehad* or independent reasoning—to reconcile Islam with the discourse of human rights, democracy, and gender equality through what was called "dynamic jurisprudence." Before his exile, Souroush was a regular contributor to the popular women's magazine, *Zanan*; his articles strove to develop a coherent theory of women's rights within Islamic jurisprudence.[101]

THE POLITICS OF REPRESSION: WOMEN'S STATUS IN THE POST-REFORM ERA

As observed by certain Iranian scholars, the 1989–2003 period reflected some positive developments for Iranian women: the government reintroduced certain measures that either mirrored the abrogated Family Protection Act or contained elements of these Pahlavi-era laws. The surprise election of Mahmoud Ahmadinejad to the office of president, however, was a watershed event. His election was a victory for the hardliners' camp and meant the end of "the reformist agenda," at least as it pertained to gender policies. Furthermore, notwithstanding the increasingly repressive approach to naysayers and regime opponents, the opposition to "Islamic despotism" of this theocracy continued, even expanded, at great personal cost. This growing opposition culminated in the Green Movement's public protests in June 2009; a consequence of the reelection of Ahmadinejad. Peaceful protests were met with brute force by the state's security forces that silenced the voices of dissent through various methods which continue at the time of this writing.

FROM LIMITED PROGRESSION TO REGRESSION: AHMADINEJAD'S "GENDER APPROACH"[102]

It has been argued that Ahmedinejab's surprise victory in 2005 was due to fraud and other electoral irregularities.[103] Others have postulated that the gradual erosion of popular support for the reformists—attributed to cronyism, endemic corruption and a failure to deliver tangible economic results—led to the resurgence of the conservatives at the ballot box. While campaigning, Ahmadinejad made sure to leverage his "humble" background and projected a cloying sincerity while frequently enunciating a deep concern for the plight of the "common people."

Regardless of the reasons for this sudden turn of events in 2005, the record of Ahmadinejad's government vis-à-vis female concerns and rights reflects a process of regression and increased repression reminiscent of the early days of the "Islamic revolution." According to Ehtehami, the presidency was the last holdout for Iran's reformists, and the victory of Ahmadinejad gave total control of state institutions to the conservative camp.[104]

During his first term in office, Ahmadinejad wasted no time in backtracking on promises made to women. Furthermore, although Ahmadinejad brought a new generation of politicians into government who wore overcoats not turbans, their ideology mirrored that of their more traditional elders associated with Khomeini's "Islamic revolution."[105] Since Ahmadinejad took office, Iranian activists (male and female) have been beaten, jailed, tortured, and killed for "disturbing the peace and/or trying to overthrow the government at the behest of foreign interests."[106] Furthermore, Ahmadinejad's government continues to send mixed messages. Ahmadinejad was the first president since the revolution to nominate women to his cabinet. By 2011, there were three women—albeit all regime hardliners—in his cabinet:[107] Nasrin Soltankhah as Minister of National Elites; Maryam Mojtahed Zadeh as Minister of Women and Family, and Marzieh Vahid Dastjerdi as Minister of Health.[108]

IMPACT OF THE 2009 GREEN REVOLUTION ON FEMALE STATUS

The results of the 2009 Presidential election revealed the clerical state's vulnerability vis-à-vis a wide swath of civil society. It also served to create and widen numerous divisive schisms within the ruling clerical elite threatening the theocracy's very survival. In many ways, the 2009 election revolved around what would constitute the "status of women" in Iranian society. Mehdi Karrubi, one of the leading presidential contenders, promised to fight for equal rights for women if elected. Calling for change, Karrubi argued that change was not possible without the restoration of the greatness and rightful status of women.[109] But it was Iran's former Prime Minister Mir Hossein Mousavi, the key challenger to incumbent Ahmadinejad—along with his wife, Zahra Rahnavard—who attracted considerable female support at the ballot box.[110] Mousavi and Rahnavard, a popular Muslim feminist, became the symbols of the "Green Movement" which followed. Roya Maoudzadeh, a young Mousavi supporter told the Associated Press before the election that what drew her most to Mousavi was his wife: "Rahnavard is a symbol of women's rights. She is inspiring women to stand up and demand their rights from Iran's male Dominated Ruling System."[111]

The massive 2009 demonstrations—with estimates of up to 3 million protestors in mid-June—against the rigged elections marked the first time since the "Iranian Revolution" that people from all walks of life filled Tehran's streets in protest. Contrary to the government's claim that the demonstrators were just a disgruntled Westernized minority, the images on television revealed women, alongside men, religious and secular, traditional and modern, young and old, poured into the streets despite the unrelenting violence (including torture) at the hands of the regime. Neda Soltan's videotaped death from a gunshot by a government militia member made her a lasting symbol of the brutal misogyny under Ahmadinejad's regime.[112]

The Green Movement shook the establishment clerics to their core. Their response was to exert more brute force against their opponents' supporters and to place Mousavi and his wife under indefinite house arrest. But the damage was done. These unprecedented public protests against the Khamenei regime demonstrated that the deep splits in civil society now reached all the way up into the ruling clerical elite. Dissension or cracks in the upper echelons of Ahmadinejad's government on the subject of women's rights in Islam were public knowledge now. In September 2010, Ahmadinejad's closest aide and chief of staff, Esfandiar Rahim Mashaie, upset Khamenei when he called for more rights for Iran's oppressed women. Mashaie was quoted as saying: "Women have been oppressed and treated unjustly in our society in the past and this oppression still exists." Mashaie's comments carry weight and underscore the growing ideological and personal rifts among the regime's hardliners over the issue of women's rights in Islam.[113]

FEMALE ACTIVISM IN AN ISLAMIC THEOCRACY: ISLAMIC FEMINISM AND RESISTANCE

By the mid-1980s, the conservative segments of Iran's women—mostly clustered in the wealthy bazaari community or from either working class or peasant backgrounds—who had despised the secular gender policies of the shah as being "un-Islamic"—realized their visions of a just Islamic society that guaranteed women their legitimate rights not only went unfulfilled but, worse, the theocracy seemed bent on denying them even their basic "Allah bestowed" rights. Even some of the more diehard female supporters of the Khomeinists objected to the seeming obsession the regime had with women's clothing as somehow constituting *the litmus test* of whether or not the revolution had succeeded or failed. Indeed, women's clothing in Iran has been one of the key overt civil society battlefields since the clerics took over. Since then many Iranian females (and some males who have defiantly worn the tie which was banned as "western") have needled the state in a variety of imaginative ways vis-à-vis their clothing. Thousands continue to defy the state's ruling on "appropriate" attire, in other words, the all-enveloping black chador, by wearing short scarves that show some hair to colorful chadors and even wearing nail polish.[114]

Although women succeeded in keeping their right to vote and run for certain public offices after the imposition of Shariah as law, they have struggled with the theocracy on three important issues: minimum marriageable age, temporary marriage, and polygamy. In 2006, female activist and Nobel Peace Prize recipient, Shirin Ebadi, helped begin a campaign to collect the signatures for the One Million Signature Campaign (also known as the Campaign for Equality); a petition protesting legalized discrimination by the Iranian government against women.[115] The petition demanded the government give women more equal footing in the laws on marriage, divorce, alimony and polygamy. It sought to end polygamy and the so-called temporary marriages permitted under Shi'ite Muslim law but viewed by many Iranians as thinly veiled prostitution.[116] Ebadi launched this campaign because she believed that Islam was not the problem but *how the clerics interpreted it was.* To Western feminists, Ebadi embodied all the commendable qualities of a modern-day feminist. A view Ebadi herself strongly objected to when she argued that the West is in some ways no better than the clerics in their desire to regulate women's lives. Rather, Ebadi argued, the state has no business dictating whether or not women should wear the veil. She believes women should have the right to choose what they want to wear.[117] Within a month, the million signature campaign for equality had been signed by 200,000 people. Yet, to date, the petition has not reached the Iranian Majlis for varied reasons to include an active repressive campaign by the State, which has led to thousands of arrests of those associated with this effort.[118]

When Ahmadinejad's government sought to remove the veto power (originally granted by the shah) of the wife on their husbands' right under Shariah to take up to four permanent wives and countless temporary concubines, it faced fierce resistance.[119] In August 2008, Ahmadinejad presented a draft bill to the Majlis to "re-Islamize" the status of women and replace what he called were the "Zionist-Crusader" inspired laws from the shah's time. Called the Family Protection Bill, it sought to restore men's "Islamic right" to divorce their wives without informing them; nor would they be obligated to pay alimony.

In the summer of 2008, wives of members of the Majlis began to receive anonymous phone calls. The female caller would ask the wife if she would permit her to be the temporary wife of her husband for just a week; she would argue that permitting this was the duty of a good Muslim wife. Many wives hung up in shock. All the callers were female activists whose investigations had uncovered that at least 65 male members of the country's 290-strong parliament had two or more wives. This action also contravened the International Covenant on Civil and Political Rights (ICCPR), which Iran had ratified. Article 23 stipulates that states must ensure that men and women have equal rights when marrying or at the dissolution of marriage.[120] To date, this bill has not been passed in the Majlis due to female activism against its passage.

Given the oppressiveness of the Iranian theocracy toward any overt social challenges, some Iranian observers have opined that the rampant divorce rate is one indicator of social (read: female) defiance toward an increasingly repressive state. Senior officials and members of parliament have increasingly referred to the issue as a crisis and a "national threat." Divorce has skyrocketed as birth rates drop sharply. Since 2000, the number of divorces awarded each year has roughly tripled from around 50,000 in 2000, to over 150,000 in 2010, according to official figures. One marriage in every seven ends in divorce nationally; in Tehran, the ratio is 1 divorce for every 3.76 marriages according to government figures. Explanations for the rising divorce rate vary. Some Iranians emphasize factors like rapid urbanization, high living costs and a jobless rate that official figures put at close to one in four among sixteen to twenty-five-year-olds. The more conservative elements blame what they view as "growing godlessness among the young and the corrupting effects of the Western media" as the source of the problem. While husbands can terminate their marriages in a matter of weeks without stating any reason, women have to establish sufficient grounds for divorce in a process that can take several years, even with professional legal advice.[121] What is noteworthy is that many of the women seeking a divorce are poor and/or even religious. Many women are also finding refuge in higher education in order to postpone marriage and earn a degree.[122]

In order to obtain a divorce, Iranian women have increasingly leveraged their legal right to a *mehrieh*—a single payment agreed to and noted in the marriage certificate that the husband must pay the wife in the event of a divorce. Under what are known as "divorces of mutual consent," a woman may forgo part or all of her mehrieh to provide a financial incentive to her husband to let her leave. Increasingly used as a weapon to thwart their future husbands from considering additional marriages or to obtain a divorce, many Iranian women and/or their families have demanded that the value of mehriehs be listed so high that it acts as a deterrent vis-à-vis a future husband's behavior. This has led some conservatives to champion the idea of capping mehriehs to reduce the divorce rate. While some clerics and government officials have promoted the idea of having a purely symbolic mehrieh, like a handful of gold coins or a Qu'ran.[123]

Despite living in a patriarchical theocracy, more Iranian women are employed or actively looking for jobs today (around 20 percent) than they were during the early years (around 7 percent) after the 1979 "Islamic Revolution." By 2011, female undergraduate students outnumbered men in Iran's universities by almost two to one. This pattern suggests that Iranian women through struggle, determination and perseverance managed to retain some semblance of control over their lives and, in some areas such as Tehran, have even gained ground (university attendance) that wasn't the case under the much more liberal governance of the last shah. But recent decisions by the Education Ministry on female higher education seem ominous. As recently as early 2012, female advocates claimed that the chasm between religious and secular women had narrowed and both camps now chafe at the embedded legal discrimination against women. It is noteworthy that Zahra Eshraghi, the granddaughter of the revolutionary leader, Ayatollah Ruhollah Khomeini, signed the One Million Signatures petition.[124] Haleh Esfandiari's recent concerns on Tehran's new education policy, however, are both noteworthy and worrisome.[125] According to various Iranian media reports, thirty-six public universities in Iran—to include Tehran University—are moving to enact discriminatory education policies which would severely constrain female access to higher education in the 2012 academic year. There does not seem to be a uniform policy; instead each university is taking its own approach resulting in the exclusion of women from seventy-seven various fields including engineering, natural science, law, social science, and the arts and humanities.[126]

There are members of parliament and elements in the Ahmadinejad's own government weren't pleased with this controversial move. In response to societal criticism, the government made the rather feeble case by arguing that the architects of such discriminatory policies vis-à-vis female higher education and access actually originate in the offices of certain universities' school administrators offices and not the Education Ministry. Most Iranians weren't fooled by such denials leading Mohammad-Mehdi Zahedi, the head of the Iranian Parliament's Education and Research committee, to demand that the Education Minister present himself to parliament to explain this policy. Since the political unrest of the summer of 2009, senior officials within the government have publicly called for university environments and the academic curriculum to more strictly conform with Islamic criteria.[127]

In August 2012, in another controversial move that impinged on women's choice in deciding family size, the government ended Iran's highly successful family planning program. It also asked women to have more children in order to double the population in the decades ahead. Some have postulated that, coupled with the restrictive new higher education policy, encouragement of large families may be the government's way of testing the waters as it moves toward eliminating limited gains women have made in their social status.[128] Given that Iran's theocracy sought to make its educational system accessible to females in order to be competitive, the move to restrict female access to most higher educational programs could be viewed as a harbinger of things to come. Iran's higher educational policy for the last two decades was a blessing for women in that it enabled them to attain a degree of social, economic and political status that would have been unimaginable a hundred years ago. Furthermore, it ensured a measure of female support for the theocracy, especially among the more conservative social groups. Ironically, the phenomenal success of women who availed themselves of the educational opportunities which came their way appears to have made rulers like Ahmadinejad nervous. Furthermore, in an "Islamic republic" such gains by females who are legally and theologically viewed as inferior to men, inevitably threatens the traditional male status quo. A scenario that is ultimately unacceptable to the clerics. To many clerics and conservative hardliners like former President Ahmadinejad, the reality of having so many well-educated, and often politically active, females in society posed a threat to regime survival, in other words, the theocracy. This dramatic reversal of education policy vis-à-vis females will undoubtedly be detrimental to state-society relations. Whether or not this policy is one of a number of measures to marginalize women remains to be seen.

CONCLUSION

The Islamic Revolution, which overthrew the Pahlavi monarchy in 1979, united disparate social groups in their desire to effect the removal of an authoritarian regime. The speed with which the clerics led by Ayatollah Khomeini moved to "Islamize" society shocked many who had initially, and wholeheartedly, participated in the "revolution" to overthrow the shah. It was not long before secular, urban, and educated women, who had enthusiastically participated in this effort to remove the shah, realized that their struggle had led them down the wrong path. By initially supporting Khomeini's "struggle" they had naively believed Khomeini's promises to bring about a more democratic and just society would improve women's status in society and within the family. Instead events led to a worse situation than they could have ever imagined. It has been surmised since—both within and without Iran—that what replaced a corrupt, but—as some have argued—well-intentioned, monarchy has been far more detrimental to Iranian women's lives, to include such realities as execution by stoning for adultery; a punishment which was unimaginable under the shah.

Opinions on the Islamic regime and its treatment of women do, however, vary with the rural and urban poor showing support for the current form of government. Nonetheless, the evidence indicates that ever since Khomeini came to power, urban "Westernized" women were singled out for abuse and have borne the brunt of the social and gender "restructuring." Women have been at the receiving end of horrific human rights abuses and executions inside the country, along with religious minorities (especially the Baha'i) and non-Persian groups like the Kurds and Baluchis.

The blueprint meant to both legitimize and guide the reign of a theocracy was the new Constitution of the Islamic Republic of 1979. It enunciated a special role for the religious elite (the *Ulema*) which were unprecedented in Persian history. Well aware that Khomeini's clique's political ambitions placed it squarely in the minority view among the Shia establishment's clergy, the Khomeinists (as the supporters of Khomeini's ideas of governance became known) did not hesitate to rely on the use of intimidation and force when necessary to silence the voices of dissenters.[129] This mechanism continues to be a favored one by the Theocracy, especially since President Mahmoud Ahmadinejad was elected into office in 2005.[130]

In sum, since the ascent of the clerics to power in Iran, the legal transformation from secular to Shariah laws has placed women in a dangerous predicament. With the legal resumption of temporary marital alliances, coupled with the designation of adultery as a death penalty by stoning offense,[131] and retribution and blood money as legal avenues to recourse for alleged victims, women have found themselves placed in enormously vulnerable positions with limited options. The enactment of such legal and marital mores in essence created a hostile, precarious environment for all Iranian women, which also psychologically inhibits them from seeking an improvement in their social and economic lives. This theocratic experiment—and its legacy—will forever be known as "the rule of brutal misogynists" cloaking their gender policies with the banner of Islam.

NOTES

1. Margaret Wente, "It's a Crime to Be a Woman in Iran," *The Globe and Mail,* July 17, 2010. Accessed at: http://www.theglobeandmail.com/news/opinions/its-a-crime-to-be-a-woman-in-iran/article1643091/

2. For more on the Fedayeen-e-Khalq, see Vanessa Martin, *Creating an Islamic State: Khomeini and the Making of a New Iran* (London: I.B. Tauris, 2000), 129–132.

3. Initially the Revolution was considered by many to be an Iranian Revolution. But it quickly morphed into an Islamic Revolution once the Komeinists began to exert brute force to ensure the establishment of a theocracy led by Khomeini himself.

4. Following the Iranian Revolution and the consolidation of their power by the clerics aligned with Ayatollah Khomeini, Iran became the first nation-state in history to apply absolute

Vilayet-e-Faqih in matters involving governance. "Guardianship" of the *Faqih* in the Islamic Republic of Iran is represented not only in the Supreme Leader (Ayatollah Khomeini was the first, followed by Ayatollah Khamenei) who must be a cleric, but other institutions of governance such as the Assembly of Experts, all members must be clerics; while in the Council of Guardians and in the courts, half of the members must be clerics. This cleric heavy rule was both controversial and unprecedented in light of Shi'a theology.

5. For more on the Vilayet-e-Faqih, see Mehran Tamadonfar, *The Islamic Polity and Political Leadership, Fundamentalism, Sectarianism, and Pragmatism* (Boulder, CO: Westview Press, 1989); Anoushiravan Ehteshami and Mahjoob Zweiri, *Iran and the Rise of Its Neoconservatives: The Politics of Tehran's Silent Revolution* (London: I.B. Tauris, 2007), 27–29; Ziba Mir-Hosseini and Richard Tapper, *Islam and Democracy in Iran: Eshkevari and the Quest for Reform* (London: I.B. Tauris, 2006), 17–23; Dariush Zahedi, *The Iranian Revolution Then and Now: Indicators of Regime Instability* (Boulder, CO: Westview Press, 2000), 68–71, 105–106; Martin (2000), 115–120; Suzanne Maloney, *Iran's Long Reach: Iran as a Pivotal State in the Muslim World* (Washington, DC: USIP, 2008), 73; Kenneth M. Pollack, *The Persian Puzzle: The Conflict Between Iran and America* (New York: Random House, 2005), 144; Con Coughlin, *Khomeini's Ghost: The Iranian Revolution and the Rise of Militant Islam* (New York: HarperCollins Publishers, 2009), 163–165; Mehran Tamadonfar, "Islam, Law, and Political Control in Contemporary Iran," *Journal for the Scientific Study of Religion* 40 (2001), 205–206, 213–214.

6. Shahra Razavi, "Islamic Politics, Human Rights and Women's Claims for Equality in Iran," *Third World Quarterly* 27 (2006), 1225.

7. For more on the IRP, see Said Amir Arjomand, *The Turban for the Crown: The Islamic Revolution in Iran* (Oxford: Oxford University Press, 1989), 141; Parvin Paidar, *Women and the Political Process in Twentieth Century Iran* (Cambridge: Cambridge University Press, 1997), 226.

8. For more on conflict and internal dissension between the clerics on their role vis-à-vis the state see Martin (2000), 60–64; Zahedi (2000), 79; Shahrough Akhavi, *Religion and Politics in Contemporary Iran: Clergy-State Relations in the Pahlavi Period* (Albany: State University of New York Press, 1980).

9. Pollack (2005), 144.

10. For more on this early period, see Shaul Bakhash, *The Reign of the Ayatollahs: Iran and the Islamic Revolution* (New York: Basic Books, 1984); A. Najmabadi, "Feminism in an Islamic Republic: Years of Hardship, Years of Growth, in *Islam, Gender, and Social Change*, edited by Y. Yazbeck Haddad and John Esposito (Oxford: Oxford University Press, 1999), 59–86.

11. Ziba Mir-Hosseini, "Sharia and National Law in Iran," *Shariah Incorporated: A Comparative Overview of the Legal Systems of Twelve Muslim Countries in Past and Present*, eds. Jan Michiel Otto (The Netherlands: Leiden University Press, 2010), 331.

12. For more on the Family Protection Law, see Ilehnaz Pakizegi, "Legal Reform and Social Positions of Iranian Women," in *Women in the Muslim World*, eds. Lois Beck and Nikki Keddie (Cambridge: Harvard University Press, 1978), 216–227; Paidar (1997), 153–157; Janet Afary, *Sexual Politics in Modern Iran* (Cambridge: Cambridge University Press, 2009), 216–218; Otto (2010), 329–330; Zahedi (2000), 76–77.

13. Nahid Yeganeh, "Women, Nationalism and Islam in Contemporary Political Discourse in Iran," *Feminist Review*, no. 44 (Summer 1993), 11.

14. For an uplifting memoir on a small secret literary group of Tehrani women led by Professor Nafisi who defied the regime and their informants by holding literary circles to discuss banned Western literature see Azar Nafisi, *Reading Lolita in Tehran* (New York: Random House, 2004).

15. On the role of Mujahidin-e-Khalq women during the Khomeini regime's "consolidation" period, see Rokhsareh S. Shoaee "The Mujahid Women of Iran: Reconciling 'Culture' and 'Gender'," *Middle East Journal* 41(Autumn 1987), 519–537.

16. For more on the politics of the *hijab* see Yeganeh (1993), 15; Nesta Ramazani, "Women in Iran: The Revolutionary Ebb and Flow," *Middle East Journal* 47 (Summer 1993), 408–409; 421–423.

17. Mark Bowden, *Guests of the Ayatollah: The First Battle in America's War with Militant Islam* (New York: Atlantic Monthly Press, 2006), 161.

18. Nasrin Alavi, *We Are Iran: The Persian Blogs* (New York: Soft Skull Press, 2005), 169–174.

19. Haleh Afshar, "Khomeini's Teachings and Their Implications for Women," *Feminist Review* 12 (October 1982), 60.

20. Afshar, 61.

21. Khomeini, *Sahifa* Vol. 4, 156–157 as cited in Vanessa Martin, *Creating an Islamic State: Khomeini and the Making of a New Iran* (London: I.B. Tauris, 2000), 154.

22. Afshar (1982), 61.

23. For more on *sigheh/muta*, see Paidar (1997), 278; Afary (2009), 284–287.

24. Guity Nashat, "Women in the Islamic Republic of Iran," *International Society for Iranian Studies* 13(1980), 183–184; Afshar (1982), 67.

25. On Iran's war widows see sociologist Ashraf Zahedi's excellent study on war widows: Ashraf Zahedi, "State Ideology and the Status of Iranian War Widows," *International Feminist Journal of Politics* 8 (June 2006): 267–286.

26. Paidar (1997), 344–345.

27. Afshar (1982), 66.

28. Afshar, 64.

29. Afshar, 66.

30. For more on the more "traditional" versus educated Iranian women (i.e., the majority of the populace) see Mary Elaine Hegland, "Traditional Iranian Women: How They Cope," *Middle East Journal* 36, no. 4 (Autumn 1982), 483–501.

31. Afshar (1982), 63.

32. Paidar (1997), 303–304.

33. N. Ramazani (1993), 411.

34. Tamadonfar (2001), 206.

35. For a comprehensive examination of the 1979 Constitution see Hamid Algar, *The Constitution of the Islamic Republic* (Berkeley, CA: Mizan Press, 1980).

36. Mir-Hosseini (in Otto, 2010), 332.

37. Paidar (1997), 270–271.

38. Tamadonfar (2001), 206; for a more detailed examination of the constitution and its implications for women see Paidar (1997), 256–262.

39. Martin (2000), 163.

40. For the text of the Constitution see R. K. Ramazani, "Document: Constitution of the Islamic Republic of Iran," *Middle East Journal* 34 (Spring 1980).

41. Valentine M. Moghadam, "A Tale of Two Countries: State, Society, and Gender Politics in Iran and Afghanistan," *The Muslim World* 94, no. 4 (October 2004), 459; *Women Living Under Muslim Laws,* ed. Harsh Kapoor, Dossier 21 (September 1998), Grabels Cedex, France, 33. Accessed at: http://www.wluml.org/fr/node/320

42. Paidar (1997), 271.

43. Otto (2010), 334.

44. Paidar (1997), 272.

45. Ayatollah Khomeini coined a phrase "taghut" to describe the pre-revolutionary Pahlavi regime. "Taghuti" was someone who worshipped idols or a Westernized person. For more on Khomeini's objectives during the "revolution" in which he coined "taghut" to describe the shah's regime see Martin (2000),150–153.

46. Paidar (1997), 273.

47. "Tawzih al-Masa'el" refers to books of religious instructions or rulings of a particular *marjah taghlid* (literal meaning: the source of emulation. It refers to an Islamic law scholar who, through rigorous study, has attained this position to practice *ijtihad* (independent reasoning) in order to interpret the Quran and Hadith to arrive at specific rulings. Here it specifically refers to Ayatollah Khomeini's interpretation on gender matters and certain family affairs. For more on his *tawzih al-Masa'el* prescriptions see Nashat (1980), 183–185.

48. Nashat (1980), 183.

49. Paidar (1997), 273.

50. Paidar, 273–274.
51. Paidar, 274.
52. Haleh Afshar, "Women, Marriage and the State in Iran," in *Women, State and Ideology: Studies from Africa and Asia*, ed. Haleh Afshar (Albany: State University of New York Press, 1987), 70–86.
53. Paidar (1997), 276.
54. Azadeh Kian, "Women and Politics in Post-Islamist Iran: the Gender Conscious Drive to Change," *Women Living under Muslim Laws*, ed. Harsh Kapoor, Dossier 21 (September 1998). Grabels Cedex, France, 35–38. Accessed at: http://www.wluml.org/fr/node/320
55. For Azam Taliqani's views see *In the Shadows of Islam*, eds. Azar Tabari and Nahid Yeganeh (London: Zed Press, 1982), 171–200.
56. Shireen Mahdavi, "Women and the Shii Ulama in Iran," *Middle Eastern Studies* 19, no. 1 (January 1983), 25.
57. Ebadi and Moaveni (2006), 42–43.
58. Paidar (1997), 348–349.
59. For more on the bill of vengeance (*Layeh-ye-Qasas*), see Farhad Kazemi, "Civil Society and Iranian Politics," *Civil Society in the Middle East*, ed. Augustus Richard Norton (Boston, MA: Brill Academic Publishers, 1995), 130–131.
60. The sentence of the court which enforced the *qisas* law of 2008 would have allowed Bahrami to personally place drops of acid into each of Movahedi's eyes in order to ensure justice for his actions toward her when she spurned his marriage proposal in 2004. Accessed at: http://articles.cnn.com/2009-02-19/world/acid.attack.victim_1_acid-attack-blind-eye?_s=PM:WORLD
61. "Iranian Women Spares Attacker Acid Punishment," *Radio Free Europe Radio Liberty*, August 2, 2011. Accessed at: http://www.rferl.org/content/iranian_woman_spares_attacker_acid_in_eyes/24283843.html
62. "'The Victim's Family Did Not Forgive Shahla Jahed until the Last Moment,' Says Lawyer," *International Campaign for Human Rights in Iran*, December 1st, 2010. Accessed at: http://www.iranhumanrights.org/2010/12/the-victims-family-did-not-forgive-shahla-jahed-until-the-last-moment-says-lawyer/
63. For coverage of Shahla Jahed's case and death see Saeed Kamali Dehghan, "Iran Executes Woman Accused of Murdering Lover's Wife," *Guardian.co.uk*. December 1, 2010. Accessed at: http://www.guardian.co.uk/world/2010/dec/01/shahla-jahed-executed-iran
64. Kian (1998), 39.
65. For more on Iran's family planning programs see Homa Hoodfar, "Devices and Desires, Population Policy and Gender Roles in the Islamic Republic," *Middle East Report* (September-October 1994), 1–17; N. Ramazani (1993), 414–415.
66. See R. K. Ramazani, "Burying the Hatchet," *Foreign Policy* 60 (Fall 1985), 52–74; N. Ramazani (1993), 409–428.
67. N. Ramazani (1993), 410.
68. For more on the female struggle to defend their rights see Haleh Esfandiari, "The Majles and Women's Issues in the Islamic Republic of Iran," *In the Eye of the Storm: Women in Post-Revolutionary Iran*, eds. Mahnaz Afkhami and Erika Friedl (New York: Syracuse University Press, 1994). See also Patricia J. Higgins, "Women in the Islamic Republic of Iran: Legal, Social, and Ideological Changes," *Signs* 10: 3 (Spring 1985), 477–494.
69. Valentine Moghadam, "Women, Work, and Ideology in the Islamic Republic," *International Journal of Middle Eastern Studies* 20 (1988), 228–233; N. Ramazani (1993), 413–414.
70. N. Ramazani (1993), 412.
71. "Glasnost" is a Russian term for "openness" and "transparency" which was used to describe the last premier of the Soviet Union's (Mikhail Gorbachev) approach to internal affairs as Gorbachev began the process of dismantling the Soviet Union.
72. "*Mehr*" is a sum of money or property that a husband pledges to his wife at the time of marriage in case of divorce.
73. For an interview with an outspoken Iranian feminist lawyer, Mehranguiz Kar, see Mehranguiz Kar and Homa Hoodfar, "Women and Personal Status Law in Iran," *Middle East Report*, no. 198 (January–March 1996), 36–38.

74. For more on child custody in the Islamic Republic, see Paidar (1997), 294–297.
75. Kar and Hoodfar (1996), 36.
76. On July 27, 2007, the U.S. designated the Iran based Martyr's Foundation as a terrorist support network and imposed financial sanctions on it and its United States branch and the finance firm Al-Qard al Hassan under Executive Order 13224. For more on the Martyr's Foundation see Immigration and Refugee Board of Canada, *Iran: Information on the Martyr's (Shahuda) Foundation (Martyrs' Foundation) and on the treatment of family members of "martyrs,"* (November 1 1995). Accessed at: http://www.unhcr.org/refworld/category,,IRBC,IRN,3ae6ac8170,0.html
77. Kar and Hoodfar (1996), 37.
78. Kar and Hoodfar (1996), 37.
79. Kar and Hoodfar (1996), 37.
80. Paidar (1997), 295.
81. Ibid, 295–296.
82. Paidar, 296.
83. N. Ramazani (1993), 417–418.
84. For more on this law, see Valentine M. Moghadam, *Modernizing Women: Gender and Social Changes in the Middle East* (Boulder: Lynne Rienner, 2003), 219.
85. Kar and Hoodfar (1996), 37–38; N. Ramazani (1993), 418.
86. For an excellent piece on early marriage see Soraya Tremayne, "Modernity and Early Marriage in Iran: A View from Within," *Journal of Middle East Women's Studies* 2 (2006), 65–94.
87. Azadeh Kian, "Women and Politics in Post-Islamist Iran: the gender conscious drive to change," *British Journal of Middle Eastern Studies* 24 (Winter 1997), 91.
88. Kian, 91.
89. For a more detailed discussion on legal matters see Ziba Mir-Hosseini, "Stretching the Limits: A Feminist Reading of the Shari'a in Post-Khomeini Iran," *Feminism and Islam: Legal and Literary Perspectives*, ed. Mia Yamani (New York: New York University Press, 1996), 285–320.
90. Kian (1998), 50.
91. *Zanan* was established by Shahla Sherkat in 1992. Sherkat was a well known journalist and magazine editor. Since 1982 she served as editor of *Zan-e-Ruz* (Today's Woman) before being forced out in 1991. Known as the "new religious intellectuals," Sherkat was the only woman among them had already begun to object to Zan-e-Ruz's conservative line (one she had been originally hired to develop). By the time of her dismissal she was eager to start her own independent journal on women and gender. She pulled together, marshaled minimal resources, and created *Zanan*. For more on *Zanan* see Razavi (2006), 1231–1232. For more on Sherkat's publishing efforts, see Margot Badran, "Iran: Closing of Zanan, Equality at Half Mast," *The American Muslim*, April 14, 2008. Accessed at: http://theamericanmuslim.org/tam.php/features/articles/iran_closing_of_zanan_equality_at_half_mast
92. Kian (1998), 51.
93. Kian, 52.
94. Kian, 53.
95. Foreign Broadcast Information Service-Near East and South Asia (FBIS-NES), July 6, 1990, 41 as cited in N. Ramazani (1993), 413.
96. Razavi (2006), 1233.
97. N. Ramazani (1993), 413.
98. On the subject of divorce and women's rights in Islam see Hojjat al-Eslam Saidzadeh, "Foundations of the Equality Perspective Modern Fiqh: The Case of Divorce," *Women Living Under Muslim Laws,* Dossier, ed. Harsh Kapoor, 21 (September 1998). Grabels Cedex, France, 60–63.
99. For an excellent synopsis of Saidzadeh's "Equality Perspective" see Ziba Mir-Hosseini, "Hojjat al-Eslam Sa'idzadeh-Iran," *Women Living under Muslim Laws,* ed. Harsh Kapoor, Dossier 21 (September 1998). Grabels Cedex, France, 56–59. Saidzadeh was widely recog-

nized to be one of the most important young modernist Islamic scholars. The regime has effectively silenced his voice through terror, intimidation, and a permanent ban of his writings.

100. Iran: Country Reports on Human Rights Practices, Bureau of Democracy, Human Rights and Labor, U.S. Department of State (February 23, 2001). Accessed at: http://www.state.gov/g/drl/rls/hrrpt/2000/nea/786.htm

101. Shahra Razavi, "Islamic Politics, Human Rights and Women's Claims for Equality in Iran," *Third World Quarterly* 27 (2006): 1227.

102. For more on Mahmoud Ahmadinejad see Kasra Naji, *Ahmadinejad: The Secret History of Iran's Radical Leader* (Berkeley: University of California Press, 2008); Yossi Melman, *The Nuclear Sphinx of Tehran: Mahmoud Ahmadinejad and the State of Iran* (New York: Carroll and Graf, 2007); Alireza Jafarzadeh, *The Iran Threat: President Ahmadinejab and the Coming Nuclear Crisis* (New York: Palgrave Macmillan, 2007).

103. The Guardian Council barred eighty-one female presidential candidates on the basis of their sex. See Xin Li, "Iranian Regime Erases Progress on Women's Rights; Fundamentalism Enforce Traditional Sex Roles under Harsh Penalties," *Washington Times* (March 8, 2006). Accessed at: http://washington-times.vlex.com/vid/erases-fundamentalists-enforce-harsh-194499151 ; Mark Gasiorowski, "The Causes and Consequences of Iran's June 2005 Presidential Election," *Strategic Insights,* IV, no. 8 (August 2005). Accessed at: http://www.nps.edu/Academics/centers/ccc/publications/OnlineJournal/2005/Aug/gasiorowskiAug05.pdf

104. Anoushiravan Ehteshami and Mahjoob Zweiri, *Iran and the Rise of the Neoconservatives: The Politics of Tehran's Silent Revolution* (London: I.B. Tauris, 2007),77.

105. Thomas Erdbrink, "Iran's Old Guard Pushed Aside: New Generation Replacing Clerics Who Had Sought Better Ties with West," *The Washington Post*, February 11, 2008. Accessed at: http://www.washingtonpost.com/wp-dyn/content/article/2008/02/10/AR2008021002698.html?nav=emailpage

106. Scott Peterson, "Iran Cracks Down on Women's Rights Activists," *Christian Science Monitor,* March 8, 2007. Accessed at: http://www.csmonitor.com/2007/0308/p12s01-wome.html ; See also "Iran's Dissenters; The Regime Marks International Women's Day By Cracking Heads," *The Washington Post,* March 11, 2007. Accessed at: http://www.highbeam.com/doc/1P2-5822331.html

107. Nazanin Shahrokni, "All the President's Women," MERIP 39 (Winter 2009). Accessed at: http://www.merip.org/mer/mer253/all-presidents-women

108. Nasrin Soltankhah is a member of the Professors' Basij and was backed in her parliamentary campaign by Basijis; Marzieh Vahid Dastjerdi is associated with the conservative Zeinab Society. See Mark Tren, "Ahmadinejad nominates women to cabinet," *The Guardian*, 16 August 2009. Accessed at: http://www.guardian.co.uk/world/2009/aug/16/ahmadinejad-nominates-women-cabinet

109. "Iran presidential hopeful Karrubi promises to defend women rights," *BBC,* May 19, 2009. Accessed at: http://www.accessmylibrary.com/article-1G1-200165852/iran-presidential-hopeful-karrubi.html

110. Although Mousavi's violent track record vis-à-vis human rights during the 1980s as prime minister is public knowledge, his popularity during the Green Revolution suggests a desperate populace and/or a "reformed" man.

111. Marek Lenarcik, "Women Campaign for Greater Rights as Iran Vote Nears," *The Washington Times,* May 31, 2009. Acccessed at: http://www.highbeam.com/doc/1G1-200924272.html

112. Azar Nafisi, "Hair and Lipstick Are Iranian Women's WMDs," *The Times,* September 13th, 2011. Accessed at: http://deconstructingislamism.com/decon/heroism-in-tehran/ ; Liora Hendelman-Baavur, "Hell Hath No Fury. Iranian Women Take the Streets in Anger and Dismay," *The Jerusalem Post,* June 25, 2009. Accessed at: http://www.highbeam.com/doc/1P1-165375917.html ; Adrian Lee, "A Very Modern Revolution," *The Express,* June 20, 2009. Accessed at: http://www.express.co.uk/posts/view/108766/A-very-modern-revolution--A-very-modern-revolution--A-very-modern-revolution-

113. Robin Pomeroy, "Mahmoud Ahmadinejad's Closest Aide Calls for More Women's Rights," *The Guardian,* September 29, 2010. Accessed at: http://www.guardian.co.uk/world/2010/sep/29/Ahmadinejad-aide-iran-womens-rights

114. Nazila Fathi, "Designer's Rainbow Brightens Iranian Women's Look," *The New York Times,* January 2, 2008. Accessed at: http://www.nytimes.com/2008/01/02/world/middleeast/02designer.html?fta=y&pagewanted=all

115. Maura Casey, "Challenging the Mullahs, One Signature at a Time," *New York Times,* February 7, 2007. Accessed at: http://www.nytimes.com/2007/02/07/opinion/07observer.html; see also "One Million Signatures Demanding Changes to Discriminatory Laws," *FIDH,* November 28, 2006. Accessed at: http://www.fidh.org/One-Million-Signatures-Demanding

116. Nazila Fathi, "Starting at Home, Iran's Women Fight for Rights," *The New York Times,* February 13, 2009. Accessed at: http://www.nytimes.com/2009/02/13/world/middleeast/13iran.html?pagewanted=all

117. Janet Bagnall, "An Extraordinary Woman: Ebadi Makes It Clear She Will Continue the Fight for Equality in Iran." *The Gazette.* November 1, 2006. Accessed at: http://www.womensequality.ca/resources.html

118. Bagnall (2006). For current updates on this campaign access: http://www.we-change.org/english/

119. Amir Taheri, "Ahmadinejad's New Enemy: Women," *New York Post,* September 6, 2008. Accessed at: http://www.nypost.com/p/news/opinion/opedcolumnists/item_SYpJU5LnKvgcVhnobRoGQN

120. "Iranian Women Fight Controversial Polygamy Bill," *Amnesty International,* November 30, 2011. Accessed at: http://www.amnesty.org/en/news/iranian-women-fight-controversial-polygamy-bill-2011-11-30

121. William Yong, "Iran's Divorce Rate Stirs Fears of Society in Crisis," *New York Times,* December 6, 2010. Accessed at: http://www.nytimes.com/2010/12/07/world/middleeast/07divorce.html?pagewanted=all

122. Nazila Fathi, "Starting at Home, Iran's Women Fight for Rights," *The New York Times,* February 13, 2009. Accessed at: http://www.nytimes.com/2009/02/13/world/middleeast/13iran.html?pagewanted=all

123. Yong (2010).

124. Fathi (2009).

125. Haleh Esfandiari, "Why Is Iran Curtailing Female Education?" *The Chronicle of Higher Education,* August 22, 2012. Accessed at: http://chronicle.com/blogs/worldwise/why-is-iran-curtailing-female-education/30260.

126. "Tensions in the Iranian Leadership over Excluding Women from Universities," *The International,* August 27, 2012. Accessed at: http://www.theinternational.org/articles/235-tensions-in-the-iranian-leadership-over-e. See also Robert Tait, "Anger as Iran Bans Women from Universities," *The Telegraph,* August 20, 2012. Accessed at: http://www.telegraph.co.uk/news/worldnews/middleeast/iran/9487761/Anger-as-Iran-bans-women-from-universities.html.

127. "Tensions in the Iranian Leadership."

128. "Tensions in the Iranian Leadership."

129. For more on this period see Azadeh Kian, "Gendered Occupation and Women's Status in Post-Revolutionary Iran," *Middle Eastern Studies,* 31 (July 1995); Valentine Moghadam, *Women, Work, and Ideology in Post-Revolutionary Iran* (East Lansing: Michigan State University, 1988); Haleh Afshar, "Women and the Politics of Fundamentalism in Iran," *Women and Politics in the Third World,* ed. Haleh Afshar (London: Routledge, 1996), 124–144; Nikki Keddie, *The Roots of Revolution: An Interpretative History of Modern Iran* (New Haven, CT: 1991); Farah Azari, "The Post-Revolutionary Women's Movement in Iran," *Women of Iran: The Conflict with Fundamentalist Islam,* ed. Farah Azari (London: Ithaca Press, 1983), 190–225.

130. For more on the rise of the "neo-conservatives" under Ahmadinejad see Anoushiravan Ehteshami and Mahjoob Zweiri, *Iran and the Rise of its Neoconservatives: The Politics of Tehran's Silent Revolution* (New York: I.B. Tauris, 2007).

131. For a recent case which garnered international attention see Michael Sheridan, "Iran Official Hints Sakineh Mohammadi Ashtiani Death By Stoning May Be Commuted," *New York Daily News,* January 2, 2011. Accessed at: http://articles.nydailynews.com/2011-01-02/news/27086171_1_stoning-sentence-face-death-iranian-authorities

Conclusion

Prospects for Pakistani, Afghan, and Iranian Women in the Twenty-first Century

> I was born a girl who should have died. But if God wills it, I may die having become the first female president of a country I love.
> —Fawzia Koofi,[1] Afghan politician and women's rights activist

> People in power and the powerful clergy are trying to throw women back fourteen centuries.
> —Organization of Women's Emancipation (Iran), 1979

> I have dedicated my life to women's rights. Wherever a woman is oppressed, I will go there and fight for her rights.
> —Mukhtar Mai,[2] Pakistani women's rights activist

The lives of women in these three neighboring countries have been characterized by tumultuous transformations since the early twentieth century. These changes have varied over time and space. Notwithstanding certain material improvements due to scientific and technological innovations which led to a better quality of life in the states under study here; the ongoing societal battles between the secular and religious camps for control over national gender policy have often been at the expense of the female populace. Furthermore, the current turmoil in the region appears to be a harbinger of things to come since the historical record, as examined here, suggests that female "status" in these conservative Muslim societies has, more often than not, been the litmus test to gauge the ruling faction's legitimation and consolidation success.

This comparative examination reveals remarkable similarities across borders, as well as certain notable differences. In all three case studies the gender policies of these governments were hostage to specific social influences and/or were tied to the very identity of the state in question. This substantiates the thesis that on gender-related social issues the state apparatus and competing social entities influence each other. It is, however, probable that on other policy matters—national security or foreign policy for instance—the state may be more immune from societal pressures and constraints; thus free to act unilaterally in the name of state survival.

The historical context used to examine the gender policies of Afghanistan, Iran, and Pakistan since the twentieth century has been illuminating and provides some insight on what the future may hold for women in Muslim majority countries in general. A comparative examination reveals the continued power struggle within civil society to dominate the gender discourse at the policy-making level within existing governmental structures. The common denominator in this "struggle" has involved *whether, and how, Shariah (Islamic) law should be instituted/applied* as all three states moved away from being either under colonial rule or influence (India/Pakistan and Persia/Iran) and/or monarchical rule (Afghanistan and Persia/Iran).

Today all three states are *Islamic Republics*[3] grappling with how to assuage warring social factions on sensitive gender-related matters (such as dress codes, marital and divorce laws) in order to ensure stability and a modicum of cohesion. The challenge for the ruling elite in these states, who wish to maintain a façade of "democracy," is how to credibly burnish their "Islamic Republic" credentials vis-à-vis the state's relationship with civil society in a manner that legitimizes and consolidates their rule.[4]

The evidence suggests that the orthodox/conservative societal elements' rigid and *literal reading* of Islamic texts as comprising the foundation of necessary Shariah law in an "Islamic Republic" constitutes the first roadblock vis-à-vis gender policies and female status. Such an approach inevitably incorporates the fundamental Islamic precept of male superiority and domination over the female into the legal process. Second, there is no specific one-size-fits-all Shariah legal template that is universally accepted and applied. Third, the often dual and competing legal systems (national and Shariah courts) have served as impediments to women's and minorities' rights, and human rights in general. Fourth, internal dissension within the state structure (especially the dual legal system) was both a blessing and a curse for females. Fifth, promulgation—and implementation—of controversial, precipitous and/or unpopular gender policies by the state (be it a monarchy, a secular Republic or an Islamic Republic) are bound to face pushback from disgruntled social forces. Sixth, regime survival and consolidation concerns (irrespective of the form of governance) take precedence over all else; thus pragmatic considerations trumped ideological preferences and, more often than not, led to backtracking and/or softening of unpopular gender policies. Seventh, females in all three countries do not constitute some sort of unified monolithic bloc given the heterogeneousness of the populace on multiple fronts (economic, social, ethnic and sectarian). This serves to impede or limit their influence on gender-related policies in the national arena and their societal leverage at the grassroots level. Eighth, female opportunities, protection and activism often have a strong familial (especially the father's) imprint and in all three case studies emerged as a key determinant of an individual female's social status irrespective of the existing societal or governmental structures. Ninth, the continued power struggle between the Islamists and the secularists amounted to psychological and physical whiplash for females who, as the weakest social link, were the most vulnerable recipients of "social experimentation" policies based on the specific whims of those in power. The remainder of this chapter will examine these findings in some detail as well as provide a synopsis on each country's gender stance and a brief prognosis in terms of female rights and position in the broader Muslim world today.

The greatest obstacle to female status in these three states struggling either with their collective identity as citizens, or with challenges associated with incorporating democratic institutional frameworks into a socially conservative milieu since the early twentieth century, has been the continued effort to "Islamize" legal systems through "Shariahization."[5] The historical record on embedding "Shariah" as the supreme law of the land in Muslim majority areas like the Middle East underscores the difficulties of such an endeavor; as well as highlights the inherent problems for females because of the absence of "gender equality" within a Shariah legal framework as understood in contemporary times. Certain fundamental, and widely accepted, injunctions of "Shariah law," which are based on the Quran and Hadith as interpreted by prominent *ulema* (Sunni and Shia scholars) advocate child marriage,[6] reduces female legal testimony to half of a male's,[7] permits wife beating,[8] smaller female inheritance,[9] polygamy,[10] and unequal rights in divorce.[11] These Islamic injunctions are based on *the literal application of a core assumption of Islamic doctrine which promotes male supremacy and dominance over the female.* The Quran's Sura an-Nisa (4:34)[12] on male authority over females:

> Men are in charge of women by what Allah has given one over the other and what they spend (for maintenance) from their wealth. Righteous women are devoutly obedient.... Then if they (the women) obey you (the men), take no further action against them.

Given the basic foundational misogyny upon which contemporary Shariah laws are built due to a literal application of Islamic theology, female access to a level playing field in these "Islamic republics"—whether in the courtroom, at home, in school, or at a workplace—will remain problematic and contingent, on a case-by-case basis, on the whims of familial male members and/or males in positions to interpret and implement Shariah compliant stipulations in an "Islamic republic."

Second, further complicating matters for females in these three countries is the confusion surrounding the enactment of Shariah derivative laws. There has always been a duality of Islamic law which, according to Muslims, originates from two major sources: divine revelation (*wahy*) as evident in the Quran; and human reason (*aql*). This duality of Islamic law is reflected in two Arabic designations: Shariah and Fiqh. Shariah literally means "the right path or way"; whereas fiqh refers to human understanding and knowledge applied with speculative reasoning (*ijtihad*).[13] Within the Sunni ulema rank and file there is no *ijma* (consensus) on what constitutes legitimate Shariah derivative legal decisions.[14] Both Pakistan and Afghanistan's Muslim Sunni communities subscribe to one school of jurisprudence (*fiqh*): the *Hanafi*,[15] which is considered the most permissive of the four Sunni schools of Islamic jurisprudence;[16] while Shia Iran follows the teachings of the *Ja'fari* fiqh. What adds to the complexity of enacting Shariah derivative laws based on either Sunni or Shia jurisprudence *as interpreted by certain ulema* is the presence of Shia minorities in Pakistan and Afghanistan comprising around 20 percent and 10 percent of the population respectively; and of Sunnis (mostly Baluch, Arabs, and Kurds) in Iran who comprise approximately 9 percent of its total population.

Historically, unlike the squabbles and legalistic disputes over various social issues between the Sunni traditionalists (*Maliki* and *Shafi*), the literalists (*Hanbali*), and the rationalists (*Hanafi*), the Shia ulema have presented a more cohesive legal front in that they all advocate *ijtihad* (independent reasoning) in court rulings. However, Ayatollah Khomeini's "*Fiqh-e-Ja'faria*," represented a theological turning point for Iran's clergy and constituted a glaring departure from the traditional quietist role (of Shia ulema). The opposition within Iran's clerical establishment to Khomeini's *Velayat-e-Faqih* (rule of the jurisprudent)[17] was suppressed by exile or house arrest of clerics opposed to this new Khomeini inspired version of Shi'ism that renounced the notion, based on the acceptance of temporal rule, which limited clerical influence solely to spiritual matters. This clerical activism in the political and legal arenas caused deep ideological schisms within Iran's clerical establishment and inevitably impacted the state's legislative and judicial behavior vis-à-vis Iranian women. While in Sunni majority Afghanistan and Pakistan, any cohesion on Shariah law due to the ulema's subscription to one school of jurisprudence (Hanafi) has been notably absent because of an ongoing turf battle between the strict literalists (*Ash'arite* traditionalism) elements within the Hanafi school and those ulema who are more inclined toward assessing matters within a broader context through the application of reason.[18]

The struggle over what interpretation of the Quran legitimately reflects the ethos of Shariah vis-à-vis female behavior has led to much confusion and/or draconian measures, such as rulings to hang or stone[19] adulterers and/or administering of one hundred or more lashes; minimum age at marriage set at nine; punishment of rape victims while setting rapists free, and so on. Worse, the "interpretations" utilized to draft Shariah laws, such as Pakistan's Hudood Ordinances of 1979, only exacerbated the inherently discriminatory essence of Shariah.

For example, when it comes to *zina* (fornication) cases, some ulema and their political supporters fought to limit state influence in marital matters by arguing that an oral divorce by the husband suffices as a legitimate action under Shariah. Muslim female activists and their supporters in Iran and Pakistan have argued that a failure to register divorces has led some husbands to falsely accuse their former wives of zina when they remarry. This deceptiveness of certain males in positions of power is indicative of how, even by traditional Shariah standards, women's rights have been trampled on under these apparently "Shariah compliant" laws. In Pakistan, for example, the passage of the "Enforcement of Shariah Act" in 1991, which was considered a political victory by the then Prime Minister Nawaz Sharif's government, was followed by a Supreme Court decision in 1992 which essentially invalidated the vital stipulation of the Muslim Family Law Ordinance of 1961. The MFLO had required a husband to give written notice of a divorce to a local union council. Citing Shariah legal tradition of oral divorce as being perfectly legitimate, the 1992 ruling ensured that divorced wives faced the real danger (barring any witnesses to the husband's verbal utterance of *"talaq"* (divorce) three times) of being accused of adultery and/or bigamy should they seek remarriage and their former husband was either vindictive and/or does not want his former spouse to be able to remarry.

Furthermore, given the severity of punishment for *hadd* offenses like adultery, murder, or rape, the burden of proof in Islam for such offenses is supposed to be set high. Thus, those witnesses or accusers bearing false testimony in hadd cases like zina or *zina bil jabr* (rape) per Shariah are expected to receive hadd punishment for such serious slander. Yet Pakistan's Hudood ordinances *do not* recommend hadd punishment for individuals making false accusations (predominantly against females); instead, in such cases punishment is determined in the taa'zir category and is left up to the discretion of the presiding judge.[20] The absence of dire consequences for slanderous accusations of adultery, fornication, or even blasphemy, in defiance of the tenets or intent of Shariah, has only served to embolden those social elements with agendas at the expense of innocent defendants, most female and/or non-Muslim, who often face a death sentence (hanging, shooting or stoning[21]) or lashes/whippings.

Third, the competing legal frameworks (national and Shariah courts)[22] have often clashed due to overlapping or even rival jurisdictions, often at women's or minorities' expense. For example, since its inception Pakistan's FSC[23] has asserted its jurisdiction over the High Courts to hear cases that fall into the "hadd" category. The disappointing outcome on the widely publicized gang rape case of Mukhtar Mai was a direct consequence of a convoluted legal system. Years of wrangling between the Lahore High Court, the Supreme Court and the Federal Shariat Court was detrimental to Mukhtar Mai's case and underscored the continued challenges women in general face vis-à-vis the convoluted Pakistani judicial system.

In Iran, upon assumption of power in 1979, Khomeini declared the Shah's Family Protection Laws as "un-Islamic" and a *kuffar* (infidel) construct. Khomeini ordered the implementation of Shariah as the law of the land. The problem for Khomeini's regime was that there were no specific "Shariah laws" to implement. Thus, as the backlog of domestic and other legal cases grew, so too did the feelings of confusion, anger, fear, and helplessness within civil society. Pressure from a broad social base led the Khomeinists to implement ad hoc judgments or to reinstate the despised Reza Shah's 1931 Civil Code and the Marriage Act of 1937 in order to placate disgruntled citizens and to keep the legal system running amid growing social chaos. It took the Iranian theocracy until 1989 before if finally managed to construct a functioning legal system. Ironically, this Shariah edifice, however, did not reflect an adherence to the Khomeinists desired "Shariah law"; rather, the legal system which emerged implemented a confusing mélange of secular (Reza Shah and his son's family laws) and religious (Shariah) laws. This result was a consequence of social push back in the Iranian majlis and compromises reached in determining the best legal course.

Controversial Shariah laws were instituted such as *Qisas* (the Laws of Retribution) and *Diyat* (blood money) in Iran under Khomeini in 1982; in Pakistan under Zia's protégé Nawaz Sharif in 1997 and prior to, and during, Taliban rule in Afghanistan in the 1990s.[24] These essentially vigilante Shariah laws superseded or were incorporated into either colonial era or the monarchical period penal codes such as the PPC (Act 45 of 1860) and the Persian Public Protection Law of 1924; while in Afghanistan, one of Pushtunwali's foundational precepts of *"badal,"*[25] which also exemplifies the tenets of Shariah's qisas and diyat laws[26] continues to be adhered to at the local level via tribal jirgas in certain Pushtun majority areas and also by other ethnic groups. This is either due to the absence of a functioning and/or a corrupt judicial system at the local level.

The Qisas and Diyat laws based on Shariah pose a serious obstacle to females seeking justice in domestic violence cases. Rather than a legal step forward for women in all three states, Qisas and Diyat laws placed "justice" in criminal cases in the hands of the victim or his/her family versus leaving it to the state to adjudicate via a court of law. Although qisas and diyat laws provided females and their guardians or heirs with the opportunity to personally punish or pardon perpetrators, it left females vulnerable to familial pressure in cases involving domestic violence (fairly commonplace) where the onus for making a decision was left to the female (and not to the courts). The female would undoubtedly be under extreme duress to pardon the family member (often spouse, brother or father) irrespective of the degree of violence committed, all in the name of saving the "family's honor."

Another detrimental impact of enacting the Qisas and Diyat laws involves jurisdiction(s) which now lay in the private realm. Behind closed doors, influential or wealthy perpetrators, invoking diyat, can purchase their freedom and avoid incarceration or any other punishment (for crimes like rape or murder) as would normally be prescribed by a criminal court. Worse, if the victim is female, under Shariah she has to produce four male witnesses of good character to successfully plead her case in order to avoid the real possibility of being charged with either slander or zina (in cases of rape) in court. Third, the value of a female or a non-Muslim in murder or other cases for the purposes of compensation amounts to only half of a Muslim male according to Islamic precepts of Shariah. Thus, the diyat or blood money paid to the female or non-Muslim's family would be substantially less than that paid on behalf of a Muslim male victim.

Fourth, the record shows that the legal apparatus of these states—especially during Shariahization measures—rarely operated as a cohesive entity; which has been both a blessing and a curse for females. The tension, dissension, and confusion within the legal edifice served to somewhat temper articulated approaches to specific gender related issues and/or served to raise unrealistic expectations or exacerbate women's fears when it came to Shariah related jurisdictional cases of rape, infidelity, or murder.

For example, Khomeini's IRP established the Special Civil Courts in 1979 to replace the Shah's family courts. The Special Civil Courts, presided over by clerics, was seen as the first judicial step toward the application of "Shariah," even though their mandate was limited to adjudicating cases involving marital matters. Much to the chagrin of the Council of Guardians (comprised of senior hardline clerics), the clerical judges in the Special Civil Courts did not work in unison. Rather, the record suggests that many of the presiding judges, applying *ijtihad* (independent reasoning), frequently sided with the wives/mothers in cases involving polygamy, child custody, or maintenance. Some judges, for example, required that in cases involving polygamy, the husband must obtain the first wife's permission, a direct conflict with the public enunciations of the Council of Guardians.

In Pakistan, the FSC has generally acted as a *moderating* entity to the relief of female activists and much to the disgust of the conservative clerics affiliated with the religious parties like the Jamaat-i-Islami.[27] What sealed the FSC's reputation for nonpartisanship and unpredictability were the 1999 public hearings held in Pakistan's major metropolitan centers on the future of the Ayub Khan–era MFLO of 1961 under the new hybrid legal system. Since opponents of the MFLO included Prime Minister Nawaz Sharif's Muslim League Party, many human rights activists worried that the FSC would be swayed to declare the MFLO null and void due to the government supporters declaring it "un-Islamic." The extensive proceedings included prominent religious scholars, lawyers, and activists, who were called to testify in front of the FSC judges. The FSC upheld the legality of the MFLO with certain caveats much to the prime minister's dismay at the embarrassing outcome, which in effect challenged the goals of his elected government. The FSC's decision to retain in the MFLO the role of local union councils in divorce cases in effect nullified the 1992 Supreme Court decision which had invalidated this requirement. On the other hand, the FSC pulled no punches when Pakistan's parliament tried to limit its jurisdiction via the Women's Protection Bill of 2006 by declaring certain key clauses of the bill "un-Islamic and unconstitutional."[28] This judicial stance indicates that the FSC, while cautious and open to reason and moderation in its rulings will fight to retain its jurisdictional turf of "Shariah compliance oversight."

Since the Taliban's ouster, Afghanistan's judicial system a decade later is still a work in progress. The 2004 Constitution, however, does require that any laws passed be in compliance with Shariah. But the respective roles of secular and Shariah law in its judiciary has not been clearly delineated. There is also an urban-rural dichotomy in social conflict resolution, including cases involving familial disputes. While in urban areas, a reliance on the law code from King Zahir Shah's rule has been a vast improvement for females, in stark contrast to the Taliban's version of Shariah justice; in many of the rural areas, familial and criminal cases are resolved through the intervention of local elders and tribal leaders. The Afghan government, however, retains the right of high justice, meaning if a jirga calls for a death sentence, it has to be referred to a government courts to adjudicate, and only then can it be carried out. But in some rural venues under Taliban control, an ad hoc system prevails defended by the Taliban and their cohorts as representing "true Shariah." In such informal and speedy venues, the draconian "Islamic justice" meted out is almost always at the expense of the female.[29]

Fifth, the historical record confirms that precipitous enactment, and implementation, of controversial social policies act like hot buttons irrespective of the form of governance in power. Such measures are bound to be met with varied societal resistance depending on the stakes. For example, Afghanistan's Amir Amanullah, in an unusual and controversial move, announced two laws, the Nizamnamah-e-Arusi and the Nikah wa Khatnasuri in 1924. The first emphasized gender equality and set a minimum age for marriage; while the latter specified certain conditions within the marital agreement that were meant to protect the bride's legal rights in the advent of a divorce.

Both measures were unpopular but the provision in the Nizamnamah that encouraged females to choose their own spouse without parental consent or approval was widely acknowledged to have pushed acceptable social boundaries to a breaking point in a conservative patriarchical culture. "Love marriages" threatened what was regarded as the crucial alliance mechanism between families or clans and were a potential financial loss; thus they were seen as a menace to the social edifice itself. In short, in contrast to the state stipulating mandatory elementary education for females or raising the acceptable marital age, this edict crossed an invisible, but well understood, line vis-à-vis social mores in the minds of most Afghans.[30] Amanullah's unpopular decrees—like banning the hijab—fell on deaf ears even in the capital, Kabul, his seat of power. Although some officials in fear of losing their positions allowed their wives to attend functions unveiled; others simply would not bend and were willing to face the consequences of defying the Amir's wishes. But the policy that sealed Amanullah's fate and forced him into exile in 1928 was a monetary one: reduction of tribal subsidies led to open rebellion and the Amir's ouster and a reversal of all his unpopular reforms like co-education and restrictions on the hijab.

Less than a decade later in Persia/Iran, Reza Khan[31]—like Amanullah, an admirer of Kemal Ataturk's "modernization" program in neighboring Turkey—banned the hijab in 1936, encouraged co-education, female employment, and European dress. Draconian enforcement measures such as compelling male government employees to bring unveiled wives to public events or risk being fined or fired and having police tear off scarves from women's heads in public venues and/or fining them, offended the sensibilities of most Iranians irrespective of socioeconomic background. Such invasive measures backfired on the state in the form of rebellion and the eventual forced abdication of Reza Shah with the help of the British. One of the first orders of business for Reza Shah's heir and son, Mohammad Reza Shah, was to lift the ban on veiling and to ease any traditional dress restrictions much to the dismay of certain female activists and to the delight of the mullahs and conservative social elements like the *bazaaris* (merchants).

When Khomeini's theocracy mandated strict hijab or head covering for all Iranian women, women found imaginative ways to be defiant in terms of how they wore their hijabs: colorful scarves exposing some of their hair, wearing heavy makeup etc. During the Taliban rule, brave Afghan women in the cities, as a means of defiance, sometimes wore colorful burkas and quarreled with the religious police if they objected. These women would argue that there were no prohibitions in Shariah when it came to color or fabric allowed in a burka. In Pakistan, with General Zia's introduction of "Islamization," female news anchors, school girls, and women in general were told to dress modestly and to cover their heads. Unlike Iran or Afghanistan, however, where the battles fought over dress codes and the hijab have been more dramatic, with overnight reversals in policy; the Pakistani state has never enforced a strict policy of mandatory hijab nor has it enacted measures to ban it. As a result, dress codes for females have varied over time and space across Pakistan; determined more by locale and familial environment.

One of the important lessons gleaned from this comparative work is that overambitious gender-related policies without widespread societal approval—whether the objective is "gender equalization" or "gender segregation"—are bound to face stiff social resistance and then either have to be forcibly implemented or rescinded by the state. Currently, in all three "Islamic republics," the ambiguity of "Shariah" itself has served to embolden social competition and/or resistance of various kinds and duration. Oppressive implementation mechanisms for "Shariah" compliance, has often resulted in resistance in all three countries toward the state apparatus. Social opposition buckled, or went into hibernation, only when the state relied on excessive brute force as evident during Taliban rule. The Taliban state brooked no public protest in areas under its control and always resorted to the use of force. Similarly, during Khomeini's "revolutionary period" and, more recently, during Iran's Green Revolution of 2009, it took large scale state approved violence—such as when Ahmadinejad's security forces opened fire on unarmed civilian protestors—to quell the unrest.

Sixth, retention of power and regime survival takes precedence over specific policies in all three states. For example, President Ayub Khan, known for his secular views and advocacy for female rights, shocked many during Pakistan's 1965 presidential election campaign when he challenged Fatima Jinnah's candidacy. Ayub declared her candidacy "un-Islamic" on the grounds that a woman could not rule in a Muslim country according to Shariah.[32] Notwithstanding his well known dislike for the ulema, Ayub sought fatwas which declared Fatima Jinnah's candidacy "*haram*" (forbidden) from several ulema. Ayub Khan's behavior was indicative of how self-preservation and pragmatic considerations often trump any publicly enunciated ideological preferences of those in power.

An earlier example of political expediency occurred during the early twentieth century India when the All Indian Muslim League pushed for female suffrage more out of necessity (strength at the ballot box) than due to any strongly held ideological convictions vis-à-vis women's right to vote. In Iran, Ayatullah Khomeini strongly opposed granting women the right to vote in 1963 on the grounds that it violated Shariah. Then, in 1979, Khomeini did a complete about face upon his return from exile when he voiced no opposition to female suffrage and, in fact, encouraged women to vote in the first presidential election of 1980.

Pakistan's—and the Muslim world's—first female head of state, Prime Minister Benazir Bhutto, did not live up to the expectations of many of her female supporters when her government failed to nullify the discriminatory Hudood ordinances as promised. Worse, on her watch, the Pakistan policy of supporting the misogynistic (even by Afghan standards) Taliban was crafted to the detriment of Afghan women. Her defenders have argued that Bhutto didn't have the support to implement widespread changes to improve female life as promised during her campaigns. In the late 1990s, when the Taliban banned women from working in hospitals (or anywhere else for that matter outside their homes) as being "haram;" this inevitably led to a sharp increase in female mortality since women were prohibited from obtaining medical care from unrelated male health professionals. The social discontent, even within the families of the Taliban's middle and senior ranks, forced the Taliban to back down from the stipulations of their own decree: a few female hospitals were reopened. In short, regime survival and/or the consolidation of power will compel those in charge to renege on specific promises and/or renounce or reform its own policies irrespective of how it may be perceived by the public and especially by their own supporters.

Seventh, female behavior in society has, more often than not, been an important litmus test in determining national identity in predominantly Muslim countries. Pakistani, Afghan, and Iranian females, however, do not comprise of some sort of monolithic united social bloc even if they share the same religious, cultural and linguistic histories. This fact has hampered societal efforts which sought state instituted reforms and/or protection of females in Muslim societies. In all three case studies, female views on "female empowerment" were contingent, or influenced, by their locale and/or their socioeconomic background. There is the urban versus rural dichotomy; the educated "Westernized" urban elite versus the semi-literate or illiterate urban/rural poor. The historical record reveals a broad chasm between women from the often more secular elite and those belonging to the traditionally conservative lower middle classes and poor who constituted the vast majority. Furthermore, the often glaring disconnect of female activists from their societies' broader social pulse; coupled with their eagerness or tendency to jump onto the "Western feminist" bandwagon through the implementation of drastic social changes has been a recipe for failure or backlash.

Whether it was Pakistan's Begum Ra'ana Liaquat Khan's successful push to create a controversial Women's Defense Force in the mid-1950s; Afghanistan's Queen Soraya's influence on her husband to ban the hijab and enforce western attire in the1920s; or Princess Ashraf's efforts at "family reform" in Iran during the 1960s; all these efforts at female "empowerment" lacked broad social approval or support. Furthermore, precipitous "social reforms" derived from alien cultural norms and mores only served to widen the existing social chasms between women. Too many female activists were impatient with the existing status quo vis-à-vis the position of women in Muslim majority societies. Due to this impatience and a failure to understand and empathize with the plight of the majority of women in their respective countries, these female activists approached any legislative success (in their favor) such as the passage of the MFLO of 1961 (Pakistan) or the Family Protection Law of 1967 (Iran) as a glass half empty event. Rather than celebrate these successes (which later, in hindsight, the female activists would come to appreciate); they clamored for further reforms without gauging the broader social pulse and reaction to such laws in a male dominated conservative milieu. Without the numbers, or widespread support, female activists in all three countries have encountered formidable road blocks and even reversal of previous legal gains due to a failure to construct a more viable and realistic list of objectives which incorporates the worldview of their more conservative sisters who constitute the social base in terms of numbers.

The social and cultural schisms between women in these societies have been successfully exploited by either the state and/or social elements to the detriment of all females irrespective of their social milieu. Increasingly in Iran at least, women's groups normally hostile to each other are finding common ground in order to bring pressure to bear on the state (in the majlis) for better economic opportunities and marital rights for all Iranian women. The chasms and divisions between females in these countries, however, remain significant and is a major roadblock or impediment toward greater female input into policy formulation at the national level.

Eighth, at the individual level, *a key determinant of female status has been the familial environment, especially the views and perceptions of the father and/or grandfather and/or brother(s) vis-à-vis the role, rights and responsibilities of their womenfolk.* This variable (familial environment) was a *critical one* in conservative Muslim societies where "female individualism" is a generally frowned upon anomaly since in Muslim majority societies "individualism" is discouraged as it is perceived to be at the expense of the larger—familial—social unit. In short, a person's (male or female) behavior within these Muslim societies is tied to a broader group's (family and/or clan and/or tribe) perception of what constitutes "honorable" conduct. Thus the views and beliefs of a female's immediate and/or extended family play a decisive role in her lifestyle and quality of life.

Women who attain significant personal milestones either in education, employment and/or marital matters in such societies *are able to achieve such social breakthroughs due to the support of one or more male relatives.* Benazir Bhutto, Pakistan's first (and only) female prime minister was encouraged and inspired by her father, Zulfiqar Ali Bhutto, to follow him into politics notwithstanding the risks and social disapproval associated with such behavior. Shirin Ebadi was able to become a world renowned human rights activist (awarded the Nobel Peace Prize) in Khomeini's Iran thanks to familial support, especially from her husband. The activism of Bilquis Edhi, Mukhtar Mai, and Malala Yousafzai of Pakistan and Shukria Barakzai and Malalai Joya of Afghanistan wouldn't have been possible without the support of their husbands and/or extended families. Zahra Rahnavard's political activism in Khomeini's Iran was due in no small part to the support and encouragement of her husband, Mir Hussein Musavi, a Khomeini protégé and Iran's prime minister from 1981 to 1989.[33] Queen Soraya of Afghanistan (1899–1968), Queen Tadj ol-Molouk (1896–1982), and Queen Farah Diba (1938–) of Persia/Iran were all able to discard the veil, obtain an education and/or become social activists *thanks to their fathers and/or husbands who protected them from the inevitable social disapproval that ensued due to their bold actions.* Even in contemporary Muslim majority societies, a female is rarely able to undertake any public action that might be construed by outsiders to be "un-Islamic" *without familial support.* Female activists almost always have some sort of male backing in order to survive (literally) and pursue social issues that are often considered controversial. *It can be argued that behind every Muslim female activist there is a man in the form of a mentor and/or protector and he is usually blood kin.*

Ninth, the historical record depicts females as the political football in the ongoing and relentless power struggle between the secularists and the Islamists in these Muslim societies. In contemporary times, "female identity and role" in a Muslim majority state remains a highly contested arena with mixed messages and disturbing empirical evidence suggesting a deterioration in the social position of females in general. Women have been, and will continue to remain, pawns for the unforeseeable future in the struggle between Islamists who claim to seek power in order to implement Shariah, and the more secular elements who wish to mitigate the impact of Shariah on the daily lives of citizens in Muslim majority countries. As a sort of litmus test of change, women's overt role in society remains vulnerable to cruel political whiplashes as evident in overnight changes in dress codes and other social behavior. This certainly was the case with Afghan women in the urban areas under Taliban rule and for Iranian women under the Khomeinists; while in Zia's Pakistan, dress codes and female behavior were implemented over time rather than overnight; nonetheless, the impact on female behavior has been a detrimental one in the long run thanks to the enactment of Shariah laws. The uncertainty vis-à-vis state behavior (policy) coupled with social pressure to conform inevitably has had a dire impact on the psyche of females in all three countries under study since the beginning of the twentieth century. This has especially been the case for females belonging to the elite and the urban middle class in Afghanistan and Iran; and for females belonging to the urban middle and working classes and in certain rural communities of Pakistan.

FEMALE PROSPECTS IN IRAN, AFGHANISTAN, AND PAKISTAN

The gender policies of these Islamic republics have much in common. Since the beginning of the twentieth century all three states—then either under colonial or monarchical rule-witnessed varied efforts by female activists and their supporters to bring about the enactment and implementation of legislature which incorporated a women's right to vote, run for office, and work outside their traditional workplaces.[34] Notwithstanding some significant political and social successes (such as female suffrage, the right to a registered divorce, to work or study or run for office) over the course of the century, females in all three countries experienced considerable legal and social setbacks once the religious elements gained influence or control over the reins of power in the latter half of the twentieth century.

In terms of specifics, the Pahlavi monarchy's approach to gender "empowerment" in Iran mirrored the imperatives of the Durrani monarchs of Afghanistan in that both sought often precipitous and controversial social changes revolving around female attire and independence which led to rebellion and pushback from conservative social elements (tribal elders, mullahs, and/or the clergy) whose power or influence both monarchies underestimated at great cost.

Since independence, the Pakistani state has grappled with its identity or raison d'être: Was it a secular state for Muslims or was it an Islamic state? The Afghan and Persian/Iranian states were not bedeviled with such identity concerns notwithstanding the heterogeneousness of their respective populaces. Thus, while Pakistan's gender policies have reflected an ongoing identity struggle between the religious elements and its elite and growing middle class to define women's position in a *Muslim* society; Afghanistan and Iran's gender policies have reflected competing socioeconomic groups (urban/ rural/tribal/ethnic dichotomies). In the latter two states the struggle between vying social groups to influence gender policies and roles has had an ideological (read: religious) patina. In Pakistan's case—a state carved out of the Indian, predominantly Hindu, subcontinent—the loss of East Pakistan in 1971 served to propel Pakistan's leadership to emphasize "Islam" as the state's raison d'être and thus began the process toward "Islamization" as a cohesive mechanism to unite the various provincial entities of this fragile state. Given the inherent misogyny of Shariah, the detrimental effects of this direction continue to this very day for Pakistani females.

Although women's status in Pakistan has evolved through gradual shifts in state policy; Iran and Afghanistan's gender policies have often been dra-

Conclusion

matic, overnight reversals (Khomeini's "Islamic Revolution" and the Taliban's "Islamic Emirate," for example).

Since independence to the PDPA takeover in 1978, Afghanistan's gender politics were a "wish list" of an urban elite divorced from the realities of the majority in a very traditional, tribal-based society. These policies, however, weren't driven by anxieties related to legitimacy, identity and consolidation as in the case of neighboring Pakistan. While Pakistani women have seen their social status deteriorate with the introduction of Shariah compliant laws, their Afghan and Iranian counterparts have experienced worse atrocities: although females in all three countries implementing "Shariah" have been whipped, imprisoned, and executed on questionable grounds; females in Afghanistan and Iran have been victims of large-scale, often state-sponsored violence which included being *officially* stoned to death (under Taliban and the Khomeinists's rule). Pakistani women, on the other hand, have had some safe guards from *within* the state apparatus.

Another similarity has involved the ongoing activism of urban women's groups such as the WAF in Pakistan, RAWA in Afghanistan, and the WSIR in Iran. Female activists, with some rare exceptions like Mukhtar Mai, come from more affluent urban households and have different priorities and conceptions on what the term "status" implies. In stark contrast, the lives of the majority of females continue to be characterized by crippling poverty, back-breaking labor, domestic violence, and economic hardship in primarily rural settings and in impoverished urban neighborhoods, *irrespective of the state's ideological proclivities.* This demographic dichotomy has constituted a critical disadvantage to the mission or objectives of female activists as they have sought to mitigate the impact of Shariah derivative legal strictures *upon their own lives.*

Critics of such female activists (fairly or unfairly) have argued that their missions are often self-serving and *counterproductive* to the overall wellbeing of females in these countries. The pursuit of unrealistic goals has, more often than not, been based on culturally alien practices for the majority of women. These goals served as distracting obstacles to the enactment of laws and the provision of essential services that constitute *more realistic and achievable first steps toward female empowerment in the long run.* From a Western vantage point such controversial goals may be perceived as commendable and necessary steps, such as the need for greater female participation in governance at the local and national level; the right to wear clothes of their own choosing (read: Western attire) without a veil; the ability to select their own spouses or to attend coeducational higher institutions or be employed in "non-traditional" female employment. But, as the historical record shows, any aggressive or controversial gender policies which are perceived by the majority of the females (and their families) to be antithetical to Islam and/or local culture are less likely to embed and become acceptable social norms.

The implications of these deep divisions between females on their identity and status are clear: they dilute the influence they, as a group, have on the state apparatus and civil society to reform laws and to improve their lives at the grassroots level. This is due to the absence of a shared perception of what will constitute this identity (of women) in an "Islamic Republic." The chasm between these socioeconomic groups remains a wide one.

PROSPECTS FOR FEMALE IN MUSLIM MAJORITY STATES

In the Muslim world, there is a widely propagated saying (claimed to be a weak hadith) that "paradise lies under the feet of a mother." Yet, while theologically and culturally motherhood in of itself is considered the most important, and respected, goal for a Muslim woman; the widespread prevalence of violence toward females of all ages in Muslim societies gives room for pause. Furthermore, there appears to be a direct correlation between widespread domestic violence and the absence or reduction in legal protections afforded to females in these Muslim majority states in the name of "Shariah law."

Critics of Shariah law in the Muslim world argue that the current trend involving implementation of legislature based on Shariah does a great disservice to females in general as it legitimizes certain kinds of punishments like stoning to death for adultery and/or fornication which belong to the seventh, and not the twenty-first, century. Furthermore, Shariah laws are often based on a *literal* interpretation of the Quran rather than the application of reason and context to this ancient text. This tendency, they argue, serves to tangibly bolster the perception that a female is not equal to a male when it comes to her legal testimony and to matters involving inheritance; worse, it permits child brides and polygamy due to a *literal* interpretation of Islamic doctrine and tradition. The current trend in Muslim majority countries toward the implementation of Shariah is increasingly seen as a commendable goal in an "Islamic republic" (for example, 88 percent of Pakistani Muslims having a favorable view of incorporating Islam into politics).[35] Given this perception, the position of females in such societies will remain a precarious one notwithstanding varied and sporadic opposition from internal forces opposed to "Shariahization" of civil society.

The dramatic political changes since early 2011 due to social upheaval in the Arab world, initially described as a harbinger of social liberalization and democratization of autocratic and/or dictatorial states, came as a surprise to the outside world. What was optimistically labeled as "the Arab Spring," however, has not turned out to be about liberalization of the political system in some strictly secular sense. As events rapidly unfolded it became clear to observers that the primary benefactors of this "spring" have been the so-called Islamists. These entities have been represented through such benignly sounding political parties such as Tunisia's Renaissance Party (*Hizb an-Nahdah*) and Egypt's Freedom and Justice Party (*Hizb Al-Hurriya Wal-Adala*) which are influenced and/or controlled by the Muslim Brotherhood (*Ikhwan Al Muslimin*) whose stated long-term objectives include the strict implementation of Shariah laws, a reestablishment of the Caliphate and jihad as a desired goal in an "Islamic democracy."[36]

Recent events in the Muslim (especially Arab) world indicate that a significant segment of the populace sought social changes along conservative, even religious, lines to include an encompassing role for Shariah in legal and legislative matters. This sentiment is echoed in the results of parliamentary and presidential elections in Egypt[37] and Tunisia, for example. Given the inherent misogyny of Shariah (based on a *literal* reading of the Quran), it can be postulated that for the foreseeable future females in parts of the Muslim world will continue to experience a reversal in various legal and social gains made under more secular, albeit autocratic and/or dictatorial, regimes.

NOTES

1. Fawzia Koofi, One *Woman's Fight to Lead Afghanistan into the Future* (New York: Palgrave Macmillan, 2012).
2. Mukhtar Mai, *In the Name of Honor* (New York: Washington Square Press, 2006).
3. The official title of these "Islamic Republics" is an oxymoron. A "republic" is a form of government in which the supreme power rests with the people through representatives or public officers who officially are granted alienable powers to represent the people in "public matters" via a constitution. According to Islamic precepts and tradition, *sovereignty belongs only to Allah and not to the people*. Thus, terrorist groups like Al Qaeda have declared such "governments" to be Western constructs and *haram* (Arabic: forbidden). It is no accident that many Sunni Muslim revivalist groups have repeatedly emphasized the need to reestablish the *only legitimate form of Muslim government:* The Caliphate, which would encompass all of *Dar al Islam* (abode of Islam). While traditionally for the Shia, such a temporal rule (a republic, monarchy) was acceptable until the return of the Mehdi as Shia's religious clerics were not to participate in any governing body. Thus Ayatollah Khomeini's *Velayat-e-Fiqh* (rule of the jurisprudents) was considered "revolutionary" and upset many prominent Shia clerics who denounced such efforts as bordering on being heretical. For those Muslim religious leaders in the Muslim world who advocate it, an "Islamic Republic" is a state under a particular theocratic form of government (Iran, for example). Others (Sunni) see it as a compromise between a purely Islamic Caliphate, republicanism and secular nationalism. *Where they all agree vis-à-vis their conception of an "Islamic republic" is that the penal code of such a state must be compatible with Shariah (Islamic) law.* Pakistan was the first Muslim majority state to adopt the adjective "Islamic" to modify its republican status under its otherwise secular constitution of 1956.
4. The reason the author calls the current system of "democratic governance" in these states a "façade," has to do with excessive fraud and/or tampering with the electoral process (Karzai in Afghanistan's 2009 Presidential Election; Ahmedinejad in Iran's 2009 Presidential Election; and the Pakistan Army's de facto control of the Pakistani state apparatus).

5. "Shariahization" is a term used here to describe ongoing internal struggles during the last four decades in certain Muslim states like Iran, Pakistan, Afghanistan, Sudan, Jordan, Algeria, Tunisia Indonesia, Malaysia, Mauritius, Egypt, etc., to replace temporal law with Shariah or Islamic law.

6. The Quranic Sura at-Talaq (65:4) on minimum marriage age for female is before puberty: *"The waiting period* (for talaq/divorce) *of those of your women who have lost all expectation of menstruation shall be three months in case you entertain any doubt; and the same shall apply to those who have not yet menstruated."* (4:6): *"And test the orphans until they reach marriageable age. Then if you perceive in them sound judgment, release their property to them. And, do not consummate it excessively and quickly (anticipating) that they will grow up."* Accessed at: http://www.muslim-marriage-guide.com/marriage-age.html;

Quotes of prominent Muslim *alim* (scholars) on child marriages: Grand Mufti of Saudi Arabia, Sheikh Abdul Aziz al-Sheikh: *"It is incorrect to say that it's not permitted to marry off girls who are 15 and younger. A girl aged 10 or 12 can be married. Those who think she's too young are wrong and they are being unfair to her. We hear a lot in the media about the marriage of underage girls. We should know that Shariah law has not brought injustice to women."* Accessed at: http://www.cnn.com/2009/WORLD/meast/01/17/saudi.child.marriage/index.html?iref=newssearch. Ayatollah Ruhollah Khomeini of Iran: *"A man can marry a girl younger than nine years of age, even if the girl is still a baby being breastfed. A man, however, is prohibited from having intercourse with a girl younger than nine, other sexual acts such as foreplay, rubbing, kissing and sodomy is allowed. A man having intercourse with a girl younger than nine years of age has not committed a crime, but only an infraction, if the girl is not permanently damaged."* Accessed at: http://www.iranian.com/main/news/2010/02/10/tahrir-ol-vasyleh.

7. The Quranic Sura al-Bakarah (2:282): *"and call to witness two witnesses, men; or if the two be not men, then one man and two women, such witness as you approve of, that if one women errs the other will remind her."*

8. The Quranic Sura an-Nisa (4:34) allows "female discipline:" *Men have authority over women because Allah has made the one superior to the other, and because they spend their wealth to maintain them. Good women are obedient. As for those from whom you fear disobedience, admonish them and send them to their beds apart, and beat them."*

9. The Quranic Sura an-Nisa (4:11): *"Allah instructs you concerning your children: for the male what is equal to the share of two females."*

10. The Quran Sura an-Nisa (4:3): *"And if you feel you will not deal justly with the orphan girls, then marry those that please you of (other) women, two, or three or four."*

11. In matters of divorce, the Quranic Sura an-Nisa (4:20) warns the husband: *"If you wish to replace a wife with another, do not take from her dowry . . . that would be unfair."* However, far too often the husband will try to blackmail the wife during divorce proceedings to avoid paying back her dowry or *mehr* and/or to avoid spousal or child supports responsibilities. Even in cases in which the wife is willing to give up any financial rights in order to gain custody of the children, some ulema have traditionally recognized, as they interpret Shariah, the right of a mother to retain custody of her son(s) until the age of seven and daughter(s) until the age of nine. Accessed at: http://iftaa.jucanada.org/divorce_/_talaq.aspx/divorce_/_talaq/if_the_husband_divorces_the_wife_who_will_get_custody_of_the_child

12. Direct quote from *The Qur'an* (Riyadh, Saudi Arabia: AbulQasim Publishing House, 1997), 105; A. J. Arberry, *The Koran* (New York: Touchston Press, 1996), 105–106.

13. Kyai Haji Abdurrahman Wajid, "God Needs No Defense," *Silenced: How Apostasy and Blasphemy Codes Are Choking Freedom Worldwide*, eds. Paul Marshall and Nina Shea (New York: Oxford University Press, 2011). As the late President of Indonesia, Abdurrehman Wahid writes: "Sharia is the way of path to God and wasn't formally codified into 'Islamic law' which only emerged in the centuries following Muhammad's death . . . Islamic law is *man made and thus subject to human interpretation and revision*" (emphasis added).

14. Mohammad Hashim Kamali, "Law and Society: The Interplay of Revelation and Reason in the Shariah," *The Oxford History of Islam* (Oxford: Oxford University Press, 1999), ed. John L. Esposito, 107–108.

15. The Hanafi School is named after Abu Hanifah al-Numan ibn Thabit (699–767) and has the largest following of the four surviving schools. Abu Hanifah advocated legal reasoning by

analogy (*qiyas*), but his reliance on personal opinion and juristic preference (*istihsan*) was anathema to the jurists who belonged to the Traditionalist (*Maliki*) and the Literalistst (*Hanbali*) Shariah camps.

16. The four Sunni schools of jurisprudence are Hanafi, Maliki, Shafi, and Hanbali. Shia Islam has three branches: The Ja'fari, Ismaili, and Zaidi.

17. Following the Iranian Revolution and the consolidation of their power by the clerics aligned with Ayatollah Khomeini, Iran became the first nation-state in history to apply absolute *Vilayet-e-Faqih* in matters involving governance. "Guardianship" of the *Faqih* in the Islamic Republic of Iran is represented not only in the Supreme Leader (Ayatollah Khomeini was the first, followed by Ayatollah Khamenei) who must be a cleric, but other institutions of governance such as the Assembly of Experts, all members must be clerics; while in the Council of Guardians and in the courts, half of the members must be clerics. This cleric heavy rule was both controversial and unprecedented in light of Shi'a theology.

18. For the purposes of this discussion, these non-Ash'arite ulema can be labeled "neo-Mu'tazilites." For an excellent work on the struggle between the Ash'arite traditionalism and the Mu'tazilites see Robert R. Reilly, *The Closing of the Muslim Mind: How Intellectual Suicide Created the Modern Islamist* (Wilmington, DE: Intercollegiate Studies Institute, 2010).

19. Stoning for adultery has been carried out in Iran by the Iranian theocracy. In rural Pakistan there have been rare cases of stoning and of being shot to death after an informal Shariah derivative decision by village elders and/or family members; while the state during Zia-ul-Haq's reign implemented one hundred lashes in some cases and/or rigorous imprisonment. In Afghanistan, under the Taliban, stoning and/or public executions for adultery were not uncommon. Even with the overthrow of the Taliban, there are reported cases of kangaroo court justice being conducted by Afghan villagers citing Shariah and the dispensation of "justice" by individuals and not the state in the name of Shariah. See Ben Farmer, "22-year-old Accused of Adultery Executed in Afghanistan." *The Telegraph*. July 8, 2012. Accessed at: http://www.telegraph.co.uk/news/worldnews/asia/afghanistan/9384963/22-year-old-accused-of-adultery-executed-in-Afghanistan.html

20. In contrast to hadd crimes, taa'zir cases are traditionally for lesser crimes and decided at the discretion of the court; thus giving judges wide latitude in determining the punishment since no specific penalty is prescribed in Islamic religious texts for taa'zir crimes. Thus, those making false accusations without specific evidence know they won't have to bear the brunt of their false testimony in a court of law if they are exposed.

21. Unlike the Iranian (since Khomeini) and Afghanistan (under the Taliban) states, the closest the Pakistani state has come to implementing a stoning sentence for zina was under General Zia ul Haq's dictatorship. But such a sentence has never been carried out, although there have been a few reported cases of stoning by Pakistanis taking the law into their own hands in rural areas as mentioned earlier.

22. In addition to the dual (secular and religious) legal frameworks, in Pushtun majority regions of Afghanistan and northern Pakistan there is also the jirga system (an assembly of tribal male members led by tribal elders) based on tribal law; and then there are international regimes as well on gender-related issues like child and forced marriages. For more on efforts to eradicate these practices from without, that is, foreign entities see "The 2011 International Congress to Eradicate Forced and Early Marriages" issued by *Yellitaare/Africa Empowerment*. December 1, 2011. Accessed at: http://bixby.ucla.edu/mattach/Report_Eradicate_Forced_Early_Marriage.pdf

23. The FSC of Pakistan was established in 1980 by General Zia ul Haq and given the power to examine and determine whether the laws of the country comply with Shariah law. Its eight Muslim judges are appointed by the President of Pakistan after consulting the Chief Justice of this Court. Three of these judges are ulema and the rest are picked from serving or retired judges of Pakistan's Supreme Court or a High Court. The judges hold office for a period of three years, which may eventually be extended by the President. Its rulings can be appealed to the Shariat Appellate Bench of the Supreme Court, which consists of three Muslim judges of the Supreme Court and two ulema who are appointed by the president. The court can also exercise revisional jurisdiction over the criminal courts in Hudood cases.

24. Under Shariah law, "retribution" by an individual or a group against another conducted as "an eye for an eye" is considered "*halal*" (prohibited) and just. The victim's family can also accept "blood money" from the defendant and/or his/her family in lieu of punishment. However, the life or injuries of a woman is only worth half that due a man for the same offense/injury according to Shariah.

25. *Badal* implemented is "an eye for an eye." Ditto for Shariah's *qisas* or retribution law.

26. Pushtunwali is Afghanistan's dominant ethnic group's (the Pushtuns) code of living or sacred commandments which predate Islam but share much of Islam's ethos.

27. The FCC was established by the President's Order No. 1 of 1980. The FSC is mandated to examine specific cases to ensure Shariah compliance vis-à-vis specific laws.

28. Iftikhar A. Khan, "Federal Shariat Court Knocks Out 3 Sections of Women's Protection Act," *Dawn*, December 23, 2010. Accessed at: http://dawn.com/2010/12/23/shariat-court-knocks-out-3-sections-of-womens-protection-act/

29. Benjamin Gottlieb, "Taliban Execution of Afghan Woman Triggers Public Outcry." *Washington Post*, July 9, 2012. Accessed at: http://www.washingtonpost.com/blogs/blogpost/post/taliban-execution-of-afghan-woman-triggers-public-outcry-video/2012/07/09/gJQA3pAXYW_blog.html

30. See Shireen Khan Burki, "The Politics of Zan From Amanullah to Karzai: Lessons for Improving Afghan Women's Status," *Land of the Unconquerable: The Lives of Contemporary Afghan Women*, eds. Jennifer Heath and Ashraf Zahedi (Berkeley: University of California Press, 2011), 47.

31. Reza Khan (1878–1944) like Amanullah and his predecessors had a love-hate relationship with the British and Russians. On the one hand he despised them for their attempts to monopolize trade and businesses; yet, on the other he admired their educational and governmental institutions. Like Ataturk and Amanullah, he showed his contempt for the illiterate mullahs and certain grasping clergy by banning the hijab and through emphasis on a secular vice a madrassa education. It can be postulated that he changed Persia's official name to "Iran" to declare to the world that the people of Persia were in fact "Aryans" (read: European stock). Given the degree of Nazi penetration in the region, it is within the realm of possibilities that this may reflect the narrative fed to him or his representatives by German agents who sought to woo regional leaders and to disrupt the British Crown's counter efforts against them.

32. "Pakistan: The Problem with Mother." *Time*. December 25, 1964. Accessed at: http://www.time.com/time/subscriber/article/0,33009,830952-2,00.html

33. Zahra Rahnavard was/is a conservative Muslim female activist with a Ph.D. who has defined her life as a constant struggle on how to merge "modernity" with traditional Islamic values.

34. Women in the region are predominantly based in rural communities where they engage in much of the back breaking labor on farms as well as in home based cottage industries like handicrafts and carpet weaving.

35. A 2010 Pew study titled: "Most Embrace a Role for Islam in Politics: Muslims around the World Divided on Hamas and Hezbollah," *Pew Research Center*, December 10, 2010. Accessed at: http://www.pewglobal.org/2010/12/02/muslims-around-the-world-divided-on-hamas-and-hezbollah/

36. Rod Nordland, "Egypt's Islamist's Tread Lightly, But Skeptics Squirm." *New York Times*, July 28, 2012. Accessed at: http://www.nytimes.com/2012/07/29/world/middleeast/egypts-islamists-tread-lightly-but-skeptics-squirm.html?pagewanted=all

37. The Muslim Brotherhood's Freedom and Justice Party won a bare majority and its President Muhammad Morsi was removed from office by the Egyptian military on July 3, 2013, after millions of Egyptians on the streets of Cairo demanded his ouster in what has been termed a "People's Revolution."

Bibliography

Abbott, Freeland. "Pakistan's New Marriage Law: A Reflection of Qur'anic Interpretation," *Asian Survey* 1 (January 1962), 26–32.
Abrahamian, Ervand. *Iranian Mojahedin.* New Haven, CT: Yale University Press, 1989.
———. *Iran between Two Revolutions.* Princeton: Princeton University Press, 1982.
Adams, C. J. "The Ideology of Maulana Maududi." In *South Asian Politics and Religion,* edited by E. D. Smith, 371–397. Princeton, NJ: Princeton University Press, 1966.
Afary, Janet. *Sexual Politics in Modern Iran.* Cambridge: Cambridge University Press, 2009.
Afkhami, Gholam Reza. *The Life and Times of the Shah.* Berkeley: University of California Press, 2009.
Afshar, Haleh. "Women and the Politics of Fundamentalism in Iran." In *Women and Politics in the Third World,* edited by Haleh Afshar, 124–144. London: Routledge, 1996.
———. "Women, Marriage and the State in Iran." In *Women, State and Ideology: Studies from Africa and Asia,* edited by Haleh Afshar, 70–86. Albany: State Universit of New York Press, 1987.
———. "Khomeini's Teachings and Their Implications for Women," *Feminist Review* 12 (October 1982), 59–72.
Afzal, Nabeela. *Women and Parliament in Pakistan, 1947–1977.* Lahore: Pakistan Study Centre, University of Punjab, 1999.
Ahmed, Akbar S. *Discovering Islam: Making Sense of Muslim History and Society.* London: Routledge, 2002.
———. *Jinnah, Pakistan and Islamic Identity: The Search for Saladin.* London: Routledge, 1997.
Ahmed, H. I. *Begum Ra'ana Liaquat Ali Khan.* Karachi: Kifayat Academy, 1975.
Ahmed-Ghosh, Huma. "A History of Women in Afghanistan: Lessons Learnt for the Future Or Yesterday and Tomorrow: Women in Afghanistan." *Journal of International Women's Studies* 4 (May 2003), 4–6.
Ahmed, Mumtaz. "Islam and the State: The Case of Pakistan." In *Religious Challenge to the State,* edited by Matthew Moen and Lowell Gustafson, 239–267. Philadelphia: Temple University Press, 1992.
———. "The Politics of War: Islamic Fundamentalism in Pakistan." In *Islamic Fundamentalism and the Gulf Crisis,* edited by James Piscatori, 178–185. Chicago: University of Chicago Press, 1991.
Ahmed, Sardar. "Joy, and Some Confusion, as Afghans Vote." *Reuters,* September 19, 2005.
Ahmed, Zafaryab. "Maudoodi's Islamic State." In *Islam, Politics and the State: The Pakistan Experience,* edited by Asghar Khan, 95–113. London: Zed Press, 1985.

Ahmedi, Farah, and Tamim Ansary. *The Story of My Life: An Afghan Girl on the Other Side of the Sky*. New York: Simon Spotlight Entertainment, 2005.
Aizenmen, N. C. "A Killing Commanded by Tradition." *Washington Times*, May 3, 2005.
Akhavi, Shahrough. *Religion and Politics in Contemporary Iran: Clergy-State Relations in the Pahlavi Period*. Albany: State University of New York Press, 1980.
Algar, Hamid. *The Constitution of the Islamic Republic*. Berkeley, CA: Mizan Press, 1980.
Alavi, Hamza. "Pakistani Women in a Changing Society." In *Economy and Culture in Pakistan: Migrants and Cities in a Muslim Society*, edited by Hastings Donnan and P. Werbner, 124–136. New York: St. Martin's Press, 1991.
———. "Ethnicity, Society and Ideology." In *Islamic Reassertion in Pakistan*, ed. Anita Weiss, 21–47. Syracuse, NY: Syracuse University Press, 1986.
———. "The State in Postcolonial Societies: Pakistan and Bangladesh." In *Imperialism and Revolution in South Asia*, edited by Kathleen Gough and Hari Sharma, 38–69. New York: Monthly Review Press, 1979.
Alavi, Nasrin. *We Are Iran: The Persian Blogs*. New York: Soft Skull Press, 2005.
Ali, Shaheen Sardar. "Testing the Limits of Family Law Reforms in Pakistan: A Critical Analysis of the Muslim Family Law Ordinance of 1961," *International Survey of Family Law* (2002): 317–335.
Ali, Tariq. *The Clash of Fundamentalism: Crusades, Jihadis, and Modernity*. London: Verso, 2002.
———. *Can Pakistan Survive?* London: Penguin Books, 1983.
Al Mujahid, Sharif. *Quaid-i-Azam Jinnah*. New Delhi: South Asian Books, 1982.
Amnesty International Annual Human Rights Report on Pakistan. *Pakistan: No Progress on Women's Rights*, New York, November 1998.
Amnesty International. Women in Pakistan: Disadvantaged and Denied Their Rights," December 1995. http://www.amnesty.org/en/library/info/ASA33/023/1995.
Anas, Imam Malik ibn. *Al-Muwatta*. Saudi Arabia: Madinah, 2005.
Ansari, Sarah. "Polygamy, Purdah and Political Representation: Engendering Citizenship in 1950s Pakistan." *Modern Asian Studies* 43 (2009), 1421–1461.
Arif, K. M. *Khaki Shadows: Pakistan 1947–1997*. Oxford: Oxford University Press, 2001.
Arif, Khalid Mahmud. *Working with Zia: Pakistan's Power Politics, 1977–1988*. Oxford: Oxford University Press, 1995.
Arjomand, Said Amir. *The Turban for the Crown: The Islamic Revolution in Iran*. Oxford: Oxford University Press, 1989.
Arney, George. *Afghanistan*. London: Mandarin, 1990.
Asghar, Raja. "NA Bill Outlaws Domestic Violence." *DAWN,* August 5, 2009.
Atkinson, Michael, and William Coleman. "Strong States and Weak States: Sectoral Policy Networks in Advanced Capitalist Economies." *British Journal of Political Science* 19 (January 1989), 47–67.
Azari, Farah. "The Post-Revolutionary Women's Movement in Iran." In *Women of Iran: The Conflict with Fundamentalist Islam*, edited by Farah Azari, 190–225. London: Ithaca Press, 1983.
Azerbaijani-Moghaddam, Sippi. "Afghan Women on the Margins of the Twenty First Century." In *Nation Building Unraveled: Aid, Peace and Justice in Afghanistan*, edited by Antonio Donini, Norah Niland, and Karin Wermeste, 95–116. West Hartford, CT: Kumarian Press, 2004.
Badran, Margot, "Iran: Closing of Zanan, Equality at Half Mast," *The American Muslim*, April 14, 2008.
Bagnall, Janet, "An Extraordinary Woman: Ebadi Makes It Clear She Will Continue the Fight for Equality in Iran." *The Gazette*. November 1, 2006.
Bahadur, Kalim. *The Jamaat-i-Islami of Pakistan*. Lahore: Progressive Books, 1978.
Bakhash, Shaul. *The Reign of the Ayatollahs: Iran and the Islamic Revolution*. New York: Basic Books, 1984.
———. *Iran's Monarchy, Bureaucracy, and Reform under the Qajars, 1858–1896*. London: Ithaca Press, 1978.

Bale, John, and David Drakaki-Smith, eds. "The International Standards of Equality and Religious Freedom: Implications for the Status of Women," *United Nations Committee for the Elimination of Discrimination against Women*, New York, 1990. Accessed at: http://untreaty.un.org/cod/avl/ha/cedaw/cedaw.html
Banani, Amin. *The Modernization of Iran: 1921–1941*. Stanford: Stanford, CA: Stanford University Press, 1961.
Baraheni, Reza. *The Crowned Cannibals: Writings on Repression in Iran*. New York: Vintage Press, 1977.
Barfield, Thomas. "Radical Political Islam in an Afghan Context." In *Political Transition in Afghanistan (Asia Program Special Report)*. Washington, DC: Woodrow Wilson Center, April 2004. Accessed at: http://www.wilsoncenter.org/sites/default/files/asiarpt122.pdf.
Baxter, Craig. *Pakistan on the Brink: Politics, Economics, and Society*. Lanham, MD: Lexington Books, 2004.
———, ed. *Zia's Pakistan: Politics, Stability in a Frontline State*. Boulder, CO: Westview Press, 1985.
Beck, Lois, and Nikki Keddie, eds. *Women in the Muslim World*. Cambridge, MA: Harvard University Press, 1978.
Bengio, Ofra, and Gabriel Ben-Ddor, eds. *Minorities and the State in the Arab World*. Boulder, CO: Lynne Rienner, 1999.
Bernard, Cheryl, and Nina Hachigan, editorss. *Democracy and Islam in the New Constitution of Afghanistan*. Santa Monica, CA: Rand, 2003.
Bettencourt, Alice. "Violence Against Women in Pakistan." *Human Rights Advocacy Clinic*, Spring 2000. Accessed at: http://8mars2009.files.wordpress.com/2009/03/violencepkstn.pdf
Bhutto, Benazir. *Daughter of the East*. London: Hamish Hamilton, 1988.
Bhutto, Zulfikar Ali. *If I Am Assassinated*. New Delhi: Vekas, 1979.
Bindra, Sukhawant Singh. *Politics of Islamization: With a Special Reference to Pakistan*. New Delhi: South Asian Books, 1990.
Binder, Leonard, ed. *The Study of the Middle East*. New York: Wiley Press, 1976.
———. *Iran: Political Development in a Changing Society*. Berkeley: University of California Press, 1962.
Boone, Jon, and Mark Tran. "Hamid Karzai Declared Winner of Afghanistan's Presidential Election." *The Guardian*, November 2, 2009.
Bose, Sugata. *Modern South Asia: History, Culture and Political Economy*. Oxford: Oxford University Press, 2006.
Bowden, Mark. *Guests of the Ayatollah: The First Battle in America's War with Militant Islam*. New York: Atlantic Monthly Press, 2006.
Bradsher, Henry. *Afghanistan and the Soviet Union*. Durham, NC: Duke Press Policy Studies, 1983.
Brodsky, Anne E. *With All Our Strength: The Revolutionary Association of the Women of Afghanistan*. New York: Routledge, 2003.
Bucha, Sana. "When Rapists Go Free," *pkarticleshub.com*, April 24, 2011. Accessed at: http://www.pkarticleshub.com/2011/04/24/when-rapists-go-free/.
Buckwalter-Poza, Rebecca. "Troubled History of Domestic Violence Legislation," *Huffington Post*, October 7, 2010.
Burki, Shahid Javed. *Zia's Eleven Years*. Boulder, CO: Westview Press, 1991.
———. *Pakistan under Bhutto, 1971–1977*. New York: St Martin's Press, 1980.
Burki, Shireen Khan. "The Politics of Zan From Amanullah to Karzai: Lessons for Improving Afghan Women's Status." In *Land of the Unconquerable: The Lives of Contemporary Afghan Women*, edited by Jennifer Heath and Ashraf Zahedi, 45–60. Berkeley: University of California Press, 2011.
Burki-Liebl, Shireen K. *The Politics of State Intervention: State Policy and the Status of Women in Pakistan (1947–2006) and Afghanistan (1919–2006)*. PhD. Diss., University of Utah, 2007.
Butt, Tariq. "Punjab Government Prepares to Regulate NGOs." *The Nation*, May 18, 1999.
Carberry, Sean. "The Afghan Battle over a Law to Protect Women." *NPR*. February 20, 2013.
Caroe, Olaf. *The Pathans*. London: Macmillan, 1964.

Carroll, Lucy. "Talaq-i-Tafwid and Stipulations in a Muslim Marriage Contract: Important Means of Protecting the Position of the South Asian Muslim Wife." *Modern Asian Studies* 16 (1982), 277–309.

———. "The Muslim Family Laws Ordinance, 1961: Provisions and Procedures," *Contributions to Indian Sociology*, 13 (1979), 117–143.

Casey, Maura. "Challenging the Mullahs, One Signature at a Time." *New York Times*, February 7, 2007. Accessed at: http://www.nytimes.com/2007/02/07/opinion/07observer.html

Chaudhary, Zafar Hussain. *Islamic Law of Hudood and Tazir—Introduction to Islamic Law of Crime*. Lahore: Nawaz Printing Press, 1983.

Chehabi, Houchang E. "Staging the Emperor's New Clothes: Dress Codes and Nation Building Under Reza Shah," *Iranian Studies* 26 (1993): 209–229.

Chip, Sylvia. "Tradition and Change: The All Pakistan Women's Association." *Islam and Modern Age* 1 (1970), 69–90.

Chip-Kraushaar, Sylvia. "The All Pakistan Women's Association and the 1961 Muslim Family Laws Ordinance." In *The Extended Family: Women and Political Participation in India and Pakistan*, edited by Gail Minault, 265–273. New Delhi: South Asian Books, 1989.

Chivvis, Dana. "Afghanistan's 2010 Parliamentary Elections: Baby Steps or Step Backwards? *AOL News*, September 20, 2010.

Choudhury, Golam Wahed. *Pakistan: Transition from Military to Civilian Rule*. Essex: Scorpion Publishing Co., 1988.

Cohen, Stephen Philip. *The Idea of Pakistan*. Washington, DC: Brookings Institution Press, 2004.

———. *The Pakistan Army*. Karachi: Oxford University Press, 1998.

Constable, Pamela. "A Precarious Shelter in Afghanistan," *Washington Post*, December 5, 2006.

Constable, Pamela and Joshua Partlow. "In Kabul, A Collective Sigh of Relief." *Washington Post*, November 3, 2009.

Cooley, John K. *Unholy Wars: Afghanistan, America and International Terrorism*. London: Pluto Press, 2000.

Coughlin, Con. *Khomeini's Ghost: The Iranian Revolution and the Rise of Militant Islam*. New York: HarperCollins, 2009.

Coulsen, Noel, and Dorvon Hinchlliffe. "Women and Law Reform in Contemporary Islam." In *Women in the Muslim World*, edited by Lois Beck and Nikki Keddie, 37–51. Cambridge: Harvard University Press, 1978.

Crile, George. *Charlie Wilson's War: The Extraordinary Story of the Largest Covert Operation in History*. New York: Grove Press, 2003.

Daoud, Zohra Yusuf. "Miss Afghanistan: A Story of a Nation." In *Women for Afghan Women Shattering Myths and Claiming the Future*, edited by Sunita Mehta, 102–112. New York: Palgrave, 2002.

Dartnell, Michael. "Post-Territorial Insurgency: The Online Activism of the Revolutionary Organization of Women of Afghanistan (RAWA)." *Small Wars and Insurgencies* 14 (Summer 2003), 151–176.

De Sarkar, Dipankar. "Women: Taliban Discrimination Blocks U.N. Aid Work in Afghanistan." *Interpress Service*, March 13, 1998.

Dehghan, Saeed Kamali, "Iran Executes Woman Accused of Murdering Lover's Wife," *Guardian.co.uk*. December 1, 2010.

Diba, Farhad. *Mohammad Mossadegh: Political Biography*. Kent, UK: Croom Helm, Ltd, 1986.

Dietl, Wilhelm. *Bridgehead Afghanistan*. New Delhi: Lancer International, 1986.

Donini, Antonio, Norah Niland, and Karin Weermester. *Nation Building Unraveled: Aid, Peace and Justice in Afghanistan*.Wermester. West Hartford, CT: Kumarian Press, 2004.

Daoud, Zohra Yusuf. "Miss Afghanistan: A Story of a Nation." In *Women for Afghan Women: Shattering Myths and Claiming the Future*, edited by Sunita Mehta, 102–111. New York: Palgrave Macmillan, 2002.

Dupree, Louis. *History of Afghanistan*. Princeton, NJ: Princeton University Press, 1980.

Dupree, Nancy Hatch. "Afghan Women Under the Taliban." In *Fundamentalism Reborn? Afghanistan and the Taliban,* edited by William Maley, 145–166. New York: New York University Press, 1998.

———. "Revolutionary Rhetoric and Afghan Women." In *Revolutions and Rebellions in Afghanistan: Anthropological Perspectives,* edited by M. Nazif Shahrani and Robert L. Canfield, 306–340. Berkeley: Institute of International Studies, University of California, 1984.

Dyer, Emily, "The War on Women Being Waged in Afghanistan." *Telegraph,* June 26, 2012.

Ebadi, Shirin. *Iran Awakening: A Memoir of Revolution and Hope.* New York: Random House, 2006.

Ebrahim, Zofeen T. "Pakistan's Domestic Violence Survivors in a Blind Alley." *Women's Feature Service,* February 15, 2010.

———. "Rights-Pakistan: Despite Sound and Fury, Hudood Laws Still Stay." *Global Information Network.* New York, September 26, 2003.

Ehteshami, Anoushiravan, and Mahjoob Zweiri. *Iran and the Rise of Its Neoconservatives: The Politics of Tehran's Silent Revolution.* London: I.B. Tauris, 2007.

Elfinstone, Mountstuart. *An Account of the Kingdom of Caubul and Its Dependences in Persia Tartary, and India.* London: Longman, Hurst, Rees, Orme and Brown, 1819.

Elwell-Sutton, Laurence Paul. *Modern Iran,* London: G. Routledge and Sons. Ltd, 1941.

Emadi, Hafizullah. *Repression, Resistance and Women in Afghanistan.* Westport: Praeger Publishers, 2002.

Erdbrink, Thomas, "Iran's Old Guard Pushed Aside: New Generation Replacing Clerics Who Had Sought Better Ties with West," *The Washington Post,* February 11, 2008.

Esfandiari, Golnaz. "New Law Seen as Setback for Afghan Women's Rights." *RFE/RL,* April 4, 2009.

———. "Afghan Protest Against Discriminatory Law." *RFE/RL,* April 16, 2009.

Esfandiari, Haleh. "Why Is Iran Curtailing Female Education?" *The Chronicle of Higher Education,* August 22, 2012. Accessed at: http://chronicle.com/blogs/worldwise/why-is-iran-curtailing-female-education/30260 .

———. "The Majles and Women's Issues in the Islamic Republic of Iran." In *In the Eye of the Storm: Women in Post-Revolutionary Iran,* edited by Mahnaz Afkhami and Erika Friedl, 61–79. New York: Syracuse University Press, 1994.

Esposito, John, ed. *Political Islam: Revolution, Radicalism or Reform?* Boulder, CO: Lynne Rienner, 1997.

———. *Women in Muslim Family Law.* Syracuse, NY: Syracuse University Press, 1982.

Evans, Martin. *Afghanistan: A New History.* Surrey, UK: Curzon Press, 2001.

Faghfoory, Mohammad H. "The Ulama-State Relations in Iran, 1921–1941." *International Journal of Middle Eastern Studies* 19 (November 1987), 413–432.

Faiez, Rahim. "Karzai Urges More Freedom for Women." *Newsvine,* March 8, 2008.

Fallain, John, and Rita Cristofari. *Zoya's Story.* New York: HarperCollins, 2002.

Farmaian, Sattareh Farman. *Daughter of Persia: A Woman's Journey from Her Father's Harem Through the Islamic Revolution.* New York: Crown Publishers, 1992.

Farmer, Ben. "Afghanistan Revises Marriage Law But Women Still Required to Submit to Sexual Intercourse." *The Telegraph,* July 9, 2009.

———. "22-Year-Old Accused of Adultery Executed in Afghanistan," *The Telegraph,* July 8, 2012.

Farooq, Umer. "A Story of Courage: Villager Rescues Women from Brutal Tribal Custom." *The Express Tribune* , January 14, 2013.

Fathi, Nazila, "Starting at Home, Iran's Women Fight for Rights," *New York Times,* February 13, 2009.

Firestone, Reuven. *Jihad: The Origins of Holy War in Islam.* New York: Oxford University Press, 1999.

Fischer, Michael M. J. "On Changing the Concept and Position of Women." In *Women in the Muslim World,* edited by Lois Beck and Nikki Keddie, 189–215. Cambridge, MA: Harvard University Press, 1978.

Fisk, Robert. "What Will the Northern Alliance Do in Our Name? I Dread to Think." *London Independent,* November 14, 2001.

Floor, William M. "The Revolutionary Character of the Iranian Ulama," *International Journal of Middle Eastern Studies* 12 (Spring 1980), 501–524.
Fuller, Graham E. *Islamic Fundamentalism in Pakistan: Its Character and Prospects.* CA: Rand, 1991.
Gaborieau, Marc. "Religion in the Pakistan Polity." In *The Contours of State and Society,* edited by Soofia Mumtaz, Jean Luc Racine, and Imran Anwar Ali, 43–55. Oxford: Oxford University Press, 2002.
Gannon, Kathy. "Afghanistan Unbound." *Foreign Affairs* 83, no. 3 (May/June 2004): 35–46.
Gardezi, Fauzia. "Islam, Feminism, and the Women's Movement in Pakistan: 1981–91." In *Against All Odds: Essays on Women, Religion and Development from India and Pakistan,* edited by Kamla Basin, Ritu Menon, and Nighat Said Khan, 51–58. New Delhi: ISIS, 1998.
Gasiorowski, Mark. "The Causes and Consequences of Iran's June 2005 Presidential Election," *Strategic Insights* IV, no. 8 (August 2005).
Geertz, Clifford. *Negara: The Theatre State in Nineteenth Century Bali.* Princeton, NJ: Princeton University Press, 1981.
Gilani, Riazul Hasan. "A Note on Islamic Family Law and Islamisation in Pakistan." In *Islamic Family Law (Arab and Islamic Laws),* edited by Chibli Mallet and Jane Connors, 339–346. London: Graham and Trotman, 1990.
Gohari, M. J. *The Taliban Ascent to Power.* New York: Oxford University Press, 2002.
Goldberg, Jeffrey. "Inside Jihad U: The Education of a Holy Warrior," *New York Times Magazine,* June 25, 2000.
Goodsen, Larry P. *Afghanistan's Endless War: State Failure, Regional Politics, and the Rise of the Taliban.* Seattle: University of Washington Press, 2001.
Goodwin, Jan. *Price of Honor: Muslim Women Lift the Veil of Silence on the Islamic World.* Boston: Little Brown, 1994.
———. *Caught in the Crossfire.* New York: E. P. Dutton, 1987.
Gottlieb, Benjamin. "Taliban Execution of Afghan Woman Triggers Public Outcry." *Washington Post,* July 9, 2012.
Goudsouzian, Tanya, and Helena Malikyar. "For Afghan Women, Some Hard Won Successes and an Ongoing Struggle," *RFE/RL,* March 8, 2010.
Graff, Irene. "Quota Systems in Pakistan under the Musharaff Regime." *Nordic Institute of Asian Studies, Asia Insights,* (March 2004): 21–22.
Graham-Harrison, Emma. "Saudi Arabia Funding $100m Mosque and Education Centre," *The Guardian,* November 2, 2012.
Gregorian, Vartan. *The Emergence of Modern Afghanistan: Politics of Reform and Modernization, 1880–1946.* Stanford, CA: Stanford University Press, 1969.
Griffin, Michael. *Reaping the Whirlwind: The Taliban Movement in Afghanistan.* London: Pluto Press, 2001.
Giustozzi, Antonio. *War, Politics and Society in Afghanistan, 1978–1992.* Washington, DC: Georgetown University Press, 2000.
Hamilton, Nora. *The Limits of State Autonomy: Post Revolutionary Mexico.* Princeton: Princeton University Press, 1982.
Haq, Farhat. "Women, Islam, and the State in Pakistan." *The Muslim World* LXXXVI, no.2 (April 1996): 158–175.
Haqqani, Husain. *Pakistan: Between Mosque and Military.* Washington, DC: Carnegie Endowment for International Peace, 2005.
Hardy, Jack. "Everything Old Is New Again: The Use of Gender-Based Terrorism against Women." *Minerva Quarterly Report on Women and the Military* 19 (Summer 2000): 3–38.
Hasan, Ali Dayan. "The Jurisdictional Dilemma," *DAWN NEWS,* March 21, 2005.
Hassan, Riaz. "Islamization: An Analysis of Religious, Political and Social Change in Pakistan." *Middle Eastern Studies* 21(July 1985), 263–284.
Heath, Jennifer, and Ashraf Zahedi, eds. *Land of the Unconquerable: The Lives of Contemporary Afghan Women.* Berkeley: University of California Press, 2011.
Hegland, Mary Elaine. "Traditional Iranian Women: How They Cope." *Middle East Journal* 36 (Autumn 1982), 483–501.

Hendelman-Baavur, Liora. "Hell Hath No Fury. Iranian Women Take the Streets in Anger and Dismay," *The Jerusalem Post,* June 25, 2009.
Higgins, Patricia J. "Women in the Islamic Republic of Iran: Legal, Social and Ideological Changes," *Signs* 10: 3 (Spring 1985): 477–494.
Hinchcliffe, Doreen. "The Iranian Family Protection Act." *The International and Comparative Law Quarterly* 17 (1968): 516–521.
Hoodfar, Homa. "Devices and Desires, Population Policy and Gender Roles in the Islamic Republic." *Middle East Report* (September–October 1994), 1–17.
Hudson, Valerie M., and Patricia Leidl. "Betrayed." *Foreign Policy,* May 10, 2010. Accessed at: http://www.foreignpolicy.com/articles/2010/05/07/the_us_is_abandoning_afghanistan_s_women
Human Rights Watch Briefing Paper. "Between Hope and Fear: Intimidation and Attacks against Women in Public Life in Afghanistan." New York: Human Rights Watch, 2004.
Hussain, Mushahid, and Akmal Hussain. *Pakistan: Problems of Governance.* Lahore: Vanguard Books, 1986.
Iacopino, Vincent. *The Taliban's War on Women: A Health and Human Rights Crisis in Afghanistan: A Report.* Boston: Physicians for Human Rights, 1998.
Ingalls, James. "The New Afghan Constitution: A Step Backwards for Democracy." *Foreign Policy in Focus,* March 13, 2004. Accessed at: www.fpif.org .
Iqbal, Javed. "The Judiciary and Constitutional Crises in Pakistan," in *Pakistan: Founder's Aspirations and Today's Realities*, ed. Hafeez Malik (Oxford: Oxford University Press, 2001), 61–81.
Iqbal, Nadeem. "Rights-Pakistan: Death Sentence Lifted on Rape Victim," *Global Information Network,* June 11, 2002.
———. "Afghanistan: Women to Demand Role in Reconstruction." *Interpress Service,* December 27, 2001. Accessed at: http://www.ipsnews.net/
Imran, Rahat, "Legal Injustices: The Zina Ordinance of Pakistan and Its Implications," *Journal of International Women's Studies* 7 (November 2005), 78–100.
Iran: Country Reports on Human Rights Practices, Bureau of Democracy, Human Rights and Labor, U.S. Department of State (February 23, 2001).
Jafarzadeh, Alireza. *The Iran Threat: President Ahmadinejab and the Coming Nuclear Crisis.* New York: Palgrave Macmillan, 2007.
Jaffrelot, Christophe, ed. *Pakistan: Nationalism without a Nation.* London: Zed Books, 2002.
Jahangir, Asma. "Women's Commission and Hudood Ordinances," *Daily Times,* September 12, 2003. Accessed at http://www.dailytimes.com.pk/default.asp?page=story_12-9-2003_pg3_2 .
Jahangir, Asma, and Hina Jilani. *A Divine Sanction? The Hudood Ordinances.* Lahore: Rhotas Books, 1990.
Jalal, Ayesha. "The Convenience of Subservience: Women and the State of Pakistan." In *Women, Islam and the State*, edited by Deniz Kandiyoti. Philadelphia: Temple University Press, 1991.
———. *The State of Martial Rule.* Cambridge: Cambridge University Press, 1990.
———. *The Sole Spokesman.* Cambridge: Cambridge University Press, 1985.
Jalalzai, Musa Khan. *Women Trafficking and Prostitution in Pakistan and Afghanistan.* Lahore: Dua Publications, 2002.
Jamal, Amina. "Feminist Selves and Feminism's Others: Feminist Representation of Jamaat-i-Islami Women in Pakistan," *Feminist Review* 81(2005), 52–73.
James, Sir Morrice. *Pakistan Chronicle.* New York: St. Martin's, 1993.
Jenkins, Laura Dudley. *Identity and Identification in India: Defining the Disadvantaged.* London: Routledge, 2003.
Jessop, Robert. *State Theory: Putting the Capitalist State in Its Place.* Oxford, UK: Polity Press, 1990.
Johnson, Chris. *Afghanistan.* UK: Oxfam, 2004.
Jones, Owen Bennett. *Pakistan: Eye of the Storm.* New Haven, CT: Yale University Press, 2002.

Joya, Malalai. "Any Hope I Had in the Ballot Box Bringing Change in Afghanistan is Gone," *The Guardian,* November 2, 2010.

———. *A Woman among Warlords: The Extraordinary Story of an Afghan Who Dared to Raise Her Voice.* New York: Scribner, 2009.

Kamili, Mohammad Hashim. "Law and Society: The Interplay of Revelation and Reason in the Shariah." In *The Oxford History of Islam,* edited by John L. Esposito, 107–154. Oxford: Oxford University Press, 1999.

———. *Law in Afghanistan: A Study of the Constitutions, Matrimonial Law, and the Judiciary.* Leiden: E.J. Brill, 1985.

Kapoor, Harsh, ed. *Women Living under Muslim Laws.* Dossier 21 (September 1998). Grabels Cedex, France, 33. Accessed at: http://www.wluml.org/fr/node/320.

Kapur, Ashok. *Pakistan in Crisis.* New York: Routledge, 1991.

Kar, Mehranguiz, and Homa Hoodfar. "Women and Personal Status Law in Iran." *Middle East Report,* no. 198 (January–March 1996), 36–38.

Kargar, Zarghuna. "Afghan Women Strive to Be Heard." *BBC News,* August 13, 2009. Accessed at: http://news.bbc.co.uk/2/hi/8198126.stm.

Katouzian, Homa. "Arbitrary Rule: A Comparative Theory of State, Politics and Society in Iran." *British Journal of Middle Eastern Studies* 24 (May 1997), 49–73.

Kaushik, Surendra Nath. *Politics of Islamization in Pakistan: A Study of the Zia Regime.* New Delhi: South Asian Publishers, 1993.

Khan, Sajda. "Conflating Cultural Practices and Islam," *Gulf News,* June 4, 2013.

Kian, Azadeh, "Women and Politics in Post-Islamist Iran: The Gender Conscious Drive to Change," *British Journal of Middle Eastern Studies* 24 (Winter 1997), 75–96.

Kazemi, Farhad. "Civil Society and Iranian Politics." In *Civil Society in the Middle East,* edited by Augustus Richard Norton, 119–152. Boston, MA: Brill Academic Publishers, 1995.

Keddie, Nikkie R. *Qajar Iran and the Rise of Reza Khan, 1796–1925.* Costa Mesa, CA: Mazda Publishers, 1999.

———. *The Roots of Revolution: An Interpretive History of Modern Iran.* New Haven, CT: Yale University Press, 1991.

———. *Sayyid Jamal ad Din "al-Afghani:" A Political Biography.* Berkeley and Los Angeles: University of California Press, 1972.

———. "The Iranian Power Structure and Social Change, 1800–1969: An Overview," *International Journal of Middle Eastern Studies* 2 (January 1971), 3–20.

———. *An Islamic Response to Imperialism: Political and Religious Writings of Sayyid Jamal ad Din "al Afghani."* Berkeley: University of California Press, 1968.

———. *Religion and Rebellion in Iran: The Tobacco Protest of 1891–1892.* London: Frank Cass, 1966.

———. "Religion and Irreligion in Early Iranian Nationalism," *Comparative Studies in Society and History* 4 (April 1962), 265–295.

Kennedy, Charles. *Pakistan, 1992.* Boulder, CO: Westview Press, 1993.

———. "Islamization and Legal Reform in Pakistan, 1979–1989." *Pacific Affairs* 63 (Spring 1990), 62–77.

Khan, Aamer Ahmed. "Pakistan's Justice System in Spotlight." *BBC News,* March 12, 2005.

Khan, Asghar, ed. *Islam, Politics, and the State: The Pakistan Experience.* Lahore: Zed Books, 1985.

Khan, Hamid. *Constitutional and Political History of Pakistan.* Oxford: Oxford University Press, 2004.

Khan, Iftikhar. "The Federal Shariat Court Knocks Out 3 Sections of Women's Protection Act." *Dawn,* December 23, 2010.

Khan, Mohammad Ayub. *Friends Not Masters: A Political Autobiography.* London: Oxford University Press, 1967.

Khan, Nighat Said. "The New Global Order: Politics and the Women's Movement." In *Pakistan: The Contours of State and Society,* edited by Soofia Mumtaz, Jean-Luc Racine, and Imran Anwar Ali, 137–154. Karachi: Oxford University Press, 2002.

Khan, Omar Asghar. "When Women Speak Out." *The News,* October 22, 1999.

Khan, Shahid Rehman. "Under Pakistan's Form of Islamic Law, Rape Is a Crime for the Victims." *Los Angeles Times,* May 25, 1986.
Khan, Shahnaz. "Zina and the Moral Regulation of Pakistani Women." *Feminist Review* 75 (2003), 75–100.
———. "Gender, Religion, Sexuality and the State: Mediating the Hudood Laws in Pakistan." *Center for Research on Violence against Women and Children.* Ontario, Canada, 2001.
Khan, Sumera. "Women Specific Bill Passed: Fourteen Year Jail Term for Acid Throwers." *The Express Tribune,* December 12, 2011.
Kian, Azadeh. "Women and Politics in Post-Islamist Iran: The Gender Conscious Drive to Change." In *Women Living under Muslim Laws,* edited by Harsh Kapoor, 35–38. Grabels Cedex, France, September 1998. Accessed at: http://www.wluml.org/fr/node/320 .
King, Angela. "United Nations and Afghanistan." In *Women for Afghan Women: Shattering Myths and Changing the Future,* edited by Sunita Mehta. New York: Palgrave Macmillan, 2002.
Kinzer, Stephen. *All the President's Men: An American Coup and the Roots of Middle East Terror.* Hoboken, NJ: Wiley, 2008.
Koofi, Fawzia. *One Women's Fight to Lead Afghanistan into the Future.* New York: Palgrave Macmillan, 2012.
Kurin, Richard. "Islamisation in Pakistan: A View from the Countryside." *Asian Survey* 25 (August 1985), 852–862.
Kux, Dennis. *The United States and Pakistan, 1947–2000: Disenchanted Allies.* Washington, DC: Woodrow Wilson Center Press, 2001.
Lambert-Hurley, Siobhan. *Muslim Women, Reform and Princely Patronage:Nawab Sultan Jahan Begum of Bhopal.* London: Routledge, 2007.
———. "Fostering Sisterhood: Muslim Women and the All India Ladies' Association." *Journal of Women's History* 16 (2004), 40–65.
Lambton, Ann. *Qajar Persia.* Austin: University of Texas Press, 1987.
Lane, Jan-Erik, ed. *State and Market: The Politics of the Public and the Private,* Beverly Hills, CA: Sage Publications, 1985.
Latifi, Ali M. "Afghan Women in Fight Over Rights Law," *Aljazeera,* May 30, 2013.
Lee, Adrian. "A Very Modern Revolution," *The Express,* June 20, 2009.
Lenarcik, Marek. "Women Campaign for Greater Rights as Iran Vote Nears." *The Washington Times,* May 31, 2009.
Lenczowski, George. *Iran under the Pahlavis.* Stanford, CA: Hoover Institute Press, 1978.
Lerner, Paula. "The Life and Death of Sitara Achakzai." *PRI's The World,* July 29, 2009. Accessed at: http://www.theworld.org/2009/07/29/the-life-and-death-of-sitara-achekzai/
Li, Xin. "Iranian Regime Erases Progress on Women's Rights; Fundamentalism Enforce Traditional Sex Roles under Harsh Penalties." *Washington Times* (March 8, 2006).
Mackey, Robert. "Malala Yousafzai, Pakistani Girl Shot by Taliban Militants, Speaks in New Videos." *The New York Times,* February 4, 2013.
Mackey, Sandra. *The Iranians: Persia, Islam and the Soul of a Nation.* New York: Penguin Group, 1996.
Mahdavi, Shireen. "Women and the Shi'i Ulama in Iran," *Middle Eastern Studies* 19 (January 1983), 17–27.
Mai, Mukhtar. *In the Name of Honor.* New York: Washington Square Press, 2006.
Maley, William, ed. *Fundamentalism Reborn? Afghanistan and the Taliban.* London: C. Hurst, 1998.
Malik, Hafeez, ed. *Pakistan: Founder's Aspirations and Today's Realities.* Oxford: Oxford University Press, 2001.
Malik, Iftikhar H. *State and Civil Society in Pakistan: Politics of Authority, Ideology and Ethnicity.* New York: Palgrave Macmillan, 1997.
———. "The State and Civil Society in Pakistan: From Crisis to Crisis." *Asian Survey* 36 (July 1996), 673–690.
Malik, Muhammad Aslam. *The Making of the Pakistan Resolution.* Oxford: Oxford University Press, 2001.

Malikyar, Helena. "Development of Family Law in Afghanistan: The Roles of the Hanafi Madhab, Customary Practices and Power Politics." *Central Asian Survey*, 16:3 (1997): 389–399.
Maloney, Suzanne. *Iran's Long Reach: Iran as a Pivotal State in the Muslim World.* Washington, DC: USIP, 2008.
Maluka, Zulfikar. K. "Reconstructing the Constitution for a COAS President: Pakistan, 1999 to 2002." In *Pakistan on the Brink: Politics, Economics, and Society,* edited by Craig Baxter, 53–100. Lanham, MD: Lexington Books, 2004.
———. *The Myth of Constitutionalism in Pakistan.* Oxford: Oxford University Press, 1995.
Mansoor, Wendy. "The Mission of RAWA: Freedom, Democracy, Human Rights." In *Women for Afghan Women: Shattering Myths and Changing the Future,* edited by Sunita Mehta, 68–84. New York: Palgrave Macmillan, 2002.
March, James, and Johan Olsen. "The New Institutionalism: Organizational Factors in Political Life." *American Political Science Review,* 48, no. 3 (September 1984): 734–749.
Marsden, Peter. *The Taliban: War, Religion and the New Order in Afghanistan.* Karachi: Oxford University Press, 1998.
Martin, Vanessa. *Creating an Islamic State: Khomeini and the Making of a New Iran.* London: I.B. Tauris, 2000.
Masrur, Mihr Nigar. *Ra'ana Liaquat Ali Khan: A Biography.* Karachi: All Pakistan's Women's Association, 1980.
Massell, Gregory. "Law and an Instrument of Revolutionary Change in a Traditional Milieu." *Law and Society Review* 2 (February 1968), 179–228.
Matinuddin, Kamal. *The Taliban Phenomenon: Afghanistan 1994–1997.* London: Oxford University Press, 1999.
Matsushige, Curtis. "Midwives Graduate from Nangarhar University." *Afghanistan Freedom Watch,* August 1, 2005.
Maududi, Abul A'la. *Purdah and the Status of Women in Islam.* New Delhi: Markizi Maktaba Islami Publisher, 1998 (originally published in 1939).
———. *The Islamic Law and Constitution.* Lahore, Pakistan: Islamic Publications, 1980.
McChesney, Robert D. *Kabul under Siege: Fayz Muhammad's Account of the 1929 Uprising.* Princeton, NJ: Marcus Weiner Publishers, 1999.
McGirk, Jan. "Women Rights in Pakistan: The Woman Who Dared to Cry Rape." *Independent News,* June 15, 2005.
McElroy, Wendy. "Muslim Woman's Courage Sets Example." *Fox News,* March 16, 2005.
Mehdi, Rubya. "The Protection of Women (Criminal Laws Amendment) Act, 2006 in Pakistan." in *Droit Cultures* (2010), 191–206. Accessed at: http://droitcultures.revues.org/2016
———. *Islamization of the Law in Pakistan.* London: Curzon Press, 1994.
———. "The Offence of Rape in the Islamic Law of Pakistan." *International Journal of Society and Law* 18 (1990), 19–29.
Melman, Yossi. *The Nuclear Sphinx of Tehran: Mahmoud Ahmadinejad and the State of Iran.* New York: Carroll and Graf, 2007.
Miles, Kay. *The Dynamo in Silk: A Brief Biographical Sketch of Begum Ra'ana Liaquat Ali Khan.* Karachi: All Pakistan Women's Association, 1974.
Minault, Gail. *Secluded Scholars: Women's Education and Muslim Social Reform in Colonial India.* Oxford: Oxford University Press, 1999.
Mir-Hosseini, Ziba. "Sharia and National Law in Iran." In *Shariah Incorporated: A Comparative Overview of the Legal Systems of Twelve Muslim Countries in Past and Present,* edited by Jan Michiel Otto, 319–372. The Netherlands: Leiden University Press, 2010.
———. "Hojjat al-Eslam Sa'idzadeh-Iran." In *Women Living under Muslim Laws,* edited by Harsh Kapoor, 56–59. Grabels Cedex, France: Dossier 21, September 1998.
———. "Stretching the Limits : A Feminist Reading of the Shari'a in Post-Khomeini Iran." In *Feminism and Islam: Legal and Literary Perspectives,* edited by Mia Yamani, 285–320. New York: New York University Press, 1996.
Mir-Hosseini, Ziba, and Richard Tapper. *Islam and Democracy in Iran: Eshkevari and the Quest for Reform.* London: I.B. Tauris, 2006.

Mirza, Anis. "Women's Role in the Pakistan Movement and the Formative Years." *Women in Public Life* (October 1972), 2–11.
Misra, Amalendu. *Afghanistan: The Labryrinth of Violence.* Cambridge, UK: Polity Press, 2004.
Moaddel, Mansoor. "Religion and Women: Islamic Modernism versus Fundamentalism." *Journal for the Scientific Study of Religion* 37 (March 1998), 108–130.
Moazam, Farhat. "The Hudood Ordinances of Pakistan." *Journal of South Asian and Middle Eastern Studies* 27 (Fall 2004), 33–52.
Moghadam, Valentine M. "A Tale of Two Countries: State, Society, and Gender Politics in Iran and Afghanistan." *The Muslim World* 94 (October 2004), 449–467.
———. *Modernizing Women: Gender and Social Changes in the Middle East.* Boulder, CO: Lynne Rienner, 2003.
———. "Hidden from History? Women Workers in Modern Iran." *Iranian Studies* 33(Summer–Autumn 2000), 377–401.
———, ed. *Identity Politics and Women: Cultural Reassertions and Feminism in International Perspectives.* Boulder, CO: Westview Press, 1994.
———. *Modernizing Women: Gender and Social Change in the Middle East.* Cairo: The American University in Cairo Press, 1993.
———, editor. *Identity Politics and Women: Cultural Reassertions and Feminisms in International Perspectives.* Boulder, CO: Westview Press, 1993.
———. *Women, Work, and Ideology in Post-Revolutionary Iran.* East Lansing: Michigan State University, 1988.
———. "Women, Work, and Ideology in the Islamic Republic." *International Journal of Middle Eastern Studies* 20 (1988), 221–243.
Moin, Baqer. *Khomeini: Life of the Ayatollah.* New York: St. Martin's Press, 1999.
Moreau, Ron, and Zahid Hussain. "I Decided to Fight Back." *Newsweek,* March 28, 2005.
Mortimer, Edward, "Pakistan-Islam as Nationality." In *Faith and Power: The Politics of Islam.* London: Vintage Books, 1982.
Mottahedeh, Roy. *The Mantle of the Prophet: Religion and Politics in Iran.* Oxford: One World, 2000.
Mumtaz, Khawar. "Identity Politics and Women: 'Fundamentalism' and Women in Pakistan." In *Identity Politics and Women: Cultural Reassertions and Feminism in International Perspectives,* edited by Valentine Moghadem, 228–242. Boulder, CO: Westview Press, 1994.
Mumtaz, Khawar, and Yameena Mitha. *Pakistan: Tradition and Change.* Oxford: Oxfam, 1996.
Mumtaz, Khawar, and Farida Shaheed. *Women of Pakistan: Two Steps Forward, One Step Back?* London: Zed Press, 1987.
Mumtaz, Soofia, Racine, Jean Luc, and Imran Anwar Ali, eds. *The Contours of State and Society.* Oxford: Oxford University Press, 2002.
Musharaff, Pervez. *In the Line of Fire: A Memoir.* New York: Free Press, 2006.
Nafisi, Azar. "Hair and Lipstick Are Iranian Women's WMDs," *The Times,* September 13, 2011.
———. *Reading Lolita in Tehran.* New York: Random House, 2004.
Naji, Kasra. *Ahmadinejad: The Secret History of Iran's Radical Leader.* Berkeley: University of California Press, 2008.
Najibullah, Farangis. "Afghan Bill Aims to Criminalize Discrimination against Women," *RFE/RL,* July 20, 2009.
———. "In Afghanistan, Traditional Values Still Threaten Women's Rights." *RFE/RL.* March 8, 2009.
———. "Teen Donation Forms Cornerstone for Girls' Education in Afghan Village." *RFE/RL,* February 8, 2009.
Najmabadi, A. "Feminism in an Islamic Republic: Years of Hardship, Years of Growth." In *Islam, Gender, and Social Change,* edited by Y. Yazbeck Haddad and John Esposito, 59–86. Oxford: Oxford University Press, 1999.
Namakydoust, Azadeh. "Covered in Messages: The Veil as a Political Tool." *The Iranian,* May 3, 2003.

Nashat, Guity. "Women in the Islamic Republic of Iran." *International Society for Iranian Studies* 13 (1980), 165–194.

Nasr, Syed Vali R. *Islamic Leviathan: Islam and the Making of State Power.* Oxford: Oxford University Press, 2001.

———. "International Politics, Domestic Imperatives, and Identity Mobilization: Sectarianism in Pakistan, *1979–1988.*" *Comparative Politics* 32 (January 2000), 171–190.

———. "The Rise of Sunni Militancy in Pakistan: The Changing Role of Islamism and Ulama in Society and Politics." *Modern Asian Studies,* 34 (January 2000), 139–180.

———. "Islamic Opposition in the Political Process: Lessons from Pakistan." In *Political Islam: Revolution, Radicalism or Reform?* edited by John Esposito, 135–156. Boulder, CO: Lynne Rienner, 1997.

———. "Pakistan: State, Agrarian Reform and Islamization." *International Journal of Politics, Culture and Society,* 10 (Winter 1996), 249–272.

———. *The Vanguard of the Islamic Revolution: The Jamaat-i-Islami of Pakistan.* Berkeley: University of California Press, 1994.

Newberg, Paula R. *Judging the State: Courts and Constitutional Politics in Pakistan.* Cambridge: Cambridge University Press, 1995.

Niland, Norah. "Justice Postponed: The Marginalization of Human Rights in Afghanistan." In *Nation-Building Unraveled: Aid, Peace and Justice in Afghanistan,* edited by Antonio Donini, Norah Niland, and Karin Wermester, 61–82. Westport, CT: Kumarian Press, 2004.

Nojumi, Neamatollah. *The Rise of the Taliban in Afghanistan: Mass Mobilization, Civil War, and the Future of the Region.* New York: Palgrave, 2002.

Nordland, Rod. "Egypt's Islamist's Tread Lightly, But Skeptics Squirm." *New York Times,* July 28, 2012.

Nordlinger, Eric. *Soldiers in Politics: Military Coups and Governments.* Englewood, NJ: Prentice Hall, 1977.

Lauryn Oates, "Demonstration Planned to Oppose Violence Against Women in Afghanistan," *The Propagandist,* June 5, 2013.

O'Shea, Chiade. "The Rape Victim Who Fought Back," *BBC News,* March 12, 2005.

Olsen, Asta. *Islam and Politics in Afghanistan.* London: Curzon Press, 1995.

Oppel, Richard A., and Abdul Waheed Wafa. "Hazara Hustle to Head of Class in Afghanistan." *New York Times,* January 3, 2010.

Paidar, Parvin. *Women and the Political Process in Twentieth Century Iran.* Cambridge: Cambridge University Press, 1995.

Pakizegi, Ilehnaz. "Legal Reform and Social Positions of Iranian Women." In *Women in the Muslim World,* edited by Lois Beck and Nikki Keddie, 216–227. Cambridge: Harvard University Press, 1978.

Pal, Izzud-Din. "Women and Islam in Pakistan." *Middle Eastern Studies* 26 (October 1990), 449–464.

Patel, Rashida. *Islamization of Laws in Pakistan?* Karachi: Faiza Publishers, 1986.

Pearl, David. "Three Decades of Executive, Legislative and Judicial Amendments to Islamic Family Law in Pakistan." In *Islamic Family Law (Arab and Islamic Laws),* edited by Chibli Mallet and Jane Connors, 321–338. London: Graham and Trotman, 1990.

Peterson, Scott. "Iran Cracks Down on Women's Rights Activists," *Christian Science Monitor,* March 8, 2007. Accessed at: http://www.csmonitor.com/2007/0308/p12s01-wome.html.

Pew Research Center. "Most Embrace a Role for Islam in Politics: Muslims around the World Divided on Hamas and Hezbollah." December 10, 2010. Accessed at: http://www.pewglobal.org/2010/12/02/muslims-around-the-world-divided-on-hamas-and-hezbollah/ .

Pollack, Kenneth M. *The Persian Puzzle: The Conflict between Iran and America.* New York: Random House, 2005.

Pomeroy, Robin. "Mahmoud Ahmadinejad's Closest Aide Calls for More Women's Rights." *The Guardian,* September 29, 2010.

Prasad, Amar Nath, and S. John Peter Joseph. *Indian Writing in English.* New Delhi: Sarup and Sons, 2006.

Putnam, Robert. *Making Democracy Work: Civic Traditions in Modern Italy.* Princeton, NJ: Princeton University Press, 1993.

Quraishi, Ahmed. "94 Self Immolation Cases Registered in Western Afghanistan." *RAWA News,* March 28, 2012.
Quraishi, Sultan J. "NGOs Under Attack in New Campaign." *The News,* May 25, 1999.
Rahimi, Fahima. *Women in Afghanistan.* Liestal: Stiftung Foundation, Stiftung Bibliotheca Afghanica, 1986.
Rajagopalan, Swarna. *State and Society in South Asia.* Boulder, CO: Lynne Rienner Press, 2001.
Ramazani, Nesta. "Women in Iran: The Revolutionary Ebb and Flow." *Middle East Journal* 47 (Summer 1993), 409–428.
Ramazani, R. K. "Burying the Hatchet." *Foreign Policy* 60 (Fall 1985), 52–74.
———. "Document: Constitution of the Islamic Republic of Iran," *Middle East Journal* 34 (Spring 1980), 181–204.
———. *The Foreign Policy of Iran, 1500–1914.* Charlottesville: University of Virginia Press, 1966.
Rasekh, Zohra. "Public Health: A Reconstruction Priority in Afghanistan." In *Women For Afghan Women,* edited by Sunita Mehta, 176–183. New York: Palgrave Macmillan, 2002.
Rashid, Ahmed. *Taliban: Militant Islam, Oil and Fundamentalism in Central Asia.* New Haven, CT: Yale University Press, 2000.
Ravandi, Morteza. *Tarikh Ejtemai Iran (The Social History of Iran).* Tehran: Amir Kabir, 1978.
Raz, Amber. "Hamid Karzai is Failing Afghan Women." *The Guardian,* May 10, 2010.
Raza, Rafi. *Zulfikar Ali Bhutto and Pakistan, 1967–1977.* Karachi: Oxford University Press, 1997.
Razavi, Shahra. "Islamic Politics, Human Rights and Women's Claims for Equality in Iran." *Third World Quarterly* 27 (2006), 1223–1237.
Rawi, Mariam. "Rule of the Rapists." *The Guadian,* February 12, 2004.
Reeves, Richard. *Passage to Peshawar: Pakistan between the Hindu Kush and the Arabian Sea.* New York: Simon and Schuster, 1984.
Rehman, Javaid. "The Sharia, Islamic Family Laws and International Human Rights Law: Examining the Theory and Practice of Polygamy and Talaq." *International Journal of Law Policy and the Family* 21 (2007), 108–127.
———. *Military, State and Society in Pakistan.* New York: St Martin's Press, 2000.
Reilly, Robert. *The Closing of the Muslim Mind: How Intellectual Suicide Created the Modern Islamist.* Wilmington, DE: Intercollegiate Studies Institute, 2010.
Rizvi, Hasan Askari. *Military, State and Society in Pakistan.* Lahore: Sang-e-Meel Publications, 2003.
———. *The Military and Politics in Pakistan, 1947–1986.* Lahore: Progressive, 1987.
Roy, Olivier. *Afghanistan, from Holy War to Civil War.* Princeton, NJ: Princeton University Press, 1995.
———. *The Failure of Political Islam.* Cambridge: I.B. Tauris, 1994.
Rubin, Barnett. *The Fragmentation of Afghanistan, State Formation and Collapse in the International System,* New Haven, CT: Yale University Press, 1995.
———. *The Search for Peace in Afghanistan, From Buffer State to Failed State.* New Haven, CT: Yale University Press, 1995.
Rubin, Barnett, and Jack Synder. *Post-Soviet Political Order, Conflict and State Building.* London: Routledge, 1998.
Saeed, Javaid. *Islam and Modernization: A Comparative Analysis of Pakistan, Egypt, and Turkey.* London: Praeger, 1994.
Saeed, Nadeem. "Swept under the Rug," *The Herald,* July 2005.
Saidzadeh, Hojjat al-Eslam. "Foundations of the Equality Perspective Modern Fiqh: the Case of Divorce." In *Women Living under Muslim Laws,* edited by Harsh Kapoor, 60–63. Dossier 21 Grabels Cedex, France, September 1998.
Saigol, Rubina. "The Shariat Bill and Its Impact on Education and Women." In *Against All Odds: Essays on Women, Religion and Development from India and Pakistan,* edited by Kamla Basin, Ritu Menon, and Nighat Said Khan, 82–94. New Delhi: ISIS, 1998.
Saikal, Amin. *Modern Afghanistan: A History of Struggle and Survival.* London: I.B. Tauris, 2004.

Sanasarian, Eliz. *Women's Rights Movement in Iran.* New York: Praeger, 1982.
Savory, Roger M. "Social Development in Iran During the Pahlavi Era." In *Iran under the Pahlavis,* edited by George Lenczowski, 85–127. Stanford, CA: Hoover Institute Press, 1978.
Sedghi, Hamideh. *Women and Politics in Iran: Veiling, Unveiling, and Reveiling.* Cambridge: Cambridge University Press, 2007.
Shafqat, Saeed. *Civil Military Relations in Pakistan. From Z. A. Bhutto to Benazir Bhutto.* Boulder, CO: Westview Press, 1998.
Shah, Niaz. A, "The Women Protection Act 2006 of Pakistan: An Analysis," *Religion and Human Rights* 5 (2010), 1–10.
———. *Women, the Koran and International Human Rights: The Experience of Pakistan.* Leiden: Martinus Nijhoff Publishers, 2006.
Shah, Waseem Ahmed. "Counter Claims." *The Herald.* April 2005.
———. "Justice Under Fire: Should the Courts Make Legal Concessions in Cases Involving Marginalised Members of Society?" *The Herald,* April 2005.
Shaheed, Farida. "Controlled or Autonomous: Identity and the Experience of the Network: Women Living under Muslim Laws." *SIGNS: Journal of Women in Culture and Sociology* 19 (1994), 997–1019.
Shahrokni, Nazanin. "All the President's Women." MERIP 39 (Winter 2009). Accessed at: http://www.merip.org/mer/mer253/all-presidents-women.
Shahidian, Hammed. "The Iranian Left and the 'Women Question' in the Revolution of 1978–79." *International Journal of Middle East Studies* 26 (May 1994), 223–247.
Sheridan, Michael. "Iran Official Hints Sakineh Mohammadi Ashtiani Death by Stoning May Be Commuted." *New York Daily News,* January 2, 2011.
Siddique, Abubakar. "Stoning of Afghan Couple for Adultery Sparks Debate on Sharia Law." *RFE/RL,* August 17, 2010.
Skaine, Rosemary. *The Women of Afghanistan under the Taliban.* NC: McFarland and Co, Inc. 2002.
Suad, Joseph, and Afsaneh Najmabadi, editors. *Encyclopedia of Women and Islamic Culture: Family Law and Politics.* Leiden: Brill Academic Publishers, 2005.
Suad, Joseph, and Susan Slyomovics, eds. *Women and Power in the Middle East.* Philadelphia: University of Pennslyvania Press, 2001.
Suratgar, Olive Hepburn. *I Sing in the Wilderness: An Intimate Account of Persia and Persians.* London: Stanford Press, 1951.
Syed, Anwar Hussein. *Pakistan: Islam, Politics and National Solidarity.* Lahore: Vanguard Books, 1984.
Tabari, Azar, and Nahid Yeganeh, eds. *In the Shadows of Islam.* London: Zed Press, 1982.
Taheri, Amir. "Ahmadinejad's New Enemy: Women." *New York Post,* September 6, 2008.
Tait, Robert. "Anger as Iran Bans Women from Universities." *The Telegraph,* August 20, 2012.
Talbot, Ian. *Pakistan: A Modern History.* New York: St. Martin's, 1998.
Tamadonfar, Mehran. "Islam, Law, and Political Control in Contemporary Iran." *Journal for the Scientific Study of Religion* 40 (2001), 205–219.
———. *The Islamic Polity and Political Leadership, Fundamentalism, Sectarianism, and Pragmatism.* Boulder, CO: Westview Press, 1989.
Thomas, Dorothy Q. "Double Jeopardy: Police Abuse of Women in Pakistan." *Human Rights Watch,* 1992.
Thomas, Lowell. *Beyond Khyber Pass: Into Forbidden Afghanistan.* New York: Grosset and Dunlap, 1925.
Tremayne, Soraya. "Modernity and Early Marriage in Iran: A View from Within." *Journal of Middle East Women's Studies* 2 (2006), 65–94.
Tren, Mark. "Ahmadinejad Nominates Women to Cabinet." *The Guardian,* August 16, 2009.
Tytler, Carolyn. "Women's Rights in Afghanistan Today." *Associated Content.* February 3 2009.
Ur-Rahman, Shamim. "Women's Bill Sets Tough Penalties." *DAWN,* Jan 30, 2010.
Vogt, Heidi. "Shahla Ata and Frozan Fana: Two Women among Those Vying for Afghan Presidency." *Huffington Post,* August 5, 2009.

Vorgetts, Fahima. "A Vision of Justice, Equality and Peace." In *Women for Afghan Women: Shattering Myths and Claiming the Future,* edited by Sunita Mehta, 93–102. New York: Palgrave Macmillan, 2002.

Wajid, Kyai Haji Abdurrahman. "God Needs No Defense." In *Silenced: How Apostasy and Blasphemy Codes Are Choking Freedom Worldwide,* edited by Paul Marshall and Nina Shea, xvii–xxii. New York: New York University Press, 2011.

Weaver, Mary Anne. *Pakistan: In the Shadows of Jihad and Afghanistan.* New York: Farrar, Straus and Giroux, 2002.

Weiss, Anita M., editor. *Islam, Gender and Sociopolitical Change: Case Studies.* New York: Oxford University Press, 1998.

———, ed. *Islamic Reassertion in Pakistan: The Application of Islamic Laws in a Modern State.* Syracuse, NY: Syracuse University Press, 1986.

Wells, Ian Bryant. *Jinnah: Ambassador of Hindu-Muslim Unity.* London: Seagull Books, 2005.

Wente, Margaret. "It's a Crime to Be a Woman in Iran." *The Globe and Mail,* July 17, 2010.

Wolpert, Stanley. *Zulfi Bhutto of Pakistan.* New York: Oxford University Press, 1993.

———. *Jinnah of Pakistan.* New York: Oxford University Press, 1984.

Yasmeen, Samina. "Islamisation and Democratisation in Pakistan: Implications for Women and Religious Minorities." *South Asia: Journal of South Asian Studies* 22 (1987), 183–198.

Yeganeh, Nahid. "Women, Nationalism and Islam in Contemporary Political Discourse in Iran." *Feminist Review* 44 (Summer 1993), 3–18.

Yong, William. "Iran's Divorce Rate Stirs Fears of Society in Crisis." *New York Times,* December 6, 2010.

Yousafzai, Sami. "The Opium Brides of Afghanistan," *Newsweek,* March 29, 2008.

Zabih, Sepehr. *The Mossadegh Era.* Chicago: Lake View Press, 1982.

Zahedi, Ashraf. "State Ideology and the Status of Iranian War Widows." *International Feminist Journal of Politics* 8 (June 2006): 267–286.

———. "Contested Meaning of the Veil and Political Ideologies of Iranian Regimes," *Journal of the Middle East Women's Studies,* 3: 3 (Fall 2007): 75–98.

Zahedi, Dariush. *The Iranian Revolution, Then and Now: The Indicators of Regime Instability.* Boulder, CO: Westview Press, 2001.

Zia, Shehla. "The Legal Status of Women in Pakistan." In *Finding Our Way: Readings on Women in Pakistan,* edited by Fareeha Zafar. Lahore: ASR Publications, 1991.

Ziring, Lawrence. *Pakistan at the Crosscurrent of History.* Oxford: One Word Press, 2003.

———. *Pakistan in the Twentieth Century: A Political History.* Karachi: Oxford University Press, 1997.

———. *The Ayub Khan Era: Politics of Pakistan, 1958–69.* Syracuse, NY: Syracuse University Press, 1971.

Index

Achakzai, Sitara, 153
Acid Control and Acid Prevention Bill of 2010, 92
Afghan women in the urban areas 1960s, 109; 1990s, 133–134; post-Taliban period, 147–148, 148, 159–162, 163; urban-rural dichotomy, 113, 115, 134–135, 168
Afghanistan's Constitution of 1964, 111–112
Afghanistan Constitution of 1975 and female status, 114–115
Afghanistan Constitution of 2004, 152; and female rights, 152; RAWA and female activists concerns, 152–153
Afkhami, Mahnaz, 4, 222
Afshar, Halah, 230
Ahmadinejad, Mahmoud, 3, 249–250, 251, 252, 254, 256, 272
al Afghani, Jamal al Din, 182
Aliabadi, Soghra, 208
Aliya, Mahde, 179
Alliance for the Repeal of Discriminatory Laws, 83
All India Muslim League, 15, 15–16, 21; female activism in, 15–16, 22
All-Pakistan Women's Association (APWA), 19, 20–21, 23–32, 32, 33, 37n47, 53, 60; activism against polygamy, 23; and maulvis, 21; and the Rashid Commission, 23–24; urban phenomenon, 20
Amanullah (king)'s modernization efforts, 101–103, 104–105, 106, 107, 108, 108–109, 109, 114, 122–123, 134, 150, 270, 271, 282n31; Bibi Gul (sister), 103, 110; Daud's views of, 106; and education policy, 102–103; first girls' school (Masturat School), 102; first women's hospital, 103; opposition to Amanullah's policies, 104, 105, 108, 123, 271; wife of (Queen Soraya), 104, 273, 275
Amnesty International, 48, 74, 79, 120, 122
Anjuman-e-Himayat-e-Islam, 14
Anjuman-e-Khawateen-e-Islam, 15
Anjuman-e-Rahnuma-e-Khanawada-e-Afghan, 110
Assembly of Experts (Majlise Khebregan-e Rahbari), 233, 256n4, 281n17
Association of Women Lawyers (Iran), 211, 212, 219
Ata, Shahla, 155
Ataturk (Mustafa Kemal), 102, 186–187, 191, 199n45, 203, 271
Aurat Foundation, 90
Aziz, Donya, 92

Bacha-e-Saqaw, 105–106
Bahonar, Javad, 227

Bahrami, Ameneh and Majid Movahedi, 239
Balkhi, Hossein, 165
Barakzai, Shukria, 166, 274
basij, 232, 237, 261n108
bazaari (Persia/Iran), 177, 178, 182, 183, 187, 188, 195, 197n3, 202, 205, 210, 211, 212, 216, 220, 224, 251, 271
Behbud, 32
Beheshti, Ayatollah Mohammad, 227, 228, 238
Behruzi, Maryam, 237
Bhutto, Benazir, 58, 67, 68–70, 70, 72, 72–73, 74, 74–75, 89, 93, 273, 274; and expectation of Pakistani females, 67, 68; opposition from religious parties, 68, 69; perception of betrayal by females, 68
Bhutto, Nusrat, 31
Bhutto, Zulfiqar Ali, 1, 29, 30–31, 32, 42, 42–43, 274; female activism during Bhutto's rule, 31–34
Bibi, Nur, 120
Bibi, Safia, 51, 52
Bibi, Zafran, 83–84, 86, 95n39
Bonn Agreement, 149, 150
Brussels Proclamation, 149–150
Bush, Laura, 148
Bux, Fehmida and Allah, 59

child marriages, 153, 160, 188, 280n7
Civil Code of 1931 (Persia), 193–194, 218, 236
Civil Code of 1935 (Persia), 234
Commission of Inquiry for Women (1994), 73; commission report, 73–74
Constitution of the Islamic Republic of Iran (1979), 232–233, 238
Constitutional Loya Jirga of 2003, 151–152
Constitutional Revolution of 1906–1911 (Persia), 178, 183, 184, 195, 232, 245; and ulema, 183–184
Council of Guardians, 227, 228, 236, 243–244, 256n4, 269, 281n17. *See also* Guardian Council

Dabbagh, Marziyyeh, 237
Dar al Islam, 13, 279n3

Dasteghayb, Gohar-al Sharia, 237, 243–244
Dastjerdi, Marzieh Vahid, 250
Daud's ambitious reform policies as Prime Minister and social/tribal opposition, 108–109; and clerics, 109; gender policies, 115; RAWA opposition to, 116; removal by Zahir Shah (king), 109; urban support for Daud's gender policies, 109
Demokratik-e-Khalq-e-Afghanistan (the People's Democratic Party of Afghanistan, PDPA), 110–111, 116–117, 120, 123, 130, 277; female resistance to, 118; gender policy of, 117; and RAWA, 119; and urban women, 118
Dostum, Abdul, 166
Doulatshahi, Mehrangiz, 217
Douletabadi, Sedigheh, 208. *See also* Zaban Zanan (Women's Language)
Dupree, Nancy, 133, 168

Ebadi, Shirin, vii, 238, 242, 252, 274
Ebrahimi, Abdul Rauf, 159
Ebtehaj-Samii, Nayyereh, 217
Elimination of the Custom of "Ghag" Law of 2013, 92
Elimination of Violence Against Women (EVAW) Decree of 2009 (Afghanistan), 164, 165, 166
Emergency Loya Jirga of 2002, 150; objectives of, 151
Enforcement of Shariah Act, 1991, 71; female views of, 71

Falsafi, Abdolghasem, 211
Family Protection Act of 1967 (Iran), 218–219, 229, 233, 236, 274; abrogation of, 236; female views of abrogation of this law, 241; Khomeini's views of, 234, 268; reinstatement of, 244
Family Protection Act of 1975 (Iran), 219; impact of, 219–220
Fana, Frozan, 155
Farmaian, Sattareh Farman, 189, 196, 221
fatwa, 28–29, 35, 182, 205, 213, 235, 237, 272

Feda'iyan-e-Islam, 205, 205–206
Fedayeen-e-Khalq (People's Fedayeen), 220, 256n2
Federal Shariat Court, 43, 51, 52, 53, 58, 60, 70, 76, 79, 83, 85, 90, 268, 270
Federation of University Women (Pakistan), 19
Fiqh-e-Jafaria, 178, 228
Flogging of Lal Mai, 53
forced marriages, 117, 154, 160, 281n22

Gailani, Fatima, 149
Ganjeh, Sedigheh, 208
GEO TV 3 and Hudood Ordinances debate, 87
Ghiyam Zanan (Women's Revolt), 208
Green Movement of 2009 (Iran), 2, 249, 250–251
Guardian Council, 233, 261n103

Habib, Mariam, 32
hadd, 47, 49, 50, 51, 88, 89, 267, 268, 281n20
Hadith, 27, 47, 49–50, 51, 54, 57, 63n1, 63n13, 258n47, 265, 278
Hanafi Fiqh, 25, 43, 57, 71, 112
Hazoor Bakhsh v.Federation of Pakistan, PLD 1981 F.S.C. 145, 44
Hezb-e-Zanan (Women's Party), 206. *See also* Showra-ye-Zanan (Women's Council)
hijab, 130, 141, 204, 205, 220, 229, 231–232, 271–272, 273, 282n31
Hikmatyar, Gulbuddin, 159
Human Rights Commission of Pakistan, 80, 90
Human Rights Watch, 48, 74, 90, 92, 135, 136, 137, 138, 142, 151–152, 154, 157–158, 171n61
Hussain, Begum Salma Tassadduque, 16
Hudood Ordinances, 2, 5, 41, 46, 47, 49, 50, 51, 52, 54, 59, 60, 61–62, 67, 68, 70, 81, 83, 84, 87–88, 89, 90, 93, 267, 273

ijma, 57, 266
ijtihad, 58, 258n47, 266, 269
Ikhwan al Muslimin (Muslim Brotherhood), 205, 279

Ikramullah, Begum Shaista, 22, 23
Iranian women struggle for suffrage, 207, 209–211, 212, 215, 216–217, 219, 232, 272, 276; pressure from Kennedy Administration, 211
Iskandari, Tayyibeh, 247
Islam, 1–2, 11, 13, 14, 22, 23, 24, 28, 106–107, 109, 132, 136, 153, 165, 179, 180, 182, 186, 188, 192, 205, 212, 216, 222, 229, 234, 237, 240, 241, 242, 247, 248–249, 251, 252, 256, 267, 276, 277, 278
Islamic, 1, 2, 4, 5, 7, 11, 12–13, 14, 16, 18, 21–22, 23, 26, 28–29, 34, 36n9, 41, 42, 43, 44, 45, 46, 47, 53, 54, 55, 57, 58, 59, 61, 62, 68, 69, 70, 71, 73, 76, 77, 78, 80–81, 84, 87, 88, 89, 90, 93, 94, 103, 105, 107, 111, 119, 120, 122, 128, 129, 132, 136, 138, 141, 143, 145n3, 152, 161, 161–162, 163, 165, 168, 177, 178, 179, 183, 186, 190, 195, 197n1, 202, 203, 205, 206, 207, 209, 210, 212, 214, 216, 220, 222–223, 224, 224n20, 227, 228, 229, 230, 231–232, 232–233, 234, 235, 236–237, 238, 239, 240, 242, 243, 244, 245, 246, 247, 248, 249, 250, 251, 252, 254, 254–256, 256n4, 260n99, 264–265, 265–266, 268, 269, 270, 272, 275, 276, 277, 278, 279, 279n3, 281n17, 281n20, 282n33
Islamic Republican Party, 227, 228, 231–232, 237, 269
Islamist, 3, 13, 19, 21, 24, 25, 41, 67, 75, 78, 91, 94, 129, 166, 168, 203, 220, 222, 227, 228, 232, 233, 246, 265, 275, 278
Islamization, 1, 5, 67, 68, 69, 70, 71, 72, 75, 79, 93, 96n67, 228, 232–233, 235, 239, 271, 276; during General Zia ul Haq's rule, 41, 42–43, 44, 45, 46, 51, 53, 54, 56, 58, 61, 62, 63n6, 63n7, 64n22, 65n65

Jahanbani, Showkat-Malek, 217
Jahan-e-Zanan (Women's World), 217
Jahed, Shahla, 239
Jalal, Massouda, 150, 155
Javed, Ghazala, vii

Jamaat-i-Islami, 12, 19, 41, 45, 57, 60, 61, 62, 70, 74, 88, 270. *See also* Mawdudi, Maulana Abul A'la
Jamhuri-ye-Eslami-ye-Iran (Islamic Republic of Iran), 227
Jehan, Nasim, 26, 30, 32
Jehangir, Asma, 62, 76–77
Jinnah, Fatima, 28–29, 35, 272
Jinnah, Muhammad Ali (Quaid-i-Azam), 11, 12, 13, 16, 28
jirga, 82, 92, 104, 105, 106, 114, 147, 150
Joya, Malalai, vii, 147, 156, 158, 159

Kakar, Tajwar, 120
Kar, Mehranguiz, 242, 259n73
Karokhail, Shinkai Zahine, 153
Karokhi, Masooda, 165
Karrubi, Mehdi, 251
Karzai, Hamid, 3, 147, 148, 150, 153, 155, 156, 159, 160, 161–162, 163, 166, 168
Kashani, Ayatullah Sayyed Abolqassem, 205
Kashf-al-Asrar (The Discovery of Secrets), 203, 203–204
Kermani, Hojatolislam Ali Movahedi, 235, 243
Khamenei, Ayatullah Ali, 228, 251, 256n4, 281n17
Khan, Ayub, 25, 27, 28–29, 29, 38n53, 270, 272
Khan, Begum Ra'ana Liaquat Ali Khan, vii, 17, 18, 20
Khan, Ghulam Ishaq, 69, 70
Khan, Malkum, 182
Khan, Nighat Said, 62
Khan, Sir Syed Ahmed, 13
Khanum, Zahra, 231
Khatami, Mohammad, 248
Khomeini, Ayatullah Ruhollah Mousavi, 178, 187, 188, 201, 203, 203–205, 211–212, 215, 221, 222, 223, 224, 224n21, 226n87, 227–235, 237, 238, 239–240, 242, 245, 248, 250–254, 255–256, 256n4, 258n45, 258n47, 266, 268, 269, 271–272, 272, 274–275, 276, 279n3, 280n7, 281n17, 281n21
Khomeinists, 228, 229, 230, 231, 233, 234, 235, 237, 239, 240, 241, 242, 249, 251, 256, 268

Khonsari, Ayatollah Ahmad, 216
Koofi, Fawzia, vii, 167, 263

Labor Law of 1984 (Afghanistan), 118
Layeh-ye-Qisas (Laws of Retribution), 237–239. *See also* Qisas and Diyat laws
Loya Jirga, 104, 106, 108, 114, 147, 149, 150, 150–152, 156, 158, 165–166, 170n20

Mai, Mukhtar, vii, 84, 85–86, 89
Majlis-e-Khawateen-i-Pakistan, 61
Majlis-e-Shoray-e-Islami (Islamic Consultative Assembly or Parliament), 183, 186–187, 202, 203, 209, 211, 212, 215, 217, 218, 219, 222
Majlis-i-Shura, 44, 46
Manuchehrian, Mehrangiz, 217
Martyrs Foundation (Iran), 242, 260n76
Mashaie, Esfandiar Rahim, 251
Maududi, 45
Mawdudi, Maulana Abul A'la, 12, 16, 19, 21, 29, 35n4, 35n5, 41. *See also* Maududi
mehr/mehrieh, 26, 194, 204, 241, 253, 259n72, 280n11
Meena (founder of RAWA), 101, 116
Meshrano Jirga, 152, 171n45
military coup of 1977 (Pakistan), 1, 41, 116
Mosahab, Shamsul-Mulk, 217
Mossadeq, Mohammad, 206, 210
Mousavi, Mir Hossein, 3, 251
Movement for the Restoration of Democracy (MRD), 58
Muassisa-e-Khayria-e-Zanan (Women's Welfare Association-WWA), 110
Musharaff, Pervez, 80, 81, 83, 84, 85, 86, 87–88, 88
Muslim Family Law Ordinance (MFLO) of 1961(Pakistan), 21, 25, 26–27, 28, 52, 59, 60, 274; challenges to MFLO, 76–79; and minimum age at marriage, 26
Mujahidin (Afghanistan), 118, 119, 120, 120–121, 121, 122, 123, 127, 128, 130, 132, 133, 137, 143, 143–144, 159, 161–162; violence towards females, 120–122

Mujahidin-e-Khalq (People's Mujahidin) of Iran, 220, 227
Mukhtar Mai Women's Welfare Organization (MMWWO), 86
Muslim Personal Law of Shariat (Pakistan), 22
Muslim League (Junejo), 58
Muslim League (Nawaz Sharif), 56, 85, 270, 272
Muslim League (Pagara Group), 41, 42
mu'ta, 153, 180, 204–205, 230
Muttahida Majlis-Amal (MMA), 82, 88

Naficy, Nezhat, 217
Najibullah, 120
Namazie, Maryam, 227
National Commission on the Status of Women (NCSW), 81, 92; report of, 81
National Front, 206, 210, 212, 220, 225n39, 234
nationalism, 12, 16, 34, 129, 178, 279n3
Nawaz, Begum Jahanara Shah, 22, 23
Nawbakht, Munireh, 247
nikah nama, 26, 27, 35
Nikah wa Khatnasuri, 103, 270
Nizam-i-Mustafa, 43, 45
Nizamnamah-e-Arusi, 103, 270
Nizamnameh-ye-Asasi-e-Dawlat-e-Aliyah-e-Afghanistan (Afghanistan's First Constitution), 102; and abolishment of slavery, 102
Nuri, Rima, 163

Office of Women's Affairs (Iran), 248
ol-Molouk, Tadj, 188, 275
One Million Signature Campaign, 252
Opium Brides (of Afghanistan), 160

Pahlavi, Ashraf, 211, 217–218, 221, 273
Pahlavi, Muhammad Reza (1919–1980), 201, 201–202, 205, 208–209, 209, 213, 217; female activists opposition to, 220. *See also* Shah, Muhammad Reza
Pahlavi, Reza (1878–1944), 177, 178, 186–191, 191; abolishment of the veil in 1936 and impact, 188–189, 195; female employment, 192; female status under, 192–193; implementation on ban of veils on women, 189–190; and modernization efforts, 187–188, 191, 192; and the mullahs, 177, 190, 191, 195; opposition from traditional middle class and rural populace, 195; polygamist, 193; and societal identity crisis, 190
Pakistan Constitution: 1956, 23; 1973, 30–31, 32, 42, 43, 44, 52, 57, 62, 67, 69, 72, 77, 81
Pakistan Constitution of 1973 and Article 25, 30; Article 27, 30; Eighth Amendment, 56, 62; Fifteenth Amendment, 79; Ninth Amendment, 57, 58
Pakistan Penal Code, 46, 63n2, 75, 88, 89, 92, 268
Pakistan People's Party (PPP), 29–30, 42, 68, 70, 72, 74, 82, 90, 91–92
Pakistan Resolution of 1940, 12, 15; and female activism, 15–16; and Muslim Girls' Student Federation, 16
Pakistan Women's Lawyers Association, 54
Pakistan's Women's National Guard (PWNG), 17–19
Pakistan's Women's Naval Reserve (PWNR), 18–19
Pakistani women's suffrage, 16, 23, 30, 32
Parliamentary Elections of 1965 (Afghanistan) and female participation, 113
Parliamentary and Provincial Council Elections of 2005 (Afghanistan), 156–158
Parliamentary Elections of 2010 (Afghanistan), 158–159
Parlika, Soraya, 162
Parsa, Farrokhroo, vii, 217, 222, 226n87
Parveen, Shahida and Muhammad Sarwar, 53
Patel, Rashida, 32
polygamy, 23, 25, 27, 37n47, 76, 77, 107, 180, 187, 193, 196, 205, 211, 218, 219, 230, 235, 238, 244, 252, 265, 269, 278
Presidential Elections of 2004 (Afghanistan), 154–155
Presidential Elections of 2009 (Afghanistan), 155; and two female candidates, Shahla Ata and Frozan

Fana, 155
Prevention of Anti-Women Practices Act 2011, 92
Prevention of Domestic Violence Bill of 2009 (Pakistan), 90–91
Protection Against Harassment of Women at Workplace Bill 2009 (Pakistan), 91–92
Protection of Women (Criminal Laws Amendment) Bill of 2006 (Pakistan), 87–89; opposition to, 90
psychological scars of Afghan populace, 160
purdah (veiling), 35n4, 105, 107, 136, 185. *See also* veil

Qajar Dynasty, 177, 186
Qajar rule, 178, 181, 183, 185; and female status, 179–181
Qanoon-e-Shahadat, 54, 55, 57, 68, 73, 93
qazf, 46, 50–51, 88, 89
Qisas and Diyat laws, 55, 56, 70, 75–76, 268
qiyas, 57, 280n15
Qomi, Ayatullah Tabataba'i, 213

Rafsanjani, Faizeh, 247
Rafsanjani, Hashemi, 227, 228, 240, 248
Rahnavard, Zahra, vii, 251, 275, 282n33
Rajai, Atefeh, 237
Rajai, Mohammad Ali, 235
rajm, 44, 46
rape, 46, 47–50, 52, 54, 83, 84, 85–86, 88, 89, 90, 120, 122, 128, 132, 135, 142, 144, 148, 153, 160–161, 164, 267, 268, 269
Rashid Commission of 1956 (Pakistan), 23–24, 25
RAWA (Revolutionary Association of Women of Afghanistan), 3, 101, 116, 119, 122, 123, 143, 148, 152, 277
Razavi, Shahra, 248
Resaleh Tawzih al Masail, 204
Revolutionary Guards Corps, 228
Rice, Condoleeza, 86

Saghafi, Khadije (Khomeini's wife), 205
Saidzadeh, Hojjat ul-Islam Seyyed Mohsin, 248–249, 260n99

Salimi, Dr. Malali, 150
Sami-Latif Bill, 71
Sarfraz, Zari, 32
Sayyaf, Abdul Rab Rasul and views on women, 159, 166
Seddiqi, Suhaila, 149
self-immolation, 2, 164, 168
Seventh Five-Year Plan (1988–1993), Pakistan, 68
Shah, Fath Ali, the second Qajar ruler, 181
Shah, Muhammad Zahir and female education, 108
Shah, Muhammad Nadir and social reforms, 106; views on Amanullah's ambitious social policy, 106
Shah, Muhammad Reza, 202. *See also* Pahlavi, Muhammad Reza
Shah, Reza, 6–7, 177, 178, 186–191, 191, 193, 195–196, 197n1, 197n7, 203, 208, 208–209, 213, 229, 234, 268, 271
Shariah, 41, 42–43, 44, 46, 47, 52, 57, 58, 61, 67, 69, 70, 70–71, 71, 75, 79, 82, 86–87, 88, 89, 93, 103, 128, 140, 148, 163, 165–166, 167, 179, 180, 183, 188, 191, 193, 194, 205, 212, 216, 228, 229, 230, 231, 233, 234, 235, 238, 239, 241, 241–243, 243–244, 245, 249, 252, 256, 264, 264–265, 265–266, 267–269, 270, 271–272, 275
Shariat Bill of 1985 (Pakistan), 57–58
Shariat Bill of 1988 (Pakistan), 58
Shariati, Dr. Ali, 222
Shariatmadari, Ayatollah Kazem, 222, 228
Sharif, Nawaz, 56, 70, 71, 75, 79, 267, 268
Sherkat, Shahla, 242, 246, 260n91
Sherzad, Zolaykha, 163
Shia Personal Status Law of 2009 (Afghanistan), 153
Shirkat Gah, 32, 33, 75, 80
Shoraye Aliye Jamiyat Zanan Iran (High Council of Women's Organizations of Iran), 211
Showra-ye-Zanan (Women's Council), 206
sigheh, 193–194, 211, 220, 230, 239
Siraj, Shafiqa (King Amanullah's sister), 150
Soltan, Neda Agha, vii, 251
Soltankhah, Nasrin, 250
Soroush, Abdolkarim, 249

Special Civil Courts, 234–235, 236, 244, 269

ta'azir, 50, 56, 64n39, 89
taghut, 235, 258n45
talaq (divorce), 24, 26, 27, 78, 204, 243, 267, 280n6
Taleghani, Azam, 236, 237–238, 247
Taliban, 2, 3, 6, 94, 118, 122, 127, 127–128, 128–129, 132, 133, 268, 270, 271–272, 273, 275, 276, 277, 281n19, 281n21; attitude towards non-Pushtun women, 135; and custom, 136; decrees of, 131–132; female access to medical care, 140–141; female education, 136–138; female employment, 138–140; female medical treatment, 132; female resistance to Taliban rule, 142–143; lives of rural women, 134; perception of rural women, 134; social repression, 129–130; wrath towards urban women, 133–134, 134
Tarbiat, Hajar, 217
Tashkilat Democratic Zanan (Democratic Association of Women), 207
Tawzih al-Masa'el, 235, 258n47
theocracy, 2, 3, 7, 12, 178, 227, 228, 231, 240, 242, 247, 249, 251, 251–252, 253, 254, 254–255, 256, 268, 271, 281n19
Tobacco Concessions of 1890 (Persia), 182
Tudeh party, 206, 209, 220, 227
Turkey, 7, 102, 111, 177, 178, 186, 187–188, 191, 197n7, 199n45, 203, 214, 271

ud-Dawleh, Anis (also known as Fatemeh), 180–181
ud-Dawleh, Khazen and Anis (daughters of Fath Ali Shah), 181
ud-Din, Nasir (Shah), 179, 180, 181–182
ujrat-e-mesel (wages for housework) laws, 244–245
ulema, 3, 7, 22–23, 23, 25, 26, 28, 29, 35, 44, 57, 58, 68, 71, 87, 88–89, 177–178, 178, 181–182, 183, 186, 186–187, 188, 190, 195, 201–203, 205, 209, 213, 215, 216, 218, 220, 222, 227, 256, 265, 266–267, 272, 280n11, 281n23
Ummi, Mahbubeh, 246

United Front for Women's Rights (Pakistan), 19
United Nations Assistance Mission in Afghanistan (UNAMA), 160
United Nations Convention on the Elimination of All Forms of Discrimination against Women (CEDAW), 61, 69, 75, 95n17, 152
United Nations Development Fund for Women (UNIFEM), 155, 163
United Nations High Commission for Human Rights, 153, 160
Usul-e-Asasi-ye-Dawlat-e-Aliyya-e-Afghanistan (Afghanistan's Second Constitution), 106

veil, 12, 21–23, 45, 53, 104, 105, 107, 108–109, 131, 134, 136, 144, 157, 180, 184, 185, 187, 188–190, 192, 195, 196–197, 201, 203, 203–204, 204–205, 206, 213, 214, 221, 222, 223, 229, 252, 271, 275, 277
Velayat-e-Faqih (rule of the jurisprudent), 228, 229, 241, 266

Wali, Sima, 149
White Revolution of 1963, 7, 202, 215–216, 220, 227; clerical opposition to, 215, 216
Wolesi Jirga, 152, 156, 158
Women's Action Forum (WAF), 34, 51, 59, 71, 143, 277; mobilization of women, 60
Women's Organization of Iran (WOI), 218, 221, 222
women's police stations in Pakistan, 74
Women's Reform Movement (Pakistan), 13, 14

Yousafzai, Malala, vii, 67, 94, 274

Zaban Zanan (Women's Voice), 185, 208
Zadeh, Maryam Mojtahed, 250
zanana, 104, 106
Zia ul Haq, General (Pakistan), 1, 5, 33, 41–42, 43, 46, 52, 57, 58, 59, 61, 62, 67, 79, 80, 86, 88, 89, 93, 271; and female intimidation, 44–49, 51, 53

zina, 44, 46–51, 53, 54, 59, 72, 77, 83, 84, 86, 88, 89, 93, 267, 269, 281n21

zina bil jabr, 47, 49, 88, 93, 267; four honorable Muslim male witnesses, 49, 50; according to Hadith, 49–50; and Hudood Ordinances' ta'azir category punishment for slander, 50–51; prosecuted rape cases in Pakistan of Jehan Mina, 47; Safia Bibi, 51–52; Shahmeem, 48; Shahnaz, 48; Shajida Parveen, 48

About the Author

Shireen K. Burki is a political scientist whose research interests specialize in state-society relations and politics in the Middle East and South Asia. She completed her doctorate in Political Science from the University of Utah in 2007. Burki was assistant professor in Conflict Management of Stabilization and Reconstruction at the National Defense University and has worked in various capacities with the U.S. military and the U.S. government. She has published in various scholarly journals such as *Terrorism and Political Violence*, *Comparative Politics*, and *Journal of Applied Security Research*.